Late Nineteenth-Century
American Development

Late Nineteenth-Century American Development

A General Equilibrium History

JEFFREY G. WILLIAMSON

Professor of Economics, University of Wisconsin

CAMBRIDGE UNIVERSITY PRESS

Published by the Syndics of the Cambridge University Press
Bentley House, 200 Euston Road, London NW1 2DB
American Branch: 32 East 57th Street, New York, N.Y. 10022

© Cambridge University Press 1974

Library of Congress Catalogue Card Number: 74-76946

ISBN: 0 521 20469 0

First published 1974

Printed in the United States of America

Contents

Part IV   The Facts of History

To
José Encarnàcion,
although he may never understand why

Preface

This book is an economist's attempt to make sense out of a critical period in American history, from the Civil War to World War I. The questions raised here are hardly new since they have always been at the heart of American historiography. My interest in the period was in no small measure stimulated by teaching graduate American economic history in 1969–70 jointly with my colleague, Ralph Andreano. Professor Andreano insisted that while cliometricians had made great strides in improving our understanding of ante bellum economic experience, the post-Civil War still remained a frontier, while the twentieth century could be considered almost virgin territory. This seems like an appropriate time to thank Professor Andreano publicly for his critical initial push towards this book.

Although the historical topics taken up in the pages following are conventional, the methods utilized are not, even for cliometricians. The counterfactual is used extensively, of course. But more to the point, the book relies very heavily on general equilibrium analysis. Furthermore, simulation is the quantitative mode which translates the formal model into a tool for historical analysis. Cliometricians have been reluctant to take this step in their work, perhaps because they are not sufficiently confident in the usefulness of general equilibrium models for empirical work in economic history. My own willingness to engage in the risky endeavor was in large part based on the striking initial success which Professor Allen Kelley and I had had in applying a formal general equilibrium model of economic dualism to Meiji Japan in our book *Dualistic Economic Development: Theory and History*, and in our 1971 paper 'Writing Economic History Backwards: Meiji Japan Revisited.' Indeed, this initial success has blossomed into a more elaborate collaborative effort on Meiji Japan (*Lessons from Japanese Development: An Analytical Economic History*). My collaboration with Professor Kelley has played an important role in the development of the present volume. Furthermore, Professor Kelley has supplied thoughtful criticism and helpful encouragement throughout. He has my grateful thanks.

Many of my economist and historian friends have been helpful at all stages of the research. At formative stages, John Bowman, Bob Brito, Glen Cain, Theodore Groves, Donald Hester, Peter Lindert, Samuel Morley, Donald Nichols, Morton Rothstein and Joseph Swanson supplied both encouragement and criticism. As the project continued, my debt to each of them increased, especially Professors Lindert, Morley and Nichols. Dennis Aigner, Lau Christensen and Zvi Griliches were unusually patient in supplying answers to questions raised in chapter 4. Stanley Engerman, a unique critic in our discipline, Robert Gallman, Donald McCloskey, William Parker, Richard Sylla, Peter Temin, Brinley Thomas and Richard Vedder all read portions of the manuscript and improved its contents immeasurably. I am also grateful for having had the opportunity to present my research to the MSSB Workshop on the application of general equilibrium models to economic history at Madison, Wisconsin in the summer of 1972. The participants in that workshop included Claudia Goldin, Glenn Hueckel, Ronald Jones, Frank Lewis, Michael Mussa, Clayne Pope and Roy Ruffin. My thanks to all of them. Research funding from the University of Wisconsin Graduate School Research Committee and the National Science Foundation (GS-3239, GS-35639) is also happily acknowledged.

The research assistance of Mr Leo De Bever was of unusually high quality at all stages of the project. Without his creative skills at programming, the research might never have been completed. In addition, William Burnett, Douglass Klein, James Roseberry and Adair Waldenberg all performed yeoman's service.

Acknowledgements must be made to the *Journal of Economic History* and *Explorations in Economic History* where early versions of portions of this book appeared. The manuscript was typed by Alice Wilcox, with competence and good humor.

Finally, I must make a confession of debt to a non-economic historian, Professor José Encarnàcion, at the University of the Philippines. He has never seen this manuscript, nor have I ever discussed it with him. Yet his influence on it has been enormous. This book is dedicated to José with the greatest fondness and respect.

Madison, Wisconsin   JEFFREY G. WILLIAMSON
1974

Part I   The Issues

1

Late Nineteenth-Century American Development: The Issues

One of the things which we have learned ... is to distinguish between those historical questions which can usefully be discussed in terms of the notion of statistical uniformity, and those which cannot.   Sir John Hicks (1969)

1.1 Late nineteenth-century American development

This book applies analytical tools and quantitative technique to the important phase of American development between the Civil War and World War I. The issues are no different from those raised by Adam Smith two centuries ago. What were the causes and consequences of American growth in the late nineteenth century?

Since our focus is on the underlying forces propelling long-term economic change, the reader warrants an explanation for the period selected. In particular, why shouldn't the investigation be pushed further back in time to the ante bellum decades? There are a number of excellent reasons why the analysis fails to confront the earlier years. Perhaps most important is that our quantitative knowledge of the earlier period is much too sparse to support the kind of quantitative analysis which the book applies. The study is unabashedly quantitative and the methodology makes very heavy demands on the quantitative record. Furthermore, the vast majority of the cliometric research completed during the past decade has dwelt with ante bellum problems. Our interest in the late nineteenth century is partly motivated by a desire to strike a better balance in the cliometric literature. Finally, the American economy grew at unusually rapid rates following the Civil War – rates which had never before been achieved for so long a period. Indeed, these four decades were critical ones during which the United States passed from a phase of primary product export and experimentation with early industrialization to a position of unsurpassed modern industrial power. For all of these reasons, the late nineteenth century deserves more detailed attention.

1

1.2 A survey of the historical terrain

The Civil War as a watershed

The demarcation of American history by major wars is common-place, but economic historians never seem to be certain why these demarcations make sense. Granted, the Civil War years generated a pronounced short-run departure from the secular trend of a notably successful developing economy. But the 'watershed' view of economic history implies far more. It is often argued that the Civil War produced an abrupt change in the structure of the Northern economy which influenced its performance for many decades to follow. Certainly the Civil War was a landmark in social and political history, but why should it play such an important role in a chronology of *economic* events? One obvious and fundamental change was centered on the vanquished region, the South. It is difficult to imagine a more fundamental change in economic institutions than the dismantling of slavery and adoption of sharecropping in an agrarian economy. But the secular impact of Slave Emancipation on the North is hardly obvious. No doubt the material and human losses in the South influenced her development in subsequent decades much like the modern experiences of Japan and Germany (although no 'economic miracles' occurred in the post-war confederacy), but the relevance of Southern war losses to subsequent Northern development is tenuous. Similarly, it is not very convincing to point to a shift in the composition of American exports from cotton to grains. Grain exports were already expanding rapidly in the 1850s and furthermore cotton was still king in the immediate post-war years. Nor is it correct to insist that mature industrialization and concentration were typical of the late nineteenth century but not of the ante bellum period. There are abundant data supporting roughly comparable rates of industrialization 1839–59 and 1869–99. Furthermore, one can easily cite evidence of Midwest farm mechanization in the 1850s, increased size of Eastern firms, vertical and horizontal integration, and so on.

In short, much of the documented 'structural' contrasts between the post-Civil War and ante bellum decades were inevitable by-products of successful economic growth, unrelated to the war decade itself. Yet, the convenient Civil War benchmark persists in our textbooks. Why?

First, the savings rate out of GNP rises at an unprecedented rate between the 1850s and the 1870s. It has been estimated that the share of gross net capital formation in GNP rises by seven percentage points during the Civil War decade. This episodic rise in the savings rate had profound implications for late nineteenth-century Northern development. Furthermore, this discontinuity in capital formation shares was hardly a temporary phenomenon since the new plateau which the savings rate reached in the 1870s is maintained for the remainder of the century. Indeed, this book will argue that the late nineteenth century can be best understood by treating the Civil War as a source of disequilibrium and viewing subsequent development in the North as a process of adjustment to the economic impact of the war.

Second, the epochal rise in the current price savings rate was reinforced by other forces centered on the Civil War decade. It is generally believed that the relative price of investment goods has continually increased from the 1870s to the present. Perhaps less well known is the enormous *decline* in capital goods' prices between the 1850s and the 1870s. Thus, while the 'savings effort' was undergoing an epochal rise during the Civil War decade those savings could increasingly command a better price on producer durables. Nowhere in the remainder of the nineteenth century, or indeed during the twentieth century, is there a comparable episode since the relative price of capital goods remained relatively stable up to the turn of the century and rose thereafter.

Third, the federal government passed tariff legislation during the Civil War that persisted as a key influence on subsequent development. The period of the 1850s was one of mild reversal from the protectionist policies of the preceding decades. The 'war tariffs' signaled an abrupt departure from a path which appeared to lead to relatively free trade. Although the 1872 Tariff Act moderated the protective tariffs of the 1860s somewhat, its life was brief since the act of 1875 witnessed a full return to the war levels. In short, after 1861 America shifted to a policy of very stiff protection. This tariff history may be well known, but perhaps its implications have not been fully appreciated. The tariff on manufactured imports should have resulted in the following: the relative price of the primary product exportable fell, thus helping precipitate farm discontent; the price of capital goods rose relative to the exportable, thus inhibiting farm mechanization; the price of imported manufactures rose by more than that of non-tradeable capital goods. Given a once and for all shift to protection of manufactured consumer goods, the relative price of capital goods fell in manufacturing thus fostering a rise in capital formation rates and yields to equity capital. No doubt there were forces other than the tariff at work, but the fact remains that real yields on municipal, state and federal bonds in the 1870s were more than double the yields which were typical of the 1850s. Nor can the tariff fully account for the episodic changes in the relative price of farm products quoted in East coast cities, but the fact remains that the relative price of wheat suffered an enormous decline from 1860 to 1865, and the recovery in 1866, 1867 and 1868 was only temporary.

Finally, the composition of capital formation expenditures changed significantly following the Civil War. Railroads accounted for an enormous share of capital formation activity throughout much of the early and mid-1870s. These expenditures coincided with other forces which in combination induced an impressive collapse in interregional commodity price differentials. In effect, farmers in the interior enjoyed a sudden improvement in their terms of trade.

Forces of disequilibrium in the North

It does indeed appear that the late 1860s ushered in a new era in the American North. The savings rate rose to a new plateau. The relative price of producer durables fell to an all time low. The rate of capital formation resumed the impressive performance typical of the late ante bellum period. The period was also one of secular price decline as policy makers struggled with Resumption following the Greenback episode. Furthermore, while the Civil War decade recorded unusually low rates of technical change, the 1870s achieved very high rates of total factor productivity growth in both agriculture and manufacturing. Finally, immigration, a significant determinant of labor force growth in the North, did not recover the levels achieved in the early mid-1850s until 1866. From 1866 to 1874, the European flood gates opened once more. In short, the underlying forces driving economic development in the North were unusually strong following the Civil War.

Inevitably, the American North found it difficult to digest this banquet after the wartime famine. The economy found itself in disequilibrium. The relative price of farm products was low. The farmer voiced strident complaint while the economy rearranged its resources in favor of industry. The adjustment was slow, of course, since the disequilibrium induced by the Civil War was profound. The financial capital market also found the adjustment difficult. Wide interest rate and rate of return differentials were the norm. This, after all, was the age for the Morgans and Rockefellers to capture large quasi-rents produced by disequilibrating forces unleashed following the war. Real wage disparities between regions and industries were magnified as the labor market fought to redirect workers to those activities especially favored by 'catching-up' growth. This, then, was the economic setting in 1870.

The end of an era

Our analysis ceases with 1910, shortly before World War I. That, too, is a conventional benchmark but it could be argued that our study should terminate even earlier at the turn of the century. Around 1900 the American economy is once again subjected to unusual episodic changes. The most familiar, of course, is the reversal in 1896 of a long-run secular decline in the general price level. Yet, there were other more fundamental forces at work which support our decision to stop the analysis shortly after the turn of the century.

First, rates of total factor productivity growth within sectors cease their gradual fall around 1900. Indeed, there is considerable evidence to suggest the dating of a 'technological epoch' between 1907 and 1920. Not only did the rate of technical progress accelerate to a new plateau, but the biases inherent in the new technologies apparently changed markedly. Secondly, the aggregate savings rate underwent another episodic rise early in the twentieth century. Third, by the turn of the century America had been transformed from her traditional role as primary product exporter to the 'industrial workshop of the world.' Finally, grain product prices enjoyed a boom after the 1890s.

In brief the American economy's historical setting was very different by 1910. It seems wise to terminate the analysis by that date.

1.3 Late nineteenth-century economic experience in the North: the issues

In what sense is the Civil War decade a watershed in Northern development? Obviously, we find it helpful to view the Civil War as a source of profound economic disequilibrium. An underlying premise of this book is that subsequent economic change in the American North up to the turn of the century, and even World War I, can be analyzed most effectively as a long-term response to these disequilibrium conditions. The response took many forms, of course, but the chapters which follow dwell at length on six of these. These six key issues have become the traditional foci for economic historians of the post-Civil War period. For the most part, the issues are either still unresolved or incorrectly resolved.

The Great Depression

English growth experience from the 1860s to the 1890s has long been the source of debate, so much so that the period has been assigned a special label, the 'Great Depression.' Post-Civil War performance in the American North after the 'catching up' phase in the 1870s is strikingly similar. Per capita output and labor productivity growth decline with a marked persistence from 1870 to the turn of the century. Nor is this simply an agricultural phenomenon, although it is agriculture's asserted poor performance that has attracted attention. Why did America undergo this secular decline in growth performance after the 1870s? Why is this trend reversed in the late 1890s?

Furthermore, why does the period also produce a long-term secular decline in nominal interest rates? A secular decline in the price level might have been sufficient to produce that result, but why then do real interest rates decline even more rapidly up to the mid-1890s? Furthermore, the very high yields on government and railroad bonds attained in the 1870s do not hold up but steadily fall up to the 1890s. Why? Indeed, why is this trend reversed at the turn of the century? To lengthen our menu still further, why do real wages surge during the same period?

Chapter 5 confronts each of these Great Depression issues in considerable detail. If the chapter successfully finds persuasive answers then we shall have learned much about nineteenth-century American development. In the process, an attempt is made to disentangle real factors from purely monetary ones. Furthermore, it confronts two popular beliefs regarding nineteenth-century American growth. First, the contribution of land availability and the 'frontier' to this growth performance is assessed. Second, American experience with technical progress is investigated. Are rates of economic growth fundamentally influenced by total factor productivity performance, or is the association primarily a twentieth-century phenomenon? The chapter concludes with detailed attention to capital formation rates and the causes of the trend reversal at the turn of the century.

National capital market integration

Financial historians have long stressed the importance of capital market institutions as an influence on national growth performance. The implication of their research is that ineffective financial intermediation can produce serious 'market failure' and inhibit industrialization. Not surprisingly, post-Civil War development has been subjected to similar scrutiny. Business histories abound on individual savings banks, the mortgage companies, national banking, and the direct securities market. Quite naturally, interest rate differentials between financial markets have commonly been used to evaluate the operation of these markets, the effectiveness of intermediation, and success with the 'integration of a national capital market.' The current view appears to be the following: After the Civil War decade, and with the extraordinary surge during 'catching up,' the capital market was forced into disequilibrium. Interregional interest rate differentials were a well-known characteristic of the American economy, even prior to the Civil War, but these differentials were unusually large in the early 1870s. Economic historians have documented a convergence of interest rates thereafter. As a result, the four decades prior to World War I are conventionally considered a period of national capital market integration.

How do we account for the evolution of a national capital market from 1870 to 1914? Chapter 6 pursues two other related issues as well. How was American experience with structural change and regional development affected by capital immobility? Can we measure the economic cost of the capital immobilities in terms of aggregate growth foregone? The chapter concludes with a tentative evaluation of the role of financial intermediation as a determinant of aggregate savings in the North.

Farmer discontent

Chapter 7 explores the behavior of farm income and land values in the Midwest during the post-Civil War period. Traditionally, the economic historian has been preoccupied with farmers' discontent up to 1896. Yet, the literature contains no universal agreement on the economic position of the farmer in the late nineteenth century, let alone whether the root causes of discontent were primarily economic. Chapter 7 establishes the uncertain facts of farm performance and evidence is reviewed on the historical movements in land values, capital gains as a component of farm income, the Midwest 'farm-gate' terms of trade, and labor productivity growth in Midwest agriculture. The chapter adopts a revisionist position which contrasts sharply with the interpretations embedded in most conventional textbooks. The key questions are: Did land rents rise over the period? Did real income of Midwestern farmers improve up to the 1890s? If so, did their income position improve relative to the remainder of the American economy? How serious was the farm problem – e.g., 'too many farmers' – in the late nineteenth century? Finally, the paradox of booming land values during a period of asserted agricultural depression is confronted. Did land values rise as a result of increasing net cash income per acre, irrational speculation, or other forces?

After this ball of conflicting and confusing evidence on farm performance is unravelled, we turn to the more fundamental issues. What determined the behavior of land rents, land values, off-farm migration and farm mechanization following the Civil War decade? Chapter 10 examines the role played by world market conditions. Chapter 9 establishes the importance of the railroads. Chapter 8 deals with both the contribution of progress with agricultural technology and land expansion at the frontier.

The role of the railroads

American economic historians unanimously agree that railroad freight rates fell sharply from 1870 to 1890. Yet, there have been few attempts to construct meaningful real transport cost series relevant for an analysis of internal trade. Chapter 9 supplies such an index and establishes its impact on regional commodity prices. This empirical effort is essential since it is generally believed that variance in commodity terms of trade across sections can explain much of the regional specialization patterns, real wage behavior, and regional experience with capital deepening. The chapter then attempts to re-evaluate the impact of the railroads on American late nineteenth-century development. In contrast with recent railroad research, the chapter does not compare the rails with competing transport modes in 1890, but rather estimates the impact of railroad development over the two decades prior to 1890. What were the 'social savings' of the railroads? What was their impact on capital formation and output growth? Did they foster or retard industrialization? Did the railroads have an important impact on farm performance in the Midwest? How were off-farm migration patterns affected by the rails? Did interregional transport improvements significantly influence Westward migration rates, or was the impact restricted primarily to the Midwest itself? Did the rails have any impact on regional and farm–non-farm wage differentials?

European trade and world markets

The interaction between trade and growth has attracted much of the economic historian's attention, and nowhere has this concern been more intense than on the experience of North America. Late nineteenth-century America has often been cited as a classic historical example where trade has been an 'engine of growth.' Economic historians have theorized about the impact of trade on growth in other guises as well. The staple theory has been an especially popular mode of analysis in Canadian economic history. When applied to tropical developing economies, the framework has another label – vent for surplus. The impact of world market conditions is at the heart of the engine-of-growth, vent-for-surplus, and staple theories of historical development. Whether the focus is on cotton in the ante bellum South or grain in the Midwest from the 1850s onwards, resource intensive regional exploitation for export is being considered concomitant with other indigenous growth forces. As a result, the historian has found it difficult to identify that share of regional growth performance attributable to the export engine.

Chapter 10 contains an accounting of the engine of growth thesis. The following questions are raised: What would have been the performance of the grain-producing Midwest in the absence of changing world market conditions after the Civil War decade? Do changing world market conditions – including rising agrarian protectionism in Europe – account for much of the observed rapid industrialization following the Civil War? Were exports an engine of or a drag on growth? The chapter concludes with a skeptical look at the 'immiserizing growth' thesis and the evidence of price inelastic demand conditions for American grains in European markets.

Immigration and economic growth

The book concludes in chapter 11 with an analysis of European emigration to America following the ebb during the Civil War. In contrast with most of the immigration literature, the chapter does not deal with immigration cycles but rather attempts to disentangle the determinants of long-term migration patterns. What share of the secular increase in the foreign-born in America after 1870 can be attributed to the 'pull' of the New World? How much to the 'push' of conditions in Europe? Are European push conditions dominated by demographic forces and the Malthusian Devil, or is this determinant of transatlantic immigration exaggerated? Were real wages and industrialization rates significantly influenced by European push conditions, or is this interdependence in the Atlantic economy also exaggerated? What were the sources of pull in America? Did the frontier really have an important influence on immigration after the Civil War? Were demographic conditions in the American North influential? All of these questions are confronted in chapter 11 and the answers are important in revising our conventional views of late nineteenth-century American development.

These then, are the historical questions which this book raises. The answers appear only reluctantly.

2
Counterfactual History

Art is a lie which makes us realize the truth.

Picasso

2.1 A survey of the methodological terrain[1]

The questions raised in the previous chapter require quantitative answers to be of real interest to the economic historian. Furthermore, the obvious complexity of the issues necessitates the use of well articulated and detailed economic models. Unfortunately, this is the price we must pay for cliometric research if that research is to be truly useful to the general economic historian as well as the economist. The reader must pay the price too, since he cannot evaluate the quality and usefulness of the answers presented in chapters 5 through 11 until he is thoroughly convinced that the methods used are sensible.

Chapter 3 constructs a model of late nineteenth-century American development which appears to be relevant for historical analysis. The model ignores much of the institutional richness and microeconomic detail of the post-Civil War economy, but it is sufficiently complex to confront the issues raised in chapter 1. No doubt the model will have its critics, but hopefully this book will generate sufficient interest to encourage others to develop just as explicitly their alternative descriptions of the late nineteenth-century American economy. In any case, the reader should hardly judge the model solely by the brief for the defense contained in chapter 3. The proof of the pudding is in the eating, and the pudding of chapter 3 can be consumed in chapter 4. There an attempt is made to establish the empirical plausibility of this model of late nineteenth-century development by comparing its predictions with historical fact. Obviously, we feel that the model survives this crucial test fairly well for otherwise the book would never have been written.

Having convinced the reader that the model conforms to reality reasonably well, it can be used to improve our understanding of late nineteenth-century economic experience. Indeed, while comparison between fact and prediction helps reconcile many paradoxes and poorly understood relationships which have puzzled economic historians of the period, the exercise is only the prologue to our economic history of this crucial phase of American growth. The main acts of the play are to be found in Part III of the book where the framework is used to uncover the 'lessons of history.' Before turning to these chapters, the reader may wish to know how we intend to proceed.

How will the model be used to identify the sources of American economic performance in the post-Civil War era? Not surprisingly, Part III relies heavily, but not solely, on the counterfactual. The present chapter briefly reports the use of the counterfactual as a tool of the 'new' economic history. It also contains a discussion of the more recent applications of general equilibrium analysis to economic history. We shall argue that many, if not most, of the economic issues raised in chapter 1 cannot be effectively answered by partial equilibrium models – the favorite mode of analysis by the new economic history. Yet, we point out that the recent general equilibrium applications are also too restrictive for our purposes, since they rely only on comparative statics. A comparative dynamic approach to late nineteenth-century American development is suggested as an alternative. We then indicate how the counterfactual can be utilized to help uncover the lessons of post-Civil War American history.

2.2 Counterfactual history and economic analysis

The method employed in chapters 5 through 11 of this book can perhaps best be understood by a simple – though relevant – example. Consider one issue of fundamental interest to the economic historian, the sources of industrialization. Industrialization can be measured either in terms of the distribution of output or the distribution of input between sectors. By convention, a change in the relative share of industry value added in gross national product is normally termed 'industrialization.' Obviously, the sectoral disaggregation can be made as detailed as desired but the non-agriculture value added share is sufficient to illustrate our argument. Movements in this statistic have been central to historical analysis since the British Industrial Revolution began. Not long ago W. W. Rostow gave it a dramatic name, the 'take-off.'[2] Measurement of industrialization performance in nineteenth-century America has been equally active.[3]

Measurement of structural change from the input side has usually dealt with employment distribution, since labor force data are available in greater abundance than capital stock data. Furthermore, changes in the relative share of industrial employment in the total labor force, $u(t)$, are often equated with urbanization.[4] In confronting this aspect of industrialization, some historians prefer to focus on the employment mix itself while others find it more useful to deal with the *process of change* in the mix; that is, the rate of off-farm migration or the rate of employment growth in industry. For expositional convenience, we shall consider the former.

Comparative static analysis of the model developed in chapter 3 is quite explicit regarding the impact of capital accumulation on $u(t)$. Successful capital formation tends to raise the relative price of labor as workers become increasingly better equipped. Industrial entrepreneurs and farmers both attempt to save on the now more expensive input by introducing labor-saving machinery wherever possible. Relative to agriculture, industry is favored by the rise in the price of men since it is the more capital-intensive activity. It also can expand without facing the relatively inelastic supply of a third factor, land. Consequently, there is a relative push of labor off the farm. In addition, this supply effect may be reinforced by demand conditions (a low income elasticity of demand for foodstuffs) if the economy in question is sufficiently large to influence world market conditions. In summary, a rise in the capital stock per worker tends to foster a rise in $u(t)$ and thus industrialization takes place. This result can be expressed formally as

$$\frac{\partial u(t)}{\partial k(t)} > 0,$$

where $k(t)$ is the economy-wide capital–labor ratio. Alternatively, our interest may center on the elasticity of $u(t)$ in response to $k(t)$,

$$\frac{\partial u(t)}{\partial k(t)} \cdot \frac{k(t)}{u(t)} > 0,$$

which varies not only with $\partial u(t)/\partial k(t)$ but also with the conditions prevailing at some point in historical time when the elasticity is being computed. For example, it may depend on the maturity of the economy as measured by $u(t)$ and $k(t)$. In any case, as long as industry remains the more capital-intensive sector, and given the relative inelasticity of land supply in agriculture, capital formation will always foster a labor transfer from agriculture to industry.

The economic historian, however, is interested in the *quantitative* dimensions involved for a specific economy. He wishes to know how government policy, the changing elasticity of land supply, technical change, and world demand might have influenced the impact of capital formation on industrialization. The *magnitude* of the rate of labor transfer resulting from a given rate of capital formation depends crucially on the structural parameters of the economy and its institutional setting.

Finally, the observed rate of industrialization obviously depends on the rate of capital formation actually achieved during a given phase of history.

The impact of capital formation on industrialization can be viewed as a combination of these effects:

$$\frac{\dot{u}(t)}{u(t)} = \frac{k(t)}{u(t)} \cdot \frac{\partial u(t)}{\partial k(t)} \cdot \frac{\dot{k}(t)}{k(t)}.$$

The theorist may be wary in evaluating the impact of a small change in $\dot{k}(t)/k(t)$ on $\dot{u}(t)/u(t)$ since his result may be sensitive to both initial conditions and structural parameters assumed in the model. Indeed, he may wish to know precisely how the structural parameters influence the impact. Chastened by the theorists' warnings, the empirical economist therefore takes care in evaluating the sensitivity of his conclusions by performing what is known as 'parametric analysis.' The economic historian is even more pragmatic. First, he has little interest in an abstract evaluation of a modelled economy's behavior. Second, he is not particularly concerned with the fact that the elasticity of $u(t)$ with respect to $k(t)$ is influenced by initial conditions and structural parameters for after all his interest is centered on a particular economy at a particular point in time: in our case, the American economy, 1870–1910. Indeed, the economic historian may wish to explore *how a given economy would have behaved under alternative historical conditions.* Suppose the rate of capital accumulation had been raised by 1 percent per annum had the American capital market operated with costless speed and perfect efficiency. How would the rate of industrialization have been affected? An answer to this question would yield an explicit measure of the industrialization foregone during a period of 'capital market imperfection.' It would help us identify the sources of late nineteenth-century American industrialization in general, as well as the asserted contribution of 'capital market integration' in particular. This experiment is called an *historical counterfactual* and it illustrates the method used in Part III to uncover the lessons of United States late nineteenth-century history.

2.3   American cliometric history

A look backwards

Explicit counterfactual analysis in American economic history did not really reveal itself fully until the appearance of Robert Fogel's research on the railroads.[5] Fogel argued that the impact of the railroads on late nineteenth-century American development could not be adequately appreciated unless one asked how the development of the economy would have been altered by its absence. It is evident that a quantitative answer to that question requires the development of an explicit economic model. The appearance of explicit models, like the one presented and defended in chapter 3 of this book, was greeted with uneasiness by most practitioners in the discipline. Nevertheless, it is now clear to us all that the 'traditional' historian differs from the cliometrician only by his reliance on *implicit* theorizing: 'The real difference between the new economic historians and their predecessors lies in the approach to the specification of models rather than in the frequency with which models are employed.'[6] Furthermore, with the appearance of *explicit* counterfactual analysis, American economic historians have made notable strides in determining the economic effects of the ante bellum tariff, slavery, railroads, the Bessemer converter, the reaper, the Revolutionary War and the availability of a frontier.[7] These effects could not have been isolated without considering how the American economy would have progressed in the absence of such institutions, processes and artifacts.[8]

General debate over the usefulness of modelling historical events is not very productive. The skeptical historian (and economist!) reading this book is urged to consider the specific harvest displayed in chapters 5 to 11 before passing judgement. There the counterfactual is applied to late nineteenth-century America by considering how her development would have been altered in the absence of factors considered by many to be critical. Among these are: elastic land supplies; rapid technical progress in agriculture; elastic European immigration rates; regional transport improvements; imperfectly functioning financial capital markets; deteriorating world market conditions for American grains; and so on. When explicit counterfactuals like these are posed of the late nineteenth-century American economy, the answers are often at variance with conventional wisdom.

Although the debate over 'theorizing' in economic history seems by hindsight to have been unproductive, the debate over *testing* of our applied theory does not. In Redlich's words 'What in theory is entirely correct becomes fictitious in the application, the result being a model rather than something related to reality.'[9] Counterfactual models need not be a direct threat to the integrity of economic history if care is taken to establish the applied theory as empirically warranted.[10] Thus, we heartily agree with the critics that considerable effort should be made to verify these 'figments' before proceeding with counterfactual analysis. This is in fact the goal of chapter 4: to convince the reader that our figment in chapter 3 is a plausible – empirically warranted – theoretical characterization of late nineteenth-century American development.

The art of asking useful questions

Were we even to agree that the model underlying a particular counterfactual history was correctly specified, we may still disagree regarding the appropriate questions to ask of the model so as to derive lessons of history in the best way. Consider briefly just two issues which have attracted much of the profession's attention: the role of the railroads and the impact of an imperfectly functioning capital market. How is counterfactual analysis to be used in confronting these two issues so deeply embedded in American historiography?

The conventional literature had always asserted that the railroads were a fundamental force in American development. Professor Fogel created quite a stir when he derived a quantitative answer to the question: By how much would annual GNP have been diminished in 1890 had the railroads been replaced by second best modes of regional transport? The answer was 'surprisingly little.' The implication of this counterfactual exercise appeared to be that the railroads were hardly essential to American development and thus they did not warrant the detailed attention which traditional scholarship had devoted to them. Yet, Fogel's counterfactual may not be entirely satisfactory in an evaluation of the role of the railroads in American growth. An equally interesting question might be: How would American economic performance have been altered if the impressive interregional transport improvements of the post-Civil War period failed to take place? Fogel's counterfactual confronts the issue of relative efficiency of transport modes *at one point in time*, 1890. The alternative counterfactual confronts the issue of efficiency improvements in all transport modes *over time*. Debate over the relative merits of these competing questions is deferred to chapter 9, but one thing is clear: the answers are very different. The impact of counterfactual analysis on economic history is conditioned not only by the skill of the researcher at model building, but also by the questions asked.

Consider a second issue of equal importance to American historiography. Economic historians have allocated much of their efforts in documenting the institutional behaviour of financial capital markets. Volumes have accumulated on the growth of savings banks, the mobility of merchant capital, the rise of life insurance and mortgage companies, the role of banking and Crédit Mobilier, the operation of international securities markets – the list extends indefinitely. The prime motivation of this research in financial history appears to be a conviction that national and regional development has been fundamentally shaped by the ability or inability of these institutions to transfer potential savings from developed surplus regions to developing deficit regions, from the metropolis to the

frontier, from stagnant senile sectors and industries to youthful and
vigorous ones. If these institutions fail to perform their functions
effectively, aggregate economic performance is suppressed. Poor
economic performance may be traced, at least in part, to the inef-
fectiveness of these institutions. A corollary clearly seems to be
that observed 'improvements' in the effective operation of
capital markets contribute in no small measure to overall economic
growth.

It is true that our understanding of the operation of financial
capital markets in the post-Civil War period is incomplete. No
consensus has emerged in accounting for interest rate differentials
across sectors and regions from the 1860s to the 1910s. Do they
reflect disequilibrium in these financial markets? Do they reflect
instead nothing more than real transaction costs associated with
financial transfer akin to real transport costs associated with the
movement of commodities? The reader will not find an answer to
these questions in chapter 6. The chapter sidesteps this issue and
asks the following counterfactual: what would have been the impact
on late nineteenth-century development had the capital market
been able to allocate national savings across sectors and regions
instantaneously and without cost? Presumably the answer is of some
interest even though our knowledge of why the rate differentials
existed remains cloudy.

In short, the contribution of cliometric history is not only limited
by the practitioners' ability to build relevant models which economize on scarce historical data. It is also, and perhaps more seriously,
limited by their creativity in phrasing useful historical questions.

2.4 General equilibrium models and historical analysis

New insights into old problems

Following the introduction of *explicit* counterfactual analysis in
American economic history a decade or so ago, a new but inevitable
debate began to take place within the ranks of the cliometricians
themselves. What was the appropriate mode of historical analysis?
Should the railroads be evaluated in a partial equilibrium vacuum –
that is, restricted to the transport sector itself, or should the analysis
of such an important historical event be evaluated in a general
equilibrium framework – that is, exploring the interdependent
impact throughout the economy?[11] Should the impact of the frontier
on American development be evaluated by partial equilibrium
analysis of agriculture alone, or should its impact be traced throughout the economy as a whole?[12] Can the impact of ante bellum tariff
policy be effectively captured using partial equilibrium analysis, or
is general equilibrium analysis essential to derive an accurate under-

standing of its influence?[13] Recent research in American economic history has shown quite convincingly that a general equilibrium approach is essential for many of the problems of interest to economic historians. The analysis contained in Part III warrants the same conclusion regarding historical research on late nineteenth-century American development.

Comparative static analysis: critique

The use of general equilibrium models in economic history has two inherent weaknesses. The first relates to their inevitable *simplicity*; the second to the conventional mode of analysis – that is, a heavy reliance on *comparative statics*. While the first pitfall cannot be avoided, the second can.

All models are 'simple' in the sense that they abstract from elements in the real world thought to be unimportant. Without a judicious use of simplification, no understanding of an economic process would be possible and a chronicle of events would be the only bequest made by the historian. Instead, the art is to develop models of historical development which capture the essential and suppress the trivial. Even those aspects of an economy thought to be absolutely fundamental can often be taken as exogenous, thereby simplifying the model yet allowing subsequent analysis of the excluded activity by treating it as a parameter change. For example, governmental activity need not be introduced into a model to explore the impact of government policy on the economy. As long as the rate of technical change in agriculture can be identified as having been influenced by government policy, the impact of that policy can be readily evaluated using a model in which technical change has a role. Similarly, if tariff policy can be shown to have had a pronounced influence on the post-Civil War domestic price structure, the impact of that policy can be easily estimated using a model where commodity prices have an influence. In any case, explicit theorizing is especially helpful in uncovering the sources of historical growth and development. Only then are the underlying assumptions made sufficiently clear so that the burden of proof can be shifted onto others who may choose to approach history with a competing model. Nor is it necessarily the case that a more complex model will more closely conform to reality. Complexity and realism are hardly synonymous when it comes to developing models of historical development.

An issue far more important than simplicity is *efficiency*: 'The attempt to transform economic history from a discipline based on implicit, weakly specified, and untested theories to one based on rigorously specified and empirically warranted theories is a prodigious and frustrating enterprise. The greatest obstacle is the

paucity of data.'[14] While researchers investigating the 1920s and
the depression of the 1930s may enjoy the luxury of evaluating large
equation systems, those of us interested in the pre-World War I
period have no such option. As the discussion in chapters 3 and 4
and appendix A indicates, the historical data for the post-Civil War
period are still of limited quantity and quality in spite of the impressive efforts of Kuznets, Gallman, Easterlin and other pioneers. The
model used in this book was developed with an eye on data availability. It was made as efficient as possible with respect to the
available historical record. The simplicity of the model was in fact
an explicit goal so as to minimize the number of parameters for
which quantitative information was required.

In our judgement, the more serious limitation of 'general equilibrium' histories lies elsewhere. With very few exceptions, these
histories rely on comparative static analysis.[15] These studies evaluate
the impact of a given 'institution, process or artifact' under the
assumption that the resource endowment, subsequent technology
and even commodity prices are fixed. Development and growth
economists would be uneasy with such an approach. The economic
historian must feel a similar disquietude. Can the dynamic effects
associated with exogenous changes in the Midwestern land stock,
world market conditions, or foreign immigration rates be ignored
in any meaningful analysis of the American economy? It seems
unlikely. However primitive, some theory of resource growth and
technological change should be appended to the static model. Comparative static analyses which identify the historical impact of
exogenous variables on income distribution, factor prices and output mix may possibly be of limited usefulness if these endogenous
variables have an impact, in turn, on rates of capital formation or
technological progress.

2.5 Comparative dynamics and the counterfactual

The simulation reported in chapter 4 is our approximation of the
developing American economy between 1870 and 1910. The correspondence between this simulated 'fiction' and historical fact is
hardly perfect, but it is sufficiently close, in our judgement, to
warrant use of the model in historical analysis. This simulation is
labelled 'actual' for the remainder of the book. What we propose to
do in Part III is to compare the 'actual history' with a sequence of
'counterfactual histories.' The discrepancy between these pairs of
simulations can then be explicitly attributed to whatever parameter
has been changed in each counterfactual. For example, the following counterfactual is posed in chapter 7: what would have been the
nature of American economic growth had the frontier shut abruptly

in 1870? The actual simulation assumes the rate of Midwest farm-land expansion documented by Tostlebe. A counterfactual world of intensive agricultural development assumes instead a fixed land stock in the Midwest set at prevailing 1870 levels. The two cases are identical in all other dimensions. The actual and counterfactual histories are then compared. Divergence in output per capita growth, regional performance, real wages, industrialization rates, migration to the 'frontier,' and so on can then be attributed explicitly to the different rates of expansion in the land stock. The experiment makes it possible to identify in quantitative terms just how much of late nineteenth-century American growth experience can be attributed to her 'unique' natural resource conditions. Similar counterfactual analysis is applied to other parameters: the rate of technical progress in agriculture, the impact of national capital market integration, the role of the railroads, the impact of world market conditions, and the role of foreign immigration.

Each of these counterfactuals is an exercise in comparative dynamics. The results are highly enlightening and very often conflict with *ex post* accountings of late nineteenth-century economic growth.

Part II The Framework

3

A Model of Late Nineteenth-Century American Regional Growth

> The real difference between the new economic historians and their predecessors lies in the approach to the specification of models rather than in the frequency with which models are employed.   Robert W. Fogel (1967)[1]

3.1 Introduction

A set of historical issues regarding American development following the 1860s has been identified in chapter 1. Chapter 2 argued that before these issues can be confronted, some theoretical framework must be constructed to facilitate historical analysis. The present chapter develops what we believe is an historically relevant model which can adequately deal with all of these issues. Section 3.2 exploits a very simple general equilibrium framework which highlights the structure of the more complex comparative static model utilized in subsequent chapters. The framework of the more complex model is discussed verbally in section 3.3 while a formal statement is presented in section 3.4. The empirical content of the model is described in section 3.5 and appendix A. Finally, the plausibility of the model is evaluated in chapter 4 where the predictions of the model are compared with the historical evidence.

3.2 Simple general equilibrium analysis and comparative statics

The model used in this book can be best understood if we first explore a simpler general equilibrium system, one which is representative of those recently applied to American and European economic history. The discussion in this section relies extensively for this purpose on the papers by Ronald Jones and Glenn Hueckel.[1]

Consider a regional economy, such as the American Midwest, producing agricultural and manufactured commodities. Let agricultural goods be used only for consumption purposes,[2] and furthermore assume that these commodities bulk large in workers' expenditures. Let manufactures be used for both consumption and investment purposes. We also impose the conventional assumptions of pure competition, full employment and constant returns to scale. Furthermore, we invoke the 'small country' assumption so that commodity prices are given exogenously to the region. The regional economy is thus considered sufficiently small to have only a negligible influence on world market prices. Under these textbook conditions trade flows are determined residually and domestic demand conditions serve only to determine external trade volumes. That is, regional demand has an influence on the size of the surplus exported but not on the regional production patterns themselves. Thus, the model is completely supply oriented. Finally, let the regional resource endowment be given exogenously. There are three primary factors of production: labor (used in both sectors), capital (used in both sectors), and land (used only in agriculture). Labor and capital are fully mobile while land is an immobile factor specific to agriculture. The following notation will prove helpful:

Q_A = agricultural output,
Q_I = industrial output,
R = land stock,
L = labor force,
K = physical stock of homogenous machines,
P_A = price of agricultural commodities,
P_I = price of industrial commodities,
d = rents (value marginal product of land),
w = wage rate (value marginal product of labor),
r = rate of return on capital (value marginal product of capital).

Full employment in this simple economy requires that

$$a_{RA}Q_A = R,$$
$$a_{KA}Q_A + a_{KI}Q_I = K,$$
$$a_{LA}Q_A + a_{LI}Q_I = L,$$

where a_{ij} is the amount of the ith factor necessary to produce the jth output. The a_{ij} are variable and respond to changes in relative factor prices. In equilibrium, factor payments exhaust total value of output, so that commodity prices and unit production costs will be equated:

$$a_{RA}d + a_{LA}w + a_{KA}r = P_A,$$
$$a_{LI}w + a_{KI}r = P_I.$$

To summarize, factor stocks are given exogenously by previous historical experience with capital accumulation, resource development, migration and natural native population growth; so too are commodity prices and production technologies. These production technologies are described by the technical response of the a_{ij}, factor input requirements per unit of output, to factor input price ratios, a measure of the relative cost of factor inputs. Factor prices, income distribution and the output mix are all determined endogenously in the system. Given factor endowments, technologies and commodity prices, we can derive wages, rents, interest rates, factor income shares and output specialization patterns for this regional economy at one point in historical time.

This system of simultaneous equations can be solved so that such endogenous variables as the real wage, the output mix, and land rents can be expressed in terms of endogenous variables and parameters describing the economy's structure.[3] To illustrate the potential of such a model for historical research, consider its application to the American Midwest in the post-Civil War era. Three exogenous variables play a very important role in historical accounts of Midwestern regional development after 1870: (i) the commodity price ratio or terms of trade; (ii) the increase in improved farmland acreage or the availability of a 'frontier,' and (iii) capital formation. Each of these exogenous variables is thought to play a key role in influencing Midwestern experience with (i) real wages and thus Westward migration, (ii) land rents, land values and farmers' discontent, and (iii) industrialization, migration off the farm, and urbanization. Let us briefly explore the insights which the model produces regarding these important facets of post-Civil War Midwestern development.

Our interest here is limited to the real wage, the output mix, and land rents per acre as in (1a), (2a) and (3a):

$$w^* - P^*_A = \frac{1}{\Delta} \left\{ \left[\theta_{KA} \frac{\lambda_{KI}}{\lambda_{LI}} \lambda_{LA} \sigma_{L,R} - \right. \right.$$
$$- (\theta_{RA} + \theta_{KA}) \lambda_{KA} \sigma_{K,R} - \theta_{RA} \lambda_{KI} \sigma_I \left. \right] (P^*_A - P^*_I) +$$
$$+ \theta_{KI} \theta_{RA} \left[K^* + R^* \left(\frac{\lambda_{LA} - \lambda_{KA}}{\lambda_{LI}} \right) - \frac{\lambda_{KI}}{\lambda_{LI}} L^* \right] \right\}, \qquad (1a)$$

$$Q^*_A - Q^*_I = \frac{1}{\lambda_{LI}} (R^* - L^* - \lambda_{LI} a^*_{RA}) +$$
$$+ \frac{1}{\Delta} \left\{ \left[\lambda_{KA} \sigma_{K,R} \left(\frac{\lambda_{LA}}{\lambda_{LI}} \sigma_{L,R} + \theta_{KI} \sigma_I \right) + \theta_{LI} \frac{\lambda_{LA} \lambda_{KI}}{\lambda_{LI}} \sigma_I \sigma_{L,K} \right] \times \right.$$
$$\times (P^*_A - P^*_I) - \left[(\theta_{KI} - \theta_{KA}) \frac{\lambda_{LA}}{\lambda_{LI}} \sigma_{L,R} + \theta_{KI} \theta_{RA} \sigma_I \right] \times$$
$$\times \left[K^* + L^* \left(\frac{\lambda_{LA} - \lambda_{KA}}{\lambda_{LI}} \right) - \frac{\lambda_{KI}}{\lambda_{LI}} L^* \right] \right\}, \qquad (2a)$$

$$d^* = \frac{1}{\Delta} \left\{ P^*_A \left(\theta_{KI} \frac{\lambda_{KI}}{\lambda_{LI}} \lambda_{LA} \sigma_{L,R} + \theta_{LI} \lambda_{KA} \sigma_{K,R} + \lambda_{KI} \sigma_I \right) - \right.$$
$$- P^*_M \left[\theta_{KA} \frac{\lambda_{KI}}{\lambda_{LI}} \lambda_{LA} \sigma_{L,R} + \theta_{LA} \lambda_{KA} \sigma_{K,R} + (\theta_{LA} + \theta_{KA}) \lambda_{KI} \sigma_I \right] +$$
$$+ (\theta_{LI} \theta_{KA} - \theta_{LA} \theta_{KI}) \left[K^* + L^* \left(\frac{\lambda_{LA} - \lambda_{KA}}{\lambda_{LI}} \right) - \frac{\lambda_{KI}}{\lambda_{LI}} N^* \right] \right\}, \qquad (3a)$$

where

$$\Delta = (\theta_{KI} - \theta_{KA}) \frac{\lambda_{KI}}{\lambda_{LI}} \lambda_{LA} \sigma_{L,R} + (\theta_{LI} - \theta_{LA}) \lambda_{KA} \sigma_{K,R} + \theta_{RA} \lambda_{KI} \sigma_I .$$

In these equations, θ_{ij} is the distributive share of factor i in sector j, λ_{ij} is the share of an input i used in the jth sector, $\sigma_{i,k}$ is the elasticity of substitution between a pair of inputs in agriculture, and σ_I is the elasticity of substitution in industry. An asterisk represents a percentage change in a variable: e.g., a positive value for $(w^* - P^*_A)$ implies that real wages tend to rise in response to a small percentage change in one of the exogenous variables of interest. Finally, Δ is assumed positive since only in that case does the production possibility curve 'bulge outwards' as in Figure 3.1 where equation (2a) is reproduced in a more familiar graphic context. The production possibility curve is drawn where technology and resource endowment are fixed. Given relative commodity prices, the output mix is determined endogenously.

Figure 3.1 replicates the standard result that a relative expansion in agricultural output takes place in response to an increase in the relative price of farm products. In the context of late nineteenth-century Midwestern development, the relative improvement in *Midwestern* farm prices could have been induced by a decline in interregional freight rates on farm products exported to Eastern cities and European markets (chapter 9). A deterioration in the Midwestern terms of trade, on the other hand, could have been induced by either 'lagging' world market conditions for American farm products, or by increasing American protectionism which raised tariffs on the import of industrial goods from Europe. The analysis using (2a) and Figure 3.1 can be reconciled if a positive $(P^*_A - P^*_I)$ implies a positive $(Q^*_A - Q^*_I)$. This result is readily forthcoming

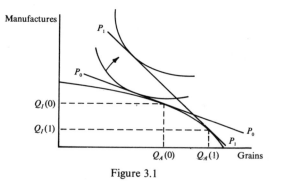

Figure 3.1

if (2a) is written for fixed endowments ($K^* = L^* = R^* = 0$) as in (2b):

$$Q^*_A - Q^*_I = -a^*_{RA} + \frac{1}{\Delta} \left\{ \left[\lambda_{KA}\sigma_{K,R} \left(\frac{\lambda_{LA}}{\lambda_{LI}}\sigma_{L,R} + \theta_{KI}\sigma_I \right) + \right. \right.$$
$$\left. \left. + \theta_{LI}\frac{\lambda_{LA}\lambda_{KI}}{\lambda_{LI}}\sigma_I\sigma_{L,K} \right] (P^*_A - P^*_I) \right\}. \qquad (2b)$$

Since Δ is positive, and $a^*_{RA} \leqq 0$, then $(Q^*_A - Q^*_I) > 0$. Although the textbook graph and the mathematics yield the same qualitative results, the explicit statement is (2b) has an obvious advantage over the graphical analysis in Figure 3.1: it is susceptible to *empirical* investigation and thus can supply a precise answer to historical questions relating to tariff policy, world market conditions or inter-regional transport costs, all of which have a direct impact on $(P^*_A - P^*_I)$.

Now consider the impact of commodity prices on real wages in the Midwest and thus on Westward migration. Certainly a rise in farm prices would reduce Midwestern real wages if expenditures on food dominate the worker's budget and if money wages are held constant. But wages do not remain constant, of course, since agriculture is a relatively labor intensive activity in the nineteenth century and its expansion should have fostered a relative increase in the regional derived demand for labor. Since our interest at the moment is in the impact of commodity prices, we can take $K^* = R^* = L^* = 0$ in (1a) and get (1b):

$$w^* - P^*_A = \frac{1}{\Delta} \left\{ \left[\theta_{KA}\frac{\lambda_{KI}}{\lambda_{LI}}\lambda_{LA}\sigma_{L,K} - \right. \right.$$
$$\left. \left. - (\theta_{RA} + \theta_{KA})\lambda_{KA}\sigma_{K,R} - \theta_{LA}\lambda_{KI}\sigma_I \right] (P^*_A - P^*_I) \right\}. \qquad (1b)$$

Expression (1b) can be made even simpler by the convenient assumption of unitary substitution elasticities (Cobb–Douglas production functions), as in (1c):

$$w^* - P^*_A = \frac{1}{\Delta} \left\{ \left[\theta_{KA}\frac{\lambda_{KI}}{\lambda_{LI}}\lambda_{LA} - \right. \right.$$
$$\left. \left. - (\theta_{RA} + \theta_{KA})\lambda_{KA} - \theta_{LA}\lambda_{KI} \right] (P^*_A - P^*_I) \right\}. \qquad (1c)$$

Even under these simplifying assumptions, we cannot tell whether a rise in Midwestern farm prices will tend to increase real wages and thus foster immigration to the region. That is, the sign of the expression in brackets preceding $(P^*_A - P^*_I)$ is ambiguous. Without utilizing empirical information on sectoral production functions and labor force distribution, we cannot conclude that improvements in Midwestern farm prices tended to raise or lower real wages there.

Thus, we cannot conclude, for example, that interregional transport improvements fostered Midwest employment expansion at the expense of the Northeast.

Finally, consider the impact of the Midwestern terms of trade on rents and land values (chapters 8, 9 and 10). Land values rose markedly in the Midwest after 1870. To what extent could these increases have been induced by improved rents per acre in response to rising farm prices as freight rates on interregional grain shipments declined? Equation (3a) can be simplified for this purpose by assuming $K^* = L^* = R^* = 0$ and Cobb–Douglas production functions, to get (3b):

$$d^* = \frac{1}{\Delta} \left\{ P^*_A \left(\theta_{KI} \frac{\lambda_{KI}}{\lambda_{LI}} \lambda_{LA} + \theta_{LI}\lambda_{KA} + \lambda_{KI} \right) - \right.$$

$$\left. - P^*_I \quad \theta_{KA} \frac{\lambda_{KI}}{\lambda_{LI}} \lambda_{LA} + \theta_{LA}\lambda_{KA} + (\theta_{LA} + \theta_{KA})\lambda_{KI} \right\}. \qquad (3b)$$

Since our interest is in the case where $P^*_A > 0$ and $P^*_I < 0$, it follows that $d^* > 0$. Presumably, land values rise as a consequence. Now the mathematics underlying equation (3b) were hardly necessary to reach the obvious intuitive conclusion that rising farm prices improve land rents. But (3b) offers a vehicle for identifying the *quantitative* impact of the price change on rents. Indeed, perhaps our intuition would not have suggested that the magnitude of the effect is stronger the larger is the employment share in agriculture and the smaller is the share of rents in farm income.

To take another example of the use to which these models may be put, consider an issue of concern to Turner and Habakkuk:[4] the importance of 'land availability' in determining American real wages. In equation (1a), take $(P^*_A - P^*_I) = 0$, $K^* = L^* = 0$, but $R^* > 0$. Under these assumptions, (1a) collapses to (1d):

$$w^* - P^*_A = \frac{1}{\Delta} \left\{ \theta_{KI}\theta_{RA}R^* \left(\frac{\lambda_{LA} - \lambda_{KA}}{\lambda_{LI}} \right) \right\}. \qquad (1d)$$

Thus real wages tend to be higher given the presence of a 'frontier' if the proportion of the American labor force employed in agriculture exceeds the proportion of the American capital stock employed there: e.g., if agriculture is more labor intensive than industry. Furthermore, (1d) can tell us by how much they would be raised if the parameters appearing in that expression can be estimated.

One final experiment with the simple general equilibrium model should prove helpful as an introduction to the analysis contained in this book. What is the impact of capital formation in the Midwest on the structural transformation of the region? Presumably, capital formation is central to the industrialization experience of the Midwest. To take explicit account of capital formation on industrialization, we need only rewrite (2a) where $P^*{}_A = P^*{}_I = 0$ and $L^* = R^* = 0$ as in (2c):

$$Q^*{}_A - Q^*{}_I = -a^*{}_{RA} - \frac{1}{\Delta} \left\{ (\theta_{KI} - \theta_{KA}) \frac{\lambda_{LA}}{\lambda_{KI}} + \theta_{KI}\theta_{RA} \right\} K^*, \qquad (2c)$$

where once again we assume Cobb–Douglas production functions. There is no ambiguity here: where $K^* > 0$, $(Q^*{}_A - Q^*{}_I) < 0$, or, in simple terms, capital formation fosters regional industrialization. Furthermore, note that this result is forthcoming regardless of the demand conditions specified. Industrialization follows in the wake of capital formation independent of Engel effects; e.g., it follows whether the income elasticity of demand for foodstuffs is less than unity or not.

The economic system we have been exploring thus far is identical with the comparative static model used in this book to describe the Midwest in the late nineteenth century, *with two important exceptions*:

(i) Since our interest is in the empirical application of this model, factor price equalization between sectors cannot be assumed since it was rarely achieved. The general equilibrium model discussed above assumes full mobility of capital. One reason why factor price equalization fails to appear in history is because capital is 'putty-clay.' Reapers cannot be converted into spindles overnight and thus there is no reason to assume full mobility except for analytical convenience. The model developed in section 3.3 assumes instead that capital once in place is fully *immobile*. Only new investment can shift the relative employment of the Midwestern capital stock and that takes time. Furthermore, our model of regional growth contains limitations on intersectoral financing of new investment by the introduction of a financial market which operates subject to positive transaction and information costs. Two borrowing rates (and net rates of return on capital) prevail in the Midwest to reflect this disequilibrium: a farm mortgage rate and an industrial bond rate. Labor migration off the farm is also inhibited by uncertainty and information costs so that farm and urban wages need not be equalized in the short run.

(ii) As it now stands, the comparative static analysis briefly developed above bears only limited resemblance to American sectional history since changes in factor returns in the Midwest generated an immediate factor supply response. Consider the real wage expression (1a) once again. Cliometricians utilizing such models presumably feel that a comparative static experiment which holds resource endowments fixed while raising the relative price of agricultural goods would be useful in understanding the impact of declining interregional transport costs on real wages in the Midwest. Suppose, however, that the real wage itself influences L^*? Are the comparative static results very helpful in this case? After all, higher real wages in the Midwest induced Westward migration. In addition, higher return to Western capital induced investment inflows from Eastern financial centers. Similar arguments could easily be constructed for other endogenous variables in the simple regional economy modelled above.

It follows that the Midwest cannot be treated in isolation. Rather, the Northeast must be explicitly introduced into our comparative static model since interregional factor mobility is clearly an important aspect of American regional development. The model developed in section 3.3 treats this regional interdependence of factor markets explicitly and attempts to capture the historically important fact that Midwestern capital formation and labor force growth were facilitated by large-scale factor migrations from the more developed Northeast. The simple model is thus expanded to encompass two interdependent regional economies with interacting factor and commodity markets. The expanded model presents us with the opportunity to introduce transport costs on interregional commodity trade and the railroad (or social savings) issue can be confronted directly.

The recent applications of general equilibrium models to problems in economic history have another limitation.[5] Even if we exclude a *foreign* migration response to American real wages (the 'pull' of employment conditions), and exclude a *foreign* investment response to rates of return on American capital as well, can the dynamic effects associated with exogenous changes in the land stock, world prices or transport costs be ignored in our two-region economy? However primitive, some theory of resource growth must be appended to the model. Comparative static analyses which identify the historical impact of exogenous variables on income distribution, factor prices and output mix may be of limited usefulness if these endogenous variables have an impact, in turn, on rates of capital formation or labor supply growth.

These introductory remarks set the stage for the remainder of this chapter. The economics of the expanded model are presented verbally whenever possible. Those readers wishing a formal presentation first are encouraged to turn to section 3.4 where the model is presented in mathematical detail.

3.3 A model of late nineteenth-century American regional growth[6]

Supply, commodity markets and interregional trade

It should be stressed at the outset that our interest is restricted to the interdependent development of the American Midwest and

Northeast. The South is excluded from our analysis. In census terminology, the Midwest includes the East North Central and the West North Central states, while the East includes the New England and Middle Atlantic states. According to Easterlin's 1880 regional estimates presented in section 3.5, the sum of our East and West accounted for 62 percent of the American labor force and 75 percent of income.

The degree to which the East and West were specialized is revealed in Easterlin's figures. Fully two-thirds of the Eastern (commodity producing) labor force was engaged in non-agricultural activity in 1880. As a consequence, a useful simplifying assumption is to treat the Northeast as fully specialized in industrial products, commodities that may be used for both investment and consumption purposes. A much more realistic characterization, of course, would include an Eastern agricultural sector as well. The addition of a (declining) agricultural sector in the East would serve only to add complexity without the advantage of greater insight. Thus, the East is characterized as producing industrial goods for local use and for export to the West. Furthermore, Eastern industrial goods must compete with foreign goods in both regional markets and the model is capable of reproducing American experience with import substitution over time, whether induced by tariff policy or by long-run changes in comparative advantage. The Midwest, on the other hand, is not fully specialized. It concentrates to be sure on the production of farm products for local consumption, and for export both to the East and to European markets. Yet an industrial goods sector does exist in the West, the output of which satisfies a portion of local consumption and investment demands.

We turn now to a discussion of the production process in each sector. As with the simpler model analyzed in section 3.2, agriculture utilizes land, labor and capital in production while manufacturing requires labor and capital only. We continue to treat capital as 'putty-clay.' Once capital goods are employed in a given production process, they cannot be transferred for use in another sector. Production is subject to constant returns to scale and diminishing marginal rates of substitution. An impressive amount of evidence on American production conditions has been accumulating suggesting that the elasticity of substitution may be fairly close to unity in both agriculture and manufacturing.[7] By appealing to these results, a Cobb–Douglas specification is adopted in all sectors:

$$Q_{IE}(t) = A(t)K_{IE}(t)^{\alpha_K}L_{IE}(t)^{\alpha_L}, \; \alpha_L + \alpha_K = 1; \qquad (1)$$

$$Q_{IW}(t) = A'(t)K_{IW}(t)^{\alpha_K}L_{IW}(t)^{\alpha_L}, \; \alpha_L + \alpha_K = 1; \qquad (2)$$

$$Q_{AW}(t) = B(t)K_{AW}(t)^{\beta_K}L_{AW}(t)^{\beta_L}R(t)^{\beta_R}, \; \beta_K + \beta_L + \beta_R = 1; \quad (3)$$

where $Q_{ij}(t)$ are the quantities of the ith good in the jth region currently produced, $K_{ij}(t)$, $L_{ij}(t)$, and $R(t)$ are, respectively, the amounts of capital, labor and land currently used in the ith sector of the jth region. Although industrial substitution elasticities are assumed identical in the two regions, the capital–labor ratios will diverge since factor price equalization across regions is not required. In addition, note that industrial efficiencies may diverge between the two regions since $A(t)$ and $A'(t)$ need not be equal. Furthermore, the impact of less rapid technical progress in agriculture can be effectively captured by less pronounced secular shifts in $B(t)$ compared to $A(t)$ and $A'(t)$. The rate of change in these efficiency levels are, of course, indices of total factor productivity growth. They are given exogenously in the model and based on Kendrick's research.

A weakness of these sectoral supply specifications is that (i) there are no biases in the form of technical progress, and (ii) no factor-intensity reversal is possible, at least in the long run. Since economists and economic historians very often use quite different terminology in exploring these concepts, it may be useful to dwell on them at some length. Economists often allege that American technological progress has been labor-saving. That is, for a fixed capital–labor ratio American technological progress tended to raise the *relative* marginal product of capital. For a given wage–rental ratio, firms sought out new optimal input mixes by increasing the relative employment of capital, thus 'saving' on labor. The issue is by no means fully resolved. Nevertheless, considerable evidence has accumulated at least consistent with the labor-saving character-ization of American technical progress.[8] We must confess that our model has not been developed to capture it. The economic historian, on the other hand, normally reserves the term 'labor-saving' for an observed historical increase in capital intensity, whether induced by innovation or factor substitution.[9] Our model is fully capable of handling labor-saving when more broadly defined in this fashion. Furthermore, the model is capable of replicating the impressive rate of mechanization in American agriculture so strikingly apparent during the latter portion of the nineteenth century.[10] This is not true of the earlier attempts to apply general equilibrium models to the ante bellum period.[11] We should also note that our model specification makes it impossible for American agriculture to mech-anize more rapidly than industry. That is to say, if substitution elasticities are identical in two industries and one is initially more capital intensive than the other, then it is well known that capital intensity ordering cannot be reversed over time as the wage–rental ratio rises. Since the elasticity of substitution is assumed unity in all sectors of our economy, it follows that agriculture cannot mechanize more rapidly than industry except for short periods of time. In the short run, say during a prosperity phase of a long swing, agriculture may mechanize more rapidly than industry since, as we shall see shortly, intersectoral factor price equalization is not required in our system and thus over short periods of time agricultural wages may rise more rapidly than interest rates when compared with industry.

One final remark regarding the implication of our technical production specification is warranted. Obviously, a Cobb–Douglas specification ensures stable factor shares in each sector over time although it need not be stable over time for the economy as a whole. What is the evidence? Edward Budd's estimates on the wages' share certainly suggests stability over most of the post-Civil War era. Between 1870 and 1900, his 'adjusted' labor share in industry rises only from 50·3 to 51·5 percent. Over the same period, labor's share also remains approximately constant in agriculture. The decade 1900–10 represents a significant departure from long-run stability since labor's share declines sharply in agriculture and rises mildly in industry.[12] The evidence, such as it is, appears to be consistent with the Cobb–Douglas specification at least over three decades of our period.

Since our concern is with long-run full employment growth, cycles in factor utilization rates are ignored.[13] Furthermore, we invoke the conventional assumption that marginal product pricing rules are satisfied in all regions and sectors of the economy (cf. p. 47):

$$w_E(t) = P_{IE}(t)\alpha_L \frac{Q_{IE}(t)}{L_{IE}(t)}, \tag{22}$$

$$w_{IW}(t) = P_{IW}(t)\alpha_L \frac{Q_{IW}(t)}{L_{IW}(t)}, \tag{23}$$

$$w_{AW}(t) = P_{AW}(t)\beta_L \frac{Q_{AW}(t)}{L_{AW}(t)}, \tag{24}$$

$$r_E(t) = P_{IE}(t)\alpha_K \frac{Q_{IE}(t)}{K_{IE}(t)}, \tag{25}$$

$$r_{IW}(t) = P_{IW}(t)\alpha_K \frac{Q_{IW}(t)}{K_{IW}(t)}, \tag{26}$$

$$r_{AW}(t) = P_{AW}(t)\beta_K \frac{Q_{AW}(t)}{K_{AW}(t)}, \tag{27}$$

$$d(t) = P_{AW}(t)\beta_R \frac{Q_{AW}(t)}{R(t)}, \tag{28}$$

where $w(t)$ are wages, $r(t)$ are rental rates on capital, and $d(t)$ are

Western land rents. Note, however, that the marginal product pricing assumption does not require factor price equalization between regions or sectors. Indeed, we shall see below that interregional and intraregional factor market disequilibrium is a distinctive characteristic of our economy. This specification should be viewed as an important departure from the conventional neoclassical model. Hopefully, it makes the framework an especially strong candidate for historical analysis.

With constant returns to scale and common efficiency levels how can the industrial sector co-exist in the two regions? The answer, of course, is to be found in the protective effect of interregional transport costs. This explanation has a venerable tradition in nineteenth-century American economic historiography[14] and use is made of it here by the introduction of commodity price differentials between regions. Per unit transport costs incurred in interregional trade are treated like exogenous tariff rates and we assume that these per unit transportation costs fully exhaust regional commodity price differentials. The freight rate on Western foodstuffs shipped East is denoted by $Z_A(t)$ and the freight rate on Eastern industrial goods shipped West by $Z_I(t)$. Thus, prices in the two regions are related by:

$$P_{IW}(t) = [1 + Z_I(t)] P_{IE}(t), Z_I(t) > 0, \qquad (37)$$

$$P_{AE}(t) = [1 + Z_A(t)] P_{AW}(t), Z_A(t) > 0. \qquad (38)$$

Clearly, $Z_A(t)$ and $Z_I(t)$ need not be equal: in fact, we shall see in appendix A that $Z_A(t)$ exceeds $Z_I(t)$ by large measure during the late nineteenth century. No explicit production function is introduced for transport activities but these exogenous freight rates are allowed to decline over time. Indeed, the purpose of chapter 9 is to evaluate the impact of declining transport costs on regional specialization, trade creation, migration and per capita income growth. This specification of transport activities is consistent with Fogel's and Fishlow's treatment since they also assume constant costs in the transport sector[15] and assume the per unit freight costs to be independent of freight volume and the demand for transport services.

In the regional factor income equations, $T_E(t)$ and $T_W(t)$ represent revenues generated from the transportation sector. These revenues must generate factor payments in the two regions. Revenue from West–East trade is expressed as

$$T_W(t) = [Z_A(t)] \{D_{AE}(t) + EX(t)\};$$

that is, the freight rate times the volume of Western grains exported to the East and abroad. Similarly, transport revenue from East–West trade can be expressed as the freight rate times the volume of

Eastern and imported industrial products shipped West:

$$T_E(t) = [Z_I(t)] \{D_{IW}(t) + I_W(t) - Q_{IW}(t)\},$$

where $D_{IW}(t)$ is the Western consumption demand for industrial goods and $I_W(t)$ is Western demand for investment goods.[16]

Foreign imports of industrial consumption and investment goods are valued at Eastern (landed at port) prices. Similarly, exports of grain products from the West must first be transported to Eastern ports and thus are valued f.o.b. at grain prices prevailing in Eastern urban markets. Following a time-honored convention, the external trade balance is assumed to be zero. Thus, short-term balance of payments disequilibria are ignored – a reasonable assumption for long-term secular analysis. Foreign capital flows are also ignored. At first glance this assumption may seem extreme, but we shall show below that net foreign capital imports formed an insignificant share of gross domestic investment in post-Civil War America. The Eastern price ratio, $P_{IE}(t)/P_{AE}(t)$, is given exogenously by world market conditions. It could be argued that American grain exports had a significant impact on the prevailing world price and the implications of this assertion will be explored in chapters 8 and 10. The possibility is ignored for the moment, however, and instead the world demand for American grain is assumed to be perfectly elastic;[17] similarly, the supply of industrial import goods is also taken to be perfectly elastic. The historians' emphasis on 'lagging export markets' for American farm products is interpreted as an exogenous deterioration of international farm products' prices, rather than as a low rate of external demand expansion for U.S. grains in foreign markets. Relative prices in the West are therefore jointly determined by changing world market conditions and interregional transport costs.

Since domestic demand plays only a passive role in the small country case, we need not devote space here to a defense of the consumption demand specifications in the model although the reader will find them stated in equations (29)–(34) and (43)–(46) in section 3.4.

Interregional factor mobility: labor migration and capital markets

To complete the static system, some migration decision rules must be formulated which are capable of replicating some key characteristics of American regional development. Since we have rejected the assumption of full factor mobility, and thus factor price equalization across regions and sectors, some alternative device must be introduced to explain labor migration and investment allocation. An historically relevant description of the operation of nineteenth-century labor and capital markets is needed.

Let us begin with labor migration and the functioning of national labor markets after the 1860s. There is no doubt that a well integrated national labor market existed in the late nineteenth century in the sense that migration was responsive to wage differentials. We are far less certain about the precise operation of that market and the explanation for the long-term persistence of money wage differentials across regions and sectors. George Borts has found, for example, that even during twentieth-century American experience regional wage differentials have increased in spite of heavy interregional migration.[18] Borts attributes the result in large measure to the high population reproduction rate in low wage areas. For our period, the region of 'high reproduction rates' is the *East* since that labor force was continually augmented by significant amounts of immigration from Europe. The evidence reviewed in subsequent chapters documents that the East was also a region of low *real* wages (but high per capita income). Contrary to the assumptions of the traditional neoclassical model, regional factor price differentials do not necessarily result in instantaneous factor reallocation. One issue we wish to confront in this book is whether growth under factor market disequilibrium is a concept which offers a better explanation of American historical experience in the post-Civil War decades. A disequilibrium framework will make it possible to observe current wage differentials of considerable magnitude over very long periods of development.

Lebergott has documented the behavior of regional (money) wage differentials for the period from Civil War to World War I. From 1860 to 1880, the rate of population redistribution was striking yet there was no tendency towards regional money wage equalization. Apparently, the disequilibrating forces associated with industrialization, land augmentation and foreign immigration were much too powerful to allow even a tendency towards equalization to assert itself. On the other hand, from 1880 to 1910 conditions must have changed markedly since regional money wage differentials declined quite sharply during those three decades.[19] The more important issue, however, relates to the behavior of *real* wages since it is the real wage which influences migration behavior. This important distinction is too often omitted from historical accounts of interregional (or international) migration. An especially thorny problem arises in constructing an appropriate regional cost-of-living deflator. In the migration specification which follows, we make a simplifying assumption which appears to have considerable historical relevance. Regional cost-of-living differentials are produced when the expenditure bundle is significantly weighted by the presence of nontraded services or by bulk commodities with high transport costs. The evidence on American internal transport costs presented in section 3.5 and appendix A suggests that the variance in regional foodstuff prices was a key determinant of regional cost-of-living differentials in the nineteenth century. Given that evidence, we shall assume that regional wages deflated by a cost-of-living index dominated by food prices are the real income variables relevant for migration decisions. Thus, regional 'real wages' are defined as

$$\tilde{w}_E(t) = \frac{w_E(t)}{COL_E(t)} \tag{51}$$

$$\tilde{w}_W(t) = \frac{\tilde{w}_W(t)}{COL_W(t)}, \tag{52}$$

where $\tilde{w}_W$ is a weighted average of Western farm and industry wages, and the regional cost-of-living indices are a weighted average of regional commodity prices, the weights themselves determined by variable budget shares.

The following formulation of late nineteenth-century American regional migration is adopted.[20] The net migration rate from the ith to jth region is $m_{ji}(t) = M_{ji}(t)/L_i(t)$ and, as in classical migration theory, the determinants of $m_{ji}(t)$ are expected net real earnings differentials. For simplicity, a one period model is hypothesized which excludes migration costs[21] (including employment search costs since full employment is assumed throughout). Thus, $m_{ji}(t)$ is determined solely by the expected East–West real wage differential, $\tilde{w}^*(t) = \tilde{w}_E^*(t) - \tilde{w}_W^*(t)$, as in Figure 3.2:

$$m_{WE}(t) = \max \{0, 1 - e^{\phi \tilde{w}^*(t)}\}, \tag{47}$$

$$m_{EW}(t) = \max \{0, 1 - e^{-\phi \tilde{w}^*(t)}\}. \tag{48}$$

Suppose further that potential migrants determine $\tilde{w}^*(t)$ by reference to actual past wage differentials where $0 \leq b \leq 1$ is an adjust-

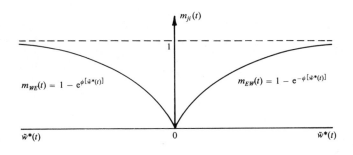

Figure 3.2

ment parameter and $[\tilde{w}_E(t) - \tilde{w}_W(t)]$ is the actual current real wage differential

$$\tilde{w}^*(t) = \tilde{w}^*(t-1) + b\{\tilde{w}_E(t) - \tilde{w}_W(t) - \tilde{w}^*(t-1)\}. \quad (54)$$

In this formulation, we may observe money wage differentials of considerable magnitude over very long periods of history in spite of massive Western settlement or migration to Western industrial employment. These differentials may be attributed to persistent cost-of-living differentials or they may be explained by a national labor market continually subjected to major shocks – e.g., changing world market conditions, declining interregional transport costs – and, as a result, in persistent disequilibrium. (Intersectoral migration within the West, i.e., migration off the farm, is treated in much the same fashion.)

This formulation of migration behavior appears very much like the usual distributed lag framework utilized to analyze international migrations in history. There are, however, a number of differences that may be worth emphasizing. First, *real* wage differentials rather than money wage or per capita income differentials are the key decision variables. Second, our formulation is in terms of migration *rates* rather than absolute flows; with few exceptions the literature seems to focus on migration levels. Kelley, for example, has the total annual flow of immigrants to Australia a function of lagged flows and proxies for earnings.[22] More recently, Wilkinson has developed a reduced form equation for international immigration to the United States, 1870–1914.[23] Wilkinson includes both a wage rate proxy and output variables in his model. A flaw in this approach will be pointed out in chapter 11, but our improved labor migration specification relies heavily on these previous contributions to the migration literature.

We now turn to investment allocation and the capital market. This concern inevitably involves attention to interregional financial flows, the development of a national capital market, and the role of financial intermediation. As we indicated in chapter 1, Davis and others have argued that nineteenth-century barriers to interregional capital mobility were significant and that certain institutional innovations introduced after the 1870s acted to reduce these barriers. Stigler, on the other hand, has argued that such barriers or capital market imperfections reflect nothing more than positive information costs. These costs are likely to have been very large for America as it underwent land-augmenting extensive development, and an effort must be made to capture them in our model. In real terms, then, what determined investment allocation in the economy? This issue has attracted perhaps more attention than any other in economics, and economic historians should be able to shed some light on it.

Gross returns to (physical) capital in a given region or sector can be decomposed into

$$r_j(t) = [i_j(t) + \delta] P_{Ij}(t).$$

The sum of interest payments to claimants on the capital stock and depreciation requirements per unit of physical capital invested, exhaust gross dollar returns to the value of capital assets at the margin. If investment goods' prices were equated between all sectors of use, then no distinction between gross returns to physical assets and gross returns to the value of capital assets would be necessary. But transport costs on investment goods in the late nineteenth century make those distinctions necessary. Note, too, that in the pages which follow we shall attempt to construct a capital market which allows $r_j P^{-1}{}_{Ij}$ to diverge across sectors and regions due to 'capital market immobilities.' We shall assume that temporary high rates of return ('excess profits') in a given sector are shared proportionately by all claimants of the capital stock and are therefore fully reflected in interest payments, $i_j(t)$. A majority of those claimants normally reside in the sector itself, of course, and thus for them the distinction between 'excess profits' and relatively high rates of return is purely semantic. Nevertheless, absentee owners earn an identical amount $i_j(t)$ on their share of the sector's assets less a payment to intermediaries. Thus we shall view $i_j(t)$ as the effective borrowing rate facing the sector as well.

Let τ be a fixed per unit search or information cost incurred with an intersectoral transfer of claims. The *net* interest rate on assets held outside the jth region is $[i_j(t) - \tau]$; that is, the effective interest rate facing the Eastern investor contemplating investment in the West is the Western interest rate less the per unit payment to intermediaries. Following the spirit of most work on financial intermediation by economic historians, we shall take τ as exogenously given by existing institutional arrangements. To be more explicit, the volume of intersectoral flows is assumed to have *no* impact on τ and furthermore the model does not consider the resource cost of intermediation nor does it confront the problem of optimal resource allocation between financial intermediation and other activities. If we find that real variables in this growing economy are sensitive to changes in τ, then a more sophisticated treatment of financial intermediation, and the price formation of τ is warranted. Finally, note that if τ is positive, then it follows that even if equilibrium and interregional financial flows cease, the discrepancy between regional interest rates (and, of course, gross rental rates) may be quite pronounced. Thus, when economic historians view *actual* regional factor price differentials over time, it is unclear whether the process of national factor market integration is to be accurately judged by these observed differentials since they may capture the effects of disequilibrium growth, declining commodity transport costs, as well as a decline in transaction (or migration) costs. The evidence relating to the evolution of a national capital market is fairly well known. Lance Davis' proxies for short-term rates document the convergence of regional interest rates throughout the period after the 1860s. These data also suggest that regional convergence is especially typical of periods of unusually slow growth, capital accumulation and structural change; e.g., the mid-1870s and 1890s. These, of course, are periods of *relative* stagnation and presumably less subject to the disequilibrating shocks generated by rapid disproportional growth. When regional investment allocation is based on partial adjustment during a unit of time and on the formation of interest rate expectations based on the immediate past, then high variance in regional interest rates and disequilibrium in the national capital market can be reproduced by the model as well.

Let $\phi_{ji}(t)$ denote the fraction of region i's gross savings allocated to gross capital formation in the jth region. Analogous to the labor migration specification, the expected East–West interest rate differential, $i^*(t) = i^*_E(t) - i^*_W(t)$, determines the interregional transfer subject to τ as in Figure 3.3:

$$\phi_{EW}(t) = \max\ \{0,\ 1 - e^{-\mu(i^*(t) - \tau)}\}, \tag{39}$$

$$\phi_{WE}(t) = \max\ \{0,\ 1 - e^{\mu(i^*(t) - \tau)}\}. \tag{40}$$

As the expected Western interest rate departs from the Eastern rate an increasing share of Eastern gross regional saving is allocated to Western capital formation and all of Western savings are reinvested there. When the expected interest rate differential equals $|\tau|$, interregional flows cease. Thus, there is some spread on regional interest rates (the shaded area in Figure 3.3) for which no interregional savings transfers would be observed. Interest rate expectations are formed by

$$i^*(t) = i^*(t-1) + \left[1 - \epsilon\right]\ \{i_E(t) - i_W(t) - i^*(t-1)\}, \tag{59}$$

where $0 \leqq \epsilon \leqq 1$, and $\bar{i}_W(t)$ refers to the average interest rate pre-

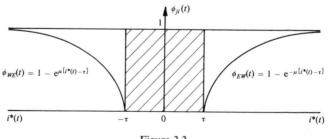

Figure 3.3

vailing in Western financial markets. The Western *intraregional* financial market is explained by a mechanism symmetrical to that formulated above for the *inter*regional financial market. Thus,

$$\hat{\phi}_{IA}(t) = \max \{0, 1 - e^{-\mu[\hat{i}^*(t) - \tau]}\}, \tag{41}$$

$$\hat{\phi}_{AI}(t) = \max \{0, 1 - e^{\mu[\hat{i}^*(t) - \tau]}\}, \tag{42}$$

where $\hat{\phi}_{IA}(t)$ is the share of gross savings in Western agriculture allocated to Western industry, and $\hat{i}^*(t)$ is the expected interest rate differential between urban and rural financial markets. This might be interpreted, for example, as the differential between industrial 'bonds' and farm 'mortgages.'

It might be helpful to present the regional factor income equations at this point. Investors outside of a region of plant location receive interest on the value of their investment less the transaction cost, τ. We assume that all interregional intermediation is performed in the East and returns to such intermediation accrue to Eastern capitalists.[24] Total regional factor income in our model can be expressed formally as[25]

$$Y_E(t) = \{r_E(t)K_{IEE}(t) + i_{AW}(t)P_{IW}(t)K_{AWE}(t) +$$
$$+ i_{IW}(t)P_{IW}(t)K_{IWE}(t) + [\tau + \delta]P_{IE}(t)K_{IEW}(t)\}$$
$$+ w_E(t)L_E(t) + T_E(t), \tag{20}$$

$$Y_W(t) = \{r_{IW}(t)K_{IWW}(t) + r_{AW}(t)K_{AWW}(t) + i_E(t) - \tau \; P_{IE}(t)K_{IEW}(t) +$$
$$+ \delta P_{IW}(t)K_{AWE}(t) + \delta P_{IW}(t)K_{IWE}(t)\} +$$
$$+ [w_{AW}(t)L_{AW}(t) + w_{IW}(t)L_{IW}(t)] + d(t)R(t) + T_W(t). \tag{21}$$

$K_{ijk}(t)$ denotes the current stock of capital assets used in the production of commodity i, in region j, claimed by residents of region k. Presumably, in early phases of regional growth the West relied heavily on Eastern financing and thus Western assets claimed by Eastern interests (accumulated by past financing) must have been relatively large while Eastern assets claimed by Westerners were negligible. Absentee ownership in early phases of regional growth was just as common as external financing was to young firms. It follows that Western regional product must have exceeded its regional income by net factor income payments to financial interests in the East. Throughout most of these four decades, this result surely tended to reinforce Western dependence on net inflows to finance railroad development, land clearing, or industrial expansion.

Capital accumulation, labor force growth and land expansion

The model discussed thus far has been limited to comparative statics. We have made no mention as yet of capital formation, labor force growth, or increases in improved farmland acreage.[26] Since we hope to use this model to improve our understanding of American *development* after the 1860s some effort must be made at this point to introduce dynamics into our framework.

This section must be prefaced with a word of warning and apology. Those optimistic readers awaiting a sophisticated statement of the determinants of technical progress, capital formation, labor force growth and improved farm acreage expansion, alas, will be sadly disappointed. Although modern growth theory has much to offer in the explanation of capital formation rates, it has made little progress on the remaining items listed above. As a result, the dynamics introduced into our model will be very primitive indeed. Yet, this is no excuse for us to ignore what tools *are* presently available and well understood. Since both the economic historian and the growth-development theorist have a great deal to learn from each other, some attempt should be made to bridge the gap between the abstract elegance of growth theory and the empirical approach of the economic historian. Even if we must retreat in frustration to a specification which simply allows the land stock and total factor productivity to grow exogenously at their *ex post* historical rates, a gain has been made. For even in this simplest of approaches, the empirical relevance of the remainder of the model can be tested against historical fact. In addition, counterfactual analysis can still be pursued to gain insight into the determinants of late nineteenth-century development. By introducing *ex post* acreage figures into the model we may abdicate an explanation of land augmentation rates, but we can still profitably explore just how differently America would have grown under alternative rates of land expansion. Indeed, we may discover in the process that the role of land in late nineteenth-century American development was not sufficiently important to warrant a serious research effort to understand the determinants of its growth.

With these introductory remarks behind us, we now turn to the sources of growth in our model.

First, consider our treatment of the growing land stock. It is generally agreed both in fact and in theory that land augmentation requires complementary investment. Martin Primack has shown just how important those investments were to nineteenth-century agricultural expansion.[27] They involve land clearing, farm construction, fencing, drainage and irrigation. The real problem, however, relates to land clearing and preparation. Not long ago, Peter Kenen[28] made an interesting theoretical contribution which captures these conditions. Kenen proposed regional production functions utilizing factor service flows from labor and 'raw' land stocks, but these stocks are unproductive until 'improved' by a series of investments like those itemized by Primack in the case of land. Kenen is suggesting that we treat the production of improved acres in much the same way that we treat capital goods production, and in the nineteenth century they both were highly labor intensive activities. In fact, interregional financial flows to the West were in part used to increase the rental value of land holdings at the frontier (either by *new* lands cleared or by the improved value of old lands). Our treatment of land augmentation will be far less sophisticated and more akin to recent applications of general equilibrium analysis to historical problems. That is, our proxy for land utilization is Tostlebe's (deflated) land value series and we use it to determine exogenously land input levels in our model. The rate of expansion in the land stock declines over time reflecting the gradual 'closing of the frontier.' Counterfactual experiments will be used to explore the impact of these land expansion rates on American growth although we offer no explanation of the land expansion rates themselves. Chapter 5 examines the contribution of diminished new improved land availability on the Great Depression from 1870 to 1896, while chapter 8 explores its impact on real wages, migration, industrialization and the Midwestern farmer himself.

Labor force growth is determined by the rates indigenous to each region as well as by the inflow of European migrants, $M(t)$:

$$L_E(t) = n_E(t)L_E(t-1) + m_{EW}(t)L_W(t-1) - m_{WE}(t)L_E(t-1) + M(t)$$
(15)

$$L_W(t) = n_W(t)L_W(t-1) + m_{WE}(t)L_E(t-1) - m_{EW}(t)L_W(t-1).$$ (16)

In effect, we assume constant labor participation rates so that the more abundant historical evidence on natural rates of population growth can be utilized. The regional rates, $n_E(t)$ and $n_W(t)$, are exogenous in our system but they are *not* assumed constant. Since they are estimated from post-Civil War demographic data these rates reflect the marked decline in both regions. Furthermore, $n_E(t) < n_W(t)$ in all years over the period. It follows that aggregate labor force growth rates are endogenously determined to the extent that they result as a weighted average of the $n_j(t)$. The weights – the regional employment distributions – are determined endogenously in the model.

No theory of international migration is embedded in our system at this point. $M(t)$ denotes the actual European in-migration flows recorded annually over the period. Note that migration to the West by European immigrants is viewed here as a two-stage process since these flows first augment the Eastern labor force. Eastern workers and new European immigrants are treated as perfect substitutes.[29] The observed rate of regional labor force growth is therefore determined jointly by regional labor migration functions, and by these exogenously determined natural rates of growth and European migration flows.

Although we make no effort to introduce a speculative theory of international migration at this point, an effort is made along these lines in chapter 11. There we allow immigration to be determined endogenously, at least in part, by employment conditions in America. It seemed wiser first to explore the empirical validity of the remainder of the model before confronting the 'push–pull' debate in the historical migration literature.

The most difficult task now remains. What determined the aggregate savings rate in the late nineteenth century and thus the rate of capital formation? On this most important issue economic historians are uncertain. In fact, one of the least understood but most interesting aspects of United States development was the secular rise in the gross savings rate in the mid-nineteenth century. Our focus, however, is the period beginning 1869–78. Davis and Gallman present four series on the gross savings rate:[30] (i) in current and in 1860 prices; (ii) including and excluding agricultural clearing. Since our model explicitly includes only *purchased* capital inputs in Western agricultural activity, the relevant series is the gross savings rate excluding agricultural clearing. In current prices, this measure of the gross savings rate rises from 0·18 to 0·20 between 1869–78 and 1894–1903.

What specification on the macro savings decision is historically most relevant for our period? In his discussion of the Civil War episode where gross savings rates in constant prices rose markedly, Temin suggests that the declining price of producer durables explains a large part of the rise.[31] For the period following 1869, we have three major hypotheses suggested by the literature: (i) the role of the 'rate of interest,' (ii) the impact of income distribution, and (iii) a naïve Keynesian specification. Each of these will be considered in turn.

Differential savings rates according to the functional source of income are common in the growth literature and have long been a cornerstone in the historical literature as well. Yet qualitative evidence on this critical matter is not sufficient, and to be more pragmatic, we have only the sketchiest evidence on savings behavior by income groups in nineteenth-century America. In any case, Davis and Gallman argue that stability in the aggregate savings rate 1869–1908 is the result of the combined forces of stability in income distribution and offsetting distributional effects.[32]

An *a priori* case has also been made that optimizing consumers will save more at higher interest rates. True, there is very little empirical evidence which supports this proposition and an equally plausible theoretical argument can be made which suggests an inverse relation. In spite of this ambiguity, the economic historian places great emphasis on bank and non-bank financial intermediation as a means by which aggregate national saving is raised. For example, Davis and Gallman have asserted: 'Foremost among the features of the 19th century economy that appear to have had an important effect on savings at that time, but which Goldsmith did not find important in 20th century, was the absolute and relative growth of financial intermediation.'[33] Davis and Gallman note that by 1880 the Western regions were served by fairly sophisticated local intermediaries and thereafter these local markets were being integrated by the penetration of commercial paper and by changes in management and legal restrictions governing investment activity by the intermediaries. The authors then argue that these indirect securities reduced variance in yield to savers, and since nineteenth-century savers were primarily concerned with safety, then increased savings should have resulted from improved intermediation. Yet at the same time, these developments tended to raise interest rates in surplus regions and lower them in deficit areas. What would have been the *net* effect on aggregate savings? Although Davis and Gallman argue *a priori* that savings were far more interest elastic in the West (the deficit region) than the East (the surplus region),[34] we know of no empirical evidence or compelling theoretical argument in favor of their proposition.

Given the absence of a resolution of both the theoretical and historical debate on the determinants of aggregate national savings, we are compelled to tread a neutral path, albeit a path well trod by growth theorists. The current price savings rate is assumed equal across sectors and regions, and furthermore, it is allowed to assume the values actually estimated by Davis and Gallman. But even if the gross savings rate were assumed constant, would this necessarily imply a constant rate of capital accumulation? Certainly not. Indeed, one contribution of modern growth theory has been to show how capital formation rates tend to diminish over time with fixed savings rates.[35] Define the aggregate capital stock as $K(t)$, gross investment as $I(t)$, the depreciation rate as δ, S as aggregate savings and $\bar{s}$ as the fixed savings rate.[36] Then the rate of accumulation can be decomposed into

$$\frac{\dot{K}(t)}{K(t)} = \frac{I(t) - \delta K(t)}{K(t)} = \frac{I(t)}{K(t)} - \delta$$

$$= \frac{S}{P_I(t)} \cdot \frac{1}{K(t)} - \delta = \bar{s} \left[\frac{\text{GNP}(t)}{P_I(t)\, K(t)} \right] - \delta,$$

where $P_I(t)$ is the current price of capital goods. In both theory and, as we shall see in chapter 5, historical fact the capital–output ratio rises with accumulation thus generating a declining *rate* of accumulation over time. Furthermore, should $P_I(t)$ decline relatively over time, then it follows that $I(t)$ should grow at rates exceeding gross national product. More simply, from a fixed savings pool more investment goods can be purchased at lower capital goods' prices (Figure 3.4) and, as a result, more rapid rates of accumulation will be forthcoming. This is precisely the effect Temin documents for the period from 1849–58 to 1869–78 when the current price $s(t)$ rose far less markedly than the constant price $\bar{s}(t)$.[37] In short, we are assuming that the price elasticity of demand for producers' durables is unity.

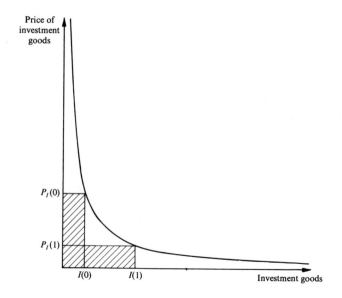

Figure 3.4

As a final caveat, the reader should be prepared for further experimentation with the determinants of American savings rates in the late nineteenth century. Chapter 6 confronts the 'capital market integration' thesis and in the course of the discussion we return once more to the more speculative explanations of American capital formation. Interest rates and income distribution jointly have fair success in accounting for American savings rate movements in the post-Civil War era. The results are far too speculative to warrant their inclusion in the basic model developed here, however.

3.4 A formal statement of the model

Notation

In constructing our model of American regional development, the following notation is used:

$Q_{IE}(t)$: Eastern output of industrial goods
$Q_{IW}(t)$: Western output of industrial goods
$Q_{AW}(t)$: Western output of agricultural goods
$K(t)$: Total capital stock
$K_{IE}(t)$: Eastern capital stock in industry
$K_{IW}(t)$: Western capital stock in industry
$K_{AW}(t)$: Western capital stock in agriculture
$K_{IEE}(t)$: Eastern industrial capital stock owned by Easterners
$K_{IEW}(t)$: Eastern industrial capital stock owned by Westerners
$K_{IWW}(t)$: Western industrial capital stock owned by Westerners
$K_{IWE}(t)$: Western industrial capital stock owned by Easterners
$K_{AWW}(t)$: Western agricultural capital stock owned by Westerners
$K_{AWE}(t)$: Western agricultural capital stock owned by Easterners
$I_{IEE}(t)$: Gross investment in Eastern industry, financed by Easterners
$I_{IEW}(t)$: Gross investment in Eastern industry, financed by Westerners
$I_{IWW}(t)$: Gross investment in Western industry, financed by Westerners
$I_{IWE}(t)$: Gross investment in Western industry, financed by Easterners
$I_{AWW}(t)$: Gross investment in Western agriculture, financed by Westerners
$I_{AWE}(t)$: Gross investment in Western agriculture, financed by Easterners
$L(t)$: Total labor supply
$L_{IE}(t)$: Labor supply in the East (all in industry)
$L_{IW}(t)$: Labor supply employed in the Western industrial sector
$L_{AW}(t)$: Labor supply employed in the Western agricultural sector
$R(t)$: Land stock in the West
$Y_E(t)$: Eastern income
$Y_W(t)$: Western income
$P_{IW}(t)$: Price of industrial goods in Western markets
$P_{AW}(t)$: Price of agricultural goods in Western markets
$P_{IE}(t)$: Price of industrial goods in Eastern markets
$P_{AE}(t)$: Price of agricultural goods in Eastern markets
$w_E(t)$: Eastern wage rate (nominal)
$w_W(t)$: Western wage rate (nominal)
$r_E(t)$: Rate of return on Eastern (capital) assets
$r_W(t)$: Rate of return on Western (capital) assets

$d(t)$: Land rental rate

$\phi_{EW}(t)$: Percentage of Western savings flowing to East

$\phi_{WE}(t)$: Percentage of Eastern savings flowing to West

$D_{AW}(t)$: Consumption demand for agricultural goods by Westerners

$D_{IW}(t)$: Consumption demand for industrial goods by Westerners

$D_{AE}(t)$: Consumption demand for agricultural goods by Easterners

$D_{IE}(t)$: Consumption demand for industrial goods by Easterners

$m_{WE}(t)$: Rate of migration from East to West, as a percentage of Eastern population

$m_{EW}(t)$: Rate of migration from West to East, as a percentage of Western population

$i^*(t)$: Expected interest rate differential, West minus East

$\tilde{w}^*(t)$: Expected real wage differential, West minus East

$M(t)$: European in-migration

$D_{AD}(t)$: Total domestic consumption demand for agricultural goods, East and West

$D_A(t)$: Total demand for agricultural goods, East, West and export

$EX(t)$: Quantum agricultural exports

$EXVAL(t)$: Value of agricultural exports, from Eastern ports

$IM(t)$: Quantum imports of industrial goods

$IMVAL(t)$: Value of industrial good imports, into Eastern ports

$COL_E(t)$: Cost-of-living index in the East

$COL_W(t)$: Cost-of-living index in the West

$\tilde{w}_W(t)$: Western real wage

$\tilde{w}_E(t)$: Eastern real wage

$T_E(t)$: Revenue generated from Eastern transportation sector

$T_W(t)$: Revenue generated from Western transportation sector

The remaining notation is introduced when needed.

The formal model

Production conditions

$$Q_{IE}(t) = A(t)K_{IE}(t)^{\alpha_K} L_{IE}(t)^{\alpha_L}, \alpha_L + \alpha_K = 1 \qquad (1)$$

$$Q_{IW}(t) = A'(t)K_{IW}(t)^{\alpha_K} L_{IW}(t)^{\alpha_L}, \alpha_L + \alpha_K = 1 \qquad (2)$$

$$Q_{AW}(t) = B(t)K_{AW}(t)^{\beta_K} L_{AW}(t)^{\beta_L} R(t)^{\beta_R}, \beta_K + \beta_L + \beta_R = 1 \qquad (3)$$

Full employment, capital accumulation and labor force growth

$$K(t) = K_{IE}(t) + K_{IW}(t) + K_{AW}(t) \qquad (4)$$

$$K_{IE}(t) = K_{IEE}(t) + K_{IEW}(t) \qquad (5)$$

$$K_{IW}(t) = K_{IWW}(t) + K_{IWE}(t) \tag{6}$$

$$K_{AW}(t) = K_{AWW}(t) + K_{AWE}(t) \tag{7}$$

$$K_{IEE}(t) = I_{IEE}(t) + (1-\delta)K_{IEE}(t-1) \tag{8}$$

$$K_{IEW}(t) = I_{IEW}(t) + (1-\delta)K_{IEW}(t-1) \tag{9}$$

$$K_{IWW}(t) = I_{IWW}(t) + (1-\delta)K_{IWW}(t-1) \tag{10}$$

$$K_{IWE}(t) = I_{IWE}(t) + (1-\delta)K_{IWE}(t-1) \tag{11}$$

$$K_{AWW}(t) = I_{AWW}(t) + (1-\delta)K_{AWW}(t-1) \tag{12}$$

$$K_{AWE}(t) = I_{AWE}(t) + (1-\delta)K_{AWE}(t-1) \tag{13}$$

$$L(t) = L_{IE}(t) + L_{IW}(t) + L_{AW}(t) \tag{14}$$

$$L_E(t) = n_E L_E(t-1) + m_{EW}(t)L_W(t-1) - m_{WE}(t)L_E(t-1) + M(t) \tag{15}$$

$$L_W(t) = n_W L_W(t-1) + m_{WE}(t)L_E(t-1) - m_{EW}(t)L_W(t-1) \tag{16}$$

$$L_{AW}(t) = L_{AW}(t-1)\left\{n_W(t-1) - \hat{m}_{IA}(t-1) - \frac{m_{WE}(t-1)L_E(t-1)}{L_W(t-1)} - \right. $$
$$\left. - m_{EW}(t-1)\right\} + \hat{m}_{AI}(t-1)L_{IW}(t-1) \tag{17}$$

$$L_{IW}(t) = L_{IW}(t-1)\left\{n_W(t-1) - \hat{m}_{AI}(t-1) + \frac{m_{WE}(t-1)L_E(t-1)}{L_W(t-1)} - \right. $$
$$\left. - m_{EW}(t-1)\right\} + \hat{m}_{IA}(t-1)L_{AW}(t-1) \tag{18}$$

$$L_W(t) = L_{AW}(t) + L_{IW}(t) \tag{19}$$

Income and factor pricing

$$Y_E(t) = \{r_E(t)K_{IEE}(t) + i_{AW}(t)P_{IW}(t)K_{AWE}(t) + i_{IW}(t)P_{IW}(t)K_{IWE}(t) + $$
$$+ \left[\tau + \delta\right]P_{IE}(t)K_{IEW}(t)\} + w_E(t)L_E(t) + T_E(t) \tag{20}$$

$$Y_W(t) = \{r_{IW}(t)K_{IWW}(t) + r_{AW}(t)K_{AWW}(t) + $$
$$+ \left[i_E(t) - \tau\right]P_{IE}(t)K_{IEW}(t) + \delta P_{IW}(t)K_{AWE}(t) + $$
$$+ \delta P_{IW}(t)K_{IWE}(t)\} + w_{AW}(t)L_{AW}(t) + w_{IW}(t)L_{IW}(t) + $$
$$+ d(t)R(t) + T_W(t) \tag{21}$$

$$w_E(t) = P_{IE}(t)\alpha_L \frac{Q_{IE}(t)}{L_{IE}(t)} \tag{22}$$

$$w_{IW}(t) = P_{IW}(t)\alpha_L \frac{Q_{IW}(t)}{L_{IW}(t)} \tag{23}$$

$$w_{AW}(t) = P_{AW}(t)\beta_L \frac{Q_{AW}(t)}{L_{AW}(t)} \tag{24}$$

$$r_E(t) = P_{IE}(t)\alpha_K \frac{Q_{IE}(t)}{K_{IE}(t)} \tag{25}$$

$$r_{IW}(t) = P_{IW}(t)\alpha_K \frac{Q_{IW}(t)}{K_{IW}(t)} \tag{26}$$

$$r_{AW}(t) = P_{AW}(t)\beta_K \frac{Q_{AW}(t)}{K_{AW}(t)} \tag{27}$$

$$d(t) = P_{AW}(t)\beta_K \frac{Q_{AW}(t)}{R(t)} \tag{28}$$

Savings levels and investment allocation

$$P_{IE}(t)I_{IEE}(t) = sY_E(t) - P_{IW}(t)\{I_{IWE}(t) + I_{AWE}(t)\} \tag{29}$$

$$P_{IE}(t)I_{IEW}(t) = s\phi_{EW}(t)Y_w(t) \tag{30}$$

$$P_{IW}(t)I_{AWW}(t) = \{S_{AW}(t)\left[1 - \hat{\phi}_{IA}(t)\right] + S_{IW}(t)\hat{\phi}_{AI}(t)\}\left[1 - \phi_{EW}(t)\right] \tag{31}$$

$$P_{IW}(t)I_{IWW}(t) = \{S_{IW}(t)\left[1 - \hat{\phi}_{AI}(t)\right] + S_{AW}(t)\hat{\phi}_{IA}(t)\}\left[1 - \phi_{EW}(t)\right] \tag{32}$$

$$I_{AWE}(t) = \{I_{IWE}(t) + I_{AWE}(t)\} \left\{ \frac{P_{IW}(t)I_{AWW}(t)}{S_{AW}(t) + S_{IW}(t)} \right\} \tag{33}$$

$$I_{IWE}(t) = \{I_{IWE}(t) + I_{AWE}(t)\} \left\{ \frac{P_{IW}(t)I_{IWW}(t)}{S_{AW}(t) + S_{IW}(t)} \right\} \tag{34}$$

$$S_{AW}(t) = sP_{AW}(t)Q_{AW}(t) \tag{35}$$

$$S_{IW}(t) = s\{Y_W(t) - P_{AW}(t)Q_{AW}(t)\} \tag{36}$$

Transport costs

$$P_{IW}(t) = \left[1 + Z_I\right]P_{IE}(t), Z_I > 0 \tag{37}$$

$$P_{AE}(t) = \left[1 + Z_A\right]P_{AW}(t), Z_A > 0 \tag{38}$$

Capital markets

$$\phi_{EW}(t) = \max\{0, 1 - e^{-\mu[i^*(t)-\tau]}\} \tag{39}$$

$$\phi_{WE}(t) = \max\{0, 1 - e^{\mu[i^*(t)-\tau]}\} \tag{40}$$

$$\hat{\phi}_{IA}(t) = \max\{0, 1 - e^{-\mu[\hat{i}^*(t)-\tau]}\} \tag{41}$$

$$\hat{\phi}_{AI}(t) = \max\{0, 1 - e^{\mu[\hat{i}^*(t)-\tau]}\} \tag{42}$$

Consumer demand

$$D_{AW}(t) = L_W(t) \left\{ d_1 \left[\frac{(1-s)Y_W(t)}{L_W(t)} \right]^{d_2} \left[\frac{P_{AW}(t)}{P_{IW}(t)} \right]^{d_3} \right\} \tag{43}$$

$$D_{IW}(t) = \frac{(1-s)Y_W(t) - P_{AW}(t)D_{AW}(t)}{P_{IW}(t)} \tag{44}$$

$$D_{AE}(t) = L_E(t) \left\{ d_1' \left[\frac{(1-s)Y_E(t)}{L_E(t)} \right]^{d_2} \left[\frac{P_{AE}(t)}{P_{IE}(t)} \right]^{d_3} \right\} \tag{45}$$

$$D_{IE}(t) = \frac{(1-s)Y_E(t) - P_{AE}(t)D_{AE}(t)}{P_{IE}(t)} \tag{46}$$

Labor migration

$$m_{WE}(t) = \max \{0, 1 - e^{\varphi \tilde{w}^*(t)}\} \tag{47}$$

$$m_{EW}(t) = \max \{0, 1 - e^{-\varphi \tilde{w}^*(t)}\} \tag{48}$$

$$\hat{m}_{AI}(t) = \max \{0, 1 - e^{\varphi \hat{w}^*(t)}\} \tag{49}$$

$$\hat{m}_{IA}(t) = \max \{0, 1 - e^{-\varphi \hat{w}^*(t)}\} \tag{50}$$

Real wages and interest rates

$$\tilde{w}_E(t) = \frac{w_E(t)}{COL_E(t)} \tag{51}$$

$$COL_E(t) = P_{AE}(t) \left[\frac{P_{AE}(t)D_{AE}(t)}{(1-s)Y_E(t)} \right] + P_{IE}(t) \left[\frac{1 - P_{AE}(t)D_{AE}(t)}{(1-s)Y_E(t)} \right]$$

$$\tilde{w}_W(t) = \frac{\overline{w}_W(t)}{COL_W(t)} \tag{52}$$

$$COL_W(t) = P_{AW}(t) \left[\frac{P_{AW}(t)D_{AW}(t)}{(1-s)Y_W(t)} \right] +$$

$$+ P_{IW}(t) \left[\frac{1 - P_{AW}(t)D_{AW}(t)}{(1-s)Y_W(t)} \right]$$

$$\overline{w}_W(t) = \frac{w_{AW}(t)L_{AW}(t) + w_{IW}(t)L_{IW}(t)}{L_W(t)} \tag{53}$$

$$\tilde{w}^*(t) = \tilde{w}^*(t-1) + b\{\tilde{w}_E(t) - \tilde{w}_W(t) - \tilde{w}^*(t-1)\} \tag{54}$$

$$\hat{w}^*(t) = \hat{w}^*(t-1) + b\left\{ \frac{w_{IW}(t)}{P_{AW}(t)} - \frac{w_{AW}(t)}{P_{AW}(t)} - \hat{w}^*(t-1)\right\} \tag{55}$$

$$i_E(t) = \frac{r_E(t)}{P_{IE}(t)} - \delta \tag{56}$$

$$i_{IW}(t) = \frac{r_{IW}(t)}{P_{IW}(t)} - \delta \tag{57}$$

$$i_{AW}(t) = \frac{r_{AW}(t)}{P_{IW}(t)} - \delta \tag{58}$$

$$i^*(t) = i^*(t-1) + (1-\epsilon)\{i_E(t) - \bar{i}_W(t) - i^*(t-1)\} \tag{59}$$

$$\bar{i}_w(t) = \frac{i_{AW}(t)K_{AW}(t) + i_{IW}(t)K_{IW}(t)}{K_{AW}(t) + K_{IW}(t)} \tag{60}$$

$$\hat{i}^*(t) = \hat{i}^*(t-1) + (1-\epsilon)\{i_{IW}(t) - i_{AW}(t) - \hat{i}^*(t-1)\} \tag{61}$$

Foreign sector and market clearing equations

$$D_{AD}(t) = Q_{AW}(t) - EX(t) \tag{62}$$

$$D_{AD}(t) = D_{AW}(t) + D_{AE}(t) \tag{63}$$

$$D_A(t) = D_{AD}(t) + EX(t) \tag{64}$$

$$Y(t) = Y_E(t) + Y_W(t) \tag{65}$$

$$s = P_{IW}(t)\left[I_{IWE}(t) + I_{IWW}(t) + I_{AWE}(t) + I_{AWW}(t)\right] + $$
$$+ P_{IE}(t)\left[I_{IEE}(t) + I_{IEW}(t)\right]/Y_E(t) + Y_W(t) \tag{66}$$

$$IM(t) = \frac{IMVAL(t)}{P_{IE}(t)} \tag{67}$$

$$EX(t) = \frac{EXVAL(t)}{P_{AE}(t)} \tag{68}$$

$$IMVAL(t) = EXVAL(t) \tag{69}$$

Transport service sector

$$T_E(t) = \gamma T(t) \tag{70}$$

$$T_W(t) = (1-\gamma)T(t) \tag{71}$$

$$T(t) = \left[Z_A(t) - 1\right]\{D_{AE}(t) + EX(t)\} + $$
$$+ \left[Z_I(t) - 1\right]\{D_{IW}(t) + I_W(t) - Q_{IW}(t)\} \tag{72}$$

3.5 The economy in 1870: an empirical survey

A framework capable of analyzing the historical issues raised in chapter 1 has now been developed and defended in the preceding sections. All models must be 'unrealistic' or they become too cumbersome for analytical purposes. We feel the system outlined above is an efficient compromise with reality and, although simple, retains the essential features of the American economy after 1870. Considerable care has been taken to convince the reader of its applicability as the building blocks were introduced. Now we must take equal care in defending our selection of initial conditions and parameter values. After all, the interest of this book is with a *quantitative* evaluation of the role of key variables in American growth; the 'sources' of growth if you prefer. The model must be given greater empirical content in order to do so. This section dwells at length on the initial conditions and estimated parameter values utilized in the quantitative analysis. If the reader, like Milton Friedman,[38] is only concerned with the predictive ability of the model he is urged to move on to chapter 4 where the historical facts are compared with our simulated economic history.

The following section briefly describes the initial conditions for the American economy in 1870 which is our starting point in re-writing history up to World War I. Appendix A discusses the parameter estimates in detail.

The initial conditions in 1870

The structure of the economy in the 1870s. Perloff and his associates tell us that only 4,585,278 workers in the American labor force of 12,505,923 were located in employments of interest to us in 1870.[39] This subset of the labor force is our reference point, and it includes only Eastern industrial employment and Midwestern employment in both industry and agriculture. That is, we explicitly exclude all regions outside the Northeast and Midwest, and ignore employment in services, mining, forestry and fishing. How was this labor force distributed in 1870? The Perloff figures are presented in Table 3.1 and this is one key facet of the 1870 industrial structure assumed for the initial period of the simulation. Almost 65 percent of our labor force is located in the West and agriculture accounts for 49 percent of the employment in the two regional economies taken together.

The implied 1870 distribution of total value added and value added of commodity output is also reported in Table 3.1. These output figures, although they appear reasonable enough, are difficult to document given the limited data available on a sectoral and regional basis for the 1870s. First, compare our assumed share of transport value added (revenue) in total value of output with Kuznets' estimated share of transport and communications in United States net national product 1869–79. For the 1870s as a

Table 3.1. *The distribution of the labor force and gross national product
assumed in 1870*

Sector or region	Labor force		Value of output		Value of commodity output	
	Level	Share	Level	Share	Level	Share
Western agriculture	49·3	·493	110·572	·358	110·572	·433
Eastern industry	35·1	·351	100·195	·325	100·195	·393
Western industry	15·6	·156	44·531	·144	44·531	·174
Transport	—	—	53.354	·173	—	—
Total	100·0	1·000	308·652	1·000	255·298	1·000

whole, Kuznets estimates the share as 18·4 percent while for 1870
our model implies a comparable figure of 17·3 percent.[40] Second,
compare the regional output distribution implied by the model for
1870 with Easterlin's 'income originating' estimates for 1880.[41]
Excluding Eastern agriculture, in 1880 Midwestern agriculture accounted for 31·5 percent of total output in the Northeast and
Midwest, a figure in rough conformity with our 35·8 percent share
for 1870. Furthermore, Easterlin finds in 1880 that 34·4 percent of
non-agricultural income was generated by the Midwestern states,
while we assume that share to be 30·7 percent in 1870. Since the
Midwest underwent significant industrialization during the 1870s,
these two figures appear to be comparable. Finally, we note that
average labor productivities implied by the model in 1870 and by
Easterlin's 1880 figures are of the same magnitude. The ratio of
agricultural to non-agricultural labor productivity is estimated as
0·58 in 1870 while Easterlin's 1880 data suggests a figure of 0·54.

In summary, the structure of our 'fictional' 1870 economy conforms very well with the limited empirical evidence available for the
1870s.

Input prices in the 1870s. The appropriate measure of the interest
rate facing Midwest farmers is the *real* rate of interest on farm
mortgages. Bowman reports the *nominal* interest rate on farm
mortgages in Illinois, Wisconsin, Iowa and Nebraska in 1870 to be,
respectively, 9·6, 8·0, 9·5 and 10·5 percent. The real farm mortgage
rate was far higher, however, since the late 1860s were years of rapid
decline in all prices. When these adjustments are made, the real
rates on farm mortgages in these four Midwestern states were

17·0, 15·4, 16·9 and 17·9 percent.[42] As a result, we take 16 percent as a representative real farm mortgage rate facing Midwestern farmers in 1870.

Recent research on Wisconsin banking by Richard Keehn suggests that farm mortgage rates offered by country banks were from 25 to 30 percent higher than the investment rates prevailing in Milwaukee.[43] On the basis of this and other evidence, 12·8 percent is taken as the relevant real interest rate facing urban manufacturing in the Midwest.

Finally, Lance Davis's research on the American capital market documents a 25 percent differential in interest rates on comparable assets quoted in Western and Eastern markets.[44] It follows that the real interest rate prevailing in Eastern financial markets was approximately 10·2 percent. Given the depreciation rates and capital goods' prices derived in the appendix A, the gross rates of return can be easily estimated. Both the interest rates and the gross rental rates are reported in Table 3.2.

Regional wages have been documented by Lebergott. In 1869, the average daily earnings of common laborers – a relatively homogenous unskilled labor input – were the following:[45] New England, $1·56; Middle Atlantic, $1·58; East North Central, $1·58; and West North Central, $1·55. Given this evidence, it certainly seems justified to assume in 1870 money wage equalization across regions. Since we can define our monetary units in any way we wish without influencing the analysis, we take Lebergott's daily wage as representing annual income per member of the 1870 labor force regardless of employment location. In appendix A, the regional commodity price differentials are documented in detail. These output price data imply a *real* wage in the West almost half again larger than that prevailing in the East. Obviously, money wage equalization was fully consistent with the continued massive Westward migration in the 1870s.

Table 3.2. *Gross rates of return and real rates of interest by sector, 1870*

Variable	Eastern industry	Western agriculture	Western industry
i_{ij}	0·102	0·160	0·128
δ	0·030	0·030	0·030
P_{Ij}	1·000	1·250	1·250
$r_{ij} = (i_{ij} + \delta)P_{Ij}$	0·132	0·197	0·237

Source: The i_{ij} estimates are discussed in the text above. The price and depreciation parameters can be found in appendix A.

Capital intensity and factor productivity in the 1870s. Since we have chosen arbitrary units in measuring both wage income and labor inputs, absolute levels of output, per capita income and capital–labor ratios have little meaning. We can, of course, compare capital–output and land value–output ratios assumed in the model with those estimated for the 1870s since these are pure numbers, independent of the monetary unit. Furthermore, the *relative* factor intensities and average factor productivities across regions and sectors should conform with the 1870 evidence.

First, consider Midwestern agriculture. Tostlebe reports gross farm income in current prices in 1869, the current 1870 value of buildings, implements and machinery, and the current 1870 value for land. In terms of our notation, these three series represent the value of Midwestern farm output, the value of farm capital, and land, respectively. Furthermore, Tostlebe constructs these estimates separately for the Great Plains, the Lake States and the Corn Belt: these three regional groupings in fact aggregate to our Midwest. The series imply for the Midwest a capital–output ratio (in value terms) of 1·053 and a land–output ratio of 8·792.[46] These ratios are utilized in the analysis and are displayed in Table 3.3.

Securing information on capital–output ratios elsewhere in the 1870 American economy is much more difficult. Kuznets has estimated the 1880 economy-wide capital–output ratio to be 2·98.[47] This seems somewhat high for our purposes. First, Kuznets includes livestock and crop inventories in his estimate of agricultural capital stock while they are excluded from our definition. When this adjustment is made, the economy-wide capital–output ratio is reduced to 2·61. Second, the regulated industrial sector – part of non-agricultural activity – underwent impressive relative growth during

Table 3.3. *Capital–output and capital–labor ratios by region and sector assumed for 1870*

Region or sector	Value of capital to value of output	Capital–labor ratio	Land–output ratio
Western agriculture	1·053	2·367	8·792
Western industry	2·848	8·128	n.a.
Eastern industry	3·409	9·743	n.a.
Western and Eastern industry	3·236	9·230	n.a.
Economy wide	2·290	5·848	n.a.

the 1870s and that sector has the highest 1880 capital–output ratio by a large margin. On these grounds alone, the capital–output ratio was likely to have been considerably lower in 1870 than 1880. Somewhat arbitrarily, we have set the economy-wide ratio at 2·29. Given the distribution of output in 1870 (Table 3.1), the economy-wide ratio implies the regional capital–output ratios reported in Table 3.3.[48]

Income distribution and the structure of demand in the 1870s. The regional and functional distributions of income implied by the model in 1870 are displayed in Table 3.4. They are presented here for completeness. A discussion of this assumed distribution is postponed to appendix A where the parameters of sectoral production functions are explicitly specified. Nevertheless, it should be noted at this point that the distribution displayed in Table 3.4 is fully consistent with the available fragments of historical data for the 1870s. That is, the implied sectoral wage shares are consistent with Budd's data;[49] the share of transport income in national production is consistent with Kuznets' data (p. 52); and the regional distribution of income conforms fairly closely with Easterlin's 1880 estimates (p. 52).

Our prime concern in this section is the implied 1870 patterns of demand. Table 3.5 reports the composition of gross national product assumed in 1870. Note first that the share of gross savings in gross national product is 18 percent. Davis and Gallman estimate that gross capital formation (excluding inventories and agricultural clearing) was 18 percent of gross national product during the decade 1869–78.[50] We have already argued that the evidence is much too limited to disaggregate savings by source and, as a result, a uniform savings rate of 18 percent is assumed for all income groups in 1870. It should be noted as well that depreciation amounts to approximately 34 percent of gross investment. This figure is reasonably close to Kuznets' calculation for the year 1870: Kuznets finds the share to be 38 percent.[51]

The remainder of income, of course, represents consumption expenditures. The share of expenditures on foodstuffs may vary across regions: indeed, our model assumes for 1870 that 55·4 percent of expenditures are devoted to foodstuffs in the East and 46·7 percent in the West. The former figure is almost identical to that reported for Massachusetts workers in 1875.[52] On the basis of Fishlow's research, the figure for the West is taken to be 46·7 percent.[53]

To complete our specification of the 1870 initial conditions an estimate of export values is required. The ratio of the value of farm exports to gross farm product is needed. This ratio averaged approx-

Table 3.4. *Assumed regional income accounts, 1870*

Income component	EAST		WEST		TOTAL	
	Variable name	Value	Variable name	Value	Variable name	Value
Wage income	$w_E L_E$	55·107	$w_{AW}L_{AW} + w_{IW}L_{IW}$	101·893	$w_E L_E + w_{AW}L_{AW} + w_{IW}L_{IW}$	157·000
Rents	—	—	dR	10·694	dR	10·694
Factor returns to transport inputs	T_E	26·677	T_W	26·677	T	53·354
Gross returns to capital assets		50·316		36·843	$r_E K_{IE} + r_{AW}K_{AW} + r_{IW}K_{IW}$	87·159
	$r_E K_{IEE}$	45·088	$r_{IW}K_{IWW}$	16·990		
	$i_{AW}P_{IW}K_{AWE}$	2·793	$r_{AW}K_{AWW}$	18·758		
	$i_{IW}P_{IW}K_{IWE}$	2·435	$(i_E - \tau)P_{IE}K_{IEW}$	—		
	$\delta P_{IE}K_{IEW}$	—	$\delta P_{IW}K_{AWE}$	0·524		
	$\tau P_{IE}K_{IEW}$	—	$\delta P_{IW}K_{IWE}$	0·571		
Gross regional income	Y_E	132·100	Y_W	176·107	Y	308·207
Depreciation	$\delta P_{IE}K_{IE}$	10·247	$\delta P_{IW}[K_{AW} + K_{IW}]$	7·297	$\delta P_{IE} + \delta P_{IW}[K_{AW} + K_{IW}]$	17·544
Net regional income		121·853		168·810		290·663
Factor returns to transport inputs	T_E	26·677	T_W	26·677	T	53·354
Net regional commodity income		95·176		142·133		237·309

Table 3.5 *Gross national product composition, 1870*

Variable	Value
Net investment	38·013
Depreciation	17·544
Current account balance in foreign sector	0
Consumption	253·095
Gross national product	308·652

imately 16·8 percent in the early 1870s,[54] while it assumes a value of 16·6 percent in our 1870 economy. The share of export receipts in gross commodity output implied by our model is 6·1 percent in 1870. This figure is far lower than the 11·5 percent share of exports in commodity output calculated from Kuznets' data for 1871.[55] The difference, of course, reflects our exclusion of the South from our regional economy.

Summary of initial conditions

Physical outputs

$$Q_{IE} = 100·195$$
$$Q_{IW} = 35·625$$
$$Q_{AW} = 110·573$$

Output prices

$$P_{IW} = 1·250$$
$$P_{AW} = 1·000$$
$$P_{IE} = 1·000$$
$$P_{AE} = 2·000$$

Income

$$Y_E = 132·100$$
$$Y_W = 176·552$$
$$T = 53·354$$

Savings and demand

$$S_W = 31·748$$
$$S_E = 23·778$$
$$D_{AW} = 70·647$$
$$D_{IW} = 59·326$$
$$D_{AE} = 30·749$$
$$D_{IE} = 46·825$$

Inputs

$$K_{IE} = 341·572$$
$$K_{IW} = 101·463$$
$$K_{AW} = 93·114$$
$$L_{IE} = 35·100$$
$$L_{IW} = 15·600$$
$$L_{AW} = 49·300$$
$$R = 972·157$$

Input prices

$$i_{AW} = 0·160$$
$$i_{IW} = 0·128$$
$$i_E = 0·102$$
$$r_E = 0·132$$
$$r_{AW} = 0·237$$
$$r_{IW} = 0·197$$
$$w_E = 1·570$$
$$w_{IW} = 1·570$$
$$w_{AW} = 1·570$$

Foreign trade

$$EX = 9·178$$
$$IM = 18·355$$
$$EXVAL = IMVAL = 18·355$$

4

American Economic History Rewritten: Fact or Fiction?

> By clearly choosing one's chisels, one can prove that inside any log there is a beautiful Madonna.
>
> Nicholas Georgescu-Roegen (1966)

4.1 An overview

This chapter is an essay in persuasion. As Henri Theil reminds us, this is true of all econometric analysis.[1]

In the preceding chapter, a model of the American economy[2] undergoing growth and structural change between Civil and World Wars was constructed and its assumptions defended. Although most economic historians may view the model as complex and sophisticated, it is, like all models, still a simple representation of complex reality. The model has also been found to satisfy Fogel's prerequisite 'efficiency' criterion since it has required a minimum amount of parametric information.[3] Hopefully, efficiency and simplicity have been purchased at a small cost. The model appears to retain the key elements of the American economy necessary to yield insight into those crucial questions of the period raised by economic historians which were highlighted in chapter 1. The proof, however, is in the predictions.

Does the model fairly accurately reproduce fact or does it instead generate total fiction? Is the model capable of rewriting American economic history between those wars? In pages 51–7, we presented a detailed quantitative description, or snapshot, of the American economy in 1870. Granted, quantitative evidence was often lacking, but qualitative evidence was normally sufficient to place fairly narrow limits on the values of requisite variables in the system. Furthermore, quantitative dimensions were successfully established on each exogenous variable for which annual observations were required. Given these initial conditions in 1870 and the estimated parameters, our model of disequilibrium growth can now tell a very precise quantitative story. Is the story purely fiction or does it closely conform to the facts? Are the simulated gross national product per capita growth rates close to those computed for the

American economy by Gallman and Kuznets? Does the shift in population to the Midwest conform with fact? Does the model predict a rate of farm mechanization consistent with the documentation of Tostlebe, Kuznets, Rogin and others? Is the predicted rate of industrialization consistent with observed experience? Does the model produce declining real interest rates, rising real land values and increasing real wages consistent with their historical behavior from the 1870s to World War I?

Section 4.2 places the econometrics of this chapter in perspective. It discusses the very special problems which economic historians must face in evaluating the predictive accuracy of large interdependent systems. The accuracy of our 'forecasts' is explored in detail in section 4.3. This is the heart of the chapter but a summary evaluation is presented in section 4.4.

4.2 Historical explanations and predictive accuracy

Models and measures of performance

Until very recently, economic historians rarely attempted to evaluate the predictive accuracy of their models. Older scholars normally used 'theory' in a taxonomic way merely as a device to make order of complex economic events. As Fogel has pointed out,[4] one can read many of the early economic historians in vain searching for an explicit maintained hypothesis with empirically verifiable content. Unfortunately, modern cliometric research offers us few guidelines as well. The new economic historian deals almost always in a world of partial equilibrium statics. He will state explicitly a maintained hypothesis of market, firm or household behavior and proceed with his analysis of an economic event. He may, perhaps, hesitate long enough to test a proposition by statistical regression. The procedure is simple enough in partial equilbrium statics although one might wish for more frequent comparisons of model performance with *competing* hypotheses even in these cases. But what do we do when our pretensions swell to encompass simultaneous equation systems and interdependent models?

General equilibrium models are now being applied to ante bellum tariff and land policy:[5] In what sense have these models been 'tested'? Should we be content with Peter Temin's qualification that 'These paradigms are presented in a provisional spirit; only time will tell if [they are] a useful way to synthesize some aspects of our history'?[6] Temin would surely agree that we should make every effort to improve on this state of affairs. Is it not precisely our task to discriminate between theories in an attempt to piece together analytical histories of evolution and growth?[7]

These lofty words, then, contain the challenge. How do we now proceed from the 'guides for general discussion' to the 'detailed work'?[8]

Prediction, forecast and historical analysis.   Simulation is the basic tool of analysis used in the present chapter. Somewhat surprisingly, this technique has rarely been used in economic history – a field for which it is ideally suited. Since this form of numerical analysis is not generally well known by economic historians, at least judging by their research, it might be useful to begin this section with a brief survey of simulation methodology.

The strength and weakness of interdependent dynamic systems lies with their large size and complex interdependence. As a counter-example, it was shown in chapter 2 that Fishlow and Fogel[9] are easily able to conceptualize the impact of declining transport costs on the American economy because they restrict their attention to comparative statics and rely on partial equilibrium analysis. Their difficulties lie only with their (manifest) inability to find creative solutions to the problems arising from a quantitative evaluation of the economic effects of the railroads when historical data are sparse. Suppose, like Fishlow, we suspect that the partial equilibrium approach may be inappropriate in evaluating a major innovation like the railroads?

A final and very significant distortion in the calculation of social saving derives from the existence of indirect benefits. Because there are second round effects of the initial reduction in transport cost, namely induced capital formation and expansion in other sectors, the position of the demand schedule for transport services is not independent of movement along it. Since all railroads are taken together as one unit, the magnitude of such a shift may be quite considerable.[10]

It is precisely the postulated strength of these 'second round effects' which has motivated the use of simple general equilibrium models in analyzing the ante bellum economy. To pursue the railroad example, our focus extends to an evaluation of the rails not simply given the present demands for transport services, but instead to include their impact on the distribution of income – over space and by function – and thus on income growth through induced labor force expansion, increased rates of capital formation, and increased land utilization. These effects can only be captured in a system which introduces the *possibility* of important feedbacks. This is the great strength of models like that developed in chapter 3.

Yet such models are defective for the same reason: because of their complexity, they cannot easily be analyzed by applying conventional graphical or mathematical technique. Given the extreme difficulty of qualitative analysis, then, large systems of simultaneous equations, whether used for business cycle forecasting or for the analysis of nineteenth-century development problems, can only be effectively explored by numerical analysis.[11]

The limitations of numerical analysis are obvious. The results are not easily generalized. The analysis will be limited to a very special economy with quite specific initial conditions and parameter values. In our case, for example, we shall not be able to generalize about the sources of industrialization. Our insights will be limited to the American economy from the 1870s to World War I. Perhaps the model developed in chapter 3 would yield quite different insights into the sources of industrialization if we were to select the conditions prevailing in the 1830s as our starting point and re-estimate the parameters of the model so that they would reflect the conditions of the antebellum period. Instead, our interest is in the period following the Civil War. Generalizations outside of that period of American growth will be left to other scholars.

There is another, more compelling reason, justifying numerical analysis of the model contained in chapter 3. The economic historian is more interested in *quantitative* than qualitative statements about the economy under scrutiny. It is all very well to speculate that the deterioration in the relative world market price for grains is consistent with the stability in real Midwestern land values during most of the 1870s, but what precisely was the quantitative impact of changing European markets? What was the relative importance of endogenously determined interest rates in the West compared to those exogenous commodity market conditions in contributing to these important changes in farm land values? Only numerical analysis can supply the quantitative dimension to such questions, and that dimension is the stuff of economic history.

There are four basic steps in the simulation procedure: model formulation, estimation, testing and analysis. Since 'good specification is vital for good economic model-building,'[12] whether the issues are historical or not,[13] this step must be treated with care. An effort was made in chapter 3 to convince the reader of the plausibility of each *component* of our model of the American economy. Furthermore, even though there are many 'omissions' in our model, that is, elements of American economic history not captured in our statements regarding the structure of the economy, this framework, like all theories, is designed to confront a particular set of problems. It is our claim – to be scrutinized in this and subsequent chapters – that these omitted elements of the historical process of change are relatively unimportant to the specific issues confronted in this book. It is the second step, however, that distinguishes historical from contemporary econometric research: how do we 'estimate' macroeconomic relationships when the requisite time series data are, for all practical purposes, non-existent? When detailed macro data are abundant, the conventional procedure is to estimate the system using time series, presumably employing simultaneous estimation procedures. We have no such option. Instead, we derived parameter estimates from decennial census information, from budget studies and from other data fragments, seeking plausible estimates from the best quantitative and qualitative information available on the post-Civil War period. The tenuous nature of these parameter estimates places even greater emphasis on the tests of the model.

How, then, are these tests to be performed? Again, the conventional procedure is to compare the predictions of the model with actual observations. That is, the model is estimated from data drawn from one time period while tested on another. This step is obviously crucial even if the components of the model pass stringent statistical tests during estimation *since there is nothing which ensures that the full model will behave adequately even if its components are plausible.* Our purpose in this chapter is to forecast (or 'backcast' if you prefer) the behavior of the American economy from the 1870s to World War I, and then to compare these predictions with fact. In one sense, this is an independent test of our model since few, if any, of the parameters were directly estimated from macro time series – and it is these series that we are attempting to replicate. In another sense, a truly independent test – by, say, 'forecasting' the 1920s – would be unproductive since the model is *specific* to the period up to 1910: the changes in economic structure following World War I are much too profound to make our pre-war model useful for understanding the 1920s. Indeed, we may even wish to use our results to suggest how and to what extent the American economy underwent significant structural changes after the mid-1890s should our ability to predict the last decade or so of the period be relatively poor.

In summary, the criterion for a good econometric model may be that it predicts well on an independent body of data but our problem is somewhat different. Our goal is to explain a particular historical period rather than to forecast future economic events based on the experience of that period. Under these conditions, it is quite appropriate to draw our parameters from the period in question and to use the time series of that period to assess the descriptive accuracy of the model. In any case, the conventional econometric criterion may not be sufficient nor in fact possible in the case of historical research:

> ... almost always the number of observations is limited, and part of them have to be used to specify [estimate] the model itself. The temptation is then great to use all or most of the observations for this purpose ... The econometrician is then forced to retreat from the prediction criterion, *and he can do no*

> *more than choose his model in such a way as to maximize the the chance that it predicts well.* The criteria for this . . . procedure are those of plausibility and *simplicity.* [14]

Thus, in the present chapter plausibility is defined to include the ability of the model to reproduce the economic history of the period under study.

Predictive performance measures: a survey of performance criteria. [15] What rules can we invoke to judge the descriptive accuracy of an historical model and thus its plausibility? Many of the standard econometric procedures reviewed below are likely to prove useless given serious constraints on data availability. Furthermore, while American economic history is replete with the short-run instability generated by business cycles and long swings in economic activity, the model is designed only to confront long-term full employment growth. A comparison of historical and predicted short-run performance is inappropriate given the scope of our model. Yet most of the measures discussed below have been developed to evaluate the predictive accuracy of short-term economic activity. Nevertheless, as a beacon in these uncharted shoals, it seems wisest to begin as if these conventional measures were applicable without qualification.

One well-known criterion for appraising the conformity of time series is turning point analysis. For output and output per capita series, which normally rise through time, the appropriate measure may be growth rates where interest focuses on predicting acceleration and retardation. For many input price series which exhibit variability in their levels, on the other hand, the actual value of the predicted variable may be the more relevant unit for turning point analysis. Failure is to be judged on two grounds: (i) predicted turning points which fail to appear in the historical data, and (ii) turning points which appear in the historical data but are not predicted. These possibilities are displayed in the following table:

		Predicted	
		Turning point	No turning point
Actual	Turning point	(i)	(iii)
	No turning point	(ii)	(iv)

Measures of failure than can be calculated as

$$\psi_1 = \frac{\text{(ii)}}{\text{(i)} + \text{(ii)}} \text{ and } \psi_2 = \frac{\text{(iii)}}{\text{(iii)} + \text{(iv)}}.$$

Ideally, one would like these ψ statistics to approach zero, but even modern Scandinavian forecasting models fail 20 to 30 percent of the time.[16] We can hardly hope for better. This simple device for evaluating the predictive accuracy of a model is especially useful when the historical data exhibit major turning points and non-linearities. As we shall see, this is indeed true of American growth during the four decades preceding World War I. We observe a major retardation in growth rates prior to 1900, a decline in real interest rates to the 1890s followed by a rise, a gain in the Midwest's share of the national labor force up to 1880 and a sharp decline thereafter, and so on. Under these historical conditions, turning point analysis is a powerful device for evaluating the plausibility of a long-run growth model. In fact, we shall rely on it heavily since most of the economic variables predicted by the model are documented only imperfectly and at scattered points in time.

A second device for evaluating model plausibility involves 'goodness-of-fit' measures. Unfortunately, it is rare indeed that sufficient historical data are available to make such measures effective. Observations are often available only at census dates so that regression analysis is of limited value. For example, in most cases our observations are limited to census dates and the degrees of freedom are much too small to allow statistical reliability in regression estimation. Comparisons of beginning and end year values are about as close as we can get to more sophisticated regression technique. For those few variables which are well documented by historical information, the 'goodness-of-fit' techniques are well defined. Suppose our purpose is to compare predicted per capita GNP growth rates per decade, $P(t)$, and the observed decennial growth rates calculated by Gallman, $A(t)$. A linear regression could then be estimated:

$$P(t) = \hat{m}_0 + \hat{m}_1 A(t).$$

Presumably, a perfect 'forecast' would have the following attributes: $\hat{m}_0 = 0$, $\hat{m}_1 = 1$ and $R^2 = 1\cdot 0$. In fact, such good fortune is rare. Note also that typically there is a bias towards $\hat{m}_1 < 1$.[17] Since larger errors are to be expected with larger changes, some allowance must be made for this systematic error. Theil makes this allowance by regressing

$$[P(t) - mA(t)]^2 = \hat{\alpha}_0 + \hat{\alpha}_1 A(t)^2.$$

Having done so, 'confidence limits' can be set by

$$P(t) = \hat{m}_1 A(t) \pm \sqrt{[\hat{\alpha}_0 + \hat{\alpha}_1 A(t)^2]}.$$

Under normality assumptions, two-thirds of the pairs of $[P(t), A(t)]$ should fall into the shaded area in Figure 4.1.[18] In any case, we can proceed to evaluate our results by testing the hypothesis that $\hat{m}_0 = 0$ and $\hat{m}_1 = 1$ using conventional significance tests.

Finally, how do we judge the accuracy of our predictions dealing with the *structure* of the economy: e.g., the distribution of labor across regions and activities, and the distribution of commodity output by sector? The model itself stresses sectoral interdependence and, as a result, the predicted shares of output or employment are always interdependent. A predictive error on one sector's employment obviously must appear as an offsetting error in another sector. In order to explore this aspect of the model's plausibility, we require a test statistic which meets the interdependence assumptions. Theil supplies us with a summary statistic, this time from information theory.[19] Suppose we denote predicted shares by $p_i(t)$ and actual shares by $a_i(t)$. Let there be n such shares predicted. Then an average measure of *information inaccuracy* is

$$T[a(t):p(t)] = \frac{1}{T} \sum_{t=1}^{T} \sum_{i=1}^{n} a_i(t) \log \frac{a_i(t)}{p_i(t)},$$

where $0 \leq a_i(t), p_i(t) \leq 1$ and $\sum_i a_i(t) = \sum_i p_i(t) = 1$. One of the

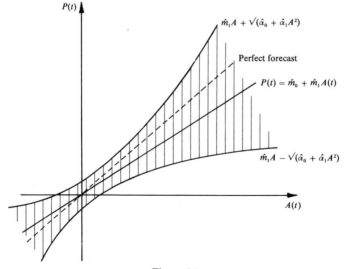

Figure 4.1

advantages of this statistic is that it weights each share prediction by its relative importance. A perfect prediction would result in $I[a:p] = 0$.

These, then, are some summary performance measures commonly used in appraising simulations. They all share the same weakness: what shall we accept as 'good' performance? The ultimate test is to compare our model's accuracy with a competing economic model of the post-Civil War period. Alas, no such competitors currently exist. Hopefully, this book may goad other researchers into supplying such competitors. Only then can we expect to edge closer towards the truth.

Data limitations and the critical quantitative series

It should come as no surprise to the practising economic historian that the critical difference between contemporary and historical work of this sort lies with the relative abundance of quantitative evidence. Our model makes many quantitative predictions that can be judged only by sketchy qualitative evidence. For example, we have no annual observations on interregional labor migration rates, and even decennial observations are weak. Yet we certainly would insist that the model generate net Westward migration during the early years of our period. Similarly, absolutely no quantitative measures of the magnitude and variance in interregional long-term capital movements exist, although we would insist that the Midwest exhibit a 'deficit' status at least during the 1870s and 1880s, with the rate of capital inflow declining towards the end of the nineteenth century and perhaps even reversing. Even in the case of aggregate output measures, Gallman's series are only approximations and further do not precisely conform with our definitions of output.

These difficulties are now discussed at greater length in section 4.3. Heavy reliance is placed on the tests of performance reviewed on pp. 67–78, because these aggregate measures of growth and structural change are important indices of American development. Yet, we place even greater stress on the input price behavior presented in the *Input prices* section since these historical series are ones in which we have relatively greater confidence. That section includes an examination of real wages, interest rates, and land values. However, some critical series in our model, sectoral and aggregate capital–labor ratios, cannot be explored as intensively as we would like since the historical data reconstructed by Kuznets and others are sparse at best.

With these caveats in mind, we now confront the question of this chapter: fact or fiction?

4.3 Fact or fiction? Simulation and economic history compared

Macro growth performance

Gross national product per worker. We begin with an examination of the aggregate output and per worker productivity measures. The basic historical series which we wish to explain is the Gallman–Kuznets index of gross national product (in 1860 prices) per member of the labor force. The aggregate output per worker series reported in Table 4.2.A are overlapping decade averages, converted to an arbitrary 1870 base. The labor force series is supplied by Lebergott. We are far less concerned with our ability to predict aggregate United States GNP growth since our model excludes regions outside the Northeast and Midwest which were undergoing rapid extensive development even after the 1880s.

First consider the long-period performance averages over these forty years. The conformity between the model and the Gallman–Kuznets indices is remarkably close. Over the thirty years preceding 1899/08, the Gallman–Kuznets data imply an average per annum growth rate of 1·47 percent while over the same period the model predicts 1·49 percent. (See Table 4.1.) The correspondence for the period 1869/78–1904/13 is less perfect but still impressive: 1·33 and 1·41 percent by Gallman–Kuznets and the model, respectively. The relatively poorer results when the five years 1899/08–1904/13 are included can be explained by two closely related factors: (i) as we shall see below, the model does not capture long swings very effectively; (ii) the model is not extended beyond 1910 and the years 1910–13 were ones of relatively sluggish per capita GNP growth. Second, the model continues to perform extremely well when the period is bisected into shorter fifteen-year movements, 1869/78–1884/93 and 1884/93–1899/1908, as in Table 4.1. The retardation in American growth rates from the early 1870s to the mid-1890s is well known and the causes of this 'Great Depression' –not to be confused

Table 4.1. *Long-period average of per annum growth rates of GNP per worker, 1870–1910*

Period	Gallman–Kuznets	Model
1869/78–1884/93	1·71%	1·69%
1884/93–1899/1908	1·24	1·29
1869/78–1899/1908	1·47	1·49
1869/78–1904/13	1·33	1·41

Source: See notes to Tables 4.2A and 4.2B.

with the 1930s – will be discussed further on in this book. A plausible model should be capable of reproducing this important facet of American nineteenth-century development. Up to the late 1880s, the Gallman–Kuznets per annum growth rate is 1·71 percent (1·69 percent in our model); during the subsequent fifteen years terminating in the middle of the first decade of the twentieth century, the Gallman–Kuznets per annum growth rate is 1·24 percent (1·29 percent in our model). Thus we have further confirmation of the model's plausibility since it predicts a major retardation in annual GNP per capita growth replicating an important characteristic of late nineteenth- and early twentieth-century American growth. In part, this major retardation was reversed after the 1890s only because of an upward shift in the savings rate. Without the increased savings rate, the retardation trend might have continued up to World War I.

Table 4.2A. *Indices of GNP per member of the labor force, 1870–1910*

Average period	Gallman–Kuznets	Model
1869–78	100·0	100·0
1874–83	114·4	105·3
1879–88	126·5	116·7
1884–93	129·0	128·5
1889–98	130·2	138·8
1894–03	140·9	149·6
1899–08	155·2	156·1
1904–13	159·0	
(1904–10)		(152·2)

Source: 1869–1908; GNP in 1860 prices from R. Gallman, 'Gross National Product in the United States, 1834–1909,' table A-1, p. 26. 1908–18; GNP in 1929 prices (converted to 1860 prices) from S. Kuznets, *Capital in the American Economy: Its Formation and Financing,* table R-12, p. 521. 1869–1918; Labor force calculated from S. Lebergott, *Manpower in Economic Growth: The United States Record Since 1800,* table A-1, p. 510.

The data presented in Table 4.2A can be utilized in another fashion to supply further evidence to the skeptical reader, reinforcing our assertion that the model reproduces aggregate GNP performance very closely. Following Theil, let the Gallman–Kuznets GNP per worker series be denoted by $A(t)$, and the simulated series by $P(t)$. For the period between 1869–78 and 1904–10, an

69

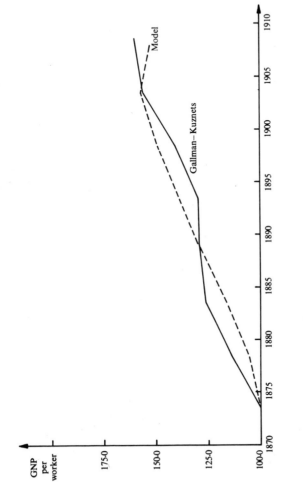

Figure 4.2 Indices of GNP per member of the labor force
(*Source*: Table 4.2A)

estimated linear regression between fact and 'fiction' yields

$$P(t) = -0.654 + 1.042A(t), R^2 = 0.891,$$
$$(2.721) \qquad (0.141)$$

where the figures in parentheses are standard errors. The R^2 is remarkably high given the well-known presence of long swings in aggregate economic activity during the late nineteenth century. More importantly, significance tests indicate that $\hat{m}_0$ is not significantly different from zero; nor is $\hat{m}_1$ significantly different from unity. Judged by the conventional forecasting literature, these results speak very well for the plausibility of the model.

Although the model reproduces the secular growth performance of the American economy very well indeed, it fails to generate long swings over shorter-term periods. The long swing or Kuznets cycle chronology has been carefully established for this phase of American growth.[20] Serious depressions have been recorded for the 1890s and the mid-1870s, while the mid-1880s produced a less significant trough. In terms of GNP growth rates, Abramovitz dates troughs in early 1874, mid-1886, early 1892 and 1911, and peaks in early 1864, 1881, late 1889 and 1899.[21] These movements are approximately reproduced by the Gallman–Kuznets series displayed in Tables 4.2A and 4.2B. Our model was not developed to confront American

Table 4.2B. *Per annum growth rates of GNP and GNP per member of the labor force, 1870–1910*

	GNP			GNP per worker		
Period	Gallman–Kuznets (1860 prices)	Model (1910 prices)	Model (variable price weights)	Gallman–Kuznets (1860 prices)	Model (1910 prices)	Model (variable price weights)
1869/78–1874/83	5·58%	5·31%	3·57%	2·66%	2·67%	1·17%
1874/83–1879/88	4·76	4·70	4·47	2·11	2·40	2·07
1879/88–1884/93	3·68	3·81	4·03	0·40	1·73	1·94
1884/93–1889/98	2·55	2·99	3·26	0·19	1·28	1·55
1889/98–1894/1903	3·39	2·62	2·90	1·61	1·19	1·47
1894/1903–1899/1908	4·31	2·70	2·29	1·94	1·23	0·85
1899/1908–1904/1913	3·68	2·16	0·57	0·50	1·02	−0·51
1869/78–1899/1908	3·33	3·62	3·36	1·47	1·76	1·49

Source: 1869–1908; GNP in 1860 prices from R. Gallman, 'Gross National Product in the United States, 1834–1909,' table A-1, p. 26. 1908–1918; GNP in 1929 prices (converted to 1860 prices) from S. Kuznets, *Capital in the American Economy: Its Formation and Financing*, table R-12, p. 521. 1869–1918; Labor force growth rates calculated from S. Lebergott, *Manpower in Economic Growth: The United States Record Since 1800*, table A-1, p. 510.

experience with long-term variation in aggregate demand, departures from full employment, and the existence of excess capacity. Thus, it is hardly surprising that we fail to generate these long swings since ours is a supply-oriented neoclassical model. Yet it should be noted that the simulated economy *does* produce a rise in growth rates to a peak in 1878–83, a steady decline to 1888–93, relative stability to 1893–8, and a sharp decline to 1903–8. There is some confirmation, therefore, of Abramovitz' suggestion that the long swing is not to be explained solely by fluctuations in aggregate demand and factor utilization. Instead, they may be in part explained by variance in rates of factor augmentation (rates of *physical* capital formation and foreign immigration) and their influence on supply.

This assertion – the importance of supply conditions on the long swing – is given further credance when our GNP and GNP per worker series are expressed in 1910 prices. A word on this procedure is necessary. The Gallman–Kuznets series is expressed in 1860 prices, a relative price structure very different from that prevailing in 1870, 1910, or 1929. As a result, our long-term growth rates are in 'current prices' to facilitate comparability of the simulated and historical series. Current price data *do not* reflect inflationary or deflationary movements in our model but only actual changes in *relative* commodity prices (e.g., variable price weights). Yet even these relative price movements have been pronounced over short time periods; the outstanding cases are the decline in relative farm product prices during the 1870s and their rise 1906–10. Interestingly enough, these short-term episodes are precisely the ones during which the model appears to predict poorly. Using 1910 prices, however, the apparent low predicted growth rates 1869/78–1874/83 are raised sharply toward the Gallman–Kuznets levels and the peculiar behavior after 1894/1908 is also partially eliminated: indeed, what had been negative growth rates per worker 1899/1908–1904/13 now become positive. The relative importance of world market conditions in generating long swings becomes even more apparent. We return to this issue in chapter 10.

Capital stock growth, the aggregate capital–output ratio and the capital–labor ratio. This section must rely on one of the most imperfectly measured economic variables – the capital stock. In spite of the pioneering efforts of Kuznets, Goldsmith, Gallman, Tostlebe and others, the historical evidence on the aggregate and sectoral capital stock is relatively poor. It follows that capital stock growth rates, capital–output ratios, and capital intensity measures are equally suspect. To make matters worse, the measured historical stocks diverge conceptually from the theoretical stocks defined in our model, and any serious attempt to improve the historical data in this dimension would take us far beyond the scope of this book. The discussion which follows will, as a result, focus only on trends in these series rather than on precise quantitative comparisons.

Table 4.3 displays both the Kuznets estimates and the model's predictions on capital stock growth rates. The historical rates are for the American economy as a whole while the predicted values are limited to the Northeast and Midwest. Yet the two series are much alike. Over the four decades as a whole, the average growth rates are 4·62 and 5·12 percent for the Kuznets and the simulated series, respectively. Presumably, our exclusion of the South and Far West explains the higher rates predicted in early decades.[22] Furthermore, with no exception, the simulated capital stock growth rates produce turning points consistent with the historical series. The model faithfully reproduces the 'catching up' in the seventies, the surge in the eighties, and the 'bust' in the nineties. The model even captures the long swing depression in the 1890s. Finally, Table 4.3 also indicates a fair degree of consistency between the historical and simulated share of capital consumption in gross savings: by 1905, the figures are almost precisely the same. All of these results tend to increase our confidence in the model's plausibility.

Let us move on to more boggy ground. It is one thing to examine historic capital stock growth areas rates with some degree of confidence. It is quite another to deal with capital–output and capital–labor ratios. The imprecision of such numbers is familiar to anyone who has had the temerity to examine the measures closely. The

Table 4.3. *Capital stock growth and the capital consumption share in gross savings, 1870–1910* (in percent)

| Period | Capital stock growth | | | Capital consumption share in gross savings | |
	Kuznets	Model	Year	Kuznets	Model
1869–79	4·55	5·26	1870–80	0·388	0·323
1879–89	4·94	5·78	1880–90	0·425	0·359
1889–99	4·75	4·82	1890–1900	0·451	0·398
1899–1909	4·34	4·09	1905	0·441	0·443
1909–19	3·27	—			
1869–1909	4·62	—			
1870–1910	—	5·12			

Source: Capital stock growth rates per annum (in billions of 1929 $, net of capital consumption) calculated from S. Kuznets, *Capital in the American Economy*, table 3, pp. 64–5. The capital consumption share is from *ibid.*, table R-29, pp. 572–4 and is based on five-year moving averages.

Table 4.4. *Capital–output and capital–labor ratios, 1870–1910 (1879–88 = 100)*

	Capital–output ratio			Capital–labor ratio		
Period	Private domestic economy: Kendrick	Private domestic non-farm economy Kendrick	Non-farm economy: model	Private domestic economy: Kendrick	Private domestic non-farm economy: Kendrick	Non-farm economy: model
1869–78	125·2	131·8	104·2	91·8	88·3	77·9
1879–88	100·0	100·0	100·0	100·0	100·0	100·0
1889	105·5	113·1	112·2	102·4	103·4	116·8
1894	116·5	130·8	119·3	121·9	136·3	131·3
1899	100·8	115·0	121·0	123·2	132·9	145·8
1904	100·8	115·9	127·7	129·4	139·2	161·0
1909	93·7	106·5	122·2	132·6	141·4	174·8

Source: Indices are exclusive of trade, construction, finance, forestry, fisheries and personal services. Calculated from J. Kendrick, *Productivity Trends in the United States*, tables A-XXII and A-XXIII, pp. 333–5 and 338–40. Kendrick includes land values in the capital stock while the model excludes them. The simulated and the Kendrick non-farm output series both include income originating in transportation.

exercise shakes the confidence of even the most avid believer in quantification. Let the avid believer examine Table 4.4 where historical and simulated indices of the capital–output and capital–labor ratio are presented. Kendrick's historic estimates for both the private domestic economy and the private domestic non-farm economy are recorded there, but the relevant comparison is between the latter and the non-farm series produced by the model. The private domestic economy series are much less useful since the underlying capital stock estimates include farm land values. Furthermore, at least in 1880 a larger share of non-agricultural wealth is located in the Northeast and Midwest than of total wealth. Thus our exclusion of the remaining regions of the United States presents less serious problems when comparing non-farm capital stocks documented by Kendrick and generated by the model. With very few exceptions, fact and fiction appear to correspond quite closely. The exceptions are the following: First, although the simulated capital–output ratio does fall between 1869–78 and 1879–88, it fails to decline at the dramatic rate produced in Kendrick's data. Second, the decline in Kendrick's capital–output ratio between 1894 and 1899 is not reproduced in the simulation. While the *rate of increase* in the capital–labor ratio declines between 1894 and 1899 in the simulated series, the *absolute level* falls in the Kendrick series over the same five years. Both of these results indicate once again that our model cannot fully capture long swings and the resulting variation in excess capacity. Yet the overall trend is close to historical fact and *every* turning point, with the exception of the late 1890s, is accurately predicted.

Changes in economic structure

Thus far, the plausibility of our disequilibrium model of historical growth has been evaluated in terms of aggregate growth performance. It is, of course, comforting and essential that the model pass these tests to make the framework a candidate for serious historical analysis. Based on this evaluation alone, the model appears to command more attention that we would devote to a 'simple paradigm' of historical growth. Yet, the majority of the analytical issues raised in chapter 1 deal with the sources of industrialization, regional development, and the operation of regional commodity and factor markets during the development process. To evaluate the plausibility of the model in these dimensions we must now turn to the model's predictions on the regional and sectoral distribution of output and inputs over time: fact or fiction?

Employment distribution and urbanization. Table 4.5 displays three key measures of factor use which have always been the focus of historian's interest and of economist's concern with the nature of industrial development. The first of these is the share of non-farm employment in the Midwest itself. The second is the share of the American (more precisely, the aggregate of the Northeastern and Midwestern) labor force employed in the Midwest. The third measures the relative importance of non-farm employment in total employment.

Table 4.5. *Sectoral employment distribution, 1870–1910*

Year	L_{IW}/L_W		$[L_{AW} + L_{IW}]/L$		$[L_{IW} + L_{IE}]/L$	
	Perloff	Model	Perloff	Model	Perloff	Model
1870	0·241	0·240	0·654	0·649	0·507	0·507
1875	—	0·260	—	0·633	—	0·535
1880	0·274	0·258	0·656	0·650	0·524	0·518
1885	—	0·240	—	0·630	—	0·521
1890	0·329	0·273	0·632	0·635	0·576	0·538
1895	—	0·329	—	0·631	—	0·576
1900	0·359	0·417	0·618	0·639	0·604	0·627
1905	—	0·467	—	0·628	—	0·663
1910	0·477	0·488	0·580	0·615	0·696	0·685

Source: H. S. Perloff *et al.*, *Regions, Resources and Economic Growth*, ch. 12. See note to Table 4.2.

The Perloff data on the non-farm employment share, $[L_{IW} + L_{IE}] /L$, is given only at census dates. The absolute increase in industry's share is 18·9 percentage points over the four decades following 1870, surely an impressive period of industrialization. The model predicts a rate of industrialization of comparable magnitude: 17·8 percentage points. Furthermore, the historical data suggest that the majority of this employment shift took place after 1890. The model replicates this characteristic of United States growth as well: both the historical and the simulated series show three-quarters of the employment shift occurring from 1890 to 1910, 12·0 and 14·7 percentage points respectively. Indeed, note that while Perloff's industrial employment share rises from 0·507 to 0·576 from 1870 to 1890 the model predicts an *identical* rise from 1870 to 1895.

The industrialization experience within the Midwest is even more dramatic, but the relative rates over time are comparable to those for the United States as a whole. Perloff documents an increase in the Midwestern non-farm employment share of 23·6 percentage points while the simulation records an increase of 24·8 percentage points. Note once again that Perloff documents a rise in L_{IW}/L_W from 0·241 to 0·329 between 1870 and 1890; the model replicates this Midwestern industrialization experience *exactly* between 1870 and 1895. Finally, it appears that the model also successfully replicates the changing distribution of the labor force by regions. It even captures critical turning points. The 1870s are years of minor increases in the American labor force employed in the Midwest, while the 1880s record a significant reversal in this trend. Although the model once again fails to capture the 1890s successfully, it does faithfully reproduce the sharp decline in the Midwest labor share from 1900 to 1910. Once again, the model is especially effective in reproducing the first two decades of historical performance: while the historic Midwestern labor force share rises to 0·632 in 1890, the model predicts 0·635 in the same year.

The distribution of output. Regional income and output data for the nineteenth century are still tentative in spite of the impressive efforts by Easterlin and others to fill this important gap. The Perloff and Easterlin measures are summarized as percentage shares at census dates in Table 4.6. Since these output shares are dominated by relative price movements in the short run, our interest is in turning points rather than levels.

With the exception of the model's predictions for the 1890s, the simulated changes in value added distribution are fairly close to those estimated by Perloff and Easterlin, at least in terms of direction of change in the regional–sectoral output mix. Over the entire forty-year period, however, we predict a much higher rise in the

Table 4.6. *Industrial structure by region, 1870–1910 (percentage shares)*

Sector	1870		1880		1890		1900		1910	
	Perloff–Easterlin	Model	Perloff–Easterlin	Model	Perloff–Easterlin	Model	Perloff–Easterlin	Model	Perloff–Easterlin	Model
West income	60·7	60·7	55·1	59·9	54·9	55·4	53·8	47·0	65·7	52·3
Agriculture	43·3	43·3	31·5	36·7	27·9	35·4	23·8	29·0	38·4	31·5
Non-agriculture	17·4	17·4	23·6	23·2	27·0	20·0	30·0	18·0	27·3	20·8
East income	39·3	39·3	44·9	40·1	45·1	44·6	46·2	53·0	34·3	47·7
Total income	100·0	100·0	100·0	100·0	100·0	100·0	100·0	100·0	100·0	100·0

Sources: These are commodity output shares.
1880 and 1900: R.A. Easterlin, 'Interregional Differences in Per Capita Income, Population and Total Income, 1840–1950,' tables A-2 and A-3, pp. 99–104.
1870, 1890 and 1910: H. S. Perloff, *et al.*, *Regions, Resources and Economic Growth*, tables 38 and 46, pp. 139 and 153.

non-farm value added share than the documented by Perloff–Easterlin: the figures are 9·9 and 3·4 percentage points, respectively. Furthermore, the predicted rate of industrialization in the Midwest 1870–1910 is considerably lower than that estimated by Perloff–Easterlin: the Perloff–Easterlin non-farm share in total Midwestern income rises from 28·7 to 46·4 percent while the model predicts a rise from 28·7 to only 39·8 percent. Yet, the model faithfully captures the industrialization of the Midwest, and the overall industrialization of the two regions combined.

With the exception of the 1890s, the model predicts each decade turning point accurately. This conformity is all the more remarkable given the instability in these output share movements. Measures such as those presented in Table 4.6 are commonly used to evaluate the *long-run* changes in economic structure and industrialization performance.[23] Yet major reversals in long-run industrialization performance can easily be reflected in these output share measures due only to short-run movements in relative commodity prices. The most striking example of this is the first decade of the twentieth century: agriculture's historic share in value added *rises* by 14·6 percentage points, a sharp reversal of the long-run trend towards industrialization indeed. So much so, in fact, that it almost eliminates all of the rise in the industrial value added share in the preceding three decades of development! It should be noted that the model *also* predicts this reversal but of a lesser magnitude. The explanation lies with the marked rise in the relative price of Midwestern agricultural products rather than any long-run endogenous mechanism in American regional development. Finally, note that the model accurately predicts the 1870s and 1880s as the decades of most impressive industrialization.

A summary evaluation of predicted structural change. Theil's information inaccuracy statistic is an ideal device to judge the accuracy of our predictions dealing with the *structure* of the economy. Denoting $a_i(t)$ as the actual share of the ith sector in the total and $p_i(t)$ as the predicted share,

$$T[a(t):p(t)] = \frac{1}{T} \sum_{t=1}^{T} \sum_{i=1}^{n} a_i(t) \log \left[\frac{a_i(t)}{p_i(t)} \right].$$

Since historical data are available only at census dates, $T = 4$ at the maximum (e.g., 1880, 1890, 1900 and 1910); in all cases, the model identifies only three sectors so that $n = 3$. Four T statistics were computed:

	Employment	*Output*
1910:	$T = 0·0013$	$T = 0·0223$
1880–1910:	$T = 0·0020$	$T = 0·0719$

In the pages immediately preceding, we argued that the model was able to predict output and input performance measures of structural change rather well, although we were more successful with the latter. This tentative conclusion is now confirmed by Theil's statistic. In the case of employment distribution, the error is always less than 1 percent. The information inaccuracy statistic for employment distribution assumes very small values even when compared with more detailed simulations of contemporary problems as they have appeared in the literature.[24]

Input prices and factor market behavior

Some of the best historical information available for testing the plausibility of our model relates to factor markets and input prices. In addition, many of the historical issues confronted by this book evolve around the behavior of real wages, interest rates, regional interest rate differentials, and land values. The next section examines the labor market, the following the capital market, and the final section the Midwestern land market, in an effort to broaden our tests of the model's performance.

Wages and the labor market. One of the most extensive, and consistent, annual wage series is Lebergott's real annual earnings of non-farm employees. The series covers all four decades and is quoted in 1914 dollars. Since the current dollar earnings data are strongly dominated by observations on Eastern industries and since the price deflator is largely based on New York prices, the index is conceptually identical with our Eastern industrial wage rate, $w_E(t)$. There is one significant difference, however, between Lebergott's real annual earnings index and $w_E(t)$. Lebergott's series refers to *employed* workers before 1900: only after 1900 is he able to adjust for the effects of unemployment on average annual earnings. Our model, on the other hand, assumes full employment; wages are fully flexible and bear the brunt of labor market adjustment. On these grounds alone, our wage series is likely to exhibit greater short-run instability up to 1900.

Lebergott's series can be improved upon in two dimensions. First, Phelps-Brown has revised the non-farm real annual earnings data. The revision includes the use of a superior cost-of-living index. Second, the data can be adjusted to include the impact of unemployment. Appendix C contains estimates of annual unemployment rates in the non-farm sector, 1870–1910. The data reported in Table 4.7 and Figure 4.3 incorporate both of these improvements. Nevertheless, the model still exhibits greater short-run instability than either the Lebergott or the adjusted Phelps-Brown wage series. Obviously, the model was never intended

Table 4.7. *Trends in real wages, 1870–1910*

Year	Real annual earnings of non-farm employees			Adjusted for un-employment	
	Lebergott: 1914 dollars (1)	Lebergott: index (2)	Phelps-Brown index (3)	Phelps-Brown index (4)	Model $w_E(t)$ (5)
1870	$375	1·57	1·57	1·57	1·57
1871	$386	1·62	1·65	1·63	1·78
1872	$416	1·74	1·67	1·71	2·05
1873	$407	1·71	1·72	1·72	2·04
1874	$403	1·69	1·72	1·67	1·71
1875	$403	1·69	1·75	1·64	1·55
1876	$393	1·65	1·77	1·63	1·56
1877	$388	1·63	1·72	1·59	1·48
1878	$397	1·66	1·77	1·65	1·79
1879	$391	1·64	1·80	1·71	1·82
1880	$395	1·65	1·82	1·79	1·73
1881	$415	1·74	1·85	1·84	1·39
1882	$431	1·81	1·92	1·92	1·47
1883	$459	1·92	2·05	2·03	1·78
1884	$478	2·00	2·15	2·06	1·86
1885	$492	2·06	2·08	1·96	1·94
1886	$499	2·09	2·15	2·13	2·02
1887	$509	2·13	2·23	2·21	2·05
1888	$505	2·12	2·28	2·25	1·88
1889	$510	2·14	2·46	2·44	2·35
1890	$519	2·17	2·53	2·54	2·32
1891	$525	2·20	2·53	2·53	1·71
1892	$527	2·21	2·56	2·58	2·06
1893	$505	2·12	2·46	2·36	2·55
1894	$484	2·03	2·35	2·21	2·66
1895	$520	2·18	2·51	2·46	2·52
1896	$521	2·18	2·53	2·38	2·94
1897	$529	2;22	2·58	2·46	2·46
1898	$527	2·21	2·56	2·51	2·47
1899	$563	2·36	2·73	2·73	2·77
1900	$573	2·40	2·79	2·70	2·98
1901	$582	2·44	2·84	2·79	3·06
1902	$612	2·56	2·96	2·96	2·44
1903	$607	2·54	2·94	2·92	2·94
1904	$606	2·54	2·86	2·75	3·11
1905	$621	2·63	2·99	2·94	3·08
1906	$627	2·63	3·17	3·28	3·17
1907	$631	2·64	3·09	3·15	2·89
1908	$631	2·64	2·84	2·57	2·36
1909	$657	2·75	3·04	2·93	2·23
1910	$669	2·80	3·06	2·92	2·19

Source: Col. (1), from S. Lebergott, *Manpower in Economic Growth*, tables A-17 and A-19, pp. 524 and 528. No adjustment for the unemployed. Col. (3), from E. H. Phelps-Brown, *A Century of Pay*, appendix 3, pp. 446–7, col. (3). Col. (4) is derived by applying to col. (3) the unemployment rate estimated in appendix C, tables C.4 and C.5.

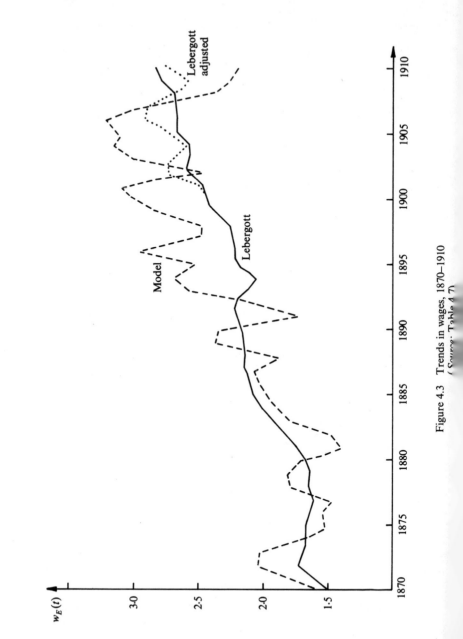

Figure 4.3 Trends in wages, 1870–1910
(Source: Table 4.7)

to capture business cycles. Yet it is comforting to find that the model *does* record the rapid expansion prior to the Panic of 1873, the boom in the 1880s, and the surge after the late 1890s. It also captures the labor market doldrums following the Panic of 1873, during the mid–late 1890s, and between 1906 and 1910.

The long-term wage movements are of greater interest. The correspondence between history and prediction is remarkable. From a common base in 1870 to the decade 1901–10, for example, the Lebergott unadjusted index rises to 2·62 while $w_E(t)$ increases to 2·75. The Phelps-Brown adjusted index rises to 2·92 in 1901–10. That is, the predicted 1901–10 value for real annual labor earnings lies exactly between the Lebergott and Phelps-Brown estimates, and neither historical series diverges from $w_E(t)$ by more than 5 percent. Overall the model appears to predict this crucial variable very well.

For those readers who prefer precision, let the Lebergott series be denoted by $A_w(t)$ and the predicted $w_E(t)$ series by $P_w(t)$. A regression between these two variables has been estimated as (the figures in parentheses are sampling errors)

$$P_w(t) = -0·039 + 1·066 \, A_w(t), \, R^2 = 0·59.$$
$$(0·300) \quad (0·139)$$

As Theil pointed out, a perfect forecast would have the estimated slope coefficient equal to unity and the intercept equal to zero. The regression results show in fact that $\hat{m}_1$ is insignificantly different from unity and $\hat{m}_0$ insignificantly different from zero. This 'goodness-of-fit' test bodes well for the model. Although only half of the variance in $P_w(t)$ is explained by $A_w(t)$, the short-run movements are of little concern to us and the R^2 could be easily raised by smoothing devices.

We turn next to measures of labor market disequilibrium. The model has been shown to replicate one detailed historical wage series, that for Eastern industrial workers. Does it perform as well for farm labor and industrial employment in the Midwest? The most effective way to answer this question is to use the scattered data reported in Lebergott's research to construct measures of wage relatives over the long term. These relatives are presented in Table 4.8. Lebergott's estimates of wages for common laborers in the Northeast and Midwest are reported in the first panel of Table 4.8A; for 1869, 1880 and 1890 they are daily wages, and for 1919 they are hourly. The regional wage relatives derived from Lebergott's data are to be compared with the model's predictions (Table 4.8A, second panel) on the average Midwestern wage relative to the Northeastern wage. The simulation reproduces the historical experience with regional wage differentials without exception. The Midwestern wage rises relative to that of the Northeast during

Table 4.8. *Measures of labor market disequilibrium, 1869–1919*

Table 4.8A. *Regional labor markets*

Region	Actual			
	Year			
	1869 (daily)	1880 (daily)	1890 (daily)	1919 (hourly)
Common laborers:				
New England	$1·56	$1·28	$1·49	$0.38
Middle Atlantic	1·58	1·27	1·45	0·45
Northeast (E)	1·57	1·27	1·47	0·41
East North Central	1·58	1·30	1·51	0·42
West North Central	1·55	1 43	1·48	0·41
Midwest (W)	1·57	1·36	1·50	0.42
Midwest ÷ Northeast (1869 = 100)	100	107	102	98
	Model			
	1870	1880	1890	1900
$w_E(t)$	$1·57	$1·72	$2·32	$2·98
$\overline{w}_W(t)$	1·57	2·05	2·51	2·93
$\overline{w}_W(t) \div w_E(t)$ (1870 = 100)	100	119	109	98

Source: S. Lebergott, *Manpower in Economic Growth*, table A-25, p. 54.

the 1870s and declines thereafter, so much so that the Midwestern laborer has a lower wage by the turn of the century. It appears that the model is quite capable of capturing American experience with regional wage differentials and, by implication, must reproduce farm wages and Midwestern industrial wages with an effectiveness equal to that of the Eastern industrial wage.[25]

Although the model reproduces regional wage differentials very closely, does it do equally well in describing labor market disequilibria *within* the Midwest? How accurately do our predictions on industry–farm wage differentials in the Midwest conform with historic differentials documented by Lebergott for the East North Central? The results are presented in Table 4.8B. The ratio of earnings in iron and steel to those of farm laborers (with board) are given in the first panel, while the predicted industry–farm wage relative is given in the second panel. The correspondence is striking. Not only are turning points reproduced without exception, but the absolute magnitudes are as close as one could possibly hope for. In summary, the model replicates late nineteenth-century labor

Table 4.8B. *Industry–farm wage differentials in the East North Central*

Sector	Actual			
	Year			
	1869/70	1879/80	1889/90	1899/1900
Iron and steel, annual earnings full time equivalent	$506	$416	$560	$579
Farm laborers, average monthly earnings with board	16·94	15·48	15·92	16·90
Iron and steel ÷ farm laborer (1869/70 = 100)	100	89	117	114
	Model			
	1870	1880	1890	1900
$w_{IW}(t)$	$1·57	$1·93	$2·84	$3·17
$w_{AW}(t)$	1·57	2·08	2·39	2·76
$w_{IW}(t) \div w_{AW}(t)$ (1870 = 100)	100	93	118	115

Source: S. Lebergott, *Manpower in Economic Growth*, tables A-29 and A-23, pp. 545 and 539. See notes to Table 4.8A.

market conditions with sufficient accuracy to satisfy the most ardent critic.

Interest rates and the capital market. A Midwestern farm mortgage rate series is displayed in Table 4.9. The series is for Iowa up to 1900, and the 1910 figure (actually 1914) represents an average of the North Central states excluding the Dakotas, Nebraska and Kansas. The nominal farm mortgage rates have been adjusted for the rate of commodity price change. Thus, they are real rather than nominal interest rates. This adjustment is critical for an understanding of the operation of the capital market and of farmers' discontent, as well as of the plausibility of our model.

There seems little doubt that our disequilibrium model replicates this aspect of American financial history very well. From 1870 to 1900, farm mortgage rates fell by remarkable proportions in the Midwest and the simulation captures the magnitude of the fall almost precisely. Iowa farm mortgage rates fall from 16·9 to 4·0 percent over these three decades, while the simulated $i_{AW}(t)$ declines from 16·0 to 3·8 percent. Furthermore, both series reverse this trend after 1900; the average farm mortgage rate in 1914 was 6·3

Table 4.9.   *Trends in real farm mortgage rates, 1870–1910*

| Year | Farm mortgage rates | | Model | |
	Actual: Midwest	$i_{AW}(t)$	$\bar{i}_W(t)$	$i_{IE}(t)$
1870	0·169	0·160	0·143	0·102
1875	—	0·122	0·123	0·111
1880	0·123	0·096	0·103	0·110
1885	—	0·072	0·086	0·120
1890	0·077	0·057	0·081	0·114
1895	—	0·048	0·080	0·110
1900	0·040	0·038	0·081	0·102
1905	—	0·036	0·082	0·100
1910	0·063	0·062	0·090	0·101

Source: 1870–1900; for Iowa and from Table 3.2. 1910; for 1914 and from L. Davis. 'The Investment Market, 1870–1914: The Evolution of a National Market,' table 7, p. 375.

percent, while $i_{AW}(t)$ generated by the model is 6·2 percent in 1910. As we shall see in chapter 5, much has been made in the literature of the secular plunge in interest rates up to the 1890s and the reversal thereafter. The model appears to reproduce these historical trends with ease.

Does the model also capture trends in capital market disequilibrium as measured by regional interest rate differentials? Recall that the model contains three interest rates prevailing in three markets which are imperfectly integrated: the Midwestern farm mortgage rate, the Midwestern rate on industrial loans, and the Eastern rate on industrial loans. The simulation produces a secular convergence in these rates over time, at least when the average Midwestern rate is compared with that prevailing in Eastern financial markets. That is, Table 4.10 shows the rate in the Midwest exceeded that in the East by 41 percent in 1870. By 1910, the relative rate in the Midwest has declined to 90 percent of the Eastern rate. This secular fall in 'the' relative Midwestern interest rate compares favorably with similar indices constructed by Lance Davis describing the integration of a national capital market. Although Davis admits that such proxies are less than perfect, he constructs regional estimates of net and gross returns to national banks and uses these as rough indices of short-term relative interest rates. The relatives displayed in Table 4.10 compare Midwest and Midatlantic rates.[26] Each of these series records a very sharp relative decline in Midwestern rates from the early 1870s to the late 1880s and early 1890s. The usual difficulties with the long swing are present, but the model predicts a decline from 1870 to 1900 in the relative Midwestern rate from 140 to 80. Over the period 1875 to 1900, Davis documents

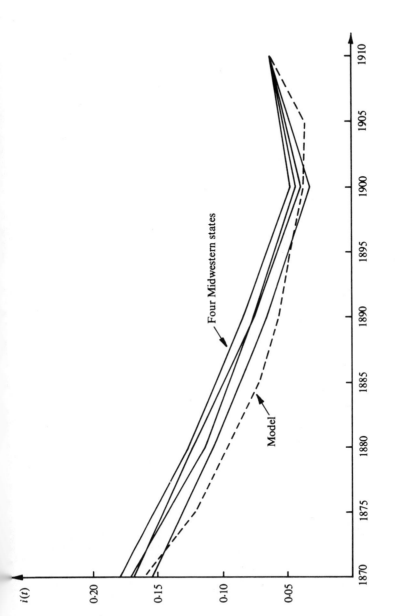

Figure 4.4   Trends in real farm mortgage rates, 1870–1910
(*Source*: Table 4.9)

Table 4.10. *Measures of capital market disequilibrium, 1870–1910*

Year	Model $\bar{i}_w(t)/i_E(t)$	Davis: Midwest relative to Middle Atlantic	
		Non-reserve city banks	Reserve city banks
1870	141	133	112
1875	111	135	133
1880	93	118	113
1885	69	124	103
1890	69	108	111
1895	72	91	78
1900	80	88	94
1905	81	96	75
1910	90	98	76

Source: L. Davis, 'The Investment Market, 1870–1914: The Evolution of a National Market,' tables 4 and 5, pp. 360–5.

a decline from 133 to 94 and 135 to 88 using two different proxies. Chapter 6 will discuss the 'capital market integration' thesis in far greater detail, but it seems apparent that the model reproduces Davis's scenario very well. It even replicates the turning point in the 1890s.

Midwestern land values. One of the anomalies of the period preceding 1900 is that a continuous state of agrarian discontent coincided with impressive secular improvements in farm land values. The evidence collected by Bowman and Tostlebe, presented in Table 4.11, indicates the magnitude of the increase of Midwest land values over these four decades, from $17·10 to $47·70 per acre. If we treat land as an asset with a permanent net rental stream over time, then land values will be determined by

$$V(t) = d(t)/i(t).$$

The model produces $d(t)$, but what is the appropriate mechanism for generating price expectations? Three land value series are presented in Table 4.11, one using current net rents, one using the expected rental rate based on average net rents over the past three years, and one which uses the past seven years in generating expectations. Although each of the land value series exhibits a significant upward movement during these four decades, their short-run behavior varies considerably as does the magnitude of the long-run improvement. The 'best' $V(t)$ prediction is produced using the three-year average. For that series, predicted land values increase to $18·40 per acre in 1880, exactly coinciding with Tostlebe's figure;

Table 4.11. *Midwestern land values, 1870–1910*

Year	Bowman (1860 prices)			Tostlebe (1910–14 prices)	Model (1910–14 prices): $V(t)$ index at		
	Iowa	Illinois	Minne-sota	Midwest	Current $d(t)$	$\frac{1}{3}\Sigma\, d(t)$ $t = -2$	$\frac{1}{7}\Sigma\, d(t)$ $t = -6$
1870	$21·60	$28·80	$19·54	$17·1	$12·3		
1875	—	—	—	—	13·4	$12·9	
1880	24·50	33·90	20·82	18·4	18·4	18·4	$18·4
1885	—	—	—	—	26·9	29·6	28·7
1890	36·30	53·90	30·40	30·0	34·2	30·4	32·9
1895	—	—	—	—	39·7	30·4	32·3
1900	55·30	62·20	38·80	30·5	46·3	28·5	24·6
1905	—	—	—	—	48·1	45·4	36·1
1910	—	—	—	47·7	29·6	34·2	29·1

Source: J. D. Bowman, 'Trends in Midwestern Farm Land Values, 1860–1900,' Appendix table A-2, col. (4), pp. 95ff. Bowman's figures refer to wheat farms only. A. S. Tostlebe, *Capital in Agriculture: Its Formation and Financing Since 1870*, tables 6 and 9, pp. 50–1 and 66–9. The model results are derived from the expression

$$V(t) = d(t)/i(t),$$

and two variants allowing for price expectations: one includes the two preceding years and the other, six preceding years. In all cases, $i(t)$ is the current farm mortgage rate. See text.

between 1880 and 1890, $V(t)$ rises from $18·40 to $30·40 compared with Tostlebe's figure of $30·00; by 1905, the predicted $V(t)$ has risen to $45·40, remarkably close to the 1910 Tostlebe figure of $47·70. Thus, the model accurately predicts long-term secular movements in $V(t)$, as well as the short-term boom in land values in the 1880s and the somewhat more moderate rise in the 1870s. Consistent with the Bowman–Tostlebe data, it also predicts a decline in the 1890s. The only weakness seems to be our prediction of only a moderate rise during the first decade of the twentieth century while in fact the boom was more marked.

Chapter 7 will have much more to say about these trends in Midwest farm land values since they have been at the heart of the debate on post-Civil War agrarian discontent. Indeed, chapter 8 will make an effort to disentangle the sources of the secular boom in land values. This section has a more limited objective. Under the plausible assumption that current farm expectations were generated on the basis of an average of the preceding three years, the model reproduces Tostlebe's Midwest farm land value series very closely indeed.

4.4 Summary: fact or fiction?

The model makes predictions on many other economic variables as
well, but to include them all here would make the present chapter
unnecessarily cumbersome. Many of these are for variables about
which we have absolutely no quantitative evidence such as the net
interregional flows of financial capital.[27] In any case, comparisons
of fact and prediction on income originating in transportation,
budget shares, labor's share, and regional labor productivity are
best introduced at appropriate points in the discussion contained
in the chapters following. These comparisons in no way alter our
judgement of the model's plausibility based on the evidence presented in the preceding section.

Overall performance

We view this book as a means by which a simple plausible model
of American multi-sectoral and interregional development can be
established and fully expect the basic model to be refined still
further. Yet the framework seems to offer far more promise as a
device for historical analysis than the term 'paradigm' would suggest. To our knowledge, this chapter contains the first attempt by
an economic historian to test the plausibility of a relatively sophisticated interdependent system.[28] The system has been able to
capture the key quantitative dimensions of American growth and
structural change over these four decades – well enough, at least,
to make us confident that the analysis remaining in this book is,
in fact, economic history. There may be other models of the late
nineteenth-century American economy which are equally plausible
and explain the period with equal or greater effectiveness. This
chapter establishes a maintained hypothesis and we shall proceed
with the historical analysis until a competing hypothesis is formulated which is judged to be a more plausible characterization of
the American economy over the four decades.

   Any competing model will find it equally critical to satisfy Fogel's
efficiency test since the quantitative record is not sufficient to supply
extensive information for elaborate structural and behavioral parameters. One class of potential competing models are the static
general equilibrium models presently being applied to the ante
bellum period and surveyed earlier in this book. These seem to us to
have less potential than the dynamic disequilibrium model formulated in chapter 3 and tested in the present chapter. The assumptions
of full factor mobility are too far removed from reality and are likely
to produce predictions far from the mark, given the instability which
violent exogenous shocks produced in the American economy over

these four decades. Nor are these competing models as useful in capturing the important spatial aspects of American regional development. More importantly, the ultimate restriction on these competing models is their static properties. One can certainly explore the impact, for example, of an exogenous change in the labor force due to foreign immigration in these models, but to the extent that capital formation rates are significantly influenced by demographic variables the conclusions from such models are likely to be very inaccurate.

Areas of poor performance and potential improvements in model specifications

The model developed in chapter 3 has three possible weaknesses. These weaknesses may go a long way in accounting for the cases of poor predicted performance. We exclude from discussion the manifest inability of the model to generate long swings and its special difficulty in accurately reproducing the 1890s. Our focus is on growth rather than cycles. The three potential weaknesses may be found in the specifications of labor force growth and capital formation, as well as our treatment of the foreign sector.

The model does not contain a sophisticated treatment of the determinants of the labor force. A more realistic treatment could be introduced at two stages. First, the purely demographic determinants of population growth might be improved. The model presently relies on exogenous forces to produce population change since the natural rates of population growth in the Northeast and Midwest are given exogenously, as is the foreign immigration from abroad. Unless we are prepared to argue that natural rates of population growth are significantly influenced by economic variables, there is little to be gained by forcing an endogenous theory of native population growth on the model. We think that the model has already been developed along these lines as far as possible by allowing differential rates East and West: at least the aggregate rate is influenced by structural change and the regional redistribution of the labor force. Second, the model might be revised to relax our simplistic assumptions regarding labor participation rates. The model assumes stability in these rates while in fact they underwent significant change over these four decades. We could, of course, introduce the observed labor participation rates exogenously but an endogenous explanation would require a much more detailed treatment of the demographic component of the model to encompass the age distribution of the population. This, too, is beyond the scope of the present study. Finally, is it feasible to introduce an endogenous explanation of foreign immigration? The possibilities may appear to be slim since the model is only able to generate endogenous *demands* for foreign migrants; the 'push' factors abroad cannot possibly be captured within the model. Yet in chapter 11 we shall devote considerable attention to endogenous determinants of foreign immigration.

The second weakness of the model lies with capital formation. These rates are determined endogenously in the model through the gross savings decision given endogenously determined income levels, through the endogenously determined capital–output ratio, through the relative price of capital goods, and through changing capital consumption requirements. The average rates of net physical capital accumulation over the four decades are predicted reasonably well, and the model reproduces the increased rate of accumulation after the early 1890s attributable to increased aggregate national savings rates. But the rise in aggregate savings rates after the early 1890s is *not* determined endogenously. What alternative theory of capital formation might *predict* the acceleration after the early 1890s? Would such a specification also account for the stable savings rates from 1870 to the 1890s? One obvious candidate was discussed in chapter 3. An alternative specification of the savings function might include the effects of interest rates and income distribution. In our model, industrialization implies a decline in labor's share (although *within* the non-farm sector the share is stable given the Cobb–Douglas specification). Since the savings rate out of wage income is thought to be lower (and in the extreme, zero) than that out of non-wage income, then industrialization up to the 1890s would have tended to raise the national savings rate. Yet the real interest rate declines markedly in the West over the same period. These two opposing influences may have been offsetting given sufficiently high interest elasticities. After the early 1890s, the real interest rate rises in all financial markets suggesting a potential source of reversal in the aggregate national savings rate. These potential refinements in the savings specification require considerable parametric information on interest elasticities and on savings rates by functional or sectoral income classes. The gains, however, may well be worth the effort and we attempt such an effort in chapter 6.

The third potential specification bias in the model may lie with the foreign sector (chapters 8 and 10). With commodity price relatives in Eastern markets now determined exogenously by world market conditions, the model in effect assumes perfectly elastic international demand for American Midwestern farm products and a 'perfectly elastic supply of competitive industrial goods from abroad. The volume of exports under these conditions plays only a residual role: world market conditions are reflected fully in East coast relative commodity price movements. It follows that domestic demand conditions play only a minimal role:[29] they only influence the volume of 'surplus' farm products available for export and the volume of competitive industrial good imports necessary to augment domestic supply. This explains why little attention was devoted to more elegant (and theoretically more attractive) consumption demand specifications in chapter 3.

Future refinements in modelling the American economy may fruitfully pursue these directions. For the present, we are content with our simpler characterization.

5
The Great Depression, 1870–96

It was not until the Civil War had been fought and won [that America] 'took off' . . .   Louis M. Hacker (1970)

5.1 The American Great Depression, 1870–96

Output expansion and growth performance

English growth experience from the 1860s to the 1890s has been the source of continued research and debate. Judged by the recent contributions of McCloskey,[1] the intensity of the debate has diminished little over the past seventy-five years. The period has long been identified in the literature as the 'Great Depression.' It has been well established that the decades up to 1896 were characterized by declining general price levels, declining nominal interest rates, and serious retardation in aggregate real output growth. These are not merely figments of historical research since they were subjects of contemporary observation as well.

Similar trends in American history are less well known,[2] and the retardation apparently is assumed to be less dramatic, but post-Civil War economic performance was very much like that of Great Britain. The severity of the 1892–6 depression has, of course, always been appreciated and it does mark the termination of these three decades of American growth. Yet the secular retardation in growth rates cannot be explained by capricious dating. After all, the depression from 1873 to 1878 was equally severe and both business cycle depressions were followed by a decade of buoyant growth. Furthermore, it should be emphasized that the Great Depression in America is more than simply an agricultural phenomena, although it is agriculture's *asserted* poor performance which has attracted the economic historian's attention.[3] The per capita output growth retardation is apparent in the series developed by Gallman and Kuznets. Output per worker growth in real terms (1860 prices) declined between the periods 1869/78–1884/93 and 1884/93–1899/1908 from 1·71 to 1·24 percent per annum.

Our focus on growth retardation over these three decades may come as some surprise to those economic historians who contrast the poor growth performance during the Civil War decade with the impressive expansion that followed. For example, in his evaluation of the Beard–Hacker thesis, Engerman states: 'Per capita output [grew] more rapidly between 1870 and 1900 than it had in the two prewar decades – at an annual rate of 2·1 percent as contrasted with the earlier 1·45 percent . . .'[4] We do not assert that growth performance was poor from 1870 to 1900. On the contrary, the impressive overall achievement deserves the attention economic historians have lavished on this 'Golden Age' of expansion and industrialization. Nevertheless, the 1870s and the first half of the 1880s are years of unusually rapid growth, while the second half of the 1880s and the 1890s are years of relatively poor performance. Gallman's GNP series (in 1860 prices, Table 4.2B) exhibits a consistent retardation in percent per annum based on overlapping decadal averages:

1869/78–1874/83	5·58
1874/83–1879/88	4·76
1879/88–1884/93	3·68
1884/93–1889/98	2·55
1889/98–1894/1903	3·39

Engerman's stimulating paper also appears to suggest that American growth performance is best measured in *per capita* terms. If welfare measures were the sole interest, per capita income might be a relevant variable, but our focus in this chapter is instead on the sources of average labor productivity growth. The more appropriate statistic in this case is GNP *per worker*. These two growth measures diverge when the labor participation rate rises as in fact it does over the period: the rate increases from 0·324 in 1870 to 0·399 in 1910.[5] As a consequence, while the rate of population growth declined markedly from the Civil War decade to the 1890s, the labor force expansion rates suffered a much less dramatic decline.[6] Some portion of the decline in GNP growth rates can be explained simply by this retardation in labor force growth. Yet real output per worker growth still underwent a notable retardation between the Civil War and the turn of the century. As we have seen, per worker GNP growth fell by about $\frac{1}{2}$ a percentage point over these three decades.

English and American experience compared

Is the magnitude of this secular retardation sufficiently large to warrant special attention? Its severity can be judged most effectively by comparison with Great Britain, a country often characterized by 'failure' over the same period. McCloskey's data for the period 1860–1910 are presented in Table 5.1. The British retardation between 1860–80 and 1880–1900 is far less apparent than that between

Table 5.1. *British growth rates, 1860–1910*

Period	Per annum growth rates		
	Real GNP	Employed labor force	GNP per worker
1860–70	3·37%	1·12%	2·25%
1870–80	2·11	1·03	1·08
1880–90	2·82	1·03	1·79
1890–1900	2·19	1·03	1·16
1900–10	0·81	1·05	−0·24

Source: D. N. McCloskey, 'Did Victorian Britain Fail?' pp. 457–8.

1870–90 and 1890–1910: in the first case, growth rates fell by only 0·2 percentage points while in the second the measured decline is one percentage point. Generally, the two economies underwent *retardation* of roughly the same magnitude, although the average growth performance was more impressive in America. This comparison confirms the quantitative importance of the American Great Depression. It also underscores the curious character of the literature on Victorian England's failure: America is often used as a standard in judging England's failure.

In chapter 4, we noted that the simulation reproduced the secular decline in growth rates with remarkable accuracy. Between the fifteen-year periods 1869/78–1884/93 and 1884/93–1899/1908, the Gallman–Kuznets per annum growth rate falls from 1·71 to 1·24 percent: the simulation reports a decline from 1·69 to 1·29 percent. The simulated output series is constructed using *variable* price weights, however. Nevertheless, the retardation in growth rates appears when *fixed* price weights are used as well. Indeed, the retardation in the simulated per capita GNP series is even more marked when 1870 or 1910 price relatives are used. Using 1870 fixed price relatives, the per capita GNP growth rate declines from 2·49 to 1·36 percent per annum from 1869/78–1884/93 to 1884/93–1899/1908. Using the 1910 fixed price relatives, the growth rate per annum declines from 2·33 to 1·25 percent. Thus, we have succeeded in replicating one important aspect of America's Great Depression. Armed with our model of disequilibrium growth, we should also be able to explain it.

We have already noted that per capita output growth for the late nineteenth century as a whole was more impressive in America. But our focus is on *retardation* over time, rather than levels, and on this score the experience was strikingly similar on both sides of the Atlantic. Nevertheless, two noteworthy discrepancies deserve emphasis. First, British growth rates start from a peak in the 1860s before undergoing the long term slide into the doldrums at the turn of the century. The American retardation, on the other hand, is dated from the 1870s. We shall argue below that the timing of the American Great Depression may differ from the British solely because of the Civil War episode. It seems likely, therefore, that American experience with the Great Depression would have been even more like that of England had the Civil War never been fought. Second, and perhaps more important, while America reversed the retardation in the late 1890s, Britain continues the retardation up to World War I. This is an important contrast and we shall return to it in section 5.5.

Interest rates, monetary variables and the Great Depression

Not only has per capita growth retardation been associated with the Great Depression, but it also has been recognized as a period of declining *nominal* interest rates. Based on historical evidence drawn from this period, Keynes coined a term for the association between the price level and nominal interest rates: the Gibson Paradox. Keynes asserted that the high correlation between nominal interest rates and the commodity price level was paradoxical since 'it seemed to contradict the prediction of classical monetary theory that the interest rate is independent of the price level.'[7] Irving Fisher offered an explanation of the paradox long before the more modern research of Cagan and Friedman: ignoring uncertainty, the nominal rate is taken to be the sum of the real return and the anticipated rate of inflation.[8] As was pointed out in chapter 4, the problem for empirical research is in measuring the anticipated rate of price change, or in the context of late nineteenth-century experience, the anticipated rate of price deflation. Although price deflation obviously fostered a fall in the money rate, price expectations were imperfect, money illusion must have prevailed to some extent, and thus the observed decline in the nominal rate was not as marked as it would have been under perfect foresight. Furthermore, it must be emphasized that it is the *changing* rate of price deflation which counts. The rate of price deflation following the Civil War greenback issues was by no means constant up to 1896. On the contrary, the rate of price deflation was far higher earlier in this period than later.

Only very recently, and with an embarassingly long lag behind the appearance of Fisher's work, has the historical literature confronted the behavior of 'the' real interest rate over long historical time periods. It is of some importance to stress that both nominal *and* real rates decline during this phase of American history: indeed, real rates decline more precipitously than do nominal rates. Under conditions of perfect certainty, one would expect historical variations in nominal rates to exceed by far those in real rates. What we actually find in the late nineteenth century is the reverse: 'The erratic behavior of the real interest is evidently a trick played on the money market by the "money illusion" when contracts are made in unstable money.'[9] In short, real interest rates plunge up to the mid-1890s and the magnitude of the decline is impressive regardless of the method used to estimate anticipated rates of price inflation. For example, the fall in Iowa real farm mortgage rates from 16·9 to 4·0 percent over three decades can hardly be called a 'myth'![10] Furthermore, the downward plunge in farm mortgage rates is reflected in other yield series as well. Table 5.2 shows both nominal and real rates declining on railroad bonds, and the latter has a more striking downward trend from 1871 to 1896 than the former.

Although Temin has been careful in identifying a fall in the real rate,[11] Friedman and Schwartz devote a very large share of their volume to this period while all but ignoring the secular decline in

Table 5.2. *Real and nominal rates, 1871–96*

	Yields on railroad bonds	
Year	Nominal	Real
1871	7·78%	12·94%
1876	6·68	8·64
1881	5·19	7·11
1886	4·55	8·47
1891	4·71	4·71
1896	4·34	7·01

Note: Index of yields of American railroad bonds from *Historical Statistics*, X332, p. 656. Anticipated rates of price inflation are estimated by computing the average annual rate of price change over the five years previous. The BLS and Warren–Pearson 'all commodity' price indices used are taken from *ibid.*, E1 and E13, pp. 115 and 117.

Observed nominal rates are converted to real rates, $r(t)$, by the following expression:

$$r(t) = \frac{i(t) - \hat{p}(t)}{1 + \hat{p}(t)},$$

where $i(t)$ is the quoted nominal rate and $\hat{p}(t)$ is the rate of change in prices. This expression assumes perfect foresight with regard to price expectations, and $\hat{p}(t)$ is computed as an average rate of growth over the preceding five years.

real interest rates. Statements like the following appear infrequently in *A Monetary History*:

> On any theory of the determination of interest rates, the declining interest rates may very plausibly be interpreted as in part a reflection of the declining prices and as in turn increasing the rate of growth of the money stock required to keep the price decline at any given level. The first follows from the discrepancy between the 'real' and 'money' rates of interest produced by anticipated changes in prices. Insofar as lenders and borrowers anticipate changes in the purchasing power of money, bond prices will tend to be higher and nominal yields lower when commodity prices are falling.... Insofar as anticipations of falling prices lag behind the actual fall in prices ... interest rates will fall together with prices.... [12]

We find no fault with this reasoning, but perhaps the more interesting issue is what determines the *real* rate? Why did it fall sharply from the end of the Civil War decade to the 1890s? The secular decline in effective interest rates was strikingly apparent in the simulation reported in chapter 4, although all interest rates do not decline equally. From 1870 to 1896 and in real terms, the Midwestern farm mortgage rate declines very sharply, while the Western and Eastern 'industrial' rates decline moderately. This divergent behavior is explained by disequilibrating forces in the national capital market – to be discussed at greater length in chapter 6, but the general decline in real rates is unmistakable.

While real interest rates are undergoing secular decline and the growth in per worker productivity exhibiting retardation, we have the 'paradox' of surging real wages. Lebergott (Table 4.7) documents a 2·07 percent per annum rise in real industrial wages between 1869/78 and 1899/1908, while during the same period Gallman's data imply a GNP per worker growth rate of 1·47 percent per annum. The simulation reported in chapter 4 reproduces these historical trends almost exactly. The comparison between real wage and GNP per worker growth rates illustrates the folly of making inferences regarding workers' standards of living by only examining aggregate output data. The historical literature on ante bellum America and Britain during the Industrial Revolution is full of consternation that real wages often failed to increase during these periods of early industrialization. There is, of course, no reason that they necessarily should. [13] In the period following 1870, we have a symmetrical result. Declining real interest rates and retarding growth performance were consistent with impressive improvements in industrial working conditions. In fact, Table 4.7 shows that real annual industrial earnings grew *more* rapidly after the early 1880s than before! It might also be noted that the same increase in real wages apparently occurred during the British retardation as well. These events have often been used to support a 'profit squeeze' explanation for the British retardation. Curiously, American economic historians have failed to notice their inconsistency with conventional British historiography. While American economic historians take a 'robber baron' view of late nineteenth-century industrialization, British economic historians stress 'profit squeeze'! In the American case at least, the presence of robber barons apparently was consistent with a relative improvement in real wages after the early 1880s and thus an improvement in wages' share in national income.

It seems to us that the issues may have become confused by the fortuitous appearance of purely monetary phenomena coincident with this period of retarding real output growth, declining real interest rates, and surging real wages. The model utilized in chapter 4 does not contain a monetary sector or a general price level. It is true that the general price level declines markedly during the Great Depression as does the nominal interest rate. Our framework is not capable of explaining the secular behavior of these monetary variables: indeed, our interest in this book is limited to real growth and structural performance of the American economy between the Civil War and World War I. Monetary variables are relevant only by the extent to which they influence real economic performance. An obvious method by which the 'monetary hypothesis' can be evaluated is to explore our ability to reproduce America's long-run retardation with a model which excludes monetary variables. The implication of the research contained in chapter 4 is that the simultaneous appearance of these real and monetary phenomena may have been purely fortuitous, since the decline in real interest rates and aggregate growth performance can be adequately captured by a growth model which excludes money and a general price level. Nevertheless, it may of course be true that money illusion seriously influenced contemporary perception of the American economy's performance and thus may account for the magnitude of social discontent which it produced.

Sources-of-growth versus the counterfactual: the supply side

These then are the historical facts to be explained. How do we proceed to supply some answers? One could follow the track blazed by Abramovitz, Solow, Denison and, most recently, McCloskey by applying conventional sources of growth accounting to the historical data.[14] To do so, we need only decompose GNP growth into

$$\frac{\dot{G}(t)}{G(t)} = \frac{\dot{T}(t)}{T(t)} + \alpha_K \frac{\dot{K}(t)}{K(t)} + \alpha_L \frac{\dot{L}(t)}{L(t)} + \alpha_R \frac{\dot{R}(t)}{R(t)}$$

or in terms of GNP per worker growth

$$\left\{ \frac{\dot{G}(t)}{G(t)} - \frac{\dot{L}(t)}{L(t)} \right\} = \frac{\dot{T}(t)}{T(t)} + \alpha_K \left\{ \frac{\dot{K}(t)}{K(t)} - \frac{\dot{L}(t)}{L(t)} \right\} +$$

$$+ \alpha_R \left\{ \frac{\dot{R}(t)}{R(t)} - \frac{\dot{L}(t)}{L(t)} \right\},$$

where $K(t)$, $L(t)$, and $R(t)$ denote economy-wide stocks of capital, labor and land, and the α's refer to economy-wide factor shares. Total factor productivity growth (the residual), is measured by the growth in $T(t)$. Given the assumption of constant economy-wide factor shares, the sources of growth method is quite capable of producing an 'accounting' of the sources of retardation in $G(t)$ growth. For example, if the Midwest land rental share in national income was 10 percent, then the decline in Midwest improved land stock per annum growth rates from almost 4·0 percent obtained in the 1870s to 1·5 achieved in the 1890s would 'account for' only 0·25 percentage points of the declined in GNP growth rates. Since *aggregate* GNP growth rates decline from 5·58 percent during 1869/74–1874/83 to 2·55 percent during 1884/93–1889/98, very little of the Great Depression would be accounted for by the declining rate of growth in the Midwestern stock of improved land. Similar computations could be generated for the observed decline in capital stock growth rates, thus decomposing the 'sources' of the decline in $G(t)$ growth, and allowing an identification of the 'causes' of the Great Depression.

Yet such calculations would fail to supply an explanation for retardations in input growth. Furthermore, the calculations may be spurious and lead to very misleading interpretations of an important phase of American economic history. Surely *interactions* between rates of factor augmentation were present during these three decades of retardation. This chapter attempts to measure their importance. Consider the following potential interactions in the land stock experiment performed above: (i) The decline in land stock expansion rates tended to increase the capital–output ratio in agriculture and thus in the economy as a whole. As we shall see below, this effect would tend to *lower* the rate of capital accumulation even for a fixed savings rate. (ii) Since rates of total factor productivity growth were consistently lower in agriculture, the increased industrialization levels induced by the declining rates of land stock growth would have fostered an *increased* rate of economy-wide total factor productivity growth (TFPG).[15] This can be seen by the economy-wide TFPG equation

$$\frac{\dot{T}(t)}{T(t)} = v_{AW}(t) \frac{\dot{B}(t)}{B(t)} + v_{IW}(t) \frac{\dot{A}'(t)}{A'(t)} + v_{IE}(t) \frac{\dot{A}(t)}{A(t)},$$

where the $v_{ij}(t)$ are the shares of each sector's output in GNP. (Three sectors are assumed to exhaust economy-wide output in this example: Midwestern agriculture with an efficiency index of $B(t)$; Midwestern industry with an efficiency index of $A'(t)$; and Eastern industry with an efficiency index of $A(t)$.) Even if the *sectoral* rates of TFPG were constant, any force which tended to increase the rate of industrialization (an accelerated reduction in $v_{AW}(t)$), would have tended to raise the observed economy-wide rate of TFPG. (iii) Furthermore, the rate of labor force growth itself may be affected by either the existing employment distribution or the real wage, both of which are influenced in turn by new land availability. The smaller is the agricultural sector (induced by reduced land abundance), the lower the rate of labor force growth given the higher rates of natural population growth prevailing in agriculture during the nineteenth century. Similarly, the lower are the rates of land expansion, the lower is the growth in real wages and thus European immigration. Thus, the decline in land stock growth would have induced a reduction in labor force growth.[16] To the extent that these and other interactions in factor growth rates are quantitatively important, then the sources of growth accounting are an inappropriate tool for historical analysis. In short, a simple accounting device may not be very helpful in understanding a complex general equilibrium problem.

Nothing has been said in the above critique about factor shares over time in computing

$$\frac{\dot{T}(t)}{T(t)} = \frac{\dot{G}(t)}{G(t)} - \left\{ \alpha_K \frac{\dot{K}(t)}{K(t)} + \alpha_L \frac{\dot{L}(t)}{L(t)} + \alpha_R \frac{\dot{R}(t)}{R(t)} \right\}.$$

Under a Cobb–Douglas specification of the *sectoral* production functions, the *sectoral* factor shares are indeed constant. Since we have adopted such a specification in chapter 3, sectoral stability in factor shares is assumed in our framework too. This does *not* imply stability in economy-wide factor shares however. If capital's share is higher in industry, then it follows that industrialization over time will tend to increase the economy-wide capital share, $\alpha_K(t)$; that is, $\alpha_K(t)$ is a *variable*, not a constant. To be precise

$$\alpha_K(t) = v_{AW}(t)\alpha_{K,AW} + \left[1 - v_{AW}(t)\right]\alpha_{K,I}.$$

Given $\alpha_{K,AW} < \alpha_{K,I}$, then it follows that industrialization raises $\alpha_K(t)$. Thus, capital formation has both a direct effect on output growth via $\dot{K}(t)/K(t)$, and an indirect (quasi-embodied) effect via a rise in $\alpha_K(t)$. Declining rates of capital formation in the American economy had a lesser impact on falling output growth since $\alpha_K(t)$ was rising. Had the output mix of the American economy remained constant, and thus had $\alpha_K(t)$ remained stable, then the retardation in output growth would have been even more marked.

These critical comments should not be construed to imply that the sources of growth 'paradox' is absent from our 'accounting' of the Great Depression, reported below, but it is surely far less important than is normally assumed. Based primarily on twentieth-century evidence, the conventional finding of the early sources of growth literature was that at least 70 percent of average labor productivity growth was to be 'explained by' technical progress or the residual.[17] A recent paper by Abramovitz and David reminds us of the contrast between nineteenth- and twentieth-century experience:

> In the United States, over the course of the nineteenth century the pace of increase of the real gross domestic product was accounted for largely by that of the traditional, conventionally defined factors of production: labor, land, and tangible reproducible capital. The long-term growth rate of total factor productivity – the crude residual portion of the output growth rate left arithmetically unexplained by the weighted sum of these conventional inputs' growth rates – lay in the low range from 0·4 to 0·6 percent per annum. This was no more than a tenth to a seventh of the secularly persistent 4·0 percent annual rate of growth in the real domestic product, and less than two-fifths of the prevailing rate at which per capita output was rising.[18]

It appears that the rates of TFPG are somewhat higher in our period than those estimated by Abramovitz and David for the nineteenth century as a whole. The implied rate of TFPG in commodity-producing sectors outside of the South and Far West lies between 0·7 and 0·8 percent per annum. The Kendrick implied 'economy-wide' rate[19] and that of Abramovitz–David may seem inconsistent, but it must be remembered that the Southern and Far Western states are excluded from our calculation in Table 5.6. In any case, it appears that the large residuals estimated on twentieth-century data may have diverted the economic historian's attention away from his more relevant focus on nineteenth-century capital formation. Furthermore, even if the *levels* of average labor productivity growth during the late nineteenth century could have been largely explained by TFPG, it is quite another matter to assert that *declining rates* of average labor productivity growth could also have been explained by a retardation in the sectoral rates of technical progress.

These arguments should place the relevance of such 'residual' calculations in considerable doubt. We choose instead to shed further light on the Great Depression by posing *counterfactuals* of our model of late nineteenth-century development.

5.2 Competing explanations of the Great Depression: the supply side

Capital formation: the Civil War as a watershed

Three prominent hypotheses have appeared in the literature to account for the Great Depression. One of these focuses on capital formation, not as a source of aggregate demand expansion, but as a source of capacity growth. Only recently has the assertion that British experience could be explained by declining rates of domestic capital formation been rejected.[20] The new quantitative evidence on Britain has now been found to be inconsistent with this thesis.[21] Yet the venerable British capital formation thesis has now reappeared in a different guise and has been applied to American experience.[22] Peter Temin has suggested that a simple neoclassical growth model may be quite consistent with the aggregate facts of American history prior to 1896. Since the simple neoclassical growth-theoretic explanation is the thesis of this chapter as well, we might do well to amplify on the discussion in chapter 3.

Due primarily to the efforts of Robert Gallman,[23] our knowledge of the economic performance of the American economy from the late 1840s to the 1870s has been much improved. The new quantitative evidence confirms a very poor growth performance during the war decade itself. From 1860 to 1870, commodity output growth reached its lowest point anywhere in the nineteenth century, 2 percent per annum. The same is true of manufacturing value added. Indeed, manufacturing output growth is sufficiently slow during the 1860s for its share in total commodity output to rise only by 1 percentage point, from 32 to 33 percent, between the 1860 and 1870 census dates. Nor is this poor performance attributable to Southern defeat and subsequent economic chaos below the Mason–Dixon line. If the Confederacy is excluded, the relative share of agriculture in total commodity output actually increases! The annual rate of growth of per capita commodity output in the victorious North was only 1 percent during the war decade, again the lowest rate in the nineteenth century.[24]

This result is hardly surprising since military conflicts are, after all, expensive in terms of human life, capital stock destruction, and foregone investment, the latter resulting from the familiar painful choice between butter (or machinery) and guns. Certainly, economic performance in the North within the war decade itself reflects this cost.[25] Frickey's index of manufacturing output shows a much slower rise from 1861 to 1865 than from 1866 to 1870. Similar findings emerge from Wayne Rasmussen's research on agriculture.[26] Our indices of capital formation activities reinforce this characterization. Gottlieb's index of non-farm residential building, about 30 percent of gross fixed investment in the mid-nineteenth century, reaches a level in 1866–70 about double that of 1861–5. Finally, the rate of purchase of farm machinery in Iowa and the sales by McCormick both rise from very low levels during the war to much higher levels after 1865. In short, there seems to be no doubt that the Civil War decade in general, and the war years (1861–5) in particular, were ones of unusually poor growth performance. The period 1866–70 reflects a resurgence in the North which eventually snowballs into a secular boom in the 1870s.

The more interesting comparison, however, is the 1850s with the 1870s. Apart from the short-term economic impact of the Civil War, does the Civil War represent a watershed in the long-term development of the nineteenth-century American economy?

Since the appearance of Gallman's capital formation shares, one of the puzzles which has attracted American economic historians has been the apparent discontinuity in measured capital formation rates between the 1850s and the 1870s.[27] Whether measured in terms of gross investment or gross savings, the capital formation shares in Table 5.3 rise by about 8 percentage points from 1849–59 to 1869–78. Furthermore, if we ignore cycles in these shares, they are fairly stable in the decades prior to and following the Civil War. How is this secular discontinuity in capital formation rates to be explained and what role does the Civil War play in the explanation?

The hypotheses raised by the literature are many and varied. Some find the explanation lying in the dislocation and disequilibrium centered on the Civil War itself while others prefer to view the capital formation shares as part of a secular process independent of the war. No doubt a portion of the secular rise is purely spurious since the measures themselves have an inherent downward bias early in the century, a bias which disappears over time. This must be so since in effect the capital formation shares exclude improvements made to farm land with farm construction materials and the farm sector gradually diminished in importance as America successfully industrialized in the mid-nineteenth century. But surely this bias accounts for only a trivial share of the 8-percentage-point rise between the 1850s and the 1870s.[28] An additional bias is introduced by wartime destruction in the South itself. The capital formation data are restricted primarily to urban-industrial investment.[29] Thus, we might plausibly assume that the vast majority of the estimated GDCF and GNCF in Table 5.3 is location specific to Northern states. The GDP and GNP figures must therefore be adjusted to exclude the Southern states. The resulting estimated investment shares for the North are presented in Table 5.3 and they also exhibit a pronounced rise from the 1850s to 1870s.

Table 5.3. *Gallman's capital formation rates adjusted, 1849–78*
(current prices)

Period	Gross capital formation (billions $)		Gross commodity output (billions $)		U.S. investment shares (percent)		Non-South investment shares (percent)	
	Domestic (GDCF) (1)	National (GNCF) (2)	Domestic (GDP) (3)	National (GNP) (4)	GDCF/GDP (5)	GNCF/GNP (6)	GDCF/GDP (7)	GNCF/GNP (8)
1849	0·282	0·257	2·46	2·43	11·5	10·6	na	na
1854	0·554	0·541	3·38	3·37	16·4	16·1	na	na
1859	0·525	0·532	4·09	4·10	12·8	13·0	na	na
1849–1859	0·453	0·443	3·31	3·30	13·6	13·4	19·4	19·1
1869–1878	1·459	1·364	6·50	6·40	22·4	21·3	27·4	26·0

Source: Cols. (1)–(4): R.E. Gallman, 'Gross National Product in the United States, 1834–1909,' tables A-1 and A-3, pp. 26 and 34. Investment limited to manufacturing durables and new construction, excluding the value of farm improvements made with farm construction materials. In addition, the output figures exclude value added by home manufacturing.

Cols. (7)–(8): GDCF and GNCF taken directly from cols. (1) and (2). GDP and GNP multiplied by estimated share of non-South in total U.S. commodity output, where the share is 0·702 in 1860 and 0·819 from 1870–1880. The shares are taken from S. Engerman, 'The Economic Impact of the Civil War,' table 1, p. 180. See text.

Elsewhere we have argued that much of this 'episodic' change in private savings rates can be explained by the manner in which the Civil War was financed.[30] The poor growth performance during the Civil War decade can be readily explained by federal long-term debt issue and the resulting diversion of private savings from capital formation activities. More to the point of this chapter, perhaps half of the 7-percentage-point rise in the Northern GNCF/GNP ratio between the 1850s and the 1870s can be attributed to debt retirement and the redistributive impact of interest payments on the debt. In addition there were other 'episodic' forces at work which generated the once-and-for-all rise in the savings rate during the Civil War decade.

Gallman's data document an even greater rise in the economy-wide investment shares between the 1850s and 1870s when constant price series are used. The explanation is apparent in Figure 5.1. Three relative price indices are presented there. The first of these is Gallman's implied ratio of capital goods' prices to the GNP price index, P_{GDCF}/P_{GNP}. Note that the relative price of investment goods declines sharply between 1859 and 1869–78. The series also exhibits a mild downward trend in relative investment goods' prices up to 1859, while relative stability is the rule after the 1870s. A roughly comparable pattern emerges when a similar index is constructed for textiles,[31] although the wide amplitude of raw cotton price fluctuations induces some spurious movements in textile prices and thus the relative price ratio. The main conclusion is abundantly evident: whether examined at the industry or national level, the average relative price of capital goods in the 1870s is far below that of the 1850s. A third index, also based on Gallman's data, is presented in Figure 5.1 which indicates which component of GDCF is undergoing the decline. Apparently, the relative price of producer durables underwent a dramatic plunge between 1859 and 1869–78. Furthermore, the decline continues up to 1879–88 and it is only an offsetting rise in construction costs which produces stability in the relative price of capital goods after the 1870s. Given these price trends, it should come as no surprise that the constant price share of producer durables investment in GDCF rises from 22 percent in 1854 to 45 percent in 1879–88.[32] We can also conclude that the direction of causation is from relative price change to investment mix change since the relative price of investment goods declines in spite of the enormous increase in capital formation rates and the abrupt shift in its composition towards producer durables.

These relative price trends are sufficiently unique to warrant a lengthy digression at this point. In 1961, R. A. Gordon published a paper which has been very influential, at least on economists with interests in growth.[33] Gordon documented a long-term secular *rise*

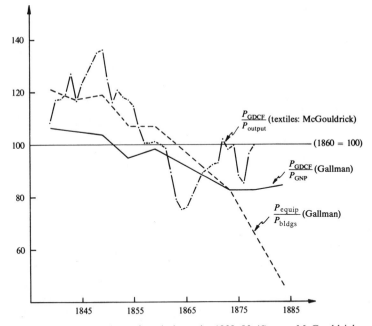

Figure 5.1   Relative prices of capital goods, 1839–83 (*Source:* McGouldrick and Gallman)

in the relative price of capital goods dating from the 1870s, although he emphasized the upward surge from the turn of the century. Granted price measurement problems are immense given product quality changes over long secular periods, but 'To deny the existence of these differential price trends is to deny the validity of the deflated estimates of the components of the GNP on which we all so heavily rely'.[34] Gordon's observation is reproduced in Table 5.4 where the long term series of P_{GDCF}/P_{GNP} (1929 = 100) is extended backward to 1839 using Gallman's data. The sharp decline in investment goods' prices during the Civil War decade is even more remarkable when viewed in terms of a century of development between 1839 and 1953. Although the indices record a mild decline in relative investment goods' prices 1839 to 1859 and 1869–78 to 1899–1908, nowhere in American economic history can we find another episode like the Civil War decade. The abrupt decline in the relative price of investment goods during that brief decade and a half appears to be unique. A watershed indeed!

The macro implications of these relative price trends can be easily unravelled. Suppose the decline was induced by one or a combination of two effects: (i) by a downward shift in the supply

Table 5.4. *Ratio of capital goods to commodity output prices, 1839–1953*
(1929 = 100)

Year	P_{GDCF}/P_{GNP}	Year	P_{GDCF}/P_{GNP}
1839	111·9	1899–1908	77·2
1849	109·4	1909–18	94·8
1859	103·4	1919–28	100·3
1869–78	86·6	1929–38	107·9
1879–88	89·3	1939–48	108·5
1889–98	81·2	1944–53	111·6

Sources: 1839–1899/1908 from R. Gallman, 'Gross National Product in the United States, 1834–1909,' tables A-1 and A-3, pp. 26 and 34. 1908/18–1944/53 from S. Kuznets, *Capital in the American Economy*, tables R-25, 26 and 29, pp. 561–4 and 572–4.

function in the capital goods' sector due to technological discovery; (ii) by the imposition of war tariffs which tended to raise the relative price of manufactured consumer goods compared to capital goods. Both of these effects would induce a decline in the relative price of producer durables over time, although the second of the two would tend to have the price decline concentrated early in the period during which the economy adjusted by induced capital formation over and above the 'normal' rate. Figure 5.2 should help clarify the induced 'catching up' effects. To simplify the diagram, only the first case is considered. The left-hand panel describes an asset market where 'capital,' or claims on capital (private bonds), are fixed in supply and demand has its normal inverse relation to its price. The market is assumed to be in equi-

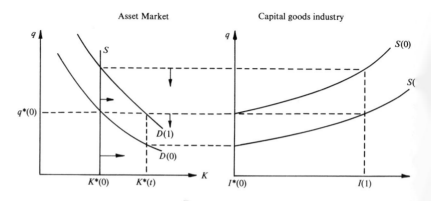

Figure 5.2 The impact of supply changes in the capital goods sector on capital formation

librium at $K^*(0)$. At this point, new capital goods are produced at a rate sufficient only to replace depreciated assets: i.e., net investment is zero. The capital goods sector is described in the right-hand panel. Now, let the supply function in the capital goods' sector shift downward due to technological discovery. If these shifts are sharp enough, a noticeable increase in investment takes place as should the investment share in GNP. The system is now in disequilibrium and we should observe the following: the relative price of capital goods declines over time; the 'heavy industry' sector (producer durables) enjoys relative expansion;[35] the rate of capital accumulation is high; and investment shares are unusually large. If further shifts take place, the process may continue for some time. This appears to be precisely what happened between the 1850s and 1870s.

This analysis also predicts that the rate of return to equity capital should rise to abnormally high levels as long as the system remains in disequilibrium. Is this in fact the case for the mid-nineteenth century? Presumably, if the rate of return to equity capital is rising, so too must be the yields on gross substitutes – such as federal, state and municipal bonds. Table 5.5 presents yield data on two such gross substitutes, Federal and New England municipal bonds. Cols. (3) and (4) estimate *real* yields adjusted by the expected rate of price inflation. Based on the relative capital goods' price data displayed in Figure 5.1 and the argument developed in Figure 5.2, we would expect real yields in the 1870s to exceed by far the real yields in the 1850s. Indeed, this is the case. The average yield on Federal bonds between 1845 and 1861 was 3·91 percent, while the comparable figure for 1867–78 is 8·85 percent. New England municipals exhibit a similar increase: from 4·08 to 9·82 percent.

Those economic historians who hold to the plausible view that aggregate savings are critically influenced by real interest rates and rates of return will welcome this evidence. The episodic rise in real interest rates following the Civil War is certainly consistent with the observed discontinuity in the national savings rate. Indeed, we shall make use of this thesis in accounting for savings rate trends after 1870 in chapter 6.

Having established an 'epochal' rise in current price savings rates and a fall in the relative price of investment goods, note the contrasting behavior thereafter. First, the current price share of gross savings excluding agricultural clearing underwent only a very mild rise from 0·18 to 0·20 between 1869/78 and 1894/1903.[36] Compared with the 'episodic' rise between the 1850s and the 1870s, the savings rate is relatively stable thereafter. Note that the retardation in growth rates during the Great Depression cannot be explained by a diminution of the 'savings effort' or of 'profit squeeze' since, if

Table 5.5. *Real and nominal yields on long-term high grade bonds, 1845–78*

Year	$r_N(t)$: Nominal yield (%)		$r(t)$: Real yield (%)	
	Federal bonds, 'selected market' (1)	New England municipal bonds (2)	Federal bonds, 'selected market' (3)	New England municipal bonds (4)
1845	5·16	4·86	0·63	0·33
1846	5·50	4·92	2·89	2·31
1847	5·77	5·14	−0·35	−0·98
1848	5·71	5·31	8·92	8·52
1849	5·16	5·31	7·21	7·36
1850	4·58	5·13	4·36	4·91
1851	4·47	5·08	4·47	5·08
1852	4·39	4·98	0·89	1·48
1853	4·02	4·99	−3·74	−2·77
1854	4·14	5·13	−6·15	−5·16
1855	4·18	5·16	−1·36	−0·38
1856	4·11	5·10	5·40	6·39
1857	4·30	5·19	2·00	2·89
1858	4·32	5·03	16·22	16·93
1859	4·72	4·81	7·72	7·81
1860	5·57	4·79	7·77	6·99
1861	6·45	5·04	9·55	8·14
1867	5·34	4·97	11·33	11·70
1868	5·28	4·62	8·79	9·45
1869	5·37	4·07	8·15	9·45
1870	5·44	4·24	12·17	13·37
1871	5·32	4·18	10·02	11·16
1872	5·36	3·70	3·11	4·77
1873	5·58	3·51	3·82	5·89
1874	5·47	3·42	6·80	8·85
1875	5·07	3·30	8·95	10·72
1876	4·59	3·66	10·19	10·12
1877	4·45	3·81	8·65	9·29
1878	4·34	3·97	14·25	14·62

Source: $r(t) = r_N(t) - \dot{P}_e(t)$, where $\dot{P}_e(t) = (0·6)\,\dot{P}(t) + (0·3)\,\dot{P}(t-1) + (0·1) \times \dot{P}(t-2)$ and P is the rate of price inflation. Cols. (1) and (2) from S. Homer, *A History of Interest Rates*, table 38, pp. 287–8. Cols. (3) and (4) use $\dot{P}_e(t)$ calculated from the Warren-Pearson index, *Historical Statistics*, E-1, p. 115.

anything, it exhibits a moderate rise over the late nineteenth century. Second, Table 5.4 shows that while the relative price of capital goods declined sharply from 1859 to the 1870s, it remained relatively stable up to the turn of the century.

Conventional neoclassical growth theory yields an explicit prediction regarding an economy's behavior in response to episodic changes in savings rates and capital goods prices. The equilibrium capital–labor and capital–output ratios rise. If for the moment we assume no technical progress and a constant rate of labor force growth, then the rate of capital stock growth declines from initial high levels to a rate asymptotically approaching the constant rate of labor force growth. As a result, the rate of real output growth per worker and the net rate of return on capital also must decline asymptotically over time. The diminution in capital stock growth will take place even with a constant savings rate. Even though it is well known in the growth literature, this point deserves stressing since it is not well appreciated in the historical literature: historically changes in savings rates have not been necessary to produce variations in rates of capital formation.[37] The source of a declining rate of capital accumulation may be, of course, the capital–output ratio which offsets the once-over increase in savings rates: that is, the rate of capital stock growth can be decomposed into

$$\frac{\dot{K}(t)}{K(t)} = \bar{s} \left\{ \frac{\text{GNP}(t)}{P_I(t)K(t)} - \delta, \right.$$

where $\bar{s}$ is the fixed savings rate, δ is a stable depreciation rate, and the expression in brackets is simply the output–capital ratio. ($P_I(t)$ is the current price of investment goods.) As the capital–output ratio rises during this disequilibrium phase of development, approaching a new and higher equilibrium, the rate of capital formation declines until it equals the rate of labor force growth: e.g., when the capital–output ratio is constant. At the higher capital–labor ratio, the real interest rate (the net rate of return on capital) is lower, and the real wage higher.

The above argument would be exactly the same if the initial change were from a sharp decline in P_I rather than an increase in $\bar{s}$. Thus, the episodic fall in investment goods prices and the rise in current savings rates were working in concert over the Civil War decade.

The available historical evidence, thin though it may be, is roughly consistent with the growth-theoretic interpretation. We saw in chapter 4 that Kuznets' data do exhibit a secular tendency towards declining rates of accumulation in the late nineteenth century. The rate of capital stock growth was 4·94 percent per annum 1879–89, and 3·94 percent per annum 1889–99. Thus, while the gross savings rate was mildly rising – clearly inconsistent with the 'profit squeeze' thesis, the rate of capital accumulation *fell* by 1 percentage point. Similar trends are forthcoming from the model. Furthermore, Kendrick's estimated capital–output ratios exhibit behavior also consistent with the predictions of neoclassical growth theory since they rise markedly after the early 1880s. From an average index of 100 during the decade 1879–88, Kendrick's private domestic non-farm capital–output ratio leaps to 131 by 1894 and still is at a high level (115) in both 1899 and 1904. Once again, the model produces similar movements (Table 4.3).

We now have one plausible explanation of the Great Depression. Historians have always rejected the rigorous elegance of growth theory as irrelevant for the serious empirical business of economic history. Yet it appears that the simple elegance of growth theory may be fully adequate to explain a phase of historical development which has kept economic historians in a state of utter anarchy and confusion for some seventy-five years. The theoretical explanation can be summarized: the economy-wide savings rate rose, and the price of producer durables fell, markedly during the Civil War decade. The initial impact was to raise capital accumulation rates and, as a result, the rate of GNP and GNP per worker growth. Engerman views the response as a 'catching up': 'The higher postwar rate may merely reflect a "catching up" process. . . . Not until almost 20 years after the war did per capita commodity output reach the level estimated by extrapolating the prewar trend, and it is at this time, that the rate of growth returns to this earlier level.'[38] The 'catching up' is attributed to the epochal rise in savings rates and/or fall in relative capital goods' prices. The subsequent retardation in the postwar growth rate was inevitable since the rate of capital accumulation diminished as the capital–labor and capital–output ratios rose. Increases in the capital–labor ratio had an inevitable effect on factor prices: yields fell and real wages rose.

Total factor productivity growth and a disappearing frontier

There are, of course, competing supply explanations of the American retardation. Two of these have attained special prominence and are well embedded in the historians' accounts of nineteenth-century performance.

One hypothesis has had an especially long tradition: the gradual 'closing of the frontier.' Surely declining output per worker growth rates are to be explained in some measure by the secular decline in the rate of natural resource augmentation during the period. Although his focus is on *average* nineteenth-century growth performance rather than the secular decline after 1870, Higgs has presented the conventional view of American land extensive growth most instructively for our purposes:

> In the United States the seemingly limitless availability of cheap land vanished the specter of diminishing returns. . . . In the twentieth century technological progress alone would conquer diminishing returns in agriculture; but in the nineteenth century, when the pace of technological progress was slower

and population growth more rapid, the availability of a vast expanse of *unoccupied land played a crucial role in permitting economic growth to continue unhampered by the drag of diminishing returns.*[39]

No doubt diminishing returns have always been operative in American agriculture, but if land augmentation uniquely favored American development then a reduction in the availability of new land surely must have placed an increasingly heavy drag on late nineteenth-century American growth. We must agree in *theory* that declining rates of land expansion may have contributed directly to the retardation in aggregate growth rates during the Great Depression, but the issue is one of *fact*. Furthermore, the influence of a 'disappearing frontier' may have had an indirect effect on capital accumulation rates via the capital–output ratio as well.

The second hypothesis relies on total factor productivity growth performance. Contemporary research on technical progress in the twentieth century has led us to believe that much of the observed long-term growth in average labor productivity is accounted for by the 'residual.' Perhaps the same might be true of the late nineteenth century. What role did changing rates of TFPG play in producing the Great Depression? In the section on sources-of-growth versus the counterfactual we cautioned against the indiscriminate use of sources-of-growth accounting in seeking answers to such questions. Table 5.6 indicates quite clearly one weakness inherent in the method. While Kendrick's estimates document sharply declining rates of TFPG in *both* industry and Midwestern agriculture, the

Table 5.6   *Total factor productivity growth in two sectors, 1869–1908* (*in percent per annum*)

Variable	1869/78–1884/93	1884/93–1899/08
TFPG in Midwestern agriculture: $\dfrac{\dot{B}(t)}{B(t)}$	0·70	0·40
TFPG in Midwestern and Eastern industry: $\dfrac{\dot{A}(t)}{A(t)}$	1·55	0·96
TFPG economy-wide: $\dfrac{\dot{T}(t)}{T(t)}$	0·83	0·72

Note: The sectoral TFPG rates are derived from J. Kendrick, *Productivity Trends in the United States.* The output weights are from H. S. Perloff *et al.*, *Regions, Resources and Economic Growth* and R. A. Easterlin, 'Interregional Differences in Per Capita Income, Population, and Total Income, 1840–1950.' See appendix A.

same cannot be said of TFPG for the two sectors combined. Simplifying the expression in that section, we see that

$$\frac{\dot{T}(t)}{T(t)} = v_{AW}(t)\frac{\dot{B}(t)}{B(t)} + \left[1 - v_{AW}(t)\right]\frac{\dot{A}(t)}{A(t)},$$

where the v's are output shares. Although both $\frac{\dot{A}(t)}{A(t)}$ and $\frac{\dot{B}(t)}{B(t)}$ sharply declined during the late nineteenth century, $\frac{\dot{T}(t)}{T(t)}$ declined only from 0·83 to 0·72 percent. The explanation for this paradoxical result is, of course, that agriculture (low in TFPG) diminished in relative importance over the period. The implication clearly seems to be that the reduction in overall TFPG contributes little to the observed retardation in average labor productivity growth. Yet, this conclusion may be premature when we recognize the possibility that the output mix itself is an endogenous variable. Presumably, the appropriate counterfactual here involves holding $\frac{\dot{A}(t)}{A(t)}$ and $\frac{\dot{B}(t)}{B(t)}$ constant and exploring its implications on late nineteenth-century development.

5.3 The causes of the Great Depression: counterfactual analysis

We now propose to shed further light on the Great Depression by posing counterfactuals of our model of late nineteenth-century development. What would have been the behavior of the American economy had the land stock maintained the high rates of expansion achieved in the early 1870s? Suppose further that the sectoral rates of total factor productivity growth documented by Kendrick had continued at the rates obtained in the early 1870s. Would the American economy have exhibited growth retardation? That is, would the Great Depression have taken place? We shall show these two forces were unimportant in accounting for the Great Depression and that the simple growth theoretic explanation accounts very well for the American economy's performance over these three decades.

Table 5.7 summarizes three counterfactual experiments. The first line repeats the actual simulation for GNP per worker growth rates as reported in chapter 4. The second and third lines display values of these variables had the land stock and sectoral total factor productivity, respectively, maintained their growth rates achieved in the early 1870s. The fourth line examines the joint impact of land stock and total factor productivity growth on output per worker expansion. Apparently, the declining historical rates of sectoral TFPG account for little or none of the secular decline in

Table 5.7   *Simulating the American Great Depression under three counterfactual
conditions*
(*GNP per worker growth rates*)

	Period	
Regime	1869/78–1884/93	1884/93–1899/1908
1. Actual land stock and total factor productivity growth	1·69%	1·24%
2. Constant land stock growth	1·83	1·45
3. Constant total factor productivity growth	1·74	1·30
4. Constant land stock growth and total factor productivity growth	1·84	1·46

growth rates during the Great Depression.[40] This seems to us an important result: *if variations in sectoral factor productivity growth are unable to account for more than marginal changes in GNP growth rates during this period of Great Depression, it appears unlikely to be important elsewhere in the nineteenth century.* This result confirms our earlier assertion that the rate of technical progress plays a far greater role in accounting for twentieth-century growth experience than for the nineteenth century.

Somewhat surprisingly, the 'closing of the frontier' contributes very little to the explanation either. It is, of course, true that growth rates would have been considerably higher throughout the three decades had land augmentation rates continued at the levels obtained during the early 1870s. It is also true that the secular decline in per capita output growth rates would have been somewhat less marked. Yet, the retardation would have persisted. This result also seems to us to have important implications for historians of nineteenth-century American development. American growth is conventionally characterized as being unique since resource extensive growth not only implied a wholly different set of institutional challenges but also 'the seemingly limitless availability of cheap land vanished the specter of diminishing returns.'[41] If so, then the sharp decline in improved land stock growth in the Midwest after 1870 surely would have accounted for a large share of the retardation in growth rates up to the turn of the century. Since we find no such effect, perhaps this unique aspect of American development has been overemphasized. In summary, *the underlying causes of the Great Depression do not appear to lie either with the sharp historical retardation in rates of land augmentation or with the decline in sectoral factor productivity growth rates.*

This analysis appears to make the growth-theoretic hypothesis even more plausible. The evidence suggests that declining rates of land exploitation and total factor productivity growth are only marginal contributors to the economic retardation. Of the 0·45 percent observed decline in per worker growth rates, 0·38 percent, or eight-tenths, is unexplained by these two forces. The explanation for the Great Depression must lie with the long run determinants of capital formation rates in the American economy as it strives to adjust to the higher saving rate achieved during the Civil War decade. What we have been observing is the American economy following a growth path from 1870 to 1896 more or less dictated by the disequilibrating conditions generated during the 1860s: in Engerman's words, we are indeed observing a 'catching up' process. This result places us directly back into what was at one time the orthodox view of the historical process of development. Since 1957, we have been led to believe that capital formation was hardly the prime vehicle of growth that orthodox economic historians had assumed was obvious. Instead, research on the residual urged a revisionist view which minimized the role of capital formation and the importance of the savings mechanism. In our analysis of the Great Depression, the old orthodox position still seems the sensible one to us.

5.4 A role for demand?

It warrants emphasizing that the monetary contraction up to 1896 was not a necessary condition of the Great Depression.[42] This provocative result inevitably follows from our ability to rewrite late nineteenth-century American economic history with a full employment model which ignores monetary variables. Our interest has only been on secular trends in the post-Civil War period. At least in this dimension, the recent econometric success in resolving the Gibson Paradox by introducing price expectations into a Keynesian macro economic model should be noted. In the long run, such a model approaches the full employment neoclassical growth framework which underlies our model of chapter 3. Sargent's empirical work with this model generates results for the period 1870–1936 'in which the interest–inflation relationship broadly resembles that characterizing the actual historical data.'[43]

Since a full employment model is effective in capturing the Great Depression, it casts considerable doubt on a second popular hypothesis – the 'underconsumptionist' or inadequate aggregate demand explanation.[44] The underconsumptionist explanation of late Victorian British and post-Civil War American decline makes a frequent appearance in the literature. The writings of two prominent cliometricians should suffice to identify the nature of the argument – John Meyer on England and Alfred Conrad on America.[45] English historians have always suspected that the failure in output growth could be explained by aggregate demand:

> The correlation between industrial and export growth was suggestive and its discovery timely . . . Aggregate demand, after all, determines output, and exports were a large part of Britain's aggregate demand. To many economists and historians it has seemed that this insight . . . could . . . be used to explain the slow growth of the British economy in the forty years after 1870.[46]

Meyer's exercise in input–output analysis is a sophisticated attempt to utilize the demand explanation of British failure. Yet McCloskey has argued persuasively that *supply* conditions were the only binding constraints on output expansion in England. Some support of McCloskey's view is to be found in fragmentary evidence on factor utilization over the period: labor 'unemployment after 1872 was low and did not increase with time.'[47] On the other hand, McCloskey shows that a neoclassical full employment model is consistent with the English historical evidence. Is there any reason to expect different results in the American case?

Alfred Conrad has argued that nineteenth-century American growth experience can be explained by a multiplier-acceleration model of income growth. For Conrad, the British emphasis on exogenous export growth performance shifts in the American case to exogenous and discontinuous movements to more capital intensive technologies:

> Technological changes that increase the capital intensity of the economy will obviously heighten the response of the accelerator mechanism: to the extent that the innovations are financed by borrowing – and this is the Schumpeterian argument – the effect will be in the direction of even greater buoyancy. The nineteenth century of this economy is punctuated by a series of developments, within industries and among industries, that increased the capital intensity of the productive process.[48]

Yet none of the neo-Keynesians have offered an explicit test of the aggregate demand thesis: in fact, there is no evidence suggesting increasing secular rates of factor unemployment in the American economy over the three decades following 1870. Lebergott's tentative estimates of unemployment during nineteenth-century crisis years suggests that 'the most we can conclude is that the extent of unemployment in the worst crisis years increased somewhat in the first half of the nineteenth century but has shown no trend since then.'[49] Certainly the cyclical depression of the 1890s obtained high unemployment rates, but Lebergott feels that the 1870s were equally poor with unemployment rates in both decades approaching 10 percent.[50] Our own efforts in chapter 4 (Table 4.7) and appendix C (Tables C.4 and C.5) to reconstruct unemployment rates for the late nineteenth century also fails to support the neo-Keynesian view. Between 1870 and 1884, the industrial unemployment rate is estimated to have been 7·4 percent. The rate was 6·9 percent between 1885 and 1899. In any case, we have not found it necessary to invoke any variant of the demand hypothesis to generate a Great Depression in late nineteenth-century American growth. A full employment neoclassical model is sufficient to the task.

5.5 Then the Wheel Turned and other puzzles

We conclude by pointing out that some stubborn puzzles persist. Much more work remains to be done to explain the rise in the savings rate during the Civil War decade. Surely this should remain as a key question for the American economic historian. Furthermore, what explains the relative stability in the savings ratio thereafter? This issue is confronted in chapter 6.

In Landes' words, another key question is why 'the wheel turned' in 1896.[51] What was the process by which the retardation up to the turn of the century was *reversed*? Why do real interest rates rise after 1896 and up to World War I? Not only did real rates rise after 1896, but the model predicts that turning point too (Table 4.9 and Figure 4.4). True, the rate of total factor productivity growth *within* sectors ceases its gradual fall around the turn of the century; this is magnified into a rise in *aggregate* total factor productivity growth as the relative demise of agriculture continues at an accelerating pace (Table 4.6). Yet, if we intend to place the cause of the 'hinge' at the doorstep of technological change – as Landes does, then we must confront the evidence collected by Brown, Kendrick, and Morishima and Saito who date the technological epoch between 1907 and 1920, rather than earlier in the late 1890s.[52] What produced the marked upward shift in aggregate savings rates during the same period? Why then does the retardation of growth rates cease, indeed, reverse in both fact and in our predictions from the model? Furthermore, any future explanation must confront the strikingly different characteristics of the 'epochal hinge' after 1896 compared with that of the Civil War decade. In the latter case, the fall in the relative price of investment goods reinforced the rise in current price savings rates. The same is not true of the post-1896 period since this dates the beginning of a long secular rise in the relative price of investment goods which persists throughout the twentieth century (Table 5.4).

These are all fundamentally important questions which should attract the future research efforts of economic historians for some time to come. It seems doubtful that the explanations will be as simple as the one offered here for the Great Depression itself.

6

Financial Intermediation, Capital Immobilities and Economic Growth

> ... is it possible to measure the economic cost of the capital
> immobilities?   Lance E. Davis (1971)

6.1 The economist's paradigm and capital mobility in history

The economist conventionally assumes instantaneous and costless 'capital' mobility when exploring problems in economic history. Capital goods are treated as putty to be remolded at will from one industrial use to another. This treatment tends to minimize the relevance of the historian's concern for institutions; in particular, it assumes that primitive economies have no difficulty finding effective means of readjustment to exogenous economic events. The mobilization of capital for new firms and expanding sectors, the migration of labor and its retraining for new employment, the development of new transport networks and marketing arrangements are all important challenges to the *status quo*. These challenges often require creative entrepreneurial response and important institutional change. The analytical economic historian employing conventional general equilibrium models is certainly aware of and sensitive to this concern with institutional response. Yet for him the process of economic readjustment may be a relevant issue only for certain problems. He must be shown that the adjustment process can have an important quantitative impact on long-term growth. He must be shown that the predictions of the simple general equilibrium model are sufficiently in error to imply that his models are 'not very useful for analyzing the process of economic growth.'[1]

A simple example should help sharpen the mobility issue. Suppose our purpose is to evaluate the historical impact of a sudden shift in world demand (reflected in relative prices) favoring primary products on economic growth and industrialization in a relatively underdeveloped region like the Midwest in the early 1870s. Indeed, suppose this abrupt shift in market conditions is induced by the sudden appearance of an interregional railroad network. General equilibrium theory yields an unambiguous answer. In Figure 6.1,

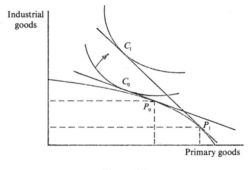

Figure 6.1

production shifts from P_0 towards primary products at P_1. Given sufficient time for resources to redistribute themselves, the industrial output share declines. An economist may be interested in the magnitude of such effects, of course, and thus may be compelled to estimate the technological parameters underlying the production possibility curve. The task is difficult but hardly impossible.[2] But for the historian, the story does not end there; indeed, the most interesting part is yet to come. How is the *growth* of the economy affected? What is the process by which the reallocation of resources takes place? Who moves to open up new farm lands? What institutions finance the move? How efficient are those institutions in effecting a speedy response to the disequilibrium conditions induced by the rails? In reality, this abrupt change in market conditions is immediately followed by an excess demand for labor and capital in the primary product sector. Wage differentials become apparent and sectoral rates of return on invested capital diverge; in short, labor and capital earn 'quasi-rents' in the expanding sector. Some *economists* find such periods of disequilibrium of sufficient interest to attempt an evaluation of the welfare losses to such an economy associated with the departure from optimal resource allocation (i.e., equilibrium). Some *historians* find such episodes of sufficient importance to document in detail the ability of the Morgans and Rockefellers to capture these quasi-rents. Furthermore, we may be interested in growth implications of this disequilibrium state. How will capital formation rates and technical change be affected?

This chapter explores just one aspect of factor market disequilibrium in history. How and in what ways was American late nineteenth-century development affected by capital immobility? What was the role of financial intermediation? Can we measure the economic cost of the capital immobilities in terms of growth foregone?

6.2 The historian, his banks and financial intermediaries

The apparent importance of intersectoral and interregional transfers

In a world of capital immobility, rate of return differentials are bound to exist. If past accumulations of capital goods are specific to a given sector after initial installation, then the equalization of rates of return on invested capital can only be achieved by current investment allocation. Even when sectors have identical savings rates out of current income (or profits), the expanding and profitable sectors normally have investment requirements considerably in excess of their self-financing capabilities. These 'excess' investment requirements must, of course, be satisfied by external borrowing and consequent intersectoral financial transfers. In the absence of external financing, the 'new' regions or sectors will find their growth seriously retarded while 'old' regions or sectors overinvest and exhibit relatively poor returns. Let us assume for the moment that the savings decision, regardless of region or sector, is independent of the interest rate. Thus, in Figure 6.2 the savings schedules in both regions (sectors) are drawn inelastic with respect to the regional (sectoral) interest rate. The regional investment demand schedules for the expanding 'deficit' savings region are denoted by I_D and that for the relatively stagnant 'surplus' savings region is I_s. The savings functions are drawn *net* of replacement requirements, so that we can define current net investment demand in a given sector as[3]

$$I^N(t) = K^*(t) - K^*(t - 1),$$

where $K^*(t)$ refers to the desired or optimal stock of capital and

$$K^*(t) = \alpha_K \frac{P(t)Q(t)}{C(t)}.$$

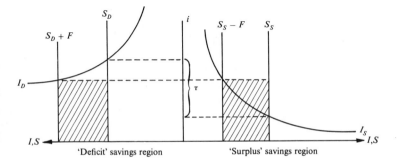

Figure 6.2

K^* is derived under a Cobb–Douglas specification (assumed in chapter 3 to hold in all sectors) and α_K is the elasticity of output with respect to capital, P is the output.price, Q is physical output, and C is the cost of capital services. If capital gains are ignored and profit taxes are non-existent, then

$$C = iP_I,$$

where P_I is the price of capital goods. Thus

$$I^N(t) = \alpha_K \left\{ \frac{P(t)Q(t)}{P_I(t)i(t)} - \frac{P(t-1)Q(t-1)}{P_I(t-1)i(t-1)} \right\}.$$

If the regional interest rate has been stable over time, then the net investment demand schedule can be written as

$$I^N(t) = \frac{\alpha_K}{i(t)} \left\{ \frac{P(t)Q(t)}{P_I(t)} - \frac{P(t-1)Q(t-1)}{P_I(t-1)} \right\} = \frac{\alpha_K}{i(t)} \{Z\}.$$

Note that the *elasticity* of the investment demand schedule is independent of the capital goods' prices facing the sector, as well as output levels, and output prices. Furthermore, the parameters of the production function itself have no influence on the elasticity of the investment demand schedule, and the elasticity is *constant* at all interest rates.[4] The investment demand schedules in the two regions depicted in Figure 6.2 have the same shape but differ only in *position* to reflect the buoyant or expansionary activity in the 'deficit' frontier region (or new industry). This point casts some doubt on an assertion by Gallman and Davis comparing 'deficit' to 'surplus' sectors in nineteenth-century American history: 'Such sectors were probably marked by a wide range of potentially profitable investment alternatives and therefore probably had fairly elastic investment demand schedules.'[5]

In the absence of interregional (intersectoral) financial transfers, current investment will be constrained by the self-financing capabilities of the two regions. An interest rate differential will appear and, as a result, there will be differentials in the rate of return to capital. The 'deficit' region will appear 'starved' for capital. Potential investors in the deficit region will accuse financial intermediaries of monopolistic practices; farmers and businessmen at the frontier will fill their journals with complaints about the scarcity of capital and the 'high cost of money.' There is certainly abundant evidence of these complaints coming from the Midwest in the mid–late nineteenth century. In Lance Davis's words:

> An examination of four of the West's most important manu-
> facturing industries (milling, meatpacking, oil refining, and
> agricultural machinery) indicates ... the effects of imperfect

capital mobility ... Although some short-term requirements were met from sources outside the region, local capital provided almost all the initial long-term finance; and most growth was financed through retained earnings ... In the 1870's ... the innovation of the Hungarian reduction milling greatly increased minimum efficient mill size and, therefore, the industry's demand for external finance. Businessmen, however, found it extremely difficult to attract depersonalized capital (either from inside or outside the region), and well into the 1880's even the largest firms were still family enterprises ... the agricultural machinery industry ... appears to have remained almost entirely self-financed until the end of the century ... The J. I. Case Company (a major producer of threshers) was entirely self-financed ... [and] McCormick remained a family enterprise until J. P. Morgan organized the International Harvester combine in 1902.[6]

Professor Davis is in good company. Almost four decades ago, Irving Fisher emphasized the presence of high interest rates in the 'deficit' Midwest, the legal barriers to capital mobility, and prevalence of quasi-rents induced by short-run disequilibrium and legal barriers to efficient capital market operation.

> Another striking proof of the demand for loans in the Middle West is shown in the experience of the New York and Connecticut life insurance companies. New York up to 1880 had a law prohibiting the life insurance companies in that state from loaning on real estate outside of New York. Connecticut had no such restriction ... and loaned extensively in the West ... Taking the period 1860–1880 as a whole, the Connecticut companies realized 1·2 percent more than did the New York companies.[7]

If the 'barriers' to capital mobility were removed in Figure 6.2, a sufficiently large interregional savings transfer, F, would take place to equalize interest rates across regions. Of course, the initial net return differentials may be so large that even a total transfer of all savings in the surplus region would fail to eliminate the differential in one year. Were the necessary transfer of savings from surplus to deficit region forthcoming, it would surely have an important impact on subsequent growth. The average (economy-wide) productivity of capital is lower without the transfer. If the financial transfer is treated as costless, then the foregone future income produced by these barriers could be readily measured. If, as is more plausible, the transfer requires at least some real resources to overcome that portion of the regional interest differential attributable to information costs, then a third sector – financial intermediaries –

must be explicitly introduced which competes for a share of aggregate savings. Clearly, the existence of interest rate differentials in history is explained by some combination of these factors.

The role of financial intermediation

What role does financial intermediation play in this process of interregional and intersectoral transfer? Financial institutions serve as intermediaries between saver and investor, and by their specialized skills foster intersectoral and interregional transfers:

> In an exchange economy individual savers are not necessarily the most efficient investors, since saving depends primarily upon income, whereas efficient investment depends upon entrepreneurial talents, knowledge, and willingness to take risks. As a result, in the absence of financial intermediaries marginal rates of return on real resources are not equated for different uses or among different users. If savers were willing to make their resources directly available to entrepreneurs the occasion for financial intermediation would not arise.[8]

Cameron presents a very useful taxonomy in listing the 'financial' requirements for economic growth and modern industrialization. These requirements can be usefully decomposed under three headings: (i) the accumulation of capital goods; (ii) the mobilization of savings for optimal investment allocation; and (iii) the efficient utilization of capital goods in production. Financial institutions are most concerned with the second of these three requirements.[9]

We may certainly agree, then, that financial intermediating activity has a crucial influence on the magnitude of the intersectoral and interregional transfers in a growing economy. Its influence becomes apparent by the costs associated with the transfers and with the ability of financial institutional development to keep these costs low (and perhaps falling). Yet the historical research on financial intermediation and banking asserts far more than this. Cameron, for example, has stated that '... if they fail to function satisfactorily ... they can effectively prevent any significant degree of industrialization.'[10] In theory, all things are possible. But empirical statements like these imply hypotheses subject to test. Similar *quantitative* statements appear elsewhere in the literature. Sylla states the financial intermediation thesis with striking forcefulness:

> The success with which capital funds are mobilized and transformed to industrial and related activities is widely regarded as a critical determinant of both the timing and the pace of industrialization in the modern era. Gerschenkron, for

example, has suggested that institutional developments which increased this type of capital mobility played an important role in the varying degrees of industrial progress of nineteenth century European countries. A functionally similar development . . . occurred in American banking and provided a powerful capital-supply stimulus for the United States' postbellum industrialization.[11]

Lance Davis has been somewhat more cautious in attaching quantitative importance to financial intermediaries than Cameron, Gerschenkron or Sylla. Yet even Davis has asserted that 'Immobile capital appears to be characteristic of most newly developing economies . . . In the United States, such immobilities *distorted the pattern of growth* throughout the entire 19th century; but they became much more important in postbellum years . . .'[12] One of the purposes of this chapter is to evaluate these assertions. No doubt financial intermediation played a key role in facilitating savings transfers between regions and sectors in nineteenth-century America. Yet it is not at all clear that its role profoundly influenced the pace and character of American development to the extent suggested by the research of financial historians. Even as late as the twentieth century, when Davis and others agree that American financial intermediaries were highly sophisticated and efficient, intersectoral transfers were remarkably small. Kuznets has documented that 80 percent of the private sector's new investment was financed internally between 1900 and 1956; from 1900 to 1920, the corporate sector financed 85 percent of its needs internally; the figure for 1930–55 is 95 percent.[13] Of course, the *marginal* impact may still be quantitatively significant. In any case, we hope to evaluate these propositions in the pages which follow.

Disequilibrium and the development of a national capital market: 1870–1910

How does the historian evaluate the efficient operation of a national capital market and its ability to facilitate intersectoral transfers? Sylla, Davis, Cameron and others all utilize measures of interest rate differentials as their criteria. Given an economy in equilibrium undisturbed by exogenous forces, interest differentials are still likely to persist since they represent real information and transaction costs: e.g., 'normal' profits earned by financial intermediaries who engage in 'interest arbitrage.' Even prior to the Civil War decade, interregional interest rate differentials were a well-known characteristic of the American economy. In fact, 'the term "disinclination of capital to migrate" was used to explain the phenomenon, and it was estimated that an interest differential of 2 percent was necessary to overcome this barrier.'[14] Thus, a fully integrated national capital market cannot be expected to produce a complete equalization of interest rates just as a fully competitive national commodity market cannot produce commodity price equalization in the face of real transportation costs. Yet the financial historian is *not* concerned with a capital market in equilibrium, but instead with a capital market *forced into disequilibrium* by economic events exogenous to it. 'Over time an economy develops certain methods of mobilizing resources and while these are usually adequate for "normal" transfers the system can be strained by extranormal pressures.'[15]

What were the sources of 'extranormal' pressures which generated disequilibrium by the late 1860s?[16] Lance Davis provides us with one statement of the conventional hypothesis:

> The increasing impact of these immobilities can be traced to the rapid rise in the demand for external finance. This rise can, in turn, be attributed to the shift of industry from East to West, to a series of technological innovations in manufacturing that increased both total capital requirements and the minimum size of initial investment, and to new developments in agriculture that required greater amounts of capital equipment.[17]

Davis appears to rest his case on the fact that after the 1860s the bulk of the nation's savings were still accruing in the East while an ever-increasing share of economic activity and investment requirements was located in the West and, to a much lesser extent, the South. Yet, if anything Davis's characterization of disequilibrium in the capital market after the Civil War is an understatement, since in many dimensions the experience is unique to American economic history. Chapter 5 pointed out that the current price savings rate rose dramatically from the 1850s to the 1870s. In addition, the relative price of producer durables plunged. Nowhere in American history can we find comparable 'episodic' changes in the underlying forces driving capital formation. Following the economic stagnation during the Civil War itself, these 'catching up' forces were in themselves sufficient to place enormous stress on the efficient functioning of all factor markets. Furthermore, the disequilibrium conditions induced by the impressive surge of pent up capital formation was reinforced by other factors. With a new flood of European immigrants, frontier settlement resumed, urbanization surged and Western cities exploded. As if this was not enough to digest, the economy had another disequilibrating force to contend with – the railroads and their impact on farm production and export in the West. Is it any wonder that capital markets had difficulty coping with the demands placed on them by the early 1870s?

We have in fact introduced Davis's characterization into our model of disequilibrium growth. Recall from chapters 3 and 4 that the West–East interest rate differential assumed in 1870 lies between 3·2 and 5·8 percent (the excess of the Western 'city' rate and the farm mortgage rate, respectively, above that of Eastern markets). The equilibrium differential would be only 1 percent in our model, since the real transactions cost is taken as 1 percent of the asset's value. The 1870 conditions in chapter 4 are set to capture the capital market disequilibrium attributable to these 'extranormal' events surrounding the Civil War decade.

The financial historian has also observed a convergence of regional interest rates following the early 1870s.[18] The convergence was sufficiently striking to warrant the term 'national capital market integration.' It should be apparent that this important phase of national capital market integration could have been generated by two forces: (i) a secular decline in the disequilibrating forces which produced the initial disequilibrium; and/or (ii) an expansion in existing financial intermediating activity which gradually removed the quasi-rents prevailing in 1870. We know, for example, that the locational shift of economic activity towards the Midwest slows down, if not actually ceases, by the early 1880s. This is documented both by the model's prediction and Perloff's data on the regional distribution of the labor force. Furthermore, although farm mechanization continues at a rapid rate both in fact and in the simulation over these four decades, the growth in Midwestern land in farms declines after the 1870s. Also, the impressive rise in the relative price of farm products (in the Midwest) during the 1870s is not repeated until very late in the century. Finally, as we have seen in chapter 5, the 'catching up' phase of the 1870s is followed by a retardation associated with the Great Depression. Thus, we might plausibly hypothesize that much of the observed national capital market integration could well be explained by forces exogenous to the capital market itself.

Davis and Sylla prefer to stress institutional developments *endogenous* to the capital market in accounting for the convergence of regional interest rates. Sylla is convinced that the explanation is to be found in government policy and monopolistic banking:

> ... the Federal government's wartime interventions in banking, which resulted in the National Banking System, were to restrain the growth of banking ... for several decades ... [and] left many of the country's bankers in relatively monopolistic positions where they could charge high interest rates ...
>
> Interregional and city-country interest rate differentials persisted because of the variations in the degree of monopoly power possessed by bankers in different areas. When barriers

to entry were eroded, competition became more uniform and bank interest rate differentials narrowed, often rather sharply.[19]

Recent research on Wisconsin nineteenth-century banking casts considerable doubt on Sylla's thesis, at least as it applies to American economy-wide experience with interest rate differentials.[20] How, then, does Davis account for the evolution of a national capital market after 1870? His explanation relies primarily on a conventional long-term supply response of a sector earning excess profits or quasi-rents. The number of financial intermediating firms expanded, their variety increased, the quality of decision-making improved and, as a result, competition among these institutions flourished. In turn, the output of the sector – the volume of intersectoral and interregional transfers – expanded, and extranormal profits eventually declined, that is, interest rate differentials in excess of transaction costs diminished. Life insurance and mortgage banking grew by leaps and bounds (the latter especially during the 1870s and 1880s), successful firms dealing in the long-term market adopted professional management, new types of life insurance policies were offered and additionally there was a gradual easing of legal restrictions which inhibited the efficient operation of the capital market. Developments in the short-term market were equally impressive:

> ... a series of new financial institutions capable of surmounting the barriers raised by distance and by the lack of adequate branch-banking legislation was innovated. In the period 1870–1914, barriers to short-term mobility were overcome (or at least reduced) by direct solicitation of interregional funds, by commercial bank rediscounting, and most important, by the evolution of a national market for commercial paper ...
>
> The profits earned by the commercial-paper houses induced additional entry, and increased competition forced the brokers to extend the area of their operations in search of prime paper and good customers ...
>
> Among the first to feel the squeeze were the western bankers who had been accustomed to high returns on their investments.[21]

In terms of the model developed in chapter 3, the financial historian is interpreted in the following fashion: The appearance of extranormal profits in financial intermediating activity by 1870 can be explained in large measure by the unusual excess demand for external financing in growing regions and sectors in the Midwest. These extranormal profits or quasi-rents in financial intermediating activity produced a supply response which took many forms. Political pressure was brought to bear to eliminate restrictions on the sector's expansion. Furthermore, the number of firms engaged in such activity rapidly expanded to facilitate the enormous and increasing demands on the sector's capacity: i.e., an increased demand for external financing. When small extranormal profits prevailed, the supply response was flexible. When larger profits appeared with increasing interest rate differentials, the short-run supply response was increasingly restricted by current capacity: only over a number of years could the sector expand sufficiently to satisfy the external financing requirements in the Midwest and thus to reduce the quasi-rents.

The model in chapter 3 attempts to capture the financial historian's hypotheses by the mechanism reproduced in Figure 6.3. Note that this formal characterization does *not* minimize the importance of institutional change. Indeed, had not the financial sector responded with the energy documented by Davis and others, the parameters underlying the intersectoral savings transfer functions would have shifted in a way to induce even higher interest rate differentials and quasi-rents. It should also be emphasized that the ϕ_{ji} functions are specified in such a fashion that (i) under 'normal' circumstances small increases in interest rate differentials induce a far greater volume of financial transfers than under 'extranormal' circumstances and that (ii) the 'disinclination of capital to migrate' is captured by the presence of τ, an initial differential or barrier which must be exceeded before any capital migrates. Both of these characteristics receive heavy emphasis in the historical literature reviewed above.

An overview of the issues

This chapter raises three questions of the late nineteenth-century American economy: How was U.S. experience with structural change and regional development affected by capital immobility? What was the role of financial intermediation? What was the

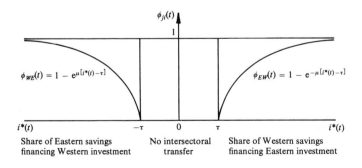

$\phi_{ji}(t)$

$\phi_{WE}(t) = 1 - e^{\mu[i^*(t)-\tau]}$

$\phi_{EW}(t) = 1 - e^{-\mu[i^*(t)-\tau]}$

| $i^*(t)$ | $-\tau$ | 0 | τ | $i^*(t)$ |

Share of Eastern savings financing Western investment — No intersectoral transfer — Share of Western savings financing Eastern investment

Figure 6.3

economic cost of the capital immobilities in terms of aggregate growth foregone? The remainder of this chapter supplies quantitative answers to these questions by utilizing the model developed in chapter 3. The predictions of the model are explored to ascertain whether it reproduces late nineteenth-century American experience with national capital market integration, quasi-rents and the rise in financial intermediation. Having established the ability of the model to 'rewrite economic history' in this dimension, the discussion turns to analysis and counterfactuals. A counterfactual American economy is examined in the *absence* of restrictions on intersectoral savings transfers. The counterfactual world approximates one with 'perfect' capital markets. How would interest differentials have behaved? Interregional financial flows? Industrialization and growth?

6.3 National capital market integration, institutional change and market failure

National capital market integration

The simulation reported in chapter 4 reproduces with considerable accuracy American 'national capital market integration' experience. The model certainly generates interest rate convergence very much like that documented by Lance Davis. Since our ability to 'rewrite' the financial history of late nineteenth-century America is essential in evaluating the analysis which follows, a brief review of the findings in chapter 4 is in order. The model contains three 'imperfectly integrated' capital markets, each with a separate interest rate: the Midwestern farm mortgage rate, the Midwestern rate on industrial loans and the Eastern rate on industrial loans. Consistent with the available historical evidence, farm mortgage rates in 1870 are by far the highest of the three and furthermore the model (Table 4.9) accurately predicts the greatest decline for farm mortgage rates up to the 1890s. Davis, however, uses regional indices of city bank rates to measure convergence and divergence of geographic interest rate differentials. Comparing the Midwest to the Atlantic states, for example, the former exceeds the latter by approximately 35 percent in the early 1870s. Davis's characterization is captured in the model by setting the ratio of Midwest to Northeast at 1·40 in 1870 (Table 4.10). By 1900, Davis documents (for non-reserve city banks) that the Midwestern rate had fallen below the Midatlantic rate: his index stands at 0·88. The model predicts a comparable figure of 0·80 in the same year. Furthermore, these trends were reversed after the 1890s since Davis's index rises to 0·98 by 1910. The model also predicts this turning point, rising to 0·90 in the same year. Granted, the correspondence between historical fact and the model's predictions is hardly perfect, but it seems close enough to suggest that the model has captured the essence of this aspect of American financial history in the late nineteenth century.

Since the parameters dictating interest rate and financial flow behavior are stable in our model, the explanation for the predicted convergence of sectoral and regional net rates of return are to be found in conditions *external* rather than internal to the sector. This result suggests that the extranormal conditions which generated the factor market disequilibrium by 1870 must have diminished by the 1890s, slowly allowing the capital market to eliminate those disequilibrium effects. Oddly enough, while Davis emphasized conditions *exogenous* to the capital market in accounting for the initial disequilibrium by the end of the Civil War decade, he explains the subsequent national capital market integration by appealing to conditions *endogenous* to the capital market. Our results suggest the contrary. The rate of labor force shift to the Midwest ceases by the early 1880s, while a retardation in this rate was apparent at least a decade earlier (Table 4.5). This surely must have diminished the pressure on excess investment demand in the West. Secular stability in the relative price of Midwestern grains after the late 1870s (Table 7.1A, Figure 7.1) must have had the same effect. Furthermore, although mechanization accelerates on Midwestern farms and labor-saving technology is continually introduced into Western industry after 1870, the prime source of capital requirements in the West, the railroads, declines as a relative share in capital formation activity during the 1870s. This historical evidence suggests that the explanation for national capital market integration may be found in economy-wide conditions exogenous to the capital market rather than to structural changes within the capital market itself. The results forthcoming from the model confirm this hypothesis.

This interpretation also accounts for Davis's 'paradox' that the process of national capital market integration was retarded, or perhaps even reversed, after the mid-1890s.[22] We noted in chapter 4 that the rate of industrialization in the Midwest accelerates after 1890. This development must have increased the relative capital requirements in the Midwest and placed pressure on local sources of finance thus 'retarding the process of capital market integration.' Other 'episodic' events should have reinforced this effect. The relative price of farm products in the Midwest surged upward in the mid-1890s after almost two decades of relative stability (Table 7.1A, Figure 7.1). Furthermore, as we pointed out in chapter 5, the 'wheel turned' after the mid-1890s: national rates of total factor productivity growth accelerated, aggregate capital formation rates rose, and a secular trend towards growth retardation was reversed. In short, after three decades of adjustment to the episodic shocks which jarred the economy during and shortly after the Civil War decade, the American economy was again shaken by abnormal exogenous forces. Under these conditions, there is nothing paradoxical about Davis's observation that the capital market integration process was retarded or even reversed after the mid-1890s. The model faithfully captures the reversal, and institutional change within the capital market is in no way related to it.

Intersectoral financial flows and market failure

Historical evidence documenting intersectoral financial flows for the late nineteenth century is practically non-existent. We do have some case histories detailing sources of finance. However, the literature can only speculate on American experience with aggregate intersectoral and interregional flows between industry and agriculture within the Midwest, and between the East and Midwest. Since our model reproduces so many other aspects of American history for which there is documentation, an examination of the model's predicted financial flows – an unobservable – might still be rewarding. These predicted intersectoral flows are displayed in Table 6.1. First, note that Western agriculture, on *net*, relies on external financing only very early in the period. After the mid-1870s, agriculture conforms to a more conventional modern characterization. In spite of its rapid output expansion, mechanization and continued rate of land exploitation, agriculture finances industrial-

Table 6.1. *Intersectoral financial flows produced by the model*

Year	Share of agriculture's savings to Western industry	Share of Western industry's savings to agriculture	Share of Western savings to East	Share of Eastern savings to West
1870	—	0·100	—	0·200
1875	0·027	—	—	0·092
1880	0·071	—	—	0·031
1885	0·094	—	0·047	—
1890	0·163	—	0·084	—
1895	0·217	—	0·081	—
1900	0·272	—	0·050	—
1905	0·282	—	0·033	—
1910	0·223	—	0·013	—

ization. That is, during the 1880s, agriculture generates a savings surplus in the Midwest and that surplus is utilized to finance industrial capital formation. Nevertheless, the model predicts that even as late as 1890 more than 80 percent of farm savings is reinvested. Beginning with the early 1890s, the share of farm savings reinvested declines to very low levels. This downward trend is reversed only with the prosperous farm conditions prior to World War I. Of equal interest is the role of Eastern savings in financing capital formation in the Midwestern non-farm sector. In the early 1870s, the model suggests that approximately 20 percent of the savings generated in the Northeast is transferred to the Western railroad network, urban capital formation, industrial capacity expansion and farm capital accumulation. This share declines markedly during the 1870s and early 1880s. In fact, the position of these two regions is reversed by the mid-1880s and the Midwest begins to finance the booming industrial expansion in the East. The share of Midwestern savings transferred to the East never assumes large proportions and the largest percentage shares are produced in the late 1880s and early 1890s.

These intersectoral financial flows respond, of course, to net rate of return differentials. The persistence of these differentials is an indication of the magnitude of the quasi-rents to be earned from intermediating activity. During the 1870s, the opportunities for a perceptive Morgan or Gould to capture these quasi-rents and to accumulate a financial fortune were clearly quite impressive. The model generates regional industrial differentials, *over and above* τ, as much as 1·5 percent in some years. The differential between Midwestern agriculture and the East was even higher. Surely these are useful proxies for 'market failure' and they have very important implications for late nineteenth-century development.

The immediate post-Civil War years have long been identified by the historian as a period of very impressive industrialization. Fogel has shown that industrialization rates during the period 1869–74 were exceeded only by 1844–9 and 1879–84.[23] It now appears that these *ex post* rates of industrialization are less a measure of American success and more a measure of failure. The argument up to this point suggests that America over-industrialized during the period, starved agriculture for capital, and, as a result, suppressed aggregate growth by using resources poorly. In short, the aggregate productivity of capital was lower in the late 1860s and early 1870s than it would have been under optimal resource allocation. The same could be said of industry in the Midwest. Not only was America undergoing inefficient (excessively rapid) industrial growth but too much of it was centered in the East.

The magnitude of the market failure and the quantitative importance of this suboptimal growth performance is approximated in section 6.4, but before implementing that experiment note that these conditions reverse by the late 1870s. The conventional farm problem so typical of twentieth-century America appears as a permanent fixture with the 1880s, at least according to our model.[24] Only at that point does it become clear that there are too many resources in agriculture. In spite of heavy out-migration of labor and intersectoral transfers of current savings out of Midwest agriculture, net rate of return differentials persist: from 1895 to 1905, the differential is especially large, in some years approaching 7 percent! Once again the rate of structural change is far from optimal, but in the latter period the rate of industrialization is far too low. One wonders to what extent this market failure inhibited American growth. What was the cost in terms of growth foregone?

6.4 American growth with 'perfect' capital markets: the impact of market failure

Lance Davis has thrown down the following challenge:

> The classical model of resource allocation assumes that within any economy capital is perfectly mobile ...
> Such a model ... is not very useful for analyzing the process of economic growth.[25]
> ... a model based on the existence of ... interregional and interindustry capital immobilities provides a better explanation for American development ...[26]
> ... is it possible to measure the economic cost of [these] capital immobilities?[27]

This section attempts to respond to Davis's challenge. The following counterfactual is posed: Would American post-Civil War development have been significantly different under conditions of perfect capital mobility? Would aggregate output growth have been raised? Was 'market failure' in American capital markets serious? Did it inhibit or foster agricultural development in any important dimension? High farm mortgage rates in the Midwest were, after all, a source of farm complaint early in our period and it does reflect capital market disequilibrium and thus market failure. Was it, therefore, a legitimate source of farmer discontent, at least during the late 1860s and early 1870s? What about the importance of the more conventional farm problem as it begins to appear during the late 1870s and early 1880s?

The counterfactual world explored here is *not* one of perfect capital mobility, since it is still assumed that capital once in place cannot be transferred to another sector. Instead, the fictional world is one in which *savings* are perfectly mobile, where capital markets are 'fully integrated,' and financial asset transfers are costless. Yet the results may be the same: complete rate of return equalization may be achieved without requiring mobility of installed plant and equipment. To approximate a perfect capital market, the parameters in the interregional and intersectoral savings transfer functions are markedly changed. Recall from chapter 3 that the share of Eastern savings invested in Western assets is written as

$$\phi_{WE}(t) = 1 - e^{\mu[i^*(t)-\tau]},$$

where expectations on returns to investment are formed by

$$i^*(t) = i^*(t-1) + \left[1 - \epsilon\right]\{i_E(t) - \bar{i}_W(t) - i^*(t-1)\}.$$

Consider an 'approximate' world of perfect mobility where transaction costs fall to zero ($\tau = 0$), lags in adjustment are minimal ($\epsilon = 0.01$), and adjustment response per unit of time is very large ($\mu = 100$). How much more effective would such an ideal capital market be in producing net rate of return equalization? Table 6.2 supplies the answer. Two versions of the perfect capital market model are presented, both with and without technical change. The usefulness of the experiment without technical change will become clearer below. The initial capital market disequilibrium is eliminated very quickly in the counterfactual world and approximate interest rate equalization prevails during most of the four decades (Table 6.2A). The interregional savings flows necessary to achieve that result are very large (Table 6.2B): e.g., on the average, approximately 40 percent of Eastern savings is flowing West during the 1870s.

Table 6.2. *Measures of interregional capital market performance: near 'perfect' markets and 'actual' historical experience compared*

Table 6.2A. *Interest rate differentials*

| Year | $\bar{i}_W(t)/i_E(t)$ | | |
| | 'Perfect' market | | 'Actual' |
	Technical progress	No technical progress	
1870	1·41	1·41	1·41
1875	1·04	1·08	1·11
1880	1·00	1·02	·93
1885	·94	·93	·69
1890	·96	·95	·69
1895	·99	·99	·72
1900	1·00	1·01	·80
1905	·99	·99	·81
1910	·96	·98	·90

Table 6.2B.   *Intersectoral financial flows*

Year	'Perfect' market				'Actual'	
	$\phi_{WE}(t)$		$\phi_{EW}(t)$		$\phi_{WE}(t)$	$\phi_{EW}(t)$
	Technical progress	No technical progress	Technical progress	No technical progress		
1870	0·20	0·20	—	—	0·20	—
1875	0·43	0·60	—	—	0·09	—
1880	—	0·66	0·43	—	0·03	—
1885	—	—	0·58	0·54	—	0·05
1890	—	—	0·42	0·39	—	0·08
1895	—	—	0·09	0·12	—	0·08
1900	0·04	0·05	—	—	—	0·05
1905	0·02	0·10	—	—	—	0·03
1910	0·27	0·19	—	—	—	0·01

Table 6.3 presents four measures of structural performance which are especially relevant in evaluating our counterfactual experiment. The series labeled 'actual' refers, with one exception, to the simulation presented in chapter 4 thus capturing the immobility specifications characteristic of the American economy in the post-Civil War era. The series labeled 'perfect' refers to our counterfactual world of approximate perfect capital markets. Both models are examined under the assumption of no technical change in industry or agriculture. To simplify exposition, our analysis focuses on the industrial sector as a whole rather than on the regional detail of industrialization.

Table 6.3.   *Measures of structural performance: Near 'perfect' and 'actual' historical experience compared (assuming no technical change)*

Year	Capital share in agriculture		Employment share in agriculture		Capital–labor ratio in agriculture		Share of agricultural output in GNP	
	'Actual'	'Perfect'	'Actual'	'Perfect'	'Actual'	'Perfect'	'Actual'	'Perfect'
1870	0·479	0·479	0·493	0·493	100·0	100·0	0·358	0·358
1875	0·530	0·484	0·465	0·465	159·6	163·8	0·375	0·374
1880	0·551	0·503	0·482	0·479	219·6	184·7	0·399	0·387
1885	0·571	0·564	0·479	0·477	286·2	243·3	0·370	0·363
1890	0·556	0·518	0·462	0·466	338·4	260·0	0·355	0·342
1895	0·530	0·473	0·424	0·431	409·9	297·1	0·325	0·309
1900	0·486	0·303	0·372	0·355	499·0	300·3	0·279	0·242
1905	0·443	0·215	0·337	0·274	576·7	334·4	0·257	0·195
1910	0·418	0·206	0·315	0·222	672·1	477·0	0·305	0·218

Increased capital mobility has a profound effect on Midwestern agriculture. Although Table 6.3 is not sufficiently detailed to reveal it, during the early 1870s (and presumably the late 1860s as well) Midwestern agriculture was starved for credit and the capital–labor ratio was suppressed. This market failure generated lower relative rates of agricultural expansion, excessive rates of industrialization, lower land rents, and lower net farm income. These conditions reverse after the mid-1870s when the market failure is of the more conventional type where too many resources are retained in agriculture. This becomes especially apparent after 1890 (Table 6.3). By 1910, agriculture's share of the U.S. capital stock was twice that which would have prevailed under 'perfect' capital mobility. As a result, the agricultural capital–labor ratio was half again as large, the employment share in agriculture was 0.315 rather than 0.222, and the share of agriculture in commodity output was 0.305 rather than 0.281. Clearly, capital market imperfections *did* have a profound effect on the structural performance of the American economy. Yet an equally important issue is the extent to which capital market imperfections inhibited *aggregate* growth performance – that is, per capita income expansion. There are two potential influences to consider in this regard: (i) The once-over resource allocative effect which increases economy-wide capital productivity through a more efficient allocation of capital goods; (ii) The positive impact of the initial fall in the capital–output ratio on the rate of capital accumulation, given the savings rate.

These combined effects are estimated to have been very small. *GNP per worker from 1871 to 1875 would have been only 1 percent higher had 'perfect' capital mobility conditions prevailed.*[28] For that matter, the cumulative impact on American growth would have been trivial as well. The average per capita income figures for 1896–1900 are 5·013 and 5·012 for the 'actual' and 'perfect' models, respectively. This experiment is performed in the absence of technical change. Since total factor productivity growth was more rapid in the non-farm sector over most of these three decades, growth in per capita income would have been higher under a regime of perfect capital markets since after the mid-1870s agriculture is growing much too rapidly and the sector is absorbing an inefficiently large share of the economy's capital resources under the presence of capital immobility conditions. A quantitative assessment of these total factor productivity effects is treated separately in section 6.5.

The results of our analysis are likely to disturb the financial historian. Although the *structural* performance of the American economy is significantly influenced by capital market disequilibrium, it does not appear that interregional and interindustry capital immobilities significantly influenced *aggregate* growth. Yet the financial historian may have legitimate reservations. Our results thus far are, according to the financial historian, derived from a model which fails to account for the full range of potential influences associated with financial intermediation. In particular, it fails to capture the potential influence of income distribution on aggregate savings, and income distribution is profoundly affected by capital market imperfections.

6.5 Financial intermediation, aggregate savings and capital formation

Aggregate savings, surplus–deficit regions and interest elasticity

The financial historian has not restricted his attention solely to the impact of financial intermediation on resource allocation. On the contrary, the literature is replete with assertions suggesting that financial institutions can increase aggregate national savings as well. These assertions have never been tested.

An *a priori* case has often been made that optimizing households will save more at higher interest rates. Since the opposite case can be argued just as plausibly, the issue is an empirical one. Until very recently, the econometric evidence based on twentieth-century data has suggested little or no impact of interest rates on savings behavior.[29] There now appears to be some quantitative support for the view that the interest elasticity of savings is indeed positive,[30] at least when applied to the Goldsmith data 1897–1949. Is there reason to expect different results for the late nineteenth century? The answer is important since it relates directly to the economic historian's interest in financial intermediation. Reduced to its barest essentials, the improvement in financial intermediating activity makes available to those with 'potential' savings an attractive form of asset accumulation which otherwise would not exist:

> In addition to altering the form of saving, the evolution of certain financial institutions can also increase an economy's propensity to save. It is obvious that, to the *extent that saving is interest-elastic* (though recent studies . . . would tend to deny this premise), the rate of saving will be lower if the market is so sectored that investments offering the greatest returns are unable to make effective bids for new saving. More important, if one assumes (as appears highly likely) that there is an increasing risk to the saver associated with the growth of cash hoards, then an increase in hoards . . . would lead to a shift from saving to consumption, a shift that would not occur if the savers had a safe depository for their funds.[31]

Since non-bank financial intermediaries substitute *known* alternative assets for investments outside the saver's immediate knowledge and earning higher yields, intermediating activity raises the net effective rate of interest facing the potential saver. It is precisely for these reasons that economic historians place such great emphasis on bank and non-bank financial intermediation as a means by which aggregate national saving is raised.[32] Furthermore, the spatial dimension of the financial intermediating thesis has been stressed in American economic historiography:

> Foremost among the features of the 19th century economy that appear to have had an important effect on savings at that time, but which Goldsmith did not find important in the 20th century, was the absolute and relative growth of financial intermediation ... there is a strong likelihood that in the context of American development the transfer of finance from deficit to surplus areas increased the volume of savings.[33]

Davis and Gallman note that by 1880 the West was served by fairly sophisticated local intermediaries and thereafter these local markets were being integrated by the penetration of commercial paper. They then argue that these indirect securities reduced variance in yield to savers, and since nineteenth-century savers were primarily concerned with safety, then increased savings should have resulted from improved intermediation. Yet at the same time, these developments tended to raise interest rates in surplus regions and lower them in deficit areas. What would have been the *net* effect on aggregate savings? The issue can be resolved only with evidence on the interest elasticity of savings. Davis and Gallman argue *a priori* that savings were far more interest inelastic in the West (the deficit region) than in the East (the surplus region). There is no empirical evidence or compelling theoretical argument in favor of their proposition, or any competing proposition for that matter. If instead we assume identical (and constant) interest elasticity of saving in the two regions, then we have the result appearing in Figure 6.4. The amount of required transfer necessary to equalize regional interest rates (if we ignore 'normal' transaction costs) will be somewhat greater than the case depicted above in Figure 6.2 since local saving is contracted in the deficit region and expanded in the surplus region in response to interest rate convergence.

The questions suggested by the literature on financial history warrant answers. How did financial intermediation affect aggregate savings? Did improvements in financial intermediating activity increase national savings? Would savings rates have been higher under conditions of perfect capital markets?

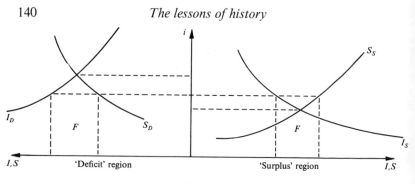

Figure 6.4

The determinants of post-Civil War American capital formation

The American economic historian's great interest in the development of financial intermediaries during and after the Civil War
decade may be motivated by the fascinating puzzle discussed in
chapters 1 and 5. Recent research has documented a rise in the
gross domestic savings rate between the 1850s and 1870s of impressive proportions. Why did the savings rate rise during the Civil War
decade? Earlier in this book we suggested an explanation which
ignores financial intermediation. This section raises a different
issue: how do we explain its relative stability up to the 1890s and
the subsequent increase up to World War I? The emphasis which
Gallman and Davis place on interregional financial intermediating
activity during the post-Civil War period is surely motivated by
these issues. Yet, by asserting regional differentials in interest elasticity perhaps they are proving too much. It may instead be sufficient
to argue the presence of an interest elastic response of saving but
non-specific to regions.

We have seen that both in historical fact and in the simulation
reported in chapter 4 the effective farm mortgage rate declines
precipitously after 1870, the Midwest 'city' rate declines moderately,
while the Eastern rate is relatively stable. These movements are
consistent with the evidence that Midwest farms became far more
reliant on external sources of finance as the late nineteenth century
progressed. These trends also suggest a negative influence on aggregate saving, at least until the late 1890s after which all effective
interest rates rise. Could there have been offsetting influences from
the early 1860s to the early 1890s which produced the stability in
aggregate savings rates? One obvious candidate is the functional
distribution of income. A fall in labor's share during the late nineteenth century may have tended to increase the aggregate savings
rate given the general acceptance of the proposition, at least on

twentieth-century data, that savings rates are lower out of wage and salary income. This would generate the required offsetting influence to that of declining interest rates up to the 1890s. An alternative device for capturing these distributional effects is to postulate lower savings rates out of farm income than non-farm income. There is considerable twentieth-century evidence supporting this view[34] and it is consistent with the fact that labor's share is higher in the nineteenth-century farm than the non-farm sector.

We have emphasized the tentative and untested nature of the hypotheses which have appeared in the historical literature on financial intermediation and capital accumulation. The empirical results which are reported below are equally tentative and exploratory. In that spirit, the model in chapter 3 will now be revised. Let the savings function for each sector be of the form

$$s_{ij}(t) = S_{ij} \, i_{ij}(t)^{\eta},$$

where η is a constant interest elasticity common to all sectors and regions. Savings rates may vary across sectors (regions) due to variance in interest rates or due to differences in the distribution of income within sectors as it is reflected in S_{ij}. The aggregate savings rate is

$$s(t) = \left[S_{AW} i_{AW}(t)^{\eta} \right] v_{AW}(t) + \left[S_I i_{IW}(t)^{\eta} \right] v_{IW}(t) + \left[S_I i_{IE}(t)^{\eta} \right] v_{IE}(t),$$

where $v_{ij}(t)$ is an income share $(\sum_j \sum_i v_{ij}(t) = 1)$ and the intercept on the savings function is the same in each regional non-farm sector. How do we 'estimate' the parameters of this savings function? We have 1870 estimates of $i_{ij}(t)$, $v_{ij}(t)$ and $s(t)$. Absolutely no historical information is available on the value of η. If we assume it to be unity, then Goldsmith's data for the period 1897–1913 would supply us with implied values for S_{AW} and S_I. 'For the first sixteen years of the period studied by Goldsmith (1897–1913) ... the farm sector's savings ratio was only 2·7 percent.'[35] Assuming $\eta = 1$ and given the average real farm mortgage rate prevailing during those sixteen years, a value for S_{AW} can be derived. An estimate of S_I can then be selected which implies a national savings rate of 18 percent in 1870. None of these parameter values are hard estimates, but if our new savings specification produces a reasonably accurate prediction of $s(t)$ from 1870 to World War I it would certainly argue for its plausibility.

The results of this experiment are presented in Table 6.4. Model II is identical to the one developed in chapter 3 except that we now have the new savings specification. The revised model yields a predicted savings rate which conforms fairly closely with the historical estimates.

Table 6.4. *Share of capital formation in GNP*

Period	Gallman–Davis	Model II (with endogenous savings)
1869–78	0·18	0·18
1874–83	0·18	0·18
1879–88	0·19	0·18
1884–93	0·20	0·19
1889–98	0·20	0·19
1894–1903	0·20	0·20

Source: Gallman and Davis, 'The Share of Savings and Investment in Gross National Product,' table 1, col. (2), p. 2.

Both series rise only very gradually over the three decades and both terminate with an average gross savings rate of 0·20 in 1894–1903. These results suggest the potential of future research on this form of the savings specification.

This experiment has generated one plausible explanation of American saving rate behavior after the Civil War. The explanation accounts for the relative stability in the savings rate up to the late 1880s and the moderate rise thereafter. After the episodic rise in savings rates during the Civil War decade, the maturing American economy was faced with two *offsetting* pressures on the aggregate savings rate: (i) the negative effect of declining rates of return during the Great Depression and (ii) the positive effect of industrialization, and the concomitant shift in the functional distribution of income away from labor (the farm sector), which favored a rise in aggregate savings rates. Nowhere in this accounting have we found it necessary to appeal to changes in savings habits.

This explanation for savings rate behavior after 1870 is consistent with our analysis of the episodic rise in capital formation rates between the 1850s and the 1870s presented in chapters 1 and 5. There we appealed to an unusual combination of factors which produced the epochal discontinuity of Northern savings rates following the Civil War. Federal debt retirement fostered an increase in the share of private savings in GNP, but this influence diminishes in importance later in the nineteenth century. A decline in the relative price of investment goods reinforced this trend, but this influence also diminishes over time as the price ratio is relatively stable after the 1870s. Finally, real interest rates in the late 1860s and during the 1870s are far higher than in the ante bellum period. This surely must have contributed to the high savings shares following the Civil War decade. On the other hand, the rate of industrialization almost ceased during the Civil War decade since the manufacturing share in total commodity output rose only from 32 to 33 percent in that decade. Thus, a positive distributional effect normally associated with industrialization was not present in the 1860s. Since federal debt retirement and relative price behavior were no longer influential on the private saving rate after the 1870s, trends in the savings ratio were left to be influenced by real interest rate and distributional effects. These were offsetting up to the 1890s and stability in the savings rate was observed as a result. After the 1890s and with the termination of the Great Depression, rapid industrialization coincides with rising real interest rates and the savings rate resumes its upward trend as a consequence.

In summary to the extent that our interpretation of American savings behavior is correct, then a further source of the Great Depression has been uncovered: not only did the decline in the net rate of return on capital over the three decades following the Civil War imply a rising capital–output ratio and thus declining rates of capital accumulation, but the fall in the net rate of return also restrained the savings rate from rising in response to rapid industrialization. The implications of this explanation of aggregate savings behavior certainly may be very important. Counterfactual analyses which confront the *dynamic* process of American development will surely be influenced by these competing savings specifications. This is especially true of those issues dealing with the impact of financial intermediation on American growth.

The role of capital market integration once again

In section 6.4 we concluded that although capital immobilities did indeed have a pronounced impact on American structural performance, they did not seriously influence aggregate growth rates. That conclusion followed under the assumption of constant savings shares and no technical change. The same counterfactual is once again posed but this time savings rates are determined endogenously according to the specification discussed in the preceding section. Furthermore, the counterfactual is posed in the presence of observed sectoral rates of total factor productivity growth. Does our evaluation of capital market imperfections now change with the addition of these dynamic relations? It does indeed, so much so that little is left of the financial intermediation thesis, at least as it applies to late nineteenth-century American history.

Consider first the potential impact on aggregate savings of capital market integration. Our endogenous savings rate model has

$$s(t) = [S_{AW} i_{AW}(t)^\eta] v_{AW}(t) + [S_I i_{IW}(t)^\eta] v_{IW}(t) + [S_I i_{IE}(t)^\eta] v_{IE}(t).$$

Even given identical *sectoral* savings elasticity in response to sectoral interest rates, aggregate savings need not be left unaffected by the convergence in interest rates. From the expression for $s(t)$, the following elasticities can be readily derived:

$$e_{AW} = \frac{\partial s}{\partial i_{AW}} \cdot \frac{i_{AW}}{s} = \eta \left[\frac{S_{AW}(t)}{S(t)}\right] < 1,$$

$$e_{IW} = \frac{\partial s}{\partial i_{IW}} \cdot \frac{i_{IW}}{s} = \eta \left[\frac{S_{IW}(t)}{S(t)}\right] < 1,$$

$$e_{IE} = \frac{\partial s}{\partial i_{IE}} \cdot \frac{i_{IE}}{s} = \eta \left[\frac{S_{IE}(t)}{S(t)}\right] < 1,$$

$$e_{AW} < e_{IW}, \; e_{AW} < e_{IE}.$$

Since the total savings in each sector is less than total national savings, the elasticity of the national savings rate with respect to a given i_{ij} is less than unity. But since total Western farm savings are believed to be a small share of total national savings, the elasticity of the national savings rate with respect to i_{AW} is relatively low. Now *all* interest rates decline up to the mid-1890s, and on these grounds alone the aggregate savings rate is suppressed. In addition, however, capital market integration implied a *more* dramatic decline in farm mortgage rates, and relative stability in 'bond' rates. The net effect of capital market integration is to attenuate the downward pressure of national savings rates induced by the decline in the whole interest rate structure. These forces are indeed complex, and an *a priori* evaluation of the impact of 'perfect capital mobility' on national savings in our general equilibrium framework is difficult to sort out. Table 6.5 yields a numerical answer, however. Aggregate

Table 6.5. *Measures of performance: perfect capital markets and actual capital markets with technical change and endogenous savings*

Year	Employment share in agriculture		Share of agricultural output in GNP		Aggregate savings rate		Per capita income	
	Actual	Perfect	Actual	Perfect	Actual	Perfect	Actual	Perfect
1870	0·493	0·493	0·358	0·358	0·180	0·180	3·087	3·087
1875	0·457	0·465	0·423	0·454	0·191	0·193	3·246	3·293
1880	0·462	0·483	0·416	0·458	0·178	0·168	3·502	3·589
1885	0·451	0·480	0·381	0·415	0·182	0·177	4·012	4·082
1890	0·412	0·453	0·319	0·364	0·186	0·178	4·318	4·360
1895	0·356	0·396	0·267	0·297	0·195	0·186	4·603	4·653
1900	0·288	0·310	0·202	0·216	0·203	0·199	5·082	5·082
1905	0·234	0·247	0·166	0·183	0·207	0·206	5·255	5·251
1910	0·196	0·213	0·193	0·223	0·204	0·204	4·212	4·217

national savings rates, at least from 1880 to 1905, would have been slightly *lower* under a regime of 'fully integrated' national capital markets.

Now consider the result of this counterfactual experiment on industrialization. Recall that Gerschenkron, Cameron and others have asserted that '... if [capital markets] fail to function satisfactorily ... they can effectively prevent any significant degree of industrialization.'[36] We find the contrary in our counterfactual experiment. Both the employment share and the output share of agriculture would have been *higher* under perfect capital markets! This result is specific to American nineteenth-century development and cannot be generalized. Furthermore, the finding is only tentative since the underlying savings function has not been established with certainty. Yet the first two columns in Table 6.5 are certainly suggestive. Agriculture receives a positive stimulus from 1870 to 1875 since it was facing a relative credit scarcity in the early 1870s. But agriculture increases its favored position during the subsequent two decades relative to actual historical conditions. That is, rapid industrialization takes place in both regimes but while the agricultural employment share falls by 13·7 percentage points between 1870 and 1895, it would have fallen by only 9·7 percentage points had perfect capital markets prevailed. A partial explanation for this surprising result is that savings rates, and thus capital accumulation, would have been reduced under a regime of perfect capital markets. True, some minor per capita income gains would have resulted in the counterfactual world of perfect capital markets. The resource allocative gains exceed the growth losses over much of the period. Only by 1900 do per capita income levels become about equal.

This analysis may tend to raise more questions than it answers. It certainly argues for a careful reassessment of the traditional literature on financial intermediation. Comparative static analysis does indeed confirm the important impact which capital market imperfections may have on resource allocation, industrial output and employment shares, and other measures of economic structure. It does *not*, however, confirm the asserted importance of these capital market imperfections on national income levels. The 'social savings' of a perfect capital market would have been disappointing. When comparative *dynamics* are considered, the asserted beneficial aspects of financial intermediation are even more doubtful. Our hope is that the tentative experiments reported here will prod economic historians into a far more careful reassessment of the role of capital market integration and financial intermediation on American nineteenth-century development.

7
Farmers' Discontent and Agricultural Performance: Facts, Issues and an Agenda

We cannot hope to unravel the mystery of the Populists . . . but a careful analysis of farmers' behavior is surely the first step along the way.

Franklin Fisher and Peter Temin (1970)

7.1 An analytical history of Midwestern agriculture

This chapter explores the behavior of farm income, prices and land values during the post-Civil War period. This has not been the focus of the traditional literature. Instead, the economic historian has been preoccupied with farmers' discontent up to 1896. The traditional focus may seem appropriate given its social and political importance in American history. Yet, the literature contains no universal agreement on the economic position of the farmer in the late nineteenth century. Indeed, it is not at all clear that the root causes of discontent were primarily, let alone purely, economic since modern historical research has undermined the asserted association between economic variables and political discontent in the agricultural sector.[1] As a result, this book makes no attempt to argue that the farmer's protest can be found only or even mainly in his economic position. Our purpose is limited instead to analysis of the economic forces which influenced the performance of the Midwest farm sector 1870 to 1910.

Before we can proceed with an evaluation of the causes of agricultural performance, the historical facts must be established and on these there is still debate. What *was* the economic position of Midwestern farmers in the late nineteenth century and how well does the framework developed in chapter 3 capture it? Fundamental to the debate over agriculture's performance are four key economic indices: (i) the Midwestern commodity terms of trade; (ii) land values; (iii) capital gains as a component of farm income; and (iv) labor productivity growth in Midwestern agriculture. A revisionist position of farmers' discontent will be adopted in our review of the contemporary evidence, a position now held by most recent students of the period but one which contrasts sharply with the interpretation

146

still embedded in most conventional textbooks dealing with late nineteenth-century American agriculture. Since our interest is not confined to establishing the historical facts of the period, the present chapter serves only to set the stage for the analysis which follows later in the book.

7.2 The uncertain historical facts

The 'plight' of the farmer

The agrarian sector was in a continuous state of political and social unrest from the end of the Civil War to the mid-1890s. The South and Far West contributed in part to this movement, but in the early years of the period it clearly centered on the Midwestern wheat and corn growing regions where in fact the greatest legislative victories were won. Farmers' discontent was best articulated through the Grange, the Greenback Party and the various Wheels, Leagues and Alliances which merged into the Populist Party at the Omaha Convention in 1892.[2] The Grange reached peak membership in 1874 while by 1880 it had become politically insignificant. Yet its impact during that decade can be gauged by the appearance of state railroad legislation first in Illinois in 1870, Minnesota in 1871, and in 1874 for both Iowa and Wisconsin. Populism obtained its greatest following, at least on the Great Plains, during the 1890s. The 1892 elections produced unusual success for Populist candidates in Kansas, Nebraska and the Dakotas. Bryan's 1896 presidential campaign, of course, represented the climacteric for the Populists. The dissent rapidly disappears following 1896, and booming agricultural prices and land values are prominent up to World War I.

These two phases of agricultural performance, 1870–96 and 1896–1910, have attracted the continued interest of American historians. While farmers' organizations espoused a variety of goals, it seems clear that their primary focus was on economic issues.[3] Very early in the 1870s, the protest began to emphasize *parity* as a means by which the (assumed) secular decline in farm prices might be reversed. Farmers perceived a deterioration in the relative price of farm products and attributed the crisis, at least in part, to the monopoly pricing power of the suppliers of key farm inputs. This included the supply of transport services as well as the supply of farm credit. The railroads and Eastern capitalists were identified as the villains.

The complaints of the farmer appear to be the following: (i) the prices of agricultural products had fallen more markedly than for other goods, thus diminishing the farmer's real income position; (ii) railroads, middlemen and grain operators were using monopolistic practices to extract the gains from cost-reducing changes in transport and marketing; (iii) farmers faced usurious rates of interest and Eastern financial interests were able to set these rates through monopsonistic power; (iv) given the overall decline in the general price level during the Great Depression, the farmer suffered special difficulty faced as he was with fixed debt repayment commitments.[4] These were the farmers' complaints. What were the facts?

First, were the net barter terms of trade really moving against Midwest agriculture up to the mid-1890s? Since all prices were generally declining during the period, the existence of depressed agricultural prices after the 1860s can only be judged by movements in the *relative* price of farm products. Two such indices are presented in Table 7.1A and Figure 7.1: one measures the ratio of industrial to agricultural prices prevailing in the Midwest, while the other is a similar East coast index. The different trends are to be explained by the dramatic fall in transport rates on Eastern and Western traffic. (These will be discussed at greater length in chapter 9.) Figure 7.1 graphically supports the revisionist view that the relative price of agricultural goods did not decline; indeed, it was

Table 7.1A. *Relative commodity prices for East and West 1870–1910*

Year	West: $\dfrac{P_{IW}}{P_{AW}} \times 100$	East: $\dfrac{P_{IE}}{P_{AE}} \times 100$	Year	West: $\dfrac{P_{IW}}{P_{AW}} \times 100$	East: $\dfrac{P_{IE}}{P_{AE}} \times 100$
1870	125	50	1890	123	68
1871	138	70	1891	88	50
1872	153	77	1892	105	55
1873	154	68	1893	126	60
1874	132	62	1894	133	70
1875	116	54	1895	121	66
1876	114	52	1896	138	70
1877	112	54	1897	113	60
1878	132	61	1898	109	57
1879	122	58	1899	118	60
1880	114	62	1900	123	66
1881	90	52	1901	124	64
1882	91	53	1902	95	56
1883	111	53	1903	113	57
1884	114	58	1904	118	61
1885	117	56	1905	116	63
1886	120	55	1906	117	67
1887	117	56	1907	105	60
1888	102	52	1908	85	52
1889	127	67	1909	78	47
			1910	75	50

Source: appendix A, Table A.27.

149

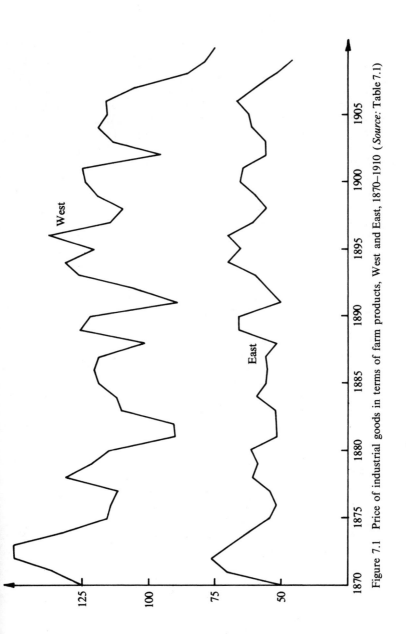

Figure 7.1 Price of industrial goods in terms of farm products, West and East, 1870–1910 (*Source:* Table 7.1)

rising in the Midwest. True, the relative price of farm products was stable in Eastern markets, but surely it was the terms of trade in the interior which counted as far as the Midwest farmer was concerned. There were, of course, marked fluctuations around this trend. The early 1870s, the late 1870s, the mid-1880s and the mid-1890s were periods of relatively depressed farm product prices in the Midwest. Yet an overall secular improvement in the Midwest is clear. Until very recently, this evidence was not very well understood by historians of the period.[5] Indeed, it was argued in chapters 1, 3 and 5 that this relative price behavior played a positive role in fostering rapid rates of capital accumulation. Since investment goods prices behaved like those of industrial goods in general, capital formation must have received a positive stimulus, forestalling an even more severe retardation in capital formation rates and thus diminishing the extent of the Great Depression. An example from Wisconsin should serve to make the point. The Wisconsin wheat spot price declined by 40 percent from 1881 to 1896.[6] Over the same fifteen years, and in spite of enormous quality improvements, the prices of the gang plow, the solid disc plow, the cultivator and the twine binder declined by at least as much and in some cases by more.[7] The source of this relative price improvement in the Midwest lay primarily in rapidly declining transport costs on Eastward grain trade (appendix A and chapter 9), rather than from market conditions in the East or Europe.

The discussion has been limited thus far to the period following 1870. It fails to take account of the Civil War decade. Although our analysis in subsequent chapters will continue to use 1870 as a starting point, an understanding of farm discontent may be seriously crippled by the exclusion of Civil War experience. Indeed, contemporary quantitative research on the Midwestern farm terms of trade often ignores the Civil War as a 'watershed' and a significant progenitor of agrarian discontent. Subsequent farm discontent may be seriously misunderstood as a result. Table 7.1B shows that the

Table 7.1B. *Relative wheat prices during the Civil War decade*

Year	Relative wheat price index	Year	Relative wheat price index
1860	1·61	1865	1·17
1861	1·60	1866	1·69
1862	1·34	1867	1·76
1863	1·23	1868	1·61
1864	1·01	1869	1·09

Source: Wholesale wheat prices divided by all commodity price index. *Historical Statistics*, E101 and E1, pp. 123–4 and 115.

relative price of wheat suffered a dramatic plunge between 1861 and 1869. True, relative wheat prices enjoyed a brief recovery in the three years following 1865, but the fact remains that it declined by 27 percent from 1861 to 1865 and by 32 percent from 1861 to 1869. This enormous deterioration in the farmer's market position was not rescued by interregional transport improvements until the late 1860s and the early 1870s. Is it any wonder that a ground swell of discontent rose when the ardor of wartime patriotism ebbed and the recovery up to 1868 was found to be only temporary? Furthermore, the striking correspondence between the permanent deterioration in the wheat farmer's terms of trade and war tariffs is hardly coincidence. In short, the Civil War is one potent source of farm discontent over prices. To ignore the war years and the impact of tariff legislation is to miss a primary cause of agrarian agitation in subsequent years.

Second, did the farmer face usurious interest rates? Whether the mortgage rates were 'usurious' or in fact monopsonistically influenced is an issue we cannot effectively confront although there is recent evidence suggesting the contrary.[8] The evidence appears to support the view that interest rates on comparable debt were higher in the Midwest than in the East, and higher especially for farm mortgages, at least in the 1870s and early 1880s. It was shown in chapters 4 and 6 that these differentials can be explained quite adequately by a competitive capital market model in disequilibrium: the simulation reproduces farm mortgage rates with considerable accuracy. In any case, both nominal and real interest rates on farm mortgages decline very sharply to 1890, remaining relatively stable to the mid–late 1890s. The real rate on farm mortgages declines from 17·0 to 7·6 percent in Illinois between 1870 and 1890 (Table 7.2). For the Midwest as a whole, they decline from 11·4 to 6·3 percent between 1880 and 1914. The high farm mortgage rates may have been a source of discontent in the late 1860s and 1870s, but they declined rapidly thereafter. The secular decline appears to be unrelated to any retreat from monopsonistic practices in the credit market.

Given the secular decline in the general price level, did the farmer suffer to the extent that he was faced with fixed repayment commitments? Of course he did, and he would have been obliged to have done so in any competitive capital market. The nominal interest rate loses all meaning as a measure of opportunity cost during a period of pronounced price change. The real interest rate is the appropriate measure of credit conditions facing the debtor or any firm seeking external financing. Surely Irving Fisher was correct in asserting that bond prices tend to be higher and nominal yields lower when commodity prices are falling since the increase in the real value of the principal is a return in addition to the

Table 7.2. *Real and nominal interest rates on Midwestern farm mortgages,*
1870–1900 (in percent)

Year	Illinois	Wisconsin	Nebraska	Iowa	Simulated $i_{AW}(t)$
			Nominal rates		
1870	9·6	8·0	10·5	9·5	
1880	7·8	7·2	9·1	8·7	n.a.
1890	6·9	5·9	7·8	7·0	
1900	5·8	4·9	6·3	5·5	
			Real rates		
1870	17·0	15·4	17·9	16·9	16·0
1880	11·4	10·8	12·7	12·3	9·6
1890	7·6	6·6	8·5	7·7	5·7
1900	4·3	3·4	4·8	4·0	3·8

Source: The nominal rates are taken from J. D. Bowman, 'Trends in Midwestern Farm Land Values, 1860–1900,' table II, chapter III, p. III–14. The real rates include the impact of the observed rate of price change, $\hat{p}(t)$, where the preceding five years is utilized as an average. The price data are based on the Warren–Pearson all commodity index. Under perfect certainty, the effective rate, $i(t)$, is related to the nominal rate by

$$i(t) = \frac{\hat{i}(t) - \hat{p}(t)}{1 + \hat{p}(t)}.$$

nominal rate of interest. These arguments seem to us so self-evident that throughout this book references to the historical interest rate are always to the *real* rate, i.e., the nominal rate adjusted by some approximation of 'expected' price changes. It seems clear that we find the traditional historians' concern with fixed repayment commitments very appropriate, but it was hardly necessary that a farmer have a high debt–asset ratio to yield that result.

Yet the 'revisionists' tend to minimize this concern with repayments.[9] They argue that since the average life of a farm mortgage ranged from three to five years, and since the terms could be renegotiated at that time, that the fixed repayment commitment could not have been a serious burden. We disagree. During the mid–late 1870s when prices were declining at a rate of 7 percent per annum, even a three-year contract would have engendered a severe 'hardship' on the farmer. Effective interest rates were far higher than nominal rates in the 1870s and 1880s, somewhat lower than nominal rates in the first decade of the twentieth century, and about equal to the nominal rate in the 1890s. The real interest rate was the relevant variable for farm decision-making and there is no doubt that it was very high indeed into the early 1880s.

Our focus, however, will be somewhat narrower in evaluating

Table 7.3. *Real and nominal interest rates on farm mortgages, Western states,*
1880–1914

Year	Region IV		Region V	
	Nominal	Real	Nominal	Real
1880	7·81	11·41	10·51	14·11
1889	7·14	7·84	8·96	9·66
1914	6·30	6·29	8·70	8·69

Source: L. Davis, 'Capital Mobility and American Growth,' table 1, p. 291 for
nominal rates. The real rates are derived using B.L.S. all commodity price index for
1904–14 and see note to Table 7.2 for earlier dates.
Region IV: Ohio, Indiana, Illinois, Michigan, Wisconsin, Minnesota, Iowa,
and Missouri. Region V: North Dakota, South Dakota, Nebraska, Kansas, Montana,
Wyoming, Colorado, New Mexico and Oklahoma.

the farmer's plight after 1870. Did land rents rise over the period?
Did the real income of Midwestern farmers improve up to the
1890s? If so, did their relative income position improve *vis-à-vis* the
remainder of the American economy? Were booming land values
the result of increasing net cash income per acre, of 'irrational'
speculation, or of other forces? While seeking answers to these questions, frequent comparisons will be made between the predictions
of the model developed in chapter 3 and historical fact, since we
hope to establish further support for the counterfactual analysis
contained in chapters 8, 9 and 10.

Labor productivity, rental incomes, land values and market failure

Measures of Midwestern labor productivity growth in agriculture
confirm the revisionist view of farm performance during this
period of agrarian protest. The results were not discussed in chapter
4, but the simulation predicts the following Midwestern farm performance from 1879 to 1899: in constant relative prices, farm income
grows at an annual rate of 1·44 percent. Compare this predicted
performance with actual historical experience. Fogel and Rutner
have estimated the per annum rate of real agricultural income per
worker growth for the North Central region to be 1·5 percent over
the same two decades.[10] The conformity between the predicted rate
of 1·44 percent and the observed rate of 1·5 percent once again
confirms the plausibility of our model. Note that this performance
closely approximates that for the economy as a whole (1·47 percent
documented by Gallman and 1·49 percent predicted by the model),[11]
negating any absolute or even relative deterioration thesis. Note
further that this rapid growth performance in Midwestern agricul-

ture is not shared elsewhere in American agriculture: comparable statistics for the North Atlantic and the South are 0·2 and 0·9 percent, respectively.

A key to understanding the position of the Midwest farm sector is the behavior of land values. Since there is so much confusion in the historical literature on the determinants of land values, it might be helpful to dwell on the economics at this point. The agriculture production function assumed in chapter 3 is

$$Q_{AW} = BK_{AW}^{\beta_K} L_{AW}^{\beta_L} R^{\beta_R}, \beta_K + \beta_L + \beta_R = 1.$$

Land's marginal physical product can be expressed as

$$\frac{\beta_R Q_{AW}}{R} = \beta_R \left\{ \frac{B[K_{AW}]^{\beta_K}[L_{AW}]^{\beta_L} R^{\beta_R}}{R} \right\}.$$

Since agriculture was surely competitive, the annual gross rental price of land, d, should be equated with land's marginal value product: i.e.,

$$d = P_{AW} \left[\beta_R \frac{Q_{AW}}{R} \right].$$

The behavior of land rents over time can thus be decomposed into

$$\dot{d} = \dot{P}_{AW} + \dot{Q}_{AW} - R;$$

the secular movement in land rents are jointly determined by changes in farm product prices and yields. Although agricultural prices and the land under cultivation are given exogenously in our formulation of the problem, farm output is endogenous and dependent upon the rate of acreage expansion and agriculture prices, among other variables. Nevertheless, it is certainly quite possible that the movements in farm product prices and increments in farms under cultivation would be offsetting so that stability or a decline in land rents would be observed should everything else have remained constant. But everything else was *not* constant, since farm employment expanded and labor was being equipped with increasingly larger doses of mechanical devices. Even if yields and thus rents per acre were stable, it does not necessarily follow that imputed farm wages were stable. For an owner-operator, an arrangement common to the Midwest, the farmer's annual earnings are determined by the sum of imputed rents and imputed wages. He may, of course, utilize hired labor, but the farmer's imputed wage can be accurately gauged by the price of hired labor. The farm wage can be derived from the production function:

$$w_{AW} = \left[\frac{P_{AW} Q_{AW}}{L_{AW}} \right] \beta_L.$$

Using our expression for rents, the farm wage can be rewritten as

$$w_{AW} = d \left[\frac{R}{L_{AW}}\right] \left[\frac{\beta_L}{\beta_R}\right].$$

We can readily see from this expression that stability in land rental income per acre does not necessarily imply stability in the farmer's imputed wage nor, as a result, stability in his annual income. The key lies in the behavior of $[R/L_{AW}]$, acreage per farm worker. Since there is a tendency towards increased farm size and farm mechanization throughout the post-Civil War period, rising real wages may have been quite consistent with stable yields and rents.

Stability in land rents certainly does not necessarily imply stability in land values either. The price of an acre of improved land must be distinguished from the annual rental price. Denote this purchase price, or current land value, by V. The purchase price is derived from conventional present value calculus, and if farmers (or speculators) use a naïve estimator of future rents wherein $d(t)$ is equal to current rents, d, then

$$V = \sum_{t=0}^{T} \frac{d(t)}{(1 + i)^t} = d \sum_{t=0}^{T} \frac{1}{(1 + i)^t}.$$

If land is treated as an asset with infinite life and a permanent income stream, then the above expression for land values becomes even simpler:

$$V = \frac{d}{i}.$$

The behavior of land values over time can thus be decomposed into productivity and interest rate effects:

$$\dot{V} = \dot{P}_{AW} + \dot{Q}_{AW} - \dot{R} - i.$$

This simple algebra helps clarify the confused literature on the behavior of land values during the Great Depression. Secular movements in land values are jointly influenced by changes in farm product prices, yields, and real interest rates. Since land yields increase moderately over the period 1870–96, relative farm prices generally improve (at least in the Midwest), and real farm mortgage rates decline, land values can be expected to rise on all three counts. The interesting issue, however, is the quantitative contribution of each of these forces to the secular boom in land values up to 1914.

Given information at census dates on land values and interest rates, the behavior of imputed land rents on farmer-owned land can be inferred: the latter variable is documented only sparsely for the nineteenth century since the owner-operator status was so predominant in the Midwest.[12] John Bowman performs this decomposition analysis for Midwestern wheat and corn counties using *nominal* rates of interest and finds that 'farm land income for wheat and corn farming combined trended upward in the Midwest for the 1860s and 1880s, downward for the 1870s and was about constant for the 1890s.'[13] Since the *real* rate of interest fell much more sharply than the nominal rate over these three decades, Bowman has presumably overstated the rise in farm land income per acre. When the calculation is performed using real interest rates, the net result is a remarkable long-run stability in imputed cash rents per acre for the Midwest as a whole and for all grains combined.

The model developed in chapter 3 generates a similar prediction. Predicted land rents per acre increase very little over the four decades as a whole in Table 7.4; they increase in the Midwest by 0·5 percent per annum from 1870 to 1910. Our predictions within decades are, with one exception, also consistent with Bowman's findings: a very modest rise in the land rental rate during the 1880s, a moderate fall during the 1890s, and stability up to 1910. The exception appears to be the 1870s since the model predicts a strong improvement in imputed land rents during the decade.

Had the farm mortgage rate remained constant, and had farmers (speculators) maintained the naïve expectation that current land rents would prevail indefinitely into the future, real land values in the Midwest would have exhibited only a mild rise between 1870 and 1895. In fact, they almost *double* between 1870 and 1900; they increase by two and one half times up to 1910! This pronounced secular boom in land values has thus often been viewed by economic historians as a 'paradox' of the Great Depression in American agriculture. Is it necessary to appeal to irrational speculation in accounting for this land value boom? Certainly not, for it can be readily explained by the movements in real farm mortgage rates.

Table 7.4. *Midwestern average land rents, in constant prices, 1860–1910*

Year	Bowman	Model (1870 = 100)
1870	⎫	100·0
1875	⎬ falling	109·0
1880	⎫	118·2
1885	⎬ rising	127·3
1890		131·8
1895	⎫ stable or	127·3
1900	⎬ mildly falling	118·0
1905	⎫ rising	119·0
1910	⎬	122·7

Source: See text.

Table 7.5. *Midwestern land values, 1870–1910*

Year	Tostlebe (1910–14 prices)	Current $d(t)$	Model (1910–14 prices): $V(t)$ Index using	
			$1/3 \sum_{t=-2} d(t)$	$1/7 \sum_{t=-6} d(t)$
1870	$17·1	$12·3	—	—
1875	—	13·4	$12·9	—
1880	18·4	18·4	18·4	$18·4
1885	—	26·9	29·6	28·7
1890	30·0	34·2	30·4	32·9
1895	—	39·7	30·4	32·3
1900	30·5	46·3	28·5	24·6
1905	—	48·1	45·4	36·1
1910	47·7	29·6	34·2	29·1

Source: See text.

Mild increases in land rents were translated into massive rises in land values by the 50 percent decline in real interest rates between 1870 and 1895. A concrete example may serve to make the point clearer. Over the three decades 1870 to 1900, our predicted land values rise by 276 percent. This can be seen by reference to the second column of Table 7.5. Had effective farm mortgage rates been constant the figures in Table 7.4 imply that land values would have increased by only 18 percent. It appears that land rents had little to do with the movements in land values up to 1900.[14]

Land speculation has been stressed in the traditional literature as a key explanation of rising land values during a period of agrarian discontent and 'depression.' Does it enrich our understanding of the underlying forces at work in Midwestern agriculture? Certainly it does, although we need not appeal to the isolated cases of 'mania,' like Kansas in the late 1880s, to get that result:

> In 1886 and 1887, many agents had so many offers from Eastern lenders that they could not get enough mortgages to cover them, yet the rates of interest remained high ... The Western farmer was tempted to extravagant specula-tion ... In other places speculation ran 'hog wild' ... There were similar booms in many smaller towns. Cities and towns were seized with a mania for public buildings and other improvements ... Railroads were built whether there was any need for them or not ... And then the pretty bubble was pricked.[15]

Characterizations of *local* speculative activity surely cannot be applied to Midwest land values as a whole. Yet, we can hardly expect our naïve expectations model to hold either, and we certainly must agree that farmers holding land were holding an income-earning asset with an explicit price. To the extent that they failed to sell this asset, they were in fact speculating that its price would rise, and in the long run they were indeed correct in their judgement:

> Historians have . . . erred by using the term 'speculator' to characterize a person who buys solely with the intent to resell and not to cultivate. The objection to this usage is that *in a private property system every owner of an asset is necessarily a speculator* in the sense that he bears the risk of reductions in the value of the asset but hopes that the value will rise.[16]

Some time ago, Chambers explored the determinants of farm land values for the first two decades of the twentieth century.[17] Net cash rents per acre were excellent predictors of farm land values in Chambers' study (applied to a period of effective interest rate stability), but only when projected rents were based on the experience of the preceding seven to ten years. In Table 7.5, a similar calculation is made using our simulated nineteenth-century data. The third column projects future rents based on the average of current rents and those of the preceding two years; the fourth column utilizes the preceding six years. The result is a much improved conformity between the model's predicted Midwest land values and those reported by Tostlebe. In fact, the model almost exactly replicates the behavior of land values during the 1880s and 1890s. The fluctuations from 1900 to 1910 are also much more like Tostlebe's estimates. Unfortunately the requisite data for the late 1860s are not available to explore the impact of the Chambers' model on the predicted $V(t)$ series for the 1870s.

The main conclusions of this section can now be summarized. First, the model appears to predict accurately the relative stability of real land rents in the Midwest up to 1895 and beyond. Furthermore, it reproduces their historical rise during the 1880s and 1900s, and the fall during the 1890s. The *causes* of this movement have yet to be explored, but at least, it has been decomposed arithmetically into average land productivity and price effects. Second, the model has reproduced with considerable accuracy the movements in land values. Part of the actual historical behavior can be explained by a simple weighted average of past land rents in generating expectations about future rents. There seems to be little scope for 'land mania' in explaining the behavior of land value movements beyond this plausible expectations framework, at least for the Midwest as a whole. Third, sharply rising real land values during a period of 'Great Depression' when real land rents were relatively stable is not at all paradoxical. This historical result can be easily reconciled by reference to the impressive fall in real farm mortgage rates up to 1895.

Fourth, note that farm rental income per acre rises at a rate far below other indices of income performance in the American economy up to 1895. Over the same period, the model shows real wages in the Midwest non-farm sector rising by 100 percent while per capita income increases by about 70 percent. Since a large source of net farm income accruing to the owner-operator is the annual rental flow, augmented by the imputed farm wage, perhaps this *was* a cause for discontent. The rental income flow accruing to owner-operators could have been increased by farm mechanization, yet the high interest rate surely inhibited the Midwestern farmer's adoption of more capital intensive technology. Perhaps he did not fully appreciate the disequilibrating conditions in the capital market which produced that result, but the farmer was certainly willing to advocate monetary reform to reduce the discrepancy between nominal and real rates of interest.[18]

These issues, however, define only a small portion of the problem. To what extent does the decline in the farm–non-farm effective interest rate differential diminish one source of discontent? To what extent was the farmer 'starved' for resource inputs very early in the period, inhibiting his expansion and thus favoring the non-farm sector? Serious suboptimality of American development is implied in that last question. Per capita income in farming was certainly less than that of non-agriculture from 1870 to 1910, even as it is today. Yet this observation is irrelevant in evaluating the optimality of resource allocation then or now. As long as production functions have different parameters sector by sector, average productivities may vary widely even if marginal value factor productivities are equalized. To put it differently, even if wages and labor's marginal value productivities are equalized, average labor productivity and thus per capita income may still be lower in agriculture. It is of some relevance to remind the reader of twentieth-century experience: 'One of the most widely-accepted conclusions regarding the distribution of income in the United States is that farm income has been substandard for many years.'[19] Farm discontent since 1929 has been vociferous, not unlike that of the pre-1896 period. Yet Christensen's recent research finds little evidence to support the modern discontent: '. . . it is clear that the returns to farm factors of production measure up very well. Furthermore, farm returns appear to be comparable with nonfarm returns regardless of the levels of government expenditures ... This would imply that the massive government expenditures in farming have done little but encourage the misallocation of resources'.[20] How would the farm sector stand up to similar scrutiny in, say, the 1870s?

The evidence presented in chapter 6 was indirect and produced by the model itself, but in Table B.5 it appears that the gross rate of return to agricultural capital far exceeds that of Eastern capital throughout the 1870s. If this accounting is supported by future research, the implications are important: resource allocation was noticeably non-optimal in the 1870s, since the farm sector was being starved for resources. The impressive rate of industrialization and urbanization in the 1870s, commonly viewed as evidence of American achievement, may reflect *failure* rather than success. Farmers may have been protesting this market failure.[21] This characterization is somewhat novel in terms of American historiography. Readers familiar with contemporary less developed economies will find a striking similarity. Development economists are now generally agreed that rapid post-World War II industrialization in much of Asia and Latin America has been non-optimal. Furthermore, the complaints voiced by the agricultural sector in those economies repeats almost word for word the farmer discontent of late nineteenth-century United States: credit is too difficult to secure, especially for the small farmer; the large farmer is reaping all the gains at the expense of the small; middlemen are robbing the farmer of his just share of the urban market price; macro policy is biased against the farm sector. A century has failed to change much in the list of grievances.

Conditions reverse after the early 1880s and it appears that the industrial sector becomes the victim of market failure. Not surprisingly, the voice of agrarian protest in the Midwest rapidly diminishes. Note, that these capital market improvements do not extend to the South: nor does farmers' protest diminish there.

Capital gains and entrepreneurial income

We have thus far emphasized one potential source of farmer discontent. Since the Midwestern farmer was an owner-operator, his net farm income (or farm entrepreneurial income) was composed of imputed rental income to his farm land and imputed wage income to his (and his family's) labor input. Imputed rental income grew at a rate far below the rate of increase in non-farm wages or per capita income in the Midwest. He may have been aware of this disparity in performance and the widening gap between himself and the remainder of the American economy, and attributed it to market failure and voiced this and other complaints through political action. Yet, few participants in the farmer discontent debate have focused on the changing wealth position of the Midwestern farmer. Rising real land values imply capital gains to those holding ownership of the land asset: 'Farmers obviously took such capital gains into account in deciding on their best course of action. A failure to consider capital gains as part of income has marred much discussion of the relative income of the farmer; that such gains were typically "automatically reinvested" is beside the point.'[22] In 1890, only 38·7 percent of the farms in the North Central area were mortgaged, and these were mortgaged up to only 35 percent of their value.[23] Yet over 60 percent of the value of physical farm assets was in land for that year.[24] On the average, the Midwestern farmer owned the majority of his land and land values increase by impressive amounts from 1870 to 1900: i.e., in Wisconsin they imply an average rate of capital gains in excess of 2·5 percent per annum (Table 7.6). Fogel and Rutner find similar rates of capital gains for the 1870s and 1880s.[25] An estimate for the contemporary farm sector (1929–69) is less than 1 percent per annum.[26] Even by contemporary standards, farmers' capital gains were enormous during the so-called Great Depression and age of Agrarian Discontent. Were this the *only* source of real income gains for the farmer, it would represent an impressive income improvement for the farmer even relative to his urban counterparts. Yet both conventional national income accounting *and* the farmer himself would seem to ignore this component of actual income. How else is one to explain Agrarian Discontent during this period? After all, the farmer wishes to farm and he can only convert capital gains to consumable income by selling the land and leaving the farm. This they were, and are, reluctant to do before retirement. Yet, this argument is not very satisfactory since the farmer can always borrow using his land as collateral before retirement. The Agrarian Paradox persists for another reason: many observers of contemporary underdeveloped economies have claimed that

Table 7.6. *Real land values of wheat farms in wheat counties, 1870–1900*

State	Census date			
	1870	1880	1890	1900
Illinois	$28·80	$33·90	$53·90	$62·20
Indiana	36·80	39·50	54·60	56·00
Iowa	21·60	24·50	36·30	55·30
Kansas	15·10	13·20	24·80	21·70
Michigan	43·80	49·30	59·00	51·80
Minnesota	19·54	20·82	30·40	38·80
Missouri	21·90	18·40	32·54	38·70
Nebraska	14·00	12·50	25·20	27·00
Ohio	46·30	55·70	64·00	60·20
Wisconsin	28·40	31·90	48·00	59·30

Source: Bowman, 'Trends in Midwestern Land Values, 1860–1900,' Appendix table A–2, pp. 95ff. The deflator used is the Warren–Pearson general wholesale price index.

savings and wealth accumulation motives are satisfied equally well by increased land values as by land improvements or other forms of new capital accumulation.[27] Given the enormous rise in farm land values up to 1910, perhaps this is one reason why Goldsmith finds the rural savings rate – that is, a rate based on income *excluding* capital gains – so low after 1897, i.e., less than 3 percent. The co-existence of impressive capital gains in agriculture and discontent remains for us an intriguing paradox.

7.3 *Ex post data versus counterfactuals: the agenda*

This chapter has attempted to unravel a ball of conflicting and confusing evidence regarding farm performance between 1870 and 1910. The *ex post* data have been rationalized and further evidence supporting the plausibility of our model of late nineteenth-century development has been collected. Yet, the underlying forces of agricultural development are not uncovered by exploiting *ex post* data alone nor will they ever be. Counterfactual analysis is required to confirm these insights.

The three chapters following depart from a rationalization of farmers' discontent, and turn instead to the more fundamental issue: what were the determinants of farm performance during the late nineteenth century? Using the historical model developed in chapter 3, the determinants of farm performance are disentangled by posing explicit counterfactuals. Chapter 9 exhumes the railroad issue. It explores the impact of transport costs on Midwestern agriculture and American industrialization by examining a counterfactual economy which maintains the transport cost conditions prevailing in 1870. By so doing, we are able to derive insight into the impact of the rails on the farmers' terms of trade, on regional trade creation and Midwestern industrialization–urbanization, on Midwestern land values, on the efficient operation of the interregional capital market, on farm wages and on off-farm migration. Social savings is only of incidental concern but the experiment does yield an explicit estimate of the output foregone in a world of no transport cost improvements. Chapter 10 uses a similar methodology but the focus there is on the impact of world market conditions.

Two further issues are confronted in chapter 8. What was the impact of declining land expansion – the disappearing 'frontier' – during the late nineteenth century? Not only is the impact of the frontier on agriculture explored, but its effect on industrialization, regional growth and real wages in industry is also estimated. This topic hardly needs motivational defense since it has occupied economic historians for some time. In addition, chapter 8 investigates the impact of agricultural productivity growth on the American economy as a whole as well as on the Midwest. This topic has also been a favorite one for economic historians (and development economists) who have searched for the causes of farm discontent, for the sources of the boom in farm land values, for the explanation of off-farm migration, and for the underlying causes of industrialization. Our results are often at variance with conventional wisdom.

8

Elements of Agricultural Performance: Land Expansion and Productivity Growth

> I cannot see how one can know in exact quantitative terms . . . something that actually never happened. The result of such investigations is . . . fictitious history – that is, not really history at all.
>
> Fritz Redlich (1968)

> It does require maturity to realize that models are to be used but not to be believed.
>
> Henri Theil (1971)

8.1 Land expansion, industrialization, and the Turner thesis

Comparative statics and the issues

The impact of land expansion on national income. American nineteenth-century growth has always been viewed by economic historians as unique at least in comparison with European experience. After all, in contrast with European development America followed a path of extensive resource exploitation. This resource 'abundance' played a role in shaping American growth and her institutions. First, the availability of unexploited natural resources at the frontier, awaiting complementary investments in labor intensive farm preparation, ensured a more equal distribution of land assets. As long as improved farm acreage remained the predominant asset in America's wealth stock, a relative equality in the distribution of landholdings (outside of the South) implied a relative equality in income distribution as well. Second, these conditions influenced the creation and development of a unique set of political, legal and economic institutions geared to the exploitation of that endowment. Third, it fostered an export specialization and foreign capital commitment to an expanding transport system to facilitate that trade. Fourth, 'the seemingly limitless availability of cheap land'[1] must have contributed at least in part to the impressive aggregate growth rates achieved by America in the last three-quarters

164

of the nineteenth century. If an abundant resource base and a rapid expansion in the arable land stock had an important impact on the nineteenth-century American economy, then as a corollary a reduction in the growth in the land stock must also have influenced American growth performance. What then was the impact of the 'disappearing frontier'?

A quantitative answer to this question was supplied in chapter 5, but only at a highly aggregative level. The focus there was on the Great Depression up to 1896. The counterfactual experiment suggested that the retardation in per capita growth rates up to the turn of the century would have persisted even had the growth in improved farmland in the Midwest maintained the high levels achieved in the early 1870s. Furthermore, the GNP per worker growth rates up to 1908 would have been only 0·21 percentage points higher had the Midwestern land stock grown at 4·0 percent per annum rather than at the far lower historical rate of 1·4 percent reached at the end of the period. We concluded that the 'closing of the frontier' had only a marginal impact on per capita growth performance.

Such counterfactual experiments are valid only to the extent that the underlying model is considered plausible. Improved land stock growth can influence per capita income expansion rates in our model only through two influences: (i) land endowment can make a *direct* contribution to labor productivity given technology and all other inputs fixed; (ii) an increase in the land endowment may make an *indirect* (positive) contribution to labor productivity by raising capital formation rates. The latter effect is achieved since the average productivity of capital is raised (i.e., the capital–output ratio is diminished). Nowhere did the counterfactual experiment in chapter 5 consider the potential impact of land expansion on national savings and thus a *direct* effect on capital formation rates. To have done so would have required far more knowledge of the determinants of American savings during the nineteenth century than we presently possess. If one accepts the validity of the savings function specified at the end of chapter 6, then high rates of resource augmentation may have had a *dampening* effect on aggregate savings rates. If savings out of income conventionally defined is considered to be lower in agriculture, then aggregate savings rates would have been higher had America increased her specialization in non-primary products, a result insured by 'less abundant natural resources.' On the other hand, lower rates of new land expansion imply higher rates of increase in average land values. The arguments presented in section 7.2 suggest that rising land values may explain the low *conventionally* measured savings rates in American agriculture. In summary, it is not at all clear how a different land expansion path would have affected American capital formation rates beyond the indirect effects considered in chapter 5. Since economic historians have been unable to guide our choice on the determinants of aggregate American savings during the late nineteenth century, the provisional estimates documented in chapter 5 must be tentatively accepted: namely, changing rates of land exploitation account for little of American growth performance after the Civil War decade.

Yet American economic historians have been far more interested in the *structural* implications of the late nineteenth-century retardation in the growth of farmland. In particular, it has long been believed that the 'disappearing frontier' played a key role in accounting for the impressive industrialization performance after the Civil War decade. The remainder of this section explores the structural dimensions of American growth after 1870 as it relates to the retardation in farmland growth. First, it examines the impact of the changing land endowment on industrialization and urbanization in both the Midwest and in America as a whole. Second, it explores the impact of increased Midwestern improved farmland on *regional* per capita income growth performance. Third, it estimates the effect of this expansion on land rents and land values in the Midwest. Finally, it documents the impact of frontier development on the labor market; that is, on wage differentials and migration rates. Before attacking these issues, however, we must first confront the federal land policy literature and establish appropriate counterfactuals.

Public land policy and the appropriate counterfactual. The large volume of historical research on land and the late nineteenth-century American economy has dealt mostly with federal land policy.[2] One key issue has been whether land was released from the public domain too rapidly thus inducing an excessive amount of capital and labor into agriculture. The literature asserts that the rapid release of federal land lowered returns to capital and labor in agriculture. It is difficult to reconstruct an economic argument which would yield that result. Obviously, if the new land is either badly managed or of lower quality then it is quite clear that average yields may decline for agriculture as a whole. But if the new land is of quality comparable to the existing old lands,[3] then the return on capital and labor can only decline if the new lands use uneconomically large doses of those complementary inputs. There is no evidence that this was the case. On the contrary, it is well known that new agricultural regions were initially faced with relatively high wages and stringent credit conditions. These factor price differentials were required to induce mobile resources into the new regions. If this *a priori* argument does not appear altogether convincing, then an examination of the Fogel and Rutner results should dispel any residual doubts. Not surprisingly, Fogel and Rutner find that the rate of return on agricultural capital compares 'quite favorably with the average yield on the common stock of manufacturing firms'[4] although the comparison holds up far better in 1869 and 1879 than afterwards when the 'farm problem' emerges. Furthermore, the returns were highest in those regions in which land was being distributed most rapidly.[5] In short, to the extent that regional variance in rates of return to capital are influenced by land policy in the 1860s and 1870s, the temporary disequilibrium observed is, if anything, one of capital *shortage* rather than surplus at the agricultural frontier.

The second focus of the literature entails the regional redistributive effect of public land policy. Eastern farms were gradually eliminated by the joint effects of (i) Western land policy, (ii) declining transport charges on interregional grain trade, and (iii) successful industrial development in the East. There is no doubt that public land policy at the frontier tended to lower rents on old land, including those farms located in the East. Resources were encouraged into the new lands by temporary wage and capital asset return differentials, and Eastern rents underwent relative decline as mobile resources responded to this incentive. But note that the diminution in Eastern rental income was simply 'a transfer to the West which is associated with the migration of part of the labor force.'[6]

This survey of the literature is brief since this section is not primarily motivated by the questions raised in the federal land policy debate. Indeed, management of the public domain had little impact on the Midwest during most of the period after the 1870s. Our interest is less on public land policy *per se* and more on the impact of Midwestern land expansion in general on American nineteenth-century performance. Ultimately our task is to improve our understanding of American industrialization and urbanization after the Civil War decade.

Economic historians have made much of the role of resource abundance on American economic growth. Indeed, the 'safety-valve' doctrine is simply another expression of the view that an expanding frontier constrained the supply of industrial labor and thus inhibited both industrialization and urbanization, while tending to raise real wages. Apparently, this effect is obvious to some historians: '. . . the effect of the frontier on the supply of labor to industry was due to the factor that has been most obvious all along; namely, the agricultural sector was expanding physically'.[7] Yet the economic historian has been far less attentive to an inevitable corollary which applies to the post-Civil War era. The corollary is simply that the increasing tendency towards relative land scarcity should explain much of American industrialization during the Gilded Age. Shannon, for example, asserts: 'As the better unused acres became scarcer, the incentive to [foreign] immigration abated and the tendency of surplus sons to move out on the frontier noticeably increased. Ultimately the saturation point was reached after which the influx of new blood did not keep pace with the exodus of the discontented.'[8] As Frank Lewis has pointed out, Shannon is appealing to a corollary of the safety valve theory so that the closing of the frontier tended to increase the movement of workers to urban employment.[9] But even if the *direction* of the impact produced by the disappearance of the frontier is obvious to some economic historians, the *relative magnitude* of that effect when compared with, say, world market conditions or agricultural productivity growth, is less transparent. This book is concerned with such magnitudes.

What counterfactuals are relevant in isolating these magnitudes? Two such counterfactuals are explored in the next section. The first fixes the improved acreage stock at 1870 levels. This describes an economy which is the polar opposite of the American case, one in which development is fully resource intensive and comparable to the European case. In short, the door of the frontier is slammed shut abruptly in 1870 rather than gradually closed as the century progresses. This counterfactual will supply an answer to the Parker and Klein question: '[How] might techniques have altered to maintain yields and reduce labor costs ... under pressure of a growing demand, if the [new] western lands had not been available?'[10] The second counterfactual world is at the other extreme. It explores the American economy during conditions of resource extensive growth typical of the first half of the century. In this counterfactual world, the 4 percent annual expansion in Midwestern improved farmland reached in the early 1870s is assumed to prevail throughout the four decades. Granted, this second counterfactual is highly unrealistic, but it should be especially useful in gauging the impact of increased land scarcity on American industrialization and the relative decline of the farm sector after 1870. By comparing this regime with fact, the contribution of retarding land stock growth rates to industrialization and urbanization in both the Midwest and America as a whole can be explicitly computed. Figure 8.1 compares these two counterfactual worlds with 'actual' historical performance.

Land expansion and late nineteenth-century American development

The impact on yields, land values and rents.   Theory supplies a ready answer to the Parker and Klein counterfactual: 'What would have happened to yields had new western lands not been available?'

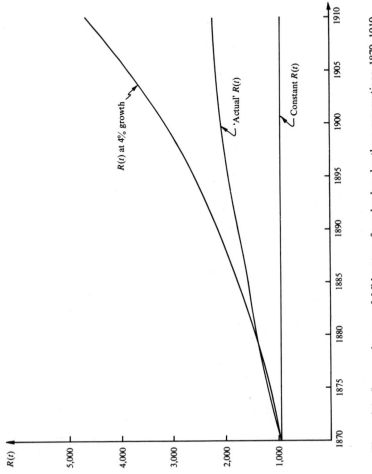

Figure 8.1 Improved acres of Midwestern farm land under three assumptions, 1870–1910

With increased scarcity, acreage would have been used more intensively far sooner in American history. Capital per worker would have increased sharply and productivity per acre would have risen in consequence. The issue is therefore not how yields might have been 'maintained' but how rapidly they would have risen compared to actual performance. Table 8.1 supplies a quantitative assessment based on the model in chapter 3. First, recall from chapter 7 the similarity between the simulated yield series and the historical series for grains as documented by Parker and Klein. The model developed in chapter 3 predicts a moderate yield improvement of 19 percent between 1870 and 1910. This prediction was welcomed as further confirmation of the model's plausibility since Parker and Klein document a rise from 1869 to 1909 of 23 percent in the Corn Belt states for wheat and 6 percent for corn.[11] Not only are these secular trends reproduced by the simulation (Table 8.1, col. 3), but turning points are captured as well. Again for wheat in the Corn Belt states, the Parker–Klein yield index rises from 1869 to 1889, it declines to 1899, then rises once more to 1909. The predicted yield series reproduces these turning points with considerable accuracy. This predicted yield series is labeled 'actual' in col. 3 of Table 8.1.

Now compare the 'actual' yield series produced by the model with the secular performance which would have been produced under land scarcity conditions. Col. 2 of Table 8.1 reports the behavior of yields in a counterfactual world where the land stock is maintained at its 1870 levels throughout the late nineteenth century. Although the direction of the impact is predictable, the magnitude is striking. Had the land in farms remained constant in the Midwest after 1870,

Table 8.1. *Index of Midwestern land yields under two land augmentation counterfactuals*

| | Midwestern farm product per acre (1870 = 100) | | |
Year	Land stock growth constant at 4% p.a.	Fixed land stock	Actual land stock growth
1870	100	100	100
1875	108	128	106
1880	112	158	114
1885	115	191	126
1890	107	207	127
1895	96	215	124
1900	81	212	115
1905	71	212	113
1910	65	220	119

Note: See text and Figure 8.1 for a detailed description of the counterfactual experiments. 'Actual' growth refers to the simulation reported in chapter 4 and discussed at length in chapter 7.

yields would have increased by 120 percent (rather than 19 percent) over the four decades. Furthermore, almost all of the increase would have taken place by 1890, a result consistent with the fact that the frontier 'disappears' by the mid-1890s in historical reality.

What would have been the sources of the yield improvement under the counterfactual conditions of late nineteenth-century land scarcity? While an index of agricultural capital utilization per acre rises by a factor of 2·8 up to 1890 in the 'actual' simulation, it would have risen 4·7 times had the land stock remained constant during these two decades. In simple terms, the capital requirements per farm in the Midwest would have increased markedly under the counterfactual conditions of land scarcity – conditions very common to twentieth-century American agriculture.

Nevertheless, it should be noted that the capital–labor ratio in Midwestern agriculture would have been almost totally unaffected by these conditions: the capital–labor ratio in Midwestern agriculture would have risen by a factor of 3·3 rather than 3·4 up to 1890. Not only would investment requirements per farm have increased under counterfactual conditions of land scarcity, but labor requirements would have increased by a like amount. The implications of this counterfactual experiment are clear. First, labor-saving mechanization in American agriculture after the Civil War decade was unrelated to changing land availability. Increasing land scarcity had little to do with the increasing mechanization of farm activities during the latter half of the nineteenth century. Instead, it was conditioned by development outside of the sector: namely, the relative increase in labor's price as capital formation and successful industrialization proceeded. True, land scarcity tended to inhibit the upward drift in real wages in the American economy during the late nineteenth century. But the experiments reported below in Table 8.5 suggest that this influence is relatively minor, at least after 1870.[12] Second, the relative stagnation in yields up to the mid-1880s is to be explained primarily by the rapid (although declining) expansion in farmland: had that expansion been absent in the post-Civil War era, land yields would have increased by half as much again.

We turn now to an examination of land rents and land values. Once again, simple comparative static theory supplies an un-ambiguous answer: given demand conditions and no land expansion, rents would have risen much more sharply than was in fact the case. Just how much more sharply they would have risen is apparent in col. 2 of Table 8.2. Had no land expansion taken place up to 1890, rents would have risen by more than two times rather than maintained their relative stability. One wonders whether farm discontent would have subsided after the mid-1870s had these counterfactual conditions of land scarcity taken place! The land value figures

Table 8.2. *Midwestern land rents under two land augmentation counterfactuals*

	Midwestern land rents (1870 = 100)		
Year	Land stock growth constant at 4% p.a.	Fixed land stock	Actual land growth
1870	100	100	100
1875	109	127	109
1880	118	164	118
1885	118	200	127
1890	109	209	132
1895	100	218	127
1900	82	218	118
1905	73	218	119
1910	64	227	123

Note: See text for a detailed description of counterfactual experiments.

present in Table 8.3 illustrate the importance of counterfactual analysis. In chapter 7, the 'sources' of land value changes were decomposed into land rent and interest rate changes. There it was argued that most of the 'paradoxical' rise in land values could be explained by the decline in effective farm mortgage rates rather than by a rise in land rents. This statistical decomposition was performed on *ex post* data. Granted land values rose by impressive amounts up to the 1900s in spite of the stability in yields and rents, but by how much more would they have risen had the Midwestern landstock remained at 1870 levels so that yields would have rapidly

Table 8.3. *Midwestern land values under two land augmentation counterfactuals*

	Midwestern land values (1870 = 100)		
Year	Land stock growth constant at 4% p.a.	Fixed land stock	Actual land growth
1870	100	100	100
1875	140	169	138
1880	187	270	190
1885	252	437	279
1890	290	601	354
1895	306	758	411
1900	318	954	479
1905	286	1031	497
1910	154	615	306

Note: These land values are computed under assumptions of infinite durability and where current land rents are assumed to prevail indefinitely. The current farm mortgage rate is used for discounting.

improved? Table 8.3 reports that, from an 1870 base of 100, land values per acre would have been almost twice as high in 1890 than they were in fact (601 versus 354), and more than twice as high in 1910 (615 versus 306). These results are roughly comparable with the land rent series in Table 8.2 suggesting that credit conditions facing agriculture (e.g., farm mortgage rates) would not have been very different in a counterfactual world of no land expansion. Obviously, the sharp retardation in farm acreage growth in the Midwest has a great deal to do with the observed movements in land values during this age of farm discontent. Had the high rates of land expansion in the early 1870s been maintained after 1895, col. 1 of Table 8.3 shows that land values would have been cut in half.

Regional income per capita, real wages and the Turner thesis. What were the effects of land expansion elsewhere in the American economy? How did the changing availability of farm acreage affect regional growth and migration to the West? The sectional distribution of gains from aggregate national development has always been an issue of keen interest to the historian of nineteenth-century American growth. Easterlin's valuable empirical research has shed considerable light on the problem.[13] Easterlin documents a rapid convergence of per capita incomes between the Northeast and North Central regions during the four decades following 1880. The Northeast has a growth rate below the national average while the North Central exceeds it. These regional per capita income trends are reproduced by the model (Table 8.4, cols. 5 and 6), once again confirming the plausibility of the model developed in chapter 3. From 1870 to 1905, the Midwest had a predicted per annum growth rate of 1·89 percent while the Northeast and Midwest combined rate is somewhat lower, 1·64 percent. One question of interest might be the role of farm land expansion on these regional income trends.

We have already seen in chapter 5 how little national per capita growth rates would have departed from observed experience under a counterfactual world of no land expansion. This result is reproduced in a different form in Table 8.4. A comparison of cols. 3 and 5 show that U.S. growth rates would have been lowered by only 0·16 percentage points under counterfactual conditions of land scarcity. What is even more striking is how little the relative regional growth rates would have been affected. The difference in per capita income growth between the Midwest and the U.S. as a whole is roughly the same in all three regimes. In the 'actual' simulation, Midwestern growth exceeds the national average by 0·25 percentage points. Under counterfactual conditions of continued land stock growth at 4 percent, the difference would have been 0·27 (Table 8.4, col. 2

Table 8.4. *Per capita income in the United States and the Midwest under two land augmentation counterfactuals*

	Per capita income					
	Land stock growth constant at 4% p.a.		Fixed land stock		Actual land growth	
Year	U.S.	West	U.S.	West	U.S.	West
1870	3·087	2·720	3·087	2·720	3·087	2·720
1875	3·306	3·095	3·260	3·038	3·310	3·100
1880	3·602	3·432	3·500	3·308	3·599	3·428
1885	4·188	4·027	4·001	3·805	4·161	3·994
1890	4·499	4·304	4·256	4·020	4·442	4·235
1895	4·856	4·699	4·536	4·339	4·761	4·588
1900	5·390	5·132	4·994	4·710	5·253	4·978
1905	5·650	5·447	5·177	4·951	5·460	5·236
1910	4·765	4·938	4·236	4·308	4·522	4·637
Aver. annual growth 1870–1905	1.74%	2.01%	1.48%	1.73%	1.64%	1.89%

Note: All figures are in current relative prices. The Western per capita figures refer to product rather than income. See text for a detailed description of the counterfactual experiments.

less col. 1). The figure is 0·25 under counterfactual land scarcity conditions (Table 8.4, col. 4 less col. 3). The implication is apparent: land availability at the frontier had little to do with the observed convergence in income per capita levels during the late nineteenth century.

The same cannot be said for regional wage differentials. Had the frontier closed abruptly in 1870, agricultural wages would have been lower by 7 percent in 1910 compared with actual levels (Table 8.5, cols. 4 and 6). Industrial wage rates in the East, on the other hand, would have been only 2 percent lower (Table 8.5, cols. 3 and 5). The different response in these two regional labor markets is attributable to lags in migration and resulting temporary disequilibria. Yet the existence of larger wage differentials does not imply that interregional migration rates or off-farm migration rates would have been unaffected by a closing of the frontier in 1870. Table 8.6 reports those effects and they are consistent with the arguments developed thus far in this section.

Historians, especially Frederick Jackson Turner[14] have normally reserved a role of some importance for the frontier:

Men would not accept inferior wages and a permanent position of social subordination when this promised land of freedom and equality was theirs for the taking. Who would rest content under oppressive legislative conditions when with

Table 8.5. *Eastern industrial and Western agricultural wages under two land augmentation counterfactuals*

| | Industrial and farm wages | | | | | |
| | Land stock growth constant at 4% p.a. | | Fixed land stock | | Actual land growth | |
Year	$W_E(t)$	$W_{AW}(t)$	$W_E(t)$	$W_{AW}(t)$	$W_E(t)$	$W_{AW}(t)$
1870	1·570	1·570	1·570	1·570	1·570	1·570
1875	1·545	1·867	1·544	1·828	1·545	1·870
1880	1·728	2·092	1·724	2·004	1·728	2·088
1885	1·943	2·277	1·933	2·134	1·943	2·254
1890	2·324	2·442	2·300	2·253	2·321	2·394
1895	2·527	2·638	2·484	2·390	2·519	2·560
1900	2·999	2·871	2·929	2·563	2·983	2·759
1905	3·102	3·073	3·011	2·713	3·077	2·918
1910	2·215	3·285	2·138	2·857	2·191	3·070

Note: These are 'money' wages unadjusted for current price relative and budget compositional changes. See text for a detailed description of the counterfactual experiments.

a slight effort he might reach a land therein to become a co-worker in the building of free cities and free states on the lines of his own ideal? In a word, then, free land meant free opportunities.[15]

Table 8.6. *Intersectoral and interregional migration rates under two land augmentation counterfactuals*

| | Migration rates Westward and off the farm | | | | | |
| | Land stock growth constant 4% p.a. | | Fixed land stock | | Actual land growth | |
Year	$m_{WE}(t)$	$m_{IA}(t)$	$m_{WE}(t)$·	$m_{IA}(t)$	$m_{WE}(t)$	$m_{IA}(t)$
1870	0·003	0·000	0·003	0·000	0·003	0·000
1875	0·003	0·000	0·003	0·002	0·003	0·000
1880	0·004	(0·008)	0·003	(0·004)	0·004	(0·008)
1885	0·005	(0·002)	0·004	0·004	0·005	(0·001)
1890	0·003	0·021	0·003	0·026	0·003	0·022
1895	0·003	0·028	0·002	0·033	0·002	0·030
1900	0·002	0·020	0·001	0·029	0·002	0·023
1905	0·002	0·015	0·001	0·025	0·002	0·019
1910	0·005	(0·034)	0·003	(0·020)	0·004	(0·027)

Note: These are out-migration rates in terms of the labor force in the sending region; $m_{WE}(t)$ denotes out-migration rates from the East to the Midwest; $m_{IA}(t)$ denotes off-farm migration rates within the Midwest. Figures in parentheses refer to reverse net migration rates. See text for a detailed description of the counterfactual experiments.

A thesis as broad and daring as this is bound to attract critics. There have been enough of these to set much of the labor-safety-valve doctrine at rest.[16] Yet the critics have grossly distorted Turner's thesis. Obviously, Eastern laborers need not have migrated Westward to engage in agriculture for the safety-valve to have operated. Urban employment was a superior option anyway. Nevertheless, 'abundant land' in the West surely must have contributed to a tight labor market everywhere in America. For the same reasons, data on farm capital requirements facing the owner-operator are equally irrelevant. Furthermore, to argue that agriculture failed to eliminate industrial unemployment during periods of depression is surely a narrow criticism of the thesis. Those forces contributing to departures from full capacity utilization affected all sectors of the economy.

A key component of Turner's thesis is, therefore, that the American frontier had an important positive effect on industrial wages. This may be a narrow economist's interpretation of an historical thesis of enormous scope, but if the narrowest interpretation fails to pass the discipline of empirical test, the larger thesis is hardly likely to survive either. To repeat, we shall adopt the most sympathetic interpretation of Turner, an interpretation which plays a central role in the more recent work of H. J. Habakkuk.[17] Land availability plays a key role in Habakkuk's treatment of Anglo-American factor price differentials and technical change. Even though the sectors undergoing the most rapid employment expansion are outside agriculture after the 1860s, Turner and Habakkuk would have us believe that the derived demand for labor in agriculture played a major role in influencing real wage behavior. In particular, Turner and Habakkuk would surely argue that the rate of expansion of farm land in the Midwest had a pronounced impact on industrial wages. No such effect is revealed in the counterfactual reported in Table 8.5. As we have seen, under the extreme counterfactual conditions of land scarcity after 1870, the real wage in industry would have been diminished by only a trivial 2 percent.[18] Even the narrowest interpretation of the Turner thesis is found to be empirically unimportant after 1870. Industrial wages were only marginally affected by agricultural frontier conditions. One cannot help but speculate that both the Turner and Habakkuk theses would suffer a similar fate if confronted with ante bellum evidence.

Agricultural employment and industrialization.   We turn now to the sources of American industrialization during the Gilded Age. It was briefly pointed out above that a corollary to the safety-valve doctrine is that the closing of the frontier played a prominent role in fostering a relative employment shift out of agriculture. This section

Table 8.7   *Agricultural labor force and Midwestern employment distribution under two land augmentation counterfactuals*

| | Distribution of the Midwestern labor force | | | | | |
| | Land stock growth constant 4% p.a. | | Fixed land stock | | Actual land growth | |
Year	$L_{AW}(t)$	$L_{IW}(t)/L_W(t)$	$L_{AW}(t)$	$L_{IW}(t)/L_W(t)$	$L_{AW}(t)$	$L_{IW}(t)/L_W(t)$
1870	49·3	0·240	49·3	0·240	49·3	0·240
1875	54·0	0·266	53·9	0·268	54·1	0·266
1880	61·4	0·258	60·9	0·264	61·4	0·258
1885	69·9	0·239	68·8	0·250	69·9	0·240
1890	73·9	0·268	70·6	0·297	73·4	0·273
1895	74·6	0·318	69·4	0·362	73·4	0·329
1900	70·5	0·400	63·3	0·457	68·4	0·417
1905	70·2	0·440	59·9	0·517	66·7	0·467
1910	73·5	0·450	59·4	0·549	68·0	0·488

Note: See text for a detailed description of the counterfactual experiments.

probes this thesis. Before applying the counterfactual analysis, however, it might be wise to protect our flanks from critics. Recall that Shannon argues that 'as the better unused acres became scarcer, the incentive to [foreign] immigration abated.'[19] In short, Shannon would object to a counterfactual which operates on land stock growth but maintains the same level of foreign immigration. This is in fact our procedure. But the international migration literature asserts that industrial employment and earnings conditions were far more important in conditioning American foreign immigration after 1870. Since Table 8.5 reports only a marginal secular impact of the land expansion counterfactuals on real industrial earnings, we felt safe in assuming independence between land stock growth and foreign immigration rates. The more detailed analysis in chapter 11 confirms this position.

The structure of the American economy is very sensitive to resource endowment, much more so than for real wages and output growth. Tables 8.7 and 8.8 present measures of employment and output distribution under the two land counterfactuals. The first table shows that the high rate of retention of farm labor up to 1890 is in part explained by continued land augmentation in the Midwest. Without any increases in Midwestern farmland after 1870, total agricultural employment would have undergone absolute reduction sooner and by 1910 the agricultural labor force would have been

Table 8.8. *Measures of industrialization under two land augmentation counterfactuals*

| | Industrialization performance | | | | | |
| | Land stock growth constant 4% p.a. | | Fixed land stock | | Actual land growth | |
Year	$L_I(t)/L(t)$	$v(t)$	$L_I(t)/L(t)$	$v(t)$	$L_I(t)/L(t)$	$v(t)$
1870	0·507	0·469	0·507	0·469	0·507	0·469
1875	0·536	0·461	0·537	0·468	0·535	0·461
1880	0·518	0·470	0·522	0·485	0·518	0·470
1885	0·521	0·474	0·529	0·500	0·521	0·477
1890	0·535	0·540	0·556	0·581	0·538	0·549
1895	0·569	0·578	0·600	0·634	0·576	0·593
1900	0·616	0·643	0·655	0·613	0·627	0·665
1905	0·645	0·666	0·697	0·751	0·663	0·697
1910	0·660	0·582	0·725	0·663	0·685	0·624

Note: The symbol $v(t)$ denotes the share of industrial output in total national 'output' where the denominator includes income from transportation and communications. See text for a detailed description of the counterfactual experiments.

13 percent lower than its actual level. Employment distribution statistics are similarly affected. Alternatively, note in Table 8.7 that had the Midwest continued to enjoy the farmland expansion rates of the early 1870s, the agricultural labor force would have been 8 percent higher by 1910. In effect, one of the reasons why America underwent a Gilded Age of Industrialization after the Civil War is that the frontier was being exhausted. An obvious result, perhaps, but the quantitative importance of this source of American industrialization in the latter half of the nineteenth century does not appear to be well appreciated in the literature.

Furthermore, the effect is actually *underestimated* in Tables 8.7 and 8.8 since, as the period progresses, the labor force and output distributions represent a significant departure from optimality. Following the argument in chapter 7, if the distribution of the labor force in 1899 had been optimal, the measured agricultural labor force and its employment share would have been far lower. (This is much less true during the 1880s.) The market failure referred to is the redundancy of labor in agriculture as indexed by wage differentials. This redundancy was induced in part by the marked decline in farm land expansion rates during the 1870s and 1880s, and the sluggish off-farm migration response.

We can readily construct a crude measure of the excess of farmers in 1899 agriculture using our counterfactual experiments. The agricultural production function specified is

$$Q_{AW} = BK_{AW}^{\beta_K}L_{AW}^{\beta_L}R^{\beta_R}$$

and labor's marginal value product there is

$$w_{AW} = P_{AW} \beta_L \{B K_{AW}^{\beta_K} L_{AW}^{\beta_L - 1} R^{\beta_R}\}.$$

Given the technology prevailing in 1899 (β_L, β_K, β_R and B), the land in farms (R), the agricultural capital utilized there (K_{AW}), and farm prices (P_{AW}), the optimal agricultural labor force consistent with any wage can be derived. Our model shows the wage in agriculture far below that of Western industry and considerably below that of Eastern industry. (See Table 4.8). Taking the wage prevailing in Western industry as the appropriate equilibrium wage in agriculture, 30 percent of the Midwestern labor force was in 'surplus'. Using instead the Eastern industrial wage as the norm, 6 percent of the farmers were redundant in the Midwest in 1899. The truth lies somewhere in between but no effort is made here to search for it since our purpose is only to establish the problem as important.[20] That is, we conclude that Tables 8.7 and 8.8 significantly understate the magnitude of the stimulating effect which the 'gradual closing of the frontier' had on American industrialization after the 1870s.

8.2 Productivity growth and Midwestern agriculture's performance

Demand, productivity growth and world markets: a defense of the 'small country' assumption

Agricultural total factor productivity growth plays a key role in most accounts of national development. The dualistic development literature,[21] for example, emphasizes its role in (i) generating an agricultural commodity surplus to feed and clothe the industrial labor force, (ii) creating a savings surplus for capital accumulation in agriculture and elsewhere in the economy, and (iii) reducing agricultural labor requirements thereby making labor available for employment in urban activities. Accounts of American nineteenth-century development seem to adopt this position. Indeed, one central hypothesis singles out agricultural productivity gains as a prime explanation for labor's shift to manufacturing in the latter half of the nineteenth century.[22] As just one example, Simon Kuznets recently asserted 'It is such a rise in [agricultural] productivity, combined with the low income elasticity of demand for products in the agricultural sector, that accounts for the marked decline in share of that sector in the total of labor and capital used.'[23] Yet, this argument invokes a 'closed economy' assumption. It treats the economy in isolation and, in its extreme form, ignores the potential of foreign trade completely.

An opposite, but more convincing, argument can be found in trade theory. Under the 'small country' assumption, trade theory predicts that if an economy has no influence on world market conditions (if price elasticities in the excess demand for exports and excess supply of imports are infinite), then agricultural productivity growth would reinforce America's comparative advantage, expand her agricultural exports and *increase* the relative importance of agricultural activity. When forced to choose between these two positions, we obviously prefer the latter view of American development.

These two views of American growth can be reconciled only by empirical evidence relating to foreign demand conditions for U.S. grains. Granted that the price elasticity of grains is normally assumed to be less than unity – it is certainly true of *domestic* demand in our model (see appendix A), but the relevant issue is the foreign demand for *United States grain* given a world of many suppliers. The extreme position often adopted is that American agriculture developed under conditions of 'immizerizing' growth. That is, the foreign demand for U.S. grains had a price elasticity of less than unity such that agricultural productivity growth was self-defeating: supply expansion generated a percentage grain price decline in excess of the physical expansion, producing a *decline* in foreign exchange receipts and in farm income. This view can hardly be taken seriously given that the relative price of grains fails to decline in the East after the early 1870s, a period of rapid agricultural productivity growth and continued land expansion. While the low price (and income) elasticities of farm products are well understood, the effects of foreign trade apparently are not. For example, we have Professor Gallman's observation: 'Did international markets provide agriculture with relief from the pressures of the changing pattern of domestic demand? There is some evidence that agriculture was able to export an increasing share of output [but] changes in foreign trade ... did not moderate the shift of U.S. commodity output away from agriculture and toward manufacturing. *Indeed, they contributed toward this shift.*'[24] Gallman is not reporting a counterfactual experiment nor is he appealing to empirical evidence on price and income elasticities. Instead, his statement is based on an examination of *ex post* data. He observes American trade shifting away from a comparative advantage in primary products and into manufactures. But this is precisely the change in American specialization we wish to explain! Presumably, the secular shift in American specialization, and thus employment distribution, is to be explained (i) by the more rapid efficiency growth outside of agriculture, (ii) by the exhaustion of new land, and (iii) by the impressive rise in the relative price of labor. The latter effect was induced by capital formation and it, in turn, induced the shift out of labor-cum-natural-resource intensive activities and into capital intensive manufacturing activities. Chester Whitney Wright understood these economic forces well enough when he wrote: '. . . the chief explanation for the rapid expansion of manufacturing . . . [was] to be found in the changes favoring lowered costs of production.'[25] Should not agriculture be treated symmetrically? If agriculture had undergone zero rates of total factor productivity growth, its competitive position in world markets would have deteriorated thus inducing a greater relative decline of employment in the sector.

Zero total factor productivity growth in agriculture?

Let us begin with a question raised by Parker and Klein: 'Would movement into the Middle West and the shift in grain production which accompanied it have occurred without the improvements in farm machinery?'[26] The counterfactual posed in the present section supplies an answer to that question. In Table 8.9, 'actual' Midwest experience with yields is compared with a counterfactual world of zero total factor productivity growth in agriculture. Instead of the moderate rise in yields up to 1890, we would have observed stability. Instead of a moderate decline in the two decades following 1890, yields would have fallen precipitiously as would land values. The discrepancy in yields is not insignificant: they are lower under zero total factor productivity growth by 25 percent in 1890, and by 45 percent in 1910.

With the lower and declining land yields, agriculture would have met its relative demise at an accelerated rate. This result can be readily seen in Tables 8.10 and 8.11 where the agricultural labor force, off-farm migration rates and measures of employment distribution are presented. Note first that the agricultural labor

Table 8.9. *Midwestern land yields under zero total factor productivity growth in agriculture: 1870–1910*

Year	Zero total factor productivity growth	Actual total factor productivity growth
1870	100	100
1875	97	106
1880	98	114
1885	101	126
1890	96	127
1895	88	124
1900	76	115
1905	69	113
1910	66	119

Note: See text for a detailed description of the counterfactual experiment.

Table 8.10. *Agricultural labor force and off-farm migration rates under zero total factor productivity growth in agriculture: 1870–1910*

	Agriculture labor force: $L_{AW}(t)$		Off-farm migration rates: $m_{IA}(t)$	
Year	Zero TFPG	Actual TFPG	Zero TFPG	Actual TFPG
1870	49·3	49·3	0·000	0·000
1875	53·6	54·0	0·005	0·000
1880	59·5	61·4	0·003	(0·008)
1885	66·0	69·9	0·011	(0·001)
1890	65·6	73·9	0·030	0·022
1895	62·5	74·6	0·038	0·030
1900	55·1	70·5	0·037	0·023
1905	49·7	70·2	0·034	0·019
1910	46·3	73·5	0·000	(0·027)

Note: The net out-migration rates in parentheses refer to reverse flows. See text for a detailed description of the counterfactual experiment.

force would have reached a peak around 1885 under zero productivity growth rather than ten years later. Indeed, in the counterfactual world total agricultural employment in the Midwest would have been some 6 percent *lower* in 1910 than four decades earlier. Another way of viewing the importance of agricultural productivity growth is to note that the agricultural labor force in the counterfactual world would have been lower by 37 percent in 1910 compared with fact. Finally, by reference to Table 8.7, it appears that agricultural productivity growth had a far more potent impact on farm employment than did land availability. The declining rate of land expansion and the rising total factor productivity levels have opposing effects,

Table 8.11. *Measures of industrialization under zero rates of total factor productivity growth in agriculture: 1870–1910*

	Midwestern industrialization: $L_{IW}(t)/L_W(t)$		American industrialization: $L_I(t)/L(t)$	
Year	Zero TFPG	Actual TFPG	Zero TFPG	Actual TFPG
1870	0·240	0·240	0·507	0·507
1875	0·272	0·266	0·539	0·535
1880	0·280	0·258	0·533	0·518
1885	0·278	0·239	0·548	0·521
1890	0·343	0·268	0·587	0·538
1895	0·420	0·318	0·639	0·576
1900	0·522	0·400	0·700	0·627
1905	0·595	0·440	0·749	0·663
1910	0·643	0·450	0·785	0·685

Note: See text for a detailed description of the counterfactural experiment.

of course, but the 37 percent agricultural employment differential might be compared with the 8 percent differential generated in a counterfactual world of constant land expansion rates. Thus, while increased land scarcity fostered industrialization, rapid productivity growth in agriculture more than offset this effect: these two conditions combined to inhibit American industrialization.

Before leaving this chapter, two final remarks are necessary. First, we have noted that rapid agricultural productivity growth inhibited industrialization in late nineteenth-century America. This statement should *not* be confused with a judgement regarding per capita income growth although historians often use industrialization statistics as a proxy for per capita income and levels of 'development.' Indeed, had no productivity growth taken place in Midwestern agriculture, per capita incomes (in current relative prices) would have been, in 1910, 17 and 15 percent lower in the West and the United States respectively. That is, while 'actual' per annum per capita income growth rates were 1·89 and 1·64 percent in the West and the United States respectively (Table 8.4), they would have fallen to 1·49 and 1·27 percent had no total factor productivity growth taken place in Midwestern agriculture. Regional convergence in income per capita levels would have occurred just as rapidly, but overall growth rates would have been considerably lower under a regime of zero total factor productivity growth in agriculture. Second, these results are based on the assumption of infinite price elasticities facing American commodities in foreign trade. Although we reject the 'immizerizing' growth thesis as implausible, nevertheless American grain supplies to world markets are likely to have exerted some downward pressure on prices. The degree to which a more complex but realistic foreign trade specification may moderate the results presented in this chapter is an issue left for future research.

9

Transportation and American Development During the Gilded Age: 1870–90

One could pose a more fascinating issue: How important was the railroad to the growth of our economy?

Stanley Lebergott (1966)

9.1 Social savings and general equilibrium analysis

The economic historian has rarely been satisfied with a partial equilibrium analysis of nineteenth-century American railroads. His interest has always been in evaluating the railroads as they interact with the whole framework of the American economy. Not only has he tended to think in general equilibrium terms (although seldom utilizing formal models), but the potential dynamic effects of the rails has always been his prime focus. Albert Fishlow's impressive book on American ante bellum railroads certainly follows in this tradition.[1] The key question central to Fishlow's book is apparent from its title: what role did transportation play in transforming the structure of the American economy? The present chapter raises the same question for the Gilded Age.

With the important exception of Fishlow, cliometricians have reduced the larger issues involving the rails as a force in American development to a more manageable exercise in partial equilibrium statics. Were the railroads an efficient investment choice? Following Robert Fogel's pathbreaking efforts, the measure which has recently caught the historian's attention is the social savings of the railroads. Although the present chapter does not dwell on Fogel's social savings computations,[2] a review of the concept may be useful in placing our own approach in perspective.

The social savings computation attempts to measure the resources saved by the introduction of a given investment or innovation. In essence, it measures the flow of benefits from a given project. Normally, economists relate this flow of benefits to the requisite costs (i.e., railroad construction) to derive a benefit–cost ratio or some other more sophisticated rate of return calculation on the investment project under consideration. If private and social costs and benefits diverge, the historian can evaluate *ex post* the extent of this gap and explore the necessity of government intervention. In addition, since historical decisions are based on imperfect information, the historian may also wish to evaluate the extent to which *ex post* experience fulfilled private or public decision-makers' expectations. These are in fact some of the issues raised in Fishlow's research on the ante bellum railroads. Fogel's focus is somewhat different. First, Fogel relates the social savings of the railroads to GNP rather than utilizing the social savings measures to compute rates of return or benefit–cost ratios. The explanation for this procedure can be readily found in Fogel's initial query: were the railroads indispensible to American development? Presumably, a ratio of the social savings produced by the interregional railroad network to GNP of, say, 1 percent implies a rejection of the 'axiom of indispensibility' since that gap represents less than one year's growth in GNP. Second, Fogel prefers to shun marginal analysis. He is not concerned with the marginal impact of an additional railroad venture but rather with the *total* impact of the railroad network in 1890.

This survey need not summarize the extensive critical debate which followed in the wake of Fogel's enormously stimulating book,[3] but Fishlow's careful review of the social savings concept deserves our attention. First, the usual index number problem must be confronted. Given a (constant) cost differential between two modes of transport, does one use traffic volume at the time of introduction of the new mode or the volume under the old mode in computing benefits? If the cost differential is large and the derived demand for transport services relatively elastic, the index number problem may become significant. This effect can be readily seen in Figure 9.1 where we invoke the assumption of constant costs. (This assumption is maintained in Fogel's and Fishlow's work and is

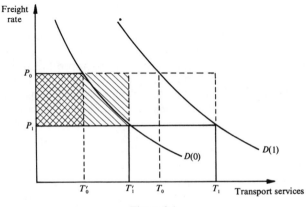

Figure 9.1

applied throughout the present chapter as well.) Shall we define social savings as $[P_0 - P_1] T_1'$, as Fogel does, or rather as $[P_0 - P_1] T_0'$? A more important issue arises when the cost differential is large and the gestation period lengthy: 'Once beyond the confines of the individual project, and with a long interval between introduction of an innovation and measurement of its effect, the distortion becomes considerably more worrisome.'[4] The difference between $[P_0 - P_1] T_1'$ and $[P_0 - P_1] T_1$, may be large enough to render the first calculation of limited usefulness. Indeed, suppose the shift in the derived demand for transport services is induced by railroad investment itself! Fishlow was certainly concerned with these second-round effects, although he was unable to adjust for them:

> A final and very significant distortion in the calculation of social savings derives from the existence of indirect benefits. Because there are second round effects of the initial reduction in transport costs, namely induced capital formation and expansion in other sectors, the position of the demand schedule for transport services is not independent of movement along it.[5]

What are these second-round effects? First, there are the full general equilibrium comparative static effects to consider. A fall in interregional transport costs generates production effects throughout the economy. The railroads fostered regional specialization and interregional commodity trade. The concomitant resource reallocation was complex. To understand it adequately, a full general equilibrium framework which specifies explicit production and consumption conditions in all regions is required. The model developed in chapter 3 is one such candidate. Indeed, it was designed mainly to confront such general equilibrium effects.[6] Second, transport improvement may have dynamic effects over and above the comparative static resource reallocation induced by the innovation. It may foster technical change in both industry and agriculture, and scale effects in industry. It may also induce greater rates of foreign immigration either through the real income effect of the rails or, more importantly, by the shift to more labor intensive economic activities. Railroad construction itself as well as the agricultural activity fostered by declining transport costs were both relatively labor intensive activities. As such, their relative expansion should have had favorable effects on real wages, employment and thus immigration. Finally, the railroads may also induce more rapid rates of capital accumulation. A full discussion of the capital formation effect is, however, postponed to section 9.3 where the dynamic effect of the rails is given quantitative content.

The discussion in this introduction should suffice to point out the potential limitations of a partial equilibrium evaluation of an innovation of such pervasive importance as the railroads. General equilibrium analysis is likely to supply greater insight into historical events of this magnitude. Furthermore, some effort, however primitive, must be made to understand their potential dynamic effects as well. These are the issues which the remainder of this chapter confronts.

9.2   *The railroads and the Midwestern terms of trade*

The discussion up to this point has focused exclusively on the economic impact of the rails on late nineteenth-century America. Yet the approach taken in this chapter contrasts sharply with that of Fishlow and Fogel. Fishlow, Fogel and other researchers have devoted much of their research efforts in documenting the *effective transport charges* for railroads and other competing modes. As a reading of the railroad literature and appendix A will attest, documenting these transport charges (whether measured as 'shadow prices' or rates actually paid) is fraught with difficulty.

American economic historians unanimously agree that railroad freight rates fell sharply from 1870 to 1890. In spite of this unanimity, there have been few attempts to construct continuous real transport cost series relevant to interregional trade within the American economy. The difficulties in constructing such series become immediately apparent in a reading of Robert Higgs' recent attempt.[7] Higgs takes *quoted* nominal freight rates on key agricultural products and deflates these rates by the prevailing prices of corn (*sic*), cotton (*sic*) and wheat. The resulting measures yield crude indices of the movements in the percentage by which farm gate prices diverge from urban market prices. His indices for wheat and especially corn *do* fall significantly from 1870 to 1890. They are not without wide short-run variance, but the long-run decline is unmistakable and pronounced. True, if these series are extended to the mid-1890s, the long-run trend is far less clear. Yet even these estimates present interpretive difficulties. Railroad rates are of interest to us *only* to the extent that they account, at least in part, for spatial commodity price differentials. It is well known that *quoted* nominal transport charges often had little relation to actual or effective rates.[8] Furthermore, farmers paid a multitude of charges for shipment to the nearest rail connection with trunk lines to Chicago as well as for storage and hauling. Given these difficulties, we have departed from the conventional approach and have instead constructed explicit measures of regional commodity price differentials. Appendix A constructs time series for these percentage price differentials between Iowa and New York City. These percentage rate differentials,

$Z_A(t)$, clearly embody more than simply railroad rates on the long haul itself, but they more appropriately capture the issues raised in the literature: What was the impact of converging regional commodity prices on American development? We do not view as improper a restatement of this more general query to the narrower question: What was the impact of the railroads on American development during the late nineteenth century? Nevertheless, this literary license should be made absolutely clear for it may account in part for the wide discrepancy between this chapter's evaluation of regional transport improvements and that of Fogel.

These percentage regional commodity price differentials are displayed in Figure 9.2. The $Z_A(t)$ series refers to rates on Eastern grain trade while the $Z_I(t)$ series refers to those on Western industrial goods trade. The $Z_j(t)$ measures the percent by which the high price region exceeds the low price region where the commodity originates. Two distinct characteristics of these $Z(t)$ series are immediately apparent. First, $Z_A(t)$ always exceeds $Z_I(t)$ since agricultural goods are high-bulk and low-value. Second, while $Z_A(t)$ declines sharply from 1870 and 1890, $Z_I(t)$ does not. Over the period as a whole, Z_I was relatively stable, although it is true that the industrial goods' freight rates were lower after 1870 in all years but two prior to 1885. They are higher thereafter. The joint behavior of $Z_A(t)$ and $Z_I(t)$ is at the heart of the railroad issue. Much of the historical regional specialization patterns, real wage behavior, and regional experience with capital-deepening in nineteenth-century America can be

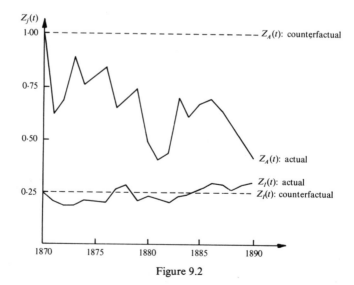

Figure 9.2

explained by the variance in commodity terms of trade across sections. Convergence in these regional commodity price relatives can be easily accounted for by transport improvements, but these improvements had far greater effects on some commodities than others. The prices of Midwestern agricultural and industrial products can be related to those in the East by the expressions

$$P_{AE} = (1 + Z_A)P_{AW},$$

$$P_{IW} = (1 + Z_I)P_{IE}.$$

Thus, the relative price of agricultural commodities in the Midwest as a ratio to that in the East can be reduced to

$$\frac{P_{AW}}{P_{IW}} \bigg/ \frac{P_{AE}}{P_{IE}} = \frac{1}{(1 + Z_A)(1 + Z_I)} < 1.$$

The *relative* price of agricultural goods in the Midwest is always below that of the East. If both Z_A and Z_I fall over time, the Midwestern terms of trade converge to the Eastern terms of trade. But if Z_I rises while Z_A is falling, the convergence is retarded: indeed, should Z_I rise sufficiently it may offset the effects of the fall in Z_A entirely. Clearly, the historian cannot analyze the historical impact of grain freight rates independent of rates on industrial goods.

The counterfactual experiment performed in this chapter can now be explicitly stated: How would the economy have developed over these two decades had these commodity price differentials remained constant at 1870 levels? We are *not* exploring a counterfactual world in 1890 which might have appeared had the railroads been eliminated as a transport mode. We are instead imposing on the economy a counterfactual world of stable 'transport rates' after 1870. By our reckoning, $Z_A(t)$ declined by 50 percent over the two decades while $Z_I(t)$ was roughly stable. Thus, Z_A in 1890 was historically one half of its counterfactual level. Actual historical experience with regional price differentials may be rationalized either by an appeal to an historical deterioration in the railroads' monopolistic tariff setting power or by an appeal to declining real costs in supplying transport services associated with increasing returns or technological improvements.[9] We are not concerned with causes of these 'rate' movements but rather with their implications. These are presented in Figure 9.3. Since we take the East coast commodity price relatives as determined by world market conditions, changing transport rates are assumed to have had an impact on the Midwestern terms of trade only.[10] In the counterfactual world of stable transport charges, the relative price of agricultural goods would have been far lower in the Midwest. Furthermore, the actual historical improvement in relative farm prices in the Midwest would not have been achieved in the counterfactual

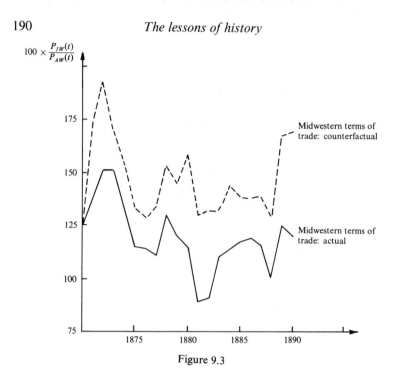

Figure 9.3

world. The relative price of farm products in the Midwest would have fallen from 1870 to 1890. In short, the Midwest farm sector would have been completely at the mercy of the deteriorating world market conditions discussed at length in chapter 10.

How would the counterfactual economy have compared with actual experience up to 1890? What was the impact of transportation improvements on the transformation of the American economy during the Gilded Age?

9.3 Transportation and American development during the Gilded Age

The railroads and economic growth: dynamics

In the introductory remarks to this chapter, we emphasized that the traditional literature on the nineteenth-century railroads stresses dynamic effects. There are numerous hypotheses which identify potential dynamic links between the railroads and economic growth. Consider the most prominent of these: capital formation rates.

The Keynesian tradition lays considerable stress on railroad activity as a key determinant of income growth in the late nineteenth century. Railroad construction itself was, after all, a large share of U.S. net capital formation: in two peak periods, 1870–4 and 1880–4, the share of net railroad investment in total net capital formation was 34 and 17 percent respectively.[11] Had net investment been lower in the absence of new railroad construction, presumably aggregate demand would have been negatively affected and income growth suppressed by departures from full capacity utilization. The conventional multiplier would assure a magnification of this impact, but the railroad literature stresses instead direct inter-industry backward linkages. It had always been assumed that expansion of railroad capacity, as well as maintenance of that capacity, had a strong impact on supplying industries – in particular, the iron industry.[12] Fogel has carefully examined this 'backward linkage' thesis and found it wanting.[13] In any case, we found in chapter 5 that our full employment neoclassical model was quite adequate in accounting for American long-run growth performance. It was not found necessary to introduce monetary variables or the possibility of departures from full capacity to account for late nineteenth-century secular growth patterns. Thus, we feel reasonably confident in ignoring the Keynesian tradition as a means of exploring the dynamic effect of the rails through capital formation rates.

The dynamic effects of the rails are introduced in two ways in our model, both of which conform to the neoclassical tradition. First, by fostering interregional trade and specialization the railroads tend to raise the marginal value product of all agricultural inputs in the Midwest. In consequence, the average productivity of capital is raised in Midwestern agriculture. That is, the capital–output ratio tends to fall in the Midwestern farm sector. The impact does not stop there, of course, since forces are set in motion economy-wide in response to rate of return differentials and eventually the capital–output ratio tends to fall in all sectors. This effect was discussed at length in chapter 5 where the rate of capital formation was decomposed into

$$\frac{\dot{K}(t)}{K(t)} = \bar{s}\left(\frac{\text{GNP}(t)}{P_I(t)K(t)} \right) - \delta = \bar{s}/P_I(t)\left(\frac{\text{GNP}(t)}{K(t)} \right) - \delta.$$

The once-over rise in GNP induced by the rails has the added dynamic effect of raising capital formation rates. From the given capital stock, GNP is increased and thus even if the savings rate, $\bar{s}$, is constant, total savings are increased and consequently capital formation rates are raised.

There is an additional impact on capital formation rates as well. Note the two terms in front of the average product of capital in the above expression: i.e., $\bar{s}/P_I(t)$. The railroads tended to raise the relative price of farm products in the Midwest. In addition, they tended to lower industrial good prices there as well, at least up to 1885. To the extent that industrial goods used for capital accumulation also fell in price, net investment would tend to increase given a fixed savings rate out of current income. This effect was discussed at length in chapter 3 but it may be helpful to present it graphically once more in Figure 9.4.

We do not insist that these are the *only* dynamic links between the railroads and American economic growth, but by exploring the quantitative impact of these within our historical model of American development we hope to enrichen our understanding of the potential importance of these dynamic effects. The research by cliometricians up to this point tends to minimize the dynamic effects of the rails and the analysis in the present section may offer some guides regarding the extent to which the importance of the rails has been underestimated in the partial equilibrium analysis of earlier work. If the dynamic effects tentatively estimated appear to be powerful, then economic historians who view the approach developed in chapter 3 as too restrictive may be goaded into presenting alternative general equilibrium models of American development which introduce an explicit role for the rails. That is certainly the prime intent of this chapter.

Table 9.1 dispels any doubt regarding the magnitude of these dynamic effects in the late nineteenth century. The table compares

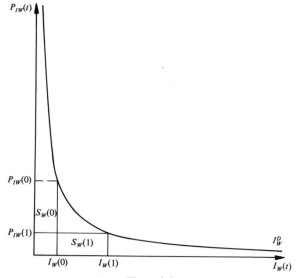

Figure 9.4

Table 9.1. *The impact of the railroads on economic growth, 1870–90*

Average annual growth rates	Actual	Constant transport costs
GNP per worker in 1870 prices	2·49%	1·81%
GNP per worker in 1910 prices	2·33	1·56
Capital stock	6·06	5·06
Midwestern capital stock	7·17	6·33

Note: Growth rates computed between averages for 1869–78 and 1884–93. See text for a full description of the counterfactual experiment.

the 'actual' growth performance of the American economy between 1869–78 and 1884–93 with that which would have taken place in a counterfactual world of constant transport costs during the Gilded Age. The differences are significant indeed. In 1870 prices, GNP per worker would have grown at a rate of 0.68 percentage points below that which was in fact achieved. Similar results are forthcoming when 1910 price weights are used: i.e., a gap of 0·77 percentage points. The main source of the lower growth performance in the counterfactual world without declining interregional transport rates lies with capital formation experience. For the United States as a whole, the rates of capital stock growth would have been lower by 1 percentage point in the counterfactual world.

The findings displayed in Table 9.1 do not adequately take account of the comparative static effect of the rails on output since the majority of the rate declines took place early in the period and the growth rates in Table 9.1 are computed from an initial base averaged over the years 1869 to 1878. Table 9.2 may be more helpful in this regard. GNP would have been lower in 1871 by 9 percent in the absence of transport improvements! The magnitude of the 'social

Table 9.2. *Railroad 'social savings', 1871–90*

	GNP in 1870 prices		
Year	Actual (1)	Constant transport costs (2)	Social savings $[(1) - (2)] \div (1)$
1871	321·2	293·0	0·09
1880	521·3	440·5	0·16
1890	776·6	614·4	0·21

Note: These 'savings' ignore intraregional gains. See texts for a full description of counterfactual experiment.

savings' – the percentage departure between actual and counter-factual GNP levels – increases over time as transport costs continue their decline and in addition as dynamic influences are brought into play. By 1890, the 'social savings' share in actual GNP would have been 21 percent. The 'axiom of indispensibility' cannot be accepted (or rejected) on the basis of such an estimate, but it certainly casts some doubt on the calculations presented thus far in the historical literature. The impressive growth performance of the American economy during the Gilded Age is indeed closely related to the interregional and intraregional transport improvements achieved from the Civil War decade to 1890. To ignore them is to miss a key factor accounting for the rapid growth in America during the Gilded Age.

Trade creation and Midwestern industrialization: statics

The comparative static effect of the railroads on the structure of the late nineteenth century is straightforward. The impact of inter-regional transport costs on the Midwest is summarized in Figure 9.5, where the analysis is equivalent to a small country faced with a deterioration in its terms of trade. The counterfactual relative prices facing the Midwest reflect the absence of interregional transport improvements. It was seen in section 9.2 that without transport improvements the relative price of farm products would have been

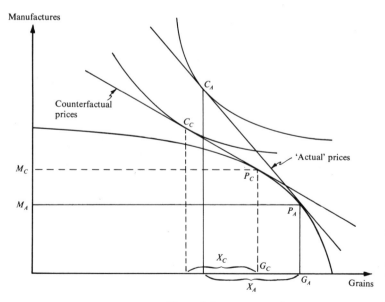

Figure 9.5

lower in the Midwest after 1870. The result would have been a relative contraction of the farm sector and, under normal local demand conditions, a reduction of grain exports from the Midwest. Given demand conditions in the East and the terms of trade prevailing there,[14] Eastern consumption of Western foodstuffs would remain unchanged. Consequently, the reduction in grain exports from the Midwest would be fully passed on as an equivalent reduction in grain exports from the United States: e.g., from East coast ports to Europe. This qualitative analysis then raises two issues relevant to late nineteenth-century American and Midwestern industrialization: (i) What was the likely *magnitude* of these comparative static effects? (ii) Are the dynamic effects sufficiently powerful to offset in the long run the estimated short-run comparative static effects? This second question follows from the analysis of the previous section. Since the absence of transport improvements after 1870 would have lowered capital formation rates, the relative price of labor (although still rising) would have risen at a lesser rate up to 1890. Thus the growth of those sectors utilizing capital intensive production methods would have been suppressed as a result. That is, the dynamic effects suggest that industrialization rates would have been lower under the counterfactual regime of no transport cost changes since industry is more capital intensive. Would the positive comparative static or the negative dynamic effects dominate over the two decades?

Table 9.3 supplies an unambiguous answer to this question. The share of agricultural value added in U.S. commodity output would have been far lower in 1890 had no improvements in interregional transport costs taken place during the Gilded Age. The differences are pronounced. While the'actual' share was 0·393 in 1890, it would have been 0·247 in the counterfactual world. The implications are

Table 9.3. *The impact of the railroads on the output mix of the American economy, 1870–90*

Year	Share of agriculture in commodity output		Share of agriculture in GNP		Share of transport and communications in GNP	
	Actual	Constant transport costs	Actual	Constant transport costs	Actual	Constant transport costs
1870	0·433	0·433	0·358	0·358	0·173	0·173
1875	0·449	0·393	0·375	0·340	0·164	0·134
1880	0·460	0·343	0·400	0·319	0·130	0·070
1885	0·437	0·328	0·371	0·301	0·152	0·082
1890	0·393	0·247	0·355	0·252	0·096	0·074

Note: See text for a full description of the counterfactual experiment.

clear. *Declining interregional transport costs had a very powerful negative influence on American industrialization during the Gilded Age.* This is hardly a conventional conclusion since most economic history texts argue the opposite: they focus primarily on (apparently weak) backward linkage effects of the railroads rather than on forward linkages and transport costs. The result can be documented in another way. In Table 9.4, we present the industrial labor share in the total labor force for both the Midwest and America as a whole. In chapter 4 (Table 4.5), it was shown that our model predicted a Midwestern industrial employment share of 0·273 in 1890 and 0·329 in 1895. Perloff's data document an historical figure of 0·329 in 1890. The experiments reported in Table 9.4 now show that the Midwest industrial employment share would have been 0·427, rather than 0·273, had no transport improvements taken place after 1870. The comparable actual and counterfactual figures for the United States as a whole are 0·637 and 0·538, respectively. No doubt revision of our model specifications and parameter estimates would alter these results, but the *magnitude* of the gap is so large as to require enormous revisions to affect significantly our findings.

The railroads inhibited industrialization during the Gilded Age, but this conclusion must not be confused with quite a different statement documented in the last section. The railroads fostered economic growth during the same period. This clarification may be unnecessary to some readers. But it should prove sobering to those economic historians who insist on using indices of employment distribution and the like as measures of economic development.

The farmer: land values, rents and yields

We have seen in the previous section the great importance of interregional transport costs to the relative expansion of the farm sector. The present section examines Midwestern agriculture in more detail.

Table 9.4.   *The impact of the railroads on employment distribution, 1870–90.*

Year	Midwestern industrial labor force share: L_{IW}/L_W		U.S. industrial labor force share L_I/L	
	Actual	Constant transport costs	Actual	Constant transport costs
1870	0·240	0·240	0·507	0·507
1875	0·266	0·311	0·535	0·564
1880	0·258	0·334	0·518	0·568
1885	0·240	0·364	0·521	0·600
1890	0·273	0·427	0·538	0·637

Note: See text for a full description of the counterfactual experiment.

In the absence of declining transport costs, would land rents have undergone the mild rise up to 1890 which is observed in fact? If instead land yields and rents would have exhibited stability, would land values have undergone a far milder improvement as well? How much of the enormous rise in Midwestern land values can be attributed to the rails, improved farm gate prices, and thus net cash income per acre?

Table 9.5 supplies some answers. First, quantum yields on the average Midwestern farm would have undergone no rise whatsoever up to 1890 in spite of continued total factor productivity growth. It was noted in chapters 7 and 8 that the rapid increase in capital equipment per acre was able to account for some of the mild increase in actual yields, but since the main impact of farm mechanization is to save labor rather than land, the marginal increases in land yields would have been absent under a counterfactual world of transport cost stability. Second, land rents as a result also would have exhibited remarkable stability up to 1890. Third, does this imply different behavior for land values? Much to our surprise, the answer is in the negative. It was established in chapter 7, of course, that declining farm mortgage rates explain most of the land value increases rather than an improvement in net cash income per acre. Nevertheless, one would have thought that zero growth in land rents would have reduced the land value 'boom' significantly. This apparent paradox is explained quite simply: farm mortgage rates decline far more rapidly in our counterfactual world of constant transport costs. It should suffice to point out that higher farm equipment prices in the counterfactual regime up to 1885 inhibit mechanization and the introduction of labor-saving devices on the farm. In fact, while the capital–labor ratio increases from 1870 to 1885 by 2·9 times in the actual simulation, it rises by only 2·3 times under constant transport costs and thus high equipment prices. (In

Table 9.5. *The impact of the railroads on land values, rents and yields in the Midwest, 1870–90 (1870 = 100)*

Year	Land values		Rents		Yields	
	Actual	Constant transport costs	Actual	Constant transport costs	Actual	Constant transport costs
1870	100	100	100	100	100	100
1875	138	141	109	100	106	98
1880	190	217	118	100	114	100
1885	279	227	127	109	126	102
1890	354	351	132	100	127	98

Note: See text for a detailed description of the counterfactual experiment.

1890 the multiples are 3·4 and 2·8, respectively.) This in turn implies a lower demand for farm credit and thus an even more rapid decline in farm mortgage rates. It appears that the diminished rise in land rents would have been offset by an accelerated decline in farm mortgage rates: the net result would have been a similar trend in land values. In summary, the farmer failed to receive a double blessing from the freight rate declines during the Railway Age. While rents, yields and farm income all rose in the Midwest as a result of the interregional transport cost reductions, land values apparently were only marginally influenced if at all.

Off-farm migration, real wages and labor market disequilibrium

Although the historical literature is primarily concerned with the impact of the railroads on output levels and industrial structure, the process by which these end results were achieved may be of interest as well. How were off-farm migration rates affected by the rails? Did interregional transport improvements significantly influence Westward migration rates, or was the impact felt primarily within the Midwest itself? Did the rails have a pronounced impact on the regional and sectoral wage structure? A comparative static equilibrium model cannot confront these issues since factor mobility is normally assumed instantaneous and costless. Since our more realistic general equilibrium model introduces constraints on factor mobility, it can more readily give some insight into the *process* by which new equilibrium conditions were achieved over time in the American economy.

Table 9.6 reports the estimated impact of the rails on farm employment. Had no interregional transport improvements taken place after 1870, the farm labor force would have been some 21 percent smaller by 1890, just two decades later. Note, however, how the reduced farm employment would have affected the labor market elsewhere in the American economy. The *total* Midwestern employed labor force would have been no different under the counterfactual conditions. The Midwestern industrial sector apparently could have fully absorbed the 'displaced' farm labor force so that the total Midwestern labor force and the Westward migration rates would have been almost exactly the same. *The conclusion is inescapable: our tentative findings suggest that although the rails had an important impact on agriculture in the Midwest, migration from the East was only marginally influenced by the subsequent regional trade creation.* The explanation for this apparently bizarre result can be found in Table 9.7. Real wages in Western urban centers were strongly *suppressed*, relative to those in the East, by interregional transport cost declines up to 1890. The farm price gains to Midwestern farmers were losses to Midwest urban labor. Typically, the

Table 9.6.   *The impact of the railroads on Midwestern employment and migration, 1870–90*

	Farm labor: $L_{AW}(t)$		Midwestern labor force: $L_W(t)$	
Year	Actual	Constant transport costs	Actual	Constant transport costs
1870	49·3	49·3	64·9	64·9
1875	54·1	50·8	73·7	73·7
1880	61·4	55·1	82·7	82·7
1885	69·9	58·3	91·9	91·7
1890	73·4	57·7	100·9	100·6

	Off-farm migration rate: $M_{IA}(t)$		East–West migration rate: $M_{WE}(t)$	
Year	Actual	Constant transport costs	Actual	Constant transport costs
1870	0·000	0·000	0·003	0·003
1875	0·000	0·015	0·003	0·003
1880	(0·008)	0·013	0·004	0·003
1885	(0·001)	0·015	0·005	0·004
1890	0·022	0·044	0·003	0·003

economic historian focuses on the Western employment creating effects associated with railway development and the consequent expansion of Midwest farming. What he fails to appreciate, however, is the symmetrical *rise* in food prices in Western urban centers. To the extent that foodstuffs loom large in urban workers' budgets,

Table 9.7.   *The impact of the railroads on wages, 1870–90*

	Real Eastern wage: $\tilde{w}_E(t)$		Regional real wage differential: $(100)\,\tilde{w}_W(t)/\tilde{w}_E(t)$		Midwest industry–agriculture wage differential: $(100)\,w_{IW}(t)/w_{AW}(t)$	
Year	Actual	Constant transport costs	Actual	Constant transport costs	Actual	Constant transport costs
1870	0·975	0·975	144·7	144·7	100·0	100·0
1875	1·048	1·002	160·4	160·9	86·3	94·9
1880	1·383	1·320	138·5	132·7	92·8	117·7
1885	1·472	1·346	143·8	146·9	109·8	113·7
1890	1·957	1·752	115·8	125·2	118·9	140·8

the food price rise produced a marked deterioration in the relative real wage in the West. The *net* inducement to migrate West was, as a result, negligible. Table 9.7 documents that the *real* wage differential between West and East would have been 2 percent higher under constant transport costs by 1895. Only in 1890 does a significant difference between the actual and counterfactual regional wage differentials appear.

The offsetting cost of living effect on real wage differentials is far less pronounced *within* the Midwest. As a result, the employment impact of transport improvements has a much more impressive influence on the Midwestern wage differential between industry and agriculture, and, as a result, on off-farm migration rates to Midwestern urban employment. The off-farm migration rate is reported in Table 9.6 and the farm–industry wage differentials in Table 9.7. In the interests of brevity, consider only one year, 1890: in the counterfactual world of constant transport costs, the industry–agriculture wage differential would have been higher by some 18 percent, and the off-farm migration rate double what it was in fact. Obviously, *urbanization in the Midwest was sharply curtailed by the interregional transport improvement during the Railway Age.*

9.4 Summary and disclaimers

This chapter has presented a fresh examination of the impact of the rails on the American economy during the Gilded Age. Our findings contrast sharply with the conventional literature, including the more recent contribution by Robert Fogel. First, 'social savings' from interregional transport improvements are estimated to be larger than Fogel's by a factor of twenty. Had no interregional transport cost improvements taken place between 1870 and 1890, GNP (in 1870 prices) would have been lower by some 20 percent. This 1890 figure is the result of two mutually reinforcing effects: (i) the comparative static losses from diminished interregional and international trade and (ii) the dynamic effects associated with the rails. Physical capital formation rates would have been considerably lower under a counterfactual world of no transport cost improvements, in both the East and the Midwest. In consequence, our model estimates that GNP per worker (1870 prices) growth rates would have been lower by about 0·6 of a percentage point per year over the two decades as a whole.

Second, declining interregional transport costs during the Gilded Age had a powerful negative influence on American industrialization, especially in the Midwest. The interregional and international trade creating effects were such as to inhibit, rather than foster, industrialization. Impressive industrialization did, of course, take place during the Gilded Age but it would have been far more pronounced had interregional transport improvements been absent. This result is to be contrasted with the (now defunct) Rostow thesis which argues that the railroads played an important role in fostering American industrialization. Although Rostow's focus was on the ante bellum period, his position commonly appears in historical accounts of the post-Civil War period. The hypothesis is rejected in the above pages where powerful forward linkages have been found to have seriously inhibited industrialization.

Third, the rise in Midwestern yields and rents can be in large measure explained by transport improvements after 1870. Yet they provide no explanation for the boom in land values up to 1890. This apparent paradox is resolved by appealing to the indirect impact of the rails on the capital market. Without rails, Midwestern farming would have expanded at far lower rates and as a result this sector's demands for external credit would have diminished. The net result would have been lower farm mortgage rates by 1890, and thus land values would have risen sufficiently on this account to offset the negative influence on yields and rents. Finally, our findings suggest that migration from the East to the West was only marginally influenced by the rails. The impetus which the rails gave to farm employment via trade creation was fully satisfied by migration within the Midwest itself. Midwestern urbanization was inhibited by transport improvements during the Railway Age, but the expansion of Eastern cities was not.

These results are only as accurate as the underlying model. This is true of any analytical economic history. As a result, the critical reader must carefully weigh the plausibility of our analysis at each of three crucial steps. First, is the counterfactual appropriate? Has the assumed decline in interregional relative commodity prices (appendix A) been accurately estimated? Can all of this decline be attributed to the rails? Is the interregional transport cost differential in 1870 larger than the railroad–no railroad cost differential estimated by Fogel in 1890? Second, is the full static general equilibrium model properly specified and estimated? No sensitivity analysis is presented in this chapter due to the large number of parameters in the system. The task would require more computer resources than are presently available to us. Yet given the magnitude of the estimated effects presented in the above pages, it seems unlikely that our results would be seriously affected by even major revisions in the parameters. Third, are the dynamic influences in the model appropriately specified? We feel somewhat less confident on this point and, as a result, anticipate sharp criticism from practitioners of the cliometric art. If a better understanding of the dynamic effects of the rails is forthcoming from such criticism, the modest efforts in this chapter will have been amply rewarded.

10

Exports, World Markets and American Development

The impact of foreign trade on growth is . . . indeterminate. . . .
Charles P. Kindleberger (1962)
The confusion [arises] through a failure to pose counter-factual questions. . . .
Edward J. Chambers and Donald F. Gordon (1966)

10.1 Engines of growth, vent for surplus and the staple theory

The interdependence between international trade and economic growth has attracted much of the economic historian's attention, and nowhere has the debate been more intense than on North American experience. The most recent addition to this large body of literature is a 1972 paper by Irving Kravis. The purpose of Kravis's paper is to examine 'the hypothesis that nineteenth century growth of the United States was export-led.'[1] His motivation is commendable since nineteenth-century America has often been cited as a classic historical example of an economy for which trade was an 'engine of growth.' Indeed, the international demand conditions facing nineteenth-century developing primary-producing nations has always been viewed as unusually favorable. Nurkse considered world demand conditions to be the fundamental difference between the twentieth- and nineteenth-century environments facing developing nations at the periphery of the world economy.[2] These external demand conditions are thought to be sufficiently different to make American historical experience irrelevant as a guide to contemporary problems in developing economies.

Economic historians have 'theorized' about the impact of trade on economic growth under other guises as well.[3] The staple theory has been an especially popular mode of analysis applied to North America. Indeed, the staple theory has been readily used to explain development in all temperate zone areas settled by European labor and capital. When applied to tropical developing economies, the theory has been called 'vent for surplus.'[4] Both of these models view the impact of trade on growth as involving the exploitation of resources which, without trade, would lack any alternative use and significant economic value. The staple version, whether applied to Canada or ante bellum America, emphasizes the discovery of 'surplus' resources.[5] Now it seems quite evident that the staple model adherent has in mind an extreme version of the conventional neoclassical analysis of the gains from trade. He appears to be analyzing a special case of an economy closed to trade where the commodity for which a potential comparative advantage exists – a primary product staple – has a relatively low domestic price: in the extreme, the price is taken to be zero. Given an exogenous event which raises the relative home price of this staple, 'discovery' leads to exploitation and expansion via exports to world markets. What is discovered, of course, is not necessarily knowledge of the staple's existence but rather an external demand for the product or an improvement in the supply of interregional and international transport for this bulk commodity. Either of these exogenous economic events raises the relative home price of the staple and thus its exploitation through export. True, a more rational process would be less abrupt: 'The quest for and discovery of resource R_i may be correlated with shifts in world demand toward the ith staple. . . .'[6] Furthermore, it follows that 'if world demand for the ith staple may increase, it may also decline.'[7]

The impact of world market conditions is, then, at the heart of the engine of growth, vent-for-surplus and staple theories of historical development. Yet, in three of the most famous applications – Canada from 1870 to 1915, the American South in the ante bellum period, and the American Midwest from the 1850s onwards – resource intensive regional development and export expansion took place concomitant with other indigenous growth forces. Precisely for this reason, the economic historian has found it very difficult to identify just how much of the observed regional growth performance may be attributed to the export engine and how much to other causes: 'This process . . . can be visualized as superimposed upon an underlying steady swell of neoclassical growth . . . Thus, export-based growth may explain a large part of the *variation* in the aggregate growth rate . . . whether or not it explains a large part of the average level of that growth rate.'[8]

Until very recently, Canadian and American economic historians have attempted to disentangle these complex forces by evaluating *ex post* data. Kravis's recent article exemplifies this approach: 'It would be plausible to regard foreign demand as the initiator of the supply changes if the level of exports was high or, if not high, at least growing relative to gross domestic product.'[9] Unfortunately, no such easy conclusions are possible without a well specified general equilibrium model. After all, an expanding export volume may be simply a passive response to independent domestic supply expansion and a low domestic income elasticity of demand for the staple in question.

To our knowledge, the first and only such attempt to pose an explicit counterfactual alternative of an economy where the historical export staple thesis is at issue can be found in the recent paper by Chambers and Gordon. Applying a general equilibrium model to the Canadian economy 1901–10, the authors are able to isolate the quantitative impact of the wheat boom on per capita income expansion.[10] There have been other recent attempts to identify the impact of trade on developing eighteenth- and nineteenth-century economies. Apart from the Chambers and Gordon paper, however, all of these focus on the impact of wartime conditions or tariff policy rather than the long-term impact of world market conditions. Robert Fogel and Stanley Engerman used partial equilibrium analysis to isolate the relative importance of domestic demand, tariffs, and domestic supply conditions in accounting for the impressive expansion of the American iron industry in the ante bellum period.[11] Clayne Pope applied a sophisticated general equilibrium model to explore the impact of tariff policy on the South in the ante bellum period.[12] Using a similar approach, Glen Hueckle attempted to isolate the economic impact of the Napoleonic Wars on the English economy.[13] Yet none of these contributions confronts the staple theory or the engine of growth thesis since their concern has not been with long-term movements in world market conditions for key staple exports.

The present chapter applies the Chambers and Gordon methodology to the American economy, 1870–1910. As we shall see in section 10.3, the framework developed in chapter 3 is somewhat more elaborate than that used by Chambers and Gordon, and, as a result, it answers much of the criticism of their model's specification.[14] Caves has argued that the simple general equilibrium model used by Chambers and Gordon fails to capture a number of key interactions embedded in the staple thesis: (i) The export-led adherents normally argue that the rate of domestic capital accumulation is positively affected by an increased rate of expansion of staple production. Our model incorporates this potential impact. (ii) During a staple boom period, the rate of economic expansion is not subject to the long-run constraints of balanced growth but rather involves the progressive elimination of a disequilibrium with windfall quasi-rents accruing along the way.[15] Since Chambers and Gordon restrict themselves to long-run competitive equilibrium analysis only, Caves feels that their numerical results are of doubtful value. Our model was specially designed to deal with short-run disequilibrium conditions and thus should alleviate Caves' anxiety on this score. (iii) In constructing their counterfactual, Chambers and Gordon fail to account for the likely diminution in foreign immigration which would have been forthcoming had world wheat markets not boomed. This issue will be confronted in detail in chapter 11.

Given this background, we now turn to the issues confronted in the present chapter: Can we isolate the impact of world market conditions on American growth from 1870 to 1910? Were exports an 'engine of growth' in late nineteenth-century American development? Do world market conditions account for any of the rapid industrialization following 1870? What would have been the performance of the Midwest in the absence of changing world market conditions for American grains?

10.2 The historical issues

The exports-as-an-engine-of-growth thesis may be well established in American historiography, but the literature dealing with the post-Civil War period certainly has its skeptics. In chapter 8 we noted that Robert Gallman was one of these: 'Did international markets provide agriculture with relief from the pressures of the changing pattern of domestic demand? There is some evidence that agriculture was able to export an increasing share of output [but] *changes in foreign trade . . . did not moderate the shift of U.S. commodity output away from agriculture and toward manufacturing. Indeed, they contributed toward this shift.'* [16] Gallman appears to argue counter to the engine of growth thesis. He seems to adopt the view that *deteriorating* world market conditions for American agricultural staples fostered industrialization. (Gallman is mute on the issue of per capita income effects, however.) Certainly, the literature on farmers' discontent is consistent with this position. Farmers perceived a deterioration in the relative price of farm products after the 1860s, and the traditional position linking agricultural hardship and falling prices has been stated succinctly by Allan Bogue:

> There is a time hallowed tradition that the years between 1866 and 1896 were years of almost unallayed agricultural depression in the United States. There is certainly evidence to support such a position. The prices of agricultural commodities fell during this period, as did prices in general, and it is generally agreed that primary producers are particularly hard hit in periods of declining prices. [17]

Chapter 7 showed that this was certainly *not* the case *in the Midwest* after 1870. Yet, this result was based on the movements of relative prices in the interior, and the Midwestern terms of trade were overwhelmingly dominated by transport improvements (chapter 9). What about East coast prices? Are economic historians correct in attributing at least a part of farm discontent to deteriorating world market conditions? It appears that before we can identify the impact of world market conditions on the late nineteenth-century American economy, we must first establish the secular movements in the relative price of America's export staples.

Since the relative deterioration of farm product prices after the late 1860s has been the focus of American historiography for some time, surely a relevant counterfactual is one which imposes stability on the international terms of trade. Figure 10.1 documents these two regimes of actual and counterfactual terms of trade movements. The terms of trade for both the East and the Midwest are displayed there. Although it was pointed out in chapters 7, 9 and in appendix A that the external terms of trade exhibited no obvious trend from the 1870s to World War I, a world of constant terms of trade would have produced quite different commodity price behavior nevertheless.

First, very early in this period the United States was subjected to a marked relative price movement which may have had a profound influence on growth throughout the remaining four decades. The relative price of agricultural products declines sharply from 1870 to 1872, *at Eastern ports*. So sharp is this short-run price movement that it dominates subsequent relative price behavior. The relevant question seems to be: To what extent were exports a 'brake' on late nineteenth-century American development? Had the terms of trade remained constant at 1870 levels, the relative price of agricultural commodities would have been higher at the Eastern seaboard than in fact it was for every year except 1891 and 1909! The same is true of the Midwest terms of trade. Indeed, had the international terms of trade remained constant up to 1872, the relative price of farm products in the Midwest would have *risen* by 25 percent rather than fallen by an equal rate. The wide disparity in these Midwestern relative price movements is, of course, to be explained by the enormous reduction in transport charges on Eastward grain trade. Clearly, there is little scope for the 'engine of growth' thesis in this period of American development since the relative price of export staples *fell* after 1870. Presumably the deterioration would have been even more pronounced if we initiated our analysis with 1866. It has been argued throughout this book that much of late nineteenth-century American growth can be understood as a response to the disequilibrating conditions associated with the Civil War decade. One aspect of the 1860s was the sharp decline in the prices of producer durables and grains starting in 1860. In the case of grains, the years 1866–8 did witness a temporary recovery in relative

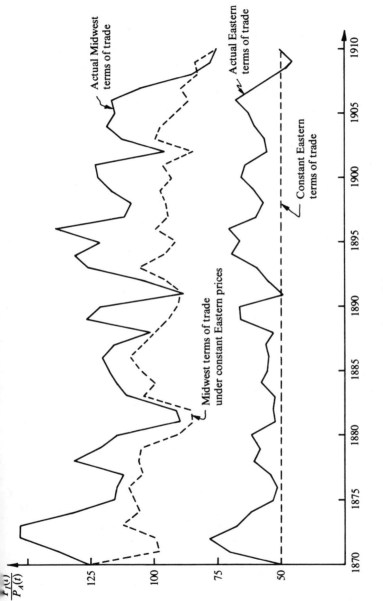

Figure 10.1

prices. Nevertheless, the decline in Eastern grain prices relative to other commodities from 1870 to 1872 must be viewed as part of a longer trend covering all of the Civil War decade. Whether the secular deterioration in East coast farm prices is to be explained by war tariffs or conditions in European markets is another matter. Given the deterioration, how did it influence subsequent American development?

Second, the significant cycles in the terms of trade series would have been eliminated under our counterfactual conditions thus imparting far greater stability to the American economy. The counterfactual experiment may, therefore, shed some light on the role of world market conditions in generating long swings in American growth at least over these four decades. The literature on American instability can be bisected into two basic positions: (i) that American cycles and long swings can be explained by large exogenous shocks to a stable system; (ii) that American cycles and long swings can be explained by small shocks to an inherently unstable system.[18] Obviously, our model is in the former tradition since departures from full employment are not possible in our system. But even in this full employment model we may be able to see far more clearly how world market conditions may have set in motion departures from full capacity during the late nineteenth century.

10.3 World markets and American development: a counterfactual

The fictitious history of constant terms of trade

This section isolates the role of foreign trade on development following the Civil War decade. The impact of trade on American growth in the late nineteenth century can only be evaluated by posing explicit counterfactuals. The general issue is to evaluate the quantitative impact on American growth had world market (trade) conditions been different. But what is the most appropriate counterfactual to pose? The impact of world market conditions can be explored best by comparing actual American economic performance with a fictitious world of constant terms of trade. How would the United States have grown from 1870 to 1910 had she faced a stable relative price of industrial imports to agricultural exports at Eastern ports? The counterfactual world being considered is one characterized by higher agricultural (export) prices throughout the period.

The impact of a counterfactual world of higher agricultural prices can be separated into static and dynamic effects. For some economic variables, e.g. the industrialization rate, these effects are

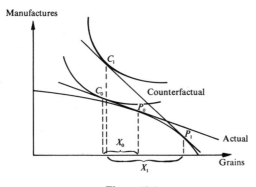

Figure 10.2

offsetting. The static effects are well understood in trade theory and they are summarized in Figure 10.2. In the counterfactual world, the relative price of 'grains' is higher, inducing a production shift out of industry and into agriculture. Exports of grains expand as well under normal demand conditions. The implication is clear: had the 1870 terms of trade been maintained throughout these four decades industrialization would have been inhibited, urbanization stifled, Westward migration accelerated but, presumably, real income gains augmented. Viewing these simple comparative static results in another way, much of the impressive industrialization which in fact took place during the Gilded Age may be explained by deteriorating world market conditions. Although the *direction* of the effect is rather clear cut, the magnitude of this influence has not been explored in the literature.

The above argument appeals only to conventional comparative static effects. What about *dynamic* effects? How might capital formation rates have been influenced by deteriorating world market conditions for American export staples? Would they have been raised or lowered? The impact must have been negative, and on two counts. First, given the capital stock in 1870 the real income loss associated with the terms of trade deterioration implies lower total savings out of this diminished income. On these grounds alone a less rapid rate of accumulation must have been forthcoming. Following the arguments of chapter 5, the rise in the economy-wide capital–output ratio associated with the windfall loss in real income must have inhibited capital formation rates. Second, the relative rise in industrial (producer durable) goods' prices early in the seventies implies less *real* investment out of a given savings pool.[19] This follows from our arguments in chapter 3 reproduced here graphically in Figure 10.3. Once again, the important issue for the eco-

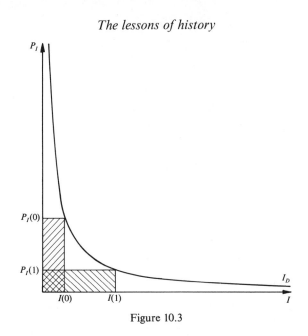

Figure 10.3

nomic historian is the *magnitude* of these potential dynamic effects. Did they lower capital formation rates significantly? Would real income growth have been noticeably different under conditions of terms of trade stability? Were the dynamic effects associated with the deterioration in the terms of trade sufficiently powerful to offset significantly the comparative static effects thus producing a less industrialized economy by 1910? That is, we have seen that the decline in relative farm prices should have tended to foster industrialization *in the short run.* In the long run, however, capital formation rates must have tended to diminish. Since industrialization is positively influenced by capital formation (being a more capital intensive process), industrialization would be inhibited on this count. Which of these two forces dominates American experience? Furthermore, if capital formation rates would have been significantly higher in the counterfactual world of constant terms of trade, to what extent can the Great Depression up to 1896 be explained by the *relative* deterioration in world market prices for farm products?

Exports and economic growth: dynamics

Table 10.1 presents a summary of the dynamic impact of world market conditions on American growth. The impact is not insignificant. For the period as a whole, capital formation rates would have been considerably higher in a counterfactual world of constant

Table 10.1. *The impact of world market conditions on GNP per capita and capital formation rates: 1869–1908*

Table 10.1A. *GNP per worker growth*

Period	1870 prices		1910 prices		Current relative prices	
	Actual	Constant terms of trade	Actual	Constant terms of trade	Actual	Constant terms of trade
1869/78–1884/93	2·49%	2·57%	2·33%	2·45%	1·69%	1·93%
1884/93–1899/1908	1·36	1·69	1·25	1·57	1·24	1·24
1869/78–1899/1908	1·91	2·11	1·76	1·99	1·49	1·57

Table 10.1B. *Capital stock growth*

Period	Actual	Constant terms of trade
1869/78–1884/93	5·87%	6·28%
1884/93–1899/1908	4·55	4·93
1869/78–1899/1908	5·18	5·57

terms of trade: from 1869/78 to 1899/1908, the per annum rate is 5·57 percent compared with the 'actual' rate of 5·18 percent. Note, however, that the tendency towards retardation is no different between the two regimes: between 1869/78–1884/93 and 1884/93–1899/1908, the rate of capital stock growth declines by 1·3 percent in both the actual and counterfactual worlds. It would appear that the Great Depression discussed in chapter 5 does not have its source in world market conditions. This conclusion is reinforced by an examination of GNP per worker growth rates presented in Table 10.1A. Whether the 1870, 1910 or current relative price weights are used the retardation in the American economy would have been roughly comparable had the external terms of trade remained stable throughout this period of Great Depression and Agrarian Discontent. This finding seems to us especially important given the attention which economic historians have lavished on British export performance in accounting for her retardation during the same four decades. Furthermore, American economic historians have also regarded agricultural performance and exports as a key to similar long-term trends on this side of the Atlantic. Our findings imply a rejection of that hypothesis.

Nevertheless, growth rates are consistently higher in the counterfactual world of constant terms of trade and our choice of price weights has nothing to do with that result. We have seen how physical capital accumulation rates would have been raised from 5·18 to 5·57 percent per annum. GNP per worker growth rates would have been similarly affected: in 1870 prices, they would have been raised from 1·91 to 2·11 percent per annum; in 1910 prices, the rates per annum would have risen from 1·76 to 1·99. Furthermore, these calculations ignore the *initial* real income losses associated with the deterioration in the terms of trade in the first years in the 1870s. Up to this point, our focus has been on growth rates from a 1869–78 base. How is the initial base affected? That is, the terms of trade shift sharply against the United States between 1870 and 1872. How did this relative price change affect American real income *initially* apart from the subsequent dynamic effects? In 1870 prices, commodity GNP outside of the South would have been 14 percent higher in 1872 had the terms of trade remained constant at 1870 levels. In 1910 prices, the figure is 8 percent. Thus, the short-run effect of instability in world market conditions on the Northeast and Midwest must have been powerful indeed. One cannot help but speculate that these world market conditions may have a great deal to do with the observed long swings in the American economy up to World War I. Although the interaction between world market conditions and domestic activity has been extensively researched for the ante bellum period,[20] externally induced instability in the post-Civil War period has not been a position commonly accepted in the long-swing literature. Our findings suggest more serious attention to this view of American instability in the late nineteenth century.

Farmers' complaints: land values, rents and yields

Although the farmers' terms of trade in the *Midwest* improved secularly from 1870 to 1910, they would have improved by even more had the 1870 foreign (East coast) terms of trade remained constant throughout the period. Under those counterfactual conditions, the full beneficial effect of interregional transport improvements would have been felt in the Midwest. This section explores the importance of world market conditions on the farmer. What would have happened to yields, rents and land values? After an answer to this question is supplied, the subsequent section turns to an evaluation of the farm sector in relation to the American economy as a whole.

Table 10.2 compares the actual and counterfactual series on land values, rents and yields in the Midwest. It seems quite clear that world market conditions were critical to farm performance. Note first that land values would have risen by 4·8 times over the four

Table 10.2. *The impact of world market conditions on the farm sector:
land values, rents and yields (1870=100)*

Year	Land values		Rents		Yields	
	Actual	Constant terms of trade	Actual	Constant terms of trade	Actual	Constant terms of trade
1870	100	100	100	100	100	100
1875	138	168	109	118	106	115
1880	190	194	118	127	114	126
1885	279	324	127	145	126	138
1890	354	317	132	145	127	143
1895	411	394	127	155	124	146
1900	479	479	118	155	115	145
1905	497	549	119	155	113	147
1910	306	483	123	164	119	157

decades rather than by three times as was in fact the case.[21] The more rapid rise in land values is explained by the behavior of rents. Land's value marginal product would have increased more markedly under the favorable price conditions. This, in turn, is to be explained both by the *direct* impact of the higher farm prices and the *indirect* effect on the marginal physical product of land and yields. Given the land stock as fixed, the rise in farm prices would have induced an output expansion by applying increased labor and capital to farm production. Yields would have risen as a result. The *magnitude* of that yield response accounts for much of the improvement in rents. Between 1870 and 1910, yields would have risen by 57 percent. Compare this figure with the percent by which yields 'actually' rise – 19 percent. Agricultural historians have noted the remarkable stability in Midwestern grain yields from 1880 to World War I. Had the (East coast) terms of trade remained constant at their 1870 levels, land yields in the Midwest would have risen by 38 percent more than in fact they did. Our findings support the view that world market conditions can explain much of the movements in yields over the late nineteenth century. In summary, world market conditions had a profound effect on the agriculture in the Midwest: they suppressed the rise in yields, rents and, thus, land values.

A final question relates to labor-saving mechanization on the farm. How would the farm sector have achieved the yield improvement? Would we have observed a neutral effect on the capital–labor ratio in agriculture, or would labor-saving farm devices have been introduced at an accelerated rate? The answers can be found in Table 10.3. Not only would equipment per farm have increased with the more favorable counterfactual price conditions, but the equip-

Table 10.3. *The impact of world market conditions on farm mechanization*
(1870=100)

	Equipment per acre		Equipment per worker	
Year	Actual	Constant terms of trade	Actual	Constant terms of trade
1870	100	100	100	100
1875	142	180	160	192
1880	188	246	220	267
1885	248	317	286	337
1890	279	367	338	402
1895	309	422	410	479
1900	324	469	499	569
1905	348	524	577	660
1910	405	609	672	754

ment per farm laborer would have risen as well. The rate of farm mechanization was very impressive under the actual historical conditions prevailing after 1870. Nevertheless, it would have received a further stimulus under the counterfactual world of constant terms of trade: the Midwestern farm capital–labor ratio index would have increased by 7·5 rather than by 6·7 times. Farm mechanization rates are determined in large measure by conditions external to the sector. Under the counterfactual conditions of lower producer durable prices, farm mechanization would have been accelerated by two mutually reinforcing effects: (i) by the relative decline in capital goods' prices, and (ii) by the relative rise in real wages induced by the higher rates of capital formation discussed in the section on *Exports and economic growth*.

The agricultural labor force and industrialization

In chapter 4 (Table 4.5) Perloff's data on the Midwestern agricultural labor force were compared with our model's predictions. The historical series are documented only by census dates.[22] In the historical data, the agricultural labor force reaches a peak in 1900 while our 'actual' series predicts a turning point five years earlier in 1895. Both series underwent impressive (but retarding) growth up to that point. We have seen above that part of this performance was attributable to world market conditions unfavorable to agriculture. Table 10.4 documents the magnitude of these effects. Had the relative world price of farm products remained at 1870 levels throughout these four decades, the agricultural labor force would have been 34 percent higher at the end of the period. Furthermore, under these

Table 10.4. *The impact of world market conditions on*
the agricultural labor force, 1870–1910

Year	Actual	Constant terms of trade
1870	49·3	49·3
1875	54·1	57·2
1880	61·4	66·1
1885	69·9	75·7
1890	73·4	81·2
1895	73·4	85·8
1900	68·4	86·9
1905	66·7	87·8
1910	68·0	91·2

counterfactual conditions there would have been *no* absolute decline in the agricultural labor force prior to 1910. The divergence
between these two regimes is clearly centered on two periods coin-
ciding with historical phases of deteriorating world market conditions for agricultural goods. The first is the decade 1870–80. The
second lies in the fifteen year period 1890–1905.

Rapid industrialization and structural change following the Civil
War decade has always been appreciated by American economic
historians. Indeed, some have argued that the transformation of
the American economy after 1869 was equal to the 'Industrial
Revolution' in the ante bellum period.[23] Yet one must search that
literature with tenacity to find some mention of the role of world
market conditions in producing that result. Indeed, the literature
treats industrialization after the Civil War as an event fully *endo-*
genous to the American economy. Just how wrong this view may be
is given dramatic support in Table 10.5. Between 1870 and 1895,
the economy-wide industrial employment share 'actually' rose
from 0·507 to 0·576. Industrialization in the Midwest was even
more impressive: the industrial employment share rose from
0·240 to 0·329. The counterfactual conditions yield strikingly different results. In the Midwest, the industrial employment share
would have *declined* from 0·240 to 0·230 up to 1895. For the economy
as a whole the figures are 0·507 and 0·505. *Had the international*
terms of trade remained at 1870 levels over the subsequent twenty-five
years, our model suggests that no industrialization would in fact have
taken place. That is, agricultural productivity growth and land
expansion would have produced balanced employment growth.
Only after 1895 would the long-term process of industrialization
have resumed. This counterfactual experiment is subject to critical
revision given the imperfect nature of the model specification and

Table 10.5. *The impact of world market conditions on industrialization, 1870–1910*

Year	Midwestern industrial employment share: L_{IW}/L_W		Economy-wide industrial employment share: L_I/L		Economy-wide share of agriculture's value added in GNP	
	Actual	Constant terms of trade	Actual	Constant terms of trade	Actual	Constant terms of trade
1870	0·240	0·240	0·507	0·507	0·358	0·358
1875	0·260	0·227	0·535	0·509	0·375	0·396
1880	0·258	0·206	0·518	0·481	0·400	0·447
1885	0·240	0·185	0·521	0·481	0·371	0·400
1890	0·273	0·206	0·538	0·490	0·355	0·421
1895	0·329	0·230	0·576	0·505	0·325	0·399
1900	0·417	0·277	0·627	0·527	0·280	0·365
1905	0·467	0·318	0·663	0·557	0·257	0·344
1910	0·488	0·335	0·685	0·578	0·306	0·371

parameter estimation underlying the calculation. Yet it seems unlikely that the magnitude of the effect of world market conditions will be significantly reversed by subsequent research. An explanation of American industrialization during the Gilded Age which relies solely, or even mainly, on factors endogenous to the economy must be rejected. In summary, much of the observed transformation of the economy up to the mid-1890s is to be explained by factors exogenous to the American economy, namely, world market conditions.

We might note that this result is consistent with Whitney's research on the American economy (1879–99), although he used a totally different model.[24] Whitney utilizes an elaborate input–output approach while our model ignores inter-industry demands completely. Since our model fails to incorporate inter-industry demands, some readers may feel that it is far too simple to evaluate effectively American industrialization experience. Apparently this is not the case, since Whitney finds that the shift in output mix had its source in final demand rather than in inter-industry requirements. More to the point of the present chapter, Whitney estimates that 90 percent of the total structural change during this period resulted from three sources, two of which are trade related: (i) lagging domestic final demand for agricultural products; (ii) replacement of imports by domestic manufactures; and (iii) weak foreign demand for agricultural products.[25] In fact, the heavy industrial sector underwent unusually rapid growth after the 1880s but the source of this expansion is not from unusually rapid rates of capital formation: 'The performance of demand for heavy capital goods over the [period 1879–99] closely paralleled the trend for all commodity production. This finding questions the prevailing historical opinion that capital investment was a major expansionary force in the late nineteenth century.'[26] Given the recent evidence gleaned by Davis and Gallman on the stability of aggregate gross savings rates after the 1870s, this result hardly seems surprising. Instead, the source of heavy industry's expansion from 1879 to 1899 is found in import substitution and export expansion. The latter is especially pronounced by the 1890s following the American commercial invasion of Europe in machinery, chemicals and fabricated metal products.[27]

Although our results are consistent with Whitney's we have gone one step further in this chapter to show that much of the industrialization, 'vented' onto the world market through exports of manufactures and import substitution for industrial products, was induced by world market conditions rather than developments endogenous to the American economy itself.

10.4 A qualification: the trade specification problem

Chapter 8 (pp. 179–81) briefly raised the trade specification issue. It was noted that many economic historians appear to analyze the American economy as if it were in isolation and closed to world trade. This book has adopted a diametrically opposing position. The 'small country' assumption has been utilized throughout. That is, America (excluding the South) is assumed to have had no influence on world market prices; price elasticities describing the excess demand for American grain exports in Europe and excess supplies of industrial imports from Europe are both taken to be very large. These competing views of American growth can be reconciled only by empirical evidence relating to foreign demand conditions for U.S. grains.

Granted that the price elasticity of grains (foodstuffs) is normally assumed to be less than unity – it is certainly true of *domestic* demand in our model (see appendix A), but the relevant issue is the foreign demand for U.S. grains given a world of many suppliers. Let

X = American (quantum) grain exports,
D = quantity of grains demanded in the rest of the world,
S = quantity of grains supplied in the rest of the world.

Then American grain exports can be formally expressed as

$$X = D - S, \qquad (1)$$

where America supplies exports to satisfy excess demands in world (European) markets at some price, P.

Expression (1) can be differentiated with respect to world grain prices (New York–Liverpool transport charges are ignored in this example):

$$\frac{dX}{dP} = \frac{dD}{dP} - \frac{dS}{dP}. \tag{2}$$

The price elasticity of demand for U.S. grains in world markets can be derived by multiplying both sides of (2) by P/X, yielding

$$\frac{dX}{dP} \cdot \frac{P}{X} = \eta_x = \frac{dD}{X} \cdot \frac{P}{dP} - \frac{dS}{X} \cdot \frac{P}{dP} \tag{3}$$

$$= \frac{dD}{X} \Big/ \frac{dP}{P} - \frac{dS}{X} \Big/ \frac{dP}{P}.$$

Expression (3) for η_x can be rewritten in terms of a weighted sum of world demand and supply elasticities:

$$\eta_x = \frac{D}{X} \left\{ \frac{dD}{D} \Big/ \frac{dP}{P} \right\} - \frac{S}{X} \left\{ \frac{dS}{S} \Big/ \frac{dP}{P} \right\} = \frac{D}{X} \{\eta_D\} - \frac{S}{X} \{\eta_s\}, \tag{4}$$

where $\eta_D < 0$, $\eta_s > 0$ and thus $\eta_x < 0$.

We can readily see that the elasticity of demand for American grains in world markets will be higher the larger are the absolute values of η_D and η_s, and the higher is D/X and S/X. That is, the demand for U.S. grains abroad will have a higher price elasticity if U.S. exports are a small share in both world demand and world supply; η_x is also higher, the larger are the demand and supply elasticities for grains in the rest of the world. In the small country case utilized throughout this book, $D/X = S/X = \infty$ and thus $\eta_x = -\infty$. Note further that even if $\eta_s = 0$,

$$\eta_x = \frac{D}{X} \{\eta_D\} < 0.$$

Similarly, demand may have a very low price elasticity yet η_x may be high: if $\eta_D = 0$,

$$\eta_x = -\frac{S}{X} \{\eta_s\} < 0.$$

The evidence presented in appendix A confirms an inelastic price elasticity of demand for foodstuffs, at least in late nineteenth-century America (e.g., $\eta_D = -0.8$). A recent study by Fisher and Temin for late nineteenth-century America yields estimates on long-run supply elasticities for wheat over seventeen states. The elasticities range widely between 0·07 and 10·76, but the average value appears to be about unity.[28] If conditions abroad were roughly similar, then $\eta_s = 1\cdot0$. Using these estimates, we only require data on D/X and S/X to infer the rough magnitude of η_x.

Our case will be made by reference to the British wheat market only, although Britain was only one part of a larger European market.[29] Between 1870 and 1900, about one-quarter of British wheat requirements were satisfied by American exports. The relevant data for wheat only (1873–1911) are presented in Table 10.6. Given the values for D/X and S/X (Table 10.6, cols. (6) and (7)) for the four decades as a whole, an estimate for η_x can be derived from expression (4):

$$\eta_x \cong 3\cdot83\ \{-0\cdot8\} - 2\cdot83\ \{1\cdot0\} = -5\cdot894.$$

In the empirical trade literature, an η_x estimate this large is considered evidence of very price elastic conditions indeed. Furthermore, we might very well argue that $\eta_x = -5\cdot9$ is a conservative *lower bound* on the price elasticity of demand for U.S. agricultural exports. Since American exports directed elsewhere were roughly equal to those absorbed by the British market, and since the remainder of Europe generated demand requirements and supplies far more than double that of Britain, the 'true' elasticity would presumably exceed $-5\cdot9$ by a large measure.

In short, it seems to us that the foreign price elasticity for U.S. foodstuff exports was very high, and that our small country characterization is quite appropriate. Rothstein is in agreement: 'Until

Table 10.6. *British wheat consumption, imports and total supply, 1873–1911* *(thousands of hundredweights)*

Period	Imports U.S. (1)	Imports Other (2)	Domestic supply (3)	Domestic consumption (4)	Total non-American supply (5)	$\frac{D}{X} = \frac{(4)}{(1)}$ (6)	$\frac{S}{X} = \frac{(5)}{(1)}$ (7)
1873–77	107,119	235,993	11,106	354,218	247,099	3·31	2·31
1878–82	172,514	286,149	10,707	469,370	296,856	2·73	1·72
1883–87	128,222	276,186	5,412	409,820	281,598	3·20	2·20
1888–92	106,936	307,502	6,804	421,242	314,306	3·93	2·96
1893–97	149,303	350,104	3,672	503,079	353,776	3·38	2·37
1898–1902	188,873	351,244	4,469	544,586	355,713	2·89	1·89
1903–06	60,439	473,672	3,481	537,592	477,153	8·95	7·95
1907–11	88,561	501,849	4,203	594,613	506,052	6·75	5·75
1873–1911						3·83	2·83

Source: Col. (1), from B. R. Mitchell and P. Deane, *Abstract of British Historical Statistics*, pp. 100–2; col. (2) , *ibid.*, pp. 98–9; col. (3), *ibid.*, pp. 88–9.

the 1880's the volume and price of American exports of breadstuffs had been influenced primarily by the size and condition of the British harvests. Increasingly, however, the *total* available supply in a more closely knit world market became the major determinant.'[30] Indeed '. . . heated debates on the extent to which Liverpool regulated prices in America filled agricultural and grain trade journals in the late 1870's and early 1880's. By the mid-1880's there was almost universal acknowledgment of the crucial role of the British market in fixing prices.'[31]

Evidence such as this leads us to reject the 'closed' characterization of American late nineteenth-century development as being totally inappropriate. We also reject as irrelevant a variant on this theme: the 'immizerizing growth' thesis. The immizerizing growth thesis views the foreign demand for U.S. grains as having a price elasticity less than unity. This unfortunate assumption, perhaps based on twentieth-century experience with the farm problem, asserts that agricultural productivity growth was self-defeating. The thesis argues that supply expansion generated a percentage grain price decline in excess of the quantum expansion thus producing a *diminution* in foreign exchange receipts and farm income. This view can hardly be taken seriously given the long-run stability in the relative international price of farm products after the mid-1870s, a period of significant total factor productivity growth in Midwestern agriculture, continued land expansion, transport improvements, and surging exports.

11

Immigration and American Growth

Fly, scatter ... anything rather than remain here.
Horace Greeley (1837)

11.1 America: Europe's safety-valve

The issues

The literature on nineteenth-century international migration has
swollen since the appearance of the classic works by Jerome,
Willcox and Ferenczi, and Dorothy Thomas.[1] The stakes appear to
be high. First, these labor migrations present a challenge to the
explanatory power of economic theory in general and the human
capital model in particular. Indeed, one of the key issues has been
the ability of individual cost-benefit calculus in accounting for the
levels, trends and timing of gross emigration rates from Europe
to the New World. Second, the economist has always viewed the
analysis of this massive trans-Atlantic migration as a means of
improving our understanding of economic–demographic interactions during phases of modern economic growth. While the
economic historian has a solid understanding of the impact of demographic variables on the structure of demand, income distribution,
and capital formation rates, he is far less confident of his knowledge regarding the response of demographic and thus long-run labor
supply variables to purely economic variables. In a closed economy,
the response is conditioned primarily by fertility choices, death
rates and the age structure of the population. In the open economy,
the complexity of family size and fertility response can be bypassed
and the impact of economic variables on labor supply examined
directly through the more immediate external migration response.
Third, the historian has an obvious interest in the role of demographic variables as progenitors of economic instability. Abramovitz, Easterlin, Kuznets and others have been persuaded that
American instability in general, and the long swing in particular,
was intimately related to foreign immigration.[2] Certainly the impact
of the immigration laws after World War I on residential construction during the twenties and the subsequent depression of the thirties
has always been appreciated.[3] It is only a small jump from this

221

historical research to Easterlin's contemporary concern with the economic importance of demographic 'echo' effects.[4]

The apparent association between external immigration rates and American instability in the pre-1930s has been primarily responsible for the economic historian's persistent attempts to identify the 'push' and 'pull' forces underlying trans-Atlantic migrations. There appears to be full agreement among economic historians as to the meaning of these descriptive terms. All participants wish to identify the relative importance of economic conditions in both sending and receiving regions in contributing to these massive migrations. Yet the participants appear to agree on nothing else. Although the consensus seems to favor the importance of pull conditions in the New World in explaining nineteenth-century migration, there is hardly unanimity. Eight major contributions which have appeared since 1961 are surveyed in Table 11.1. Of these, three favor pull, three favor combined effects, one favors push, and one fails to reach *any* conclusion. Thus, while Easterlin concludes that '. . . we are led back to Kuznets' view that emigration was responding to a common external force . . . a swing in the demand for labor [in the United States] which generated a common response among the European countries',[5] Wilkinson asserts that '. . . if the 'pull' factor underlying international migration . . . refers to the expansions and contractions of United States output there is little evidence that it was significant'.[6] The present chapter enters the migration debate at precisely this point. It attempts to decompose the sources of late nineteenth-century American immigration into push and pull forces. In contrast to the bulk of past research, however, our emphasis will be on long-term forces rather than cycles or long swings. As we shall see, the results of the research in this chapter are essential to the remainder of the book.

The key historical question is: What was the contribution of American economic conditions to gross migration rates? The answer should shed light on many issues which are central to nineteenth-century trans-Atlantic development. For example, Habakkuk's thesis[7] depends critically on migration behavior. Habakkuk has argued that much of the observed differences in Anglo-American industrialization, technique choices and capital formation can be explained by the relative cheapness of skilled compared to unskilled labor. How did the character of nineteenth-century immigration influence this asserted small skill differential in American wages compared to the British, specifically, and the European, more generally? In addition, if pull forces in America were important determinants of trans-Atlantic migrations, then what were the underlying sources of those forces? How important was the American frontier as a European safety-valve? Is its asserted importance exaggerated? How much of the secular rise in foreign immigration can be attributed to the demographic forces in America, forces which produced a sharply declining rate of native labor force growth throughout the nineteenth century? Is it possible that these American demographic forces are at least as important as the 'Malthusian Devil' operating in Europe?

The present chapter attempts to supply some tentative answers to these important historical issues. They are inherently interesting in and of themselves, of course, but they are essential to chapters 5 through 10. The counterfactual analysis reported elsewhere in this book assumes that American pull conditions were sufficiently weak in the late nineteenth century for immigration response to changing U.S. economic conditions to be ignored in counterfactual analysis without serious bias. Thus it is fitting to conclude this book with the question: what was the contribution of long-term economic conditions in America to historical immigration rates? The going is rough. We must first consider potential revisions of the model developed in chapter 3 and then engage in some very messy econometrics.

A simple model of the nineteenth-century American labor market

The conventional approach by the economic historian investigating secular growth is to treat immigration as an exogenous variable. The framework in chapter 3 adopted this approach. Total labor supply in the American economy was characterized as increasing over time in response to two forces: (i) endogenous native population (labor force) growth rates; (ii) exogenous foreign immigration. The immigration series utilized has been the Kuznets–Rubin annual gross immigration estimates. In addition, the possibility of direct migration of these foreign immigrants to Western employment, agricultural or otherwise, has been ignored. Instead, foreign immigration has been treated as a two-stage process, although in fact this may be an oversimplification. Foreign immigration, $M(t)$, first augments the Eastern industrial labor force after which both 'foreigners' and native Easterners migrate if regional real wage differentials offer sufficient incentive. In Lebergott's words

> If we recognize that endless amounts of free or nearly free land were available throughout the nineteenth century, offering brighter opportunities at nearly any time than the European migrant could have had at home, we may question why short-term variations even in American opportunities affected migration at all substantially. The answer would appear to lie in the fact that migrants first took jobs . . . in Eastern cities . . . Having

accumulated a minimum competence, only then could they move on both geographically and economically.[8]

This treatment implies that foreign immigration is determined primarily by employment and wage conditions in non-agricultural sectors in the East. As a result, our attempt to make foreign immigration endogenous to the framework developed in chapter 3 will entail a respecification of the description of Eastern labor market behavior only.

To ease this section's exposition, let us treat the Eastern labor market in isolation for a given year as in Figure 11.1. The short-run labor demand function in the East, $D_E(t)$, has the usual properties: it is derived from the production function describing Eastern industry with capacity and technology fixed. The short-run labor supply function, $S'_E(t)$, is upward sloping reflecting the increased attraction of Eastern employment as real wages rise there relative to the West. This supply function is relatively inelastic given short-run limitations (e.g., search costs and risks) to interregional migration as they have been specified in chapter 3. If European migrations were really exogenous to the American labor market, as assumed in previous chapters, then *total* Eastern labor supply, $S_E(t)$, would be derived by the linear addition of observed foreign immigration to $S'_E(t)$: that is, $M(t)$ would not be influenced by job vacancy or wage conditions in the East. Obviously, the Eastern wage was depressed by the influx of foreign immigrants, but it would have been depressed by a lesser degree if $M(t)$ had been influenced by pull factors (i.e., influenced by employment conditions in the American East). That is, if the rate of foreign immigration tended to diminish with declining real wages and rising unemployment rates in the American

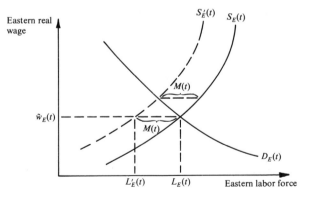

Figure 11.1

Northeast, then an exogenous increase in the average propensity to migrate to American cities would have had a less dramatic effect on both real wages and *actual* migration.

Suppose we now allow foreign immigration to be influenced by 'pull' factors in the United States. Nowhere in the historical literature is there a rejection of the thesis that American urban employment conditions had a positive influence on foreign immigration. Rather, the literature cannot agree on an answer to the question: how much? Let the endogenous $M(t)$ specification be

$$M(t) = \delta_1 \tilde{w}_E(t) - \delta'_0,$$

where δ_1 measures the response of $M(t)$ to real wages in Eastern industrial employment. Since we have not specified the magnitude of δ_1 we can temporarily sidestep the issue of 'how much.' The real wage variable presumably is identical to that explaining American interregional migration. Push factors abroad are captured by δ'_0 in this simple model. These include European harvest conditions, the 'Malthusian Devil,' migration costs, conscription in the Tsar's army and other influences on European employment conditions and living standards of the average worker. Assume for the moment that emigration to America has no impact on employment conditions in Europe.

Given an estimate of δ_1 and δ'_0, the revised description of the Eastern labor market can be graphically described as in Figure 11.2. Push effects in Europe are captured by rightward shifts in the $M(t)$ function, but let us instead concentrate on the pull of American labor market conditions. A shift in the derived demand for labor to the right due to capacity expansion would produce both an increased inflow of migrants and a rise in the real wage. If potential European migrants are very sensitive to employment conditions in America, e.g., if δ_1 is large, then $S_E(t)$ is more elastic than in the previous case where pull effects were ignored ($\delta_1 = 0$), and the resulting inflow of migrants will be all the larger and the real wage increase stifled. Furthermore, the less elastic is D_E with respect to the real wage, the more potent will be the measured pull on foreign labor, and the higher will be the resulting wage, from a given output or capacity expansion in the United States. Labor-saving technological change would have an effect opposite to capacity expansion. Presumably it was the combination of these effects that determined the strength of America's pull on European workers. That is, strong pull effects would have dominated if (i) capacity expansion was rapid, (ii) if technological progress was not labor-saving, (iii) if the American labor demand function was wage inelastic, and (iv) if migrant response to real wage differentials was highly elastic. We shall argue in the next section that the migration literature does not allow us to

226

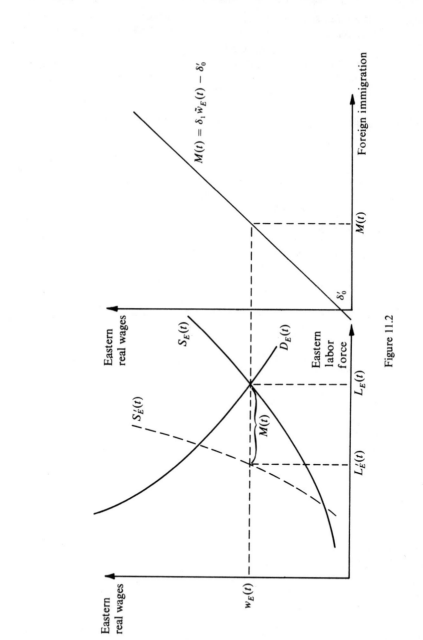

Figure 11.2

identify these component effects. It is important that we do so, since it is only (iv) which is relevant to the earlier counterfactuals raised in this book.

Symmetric arguments can be made for American 'native' labor force growth. A leftward shift in S'_E, due either to long-term demographic forces or to the operation of the Western frontier as a safety-valve, would have raised Eastern wages and increased the measured pull of American industrial employment conditions. This comparative static experiment can be readily translated into a more intriguing historical issue: to what extent did the pronounced decline in native labor force growth rates in America after the Civil War induce increased European emigration? Raising this issue does not reflect an effort to revive the 'Walker thesis.' The Walker thesis asserts that in the absence of immigration an offsetting rise in native population would have taken place in nineteenth-century America.[9] In contrast, we are asking whether domestic demographic factors influenced foreign immigration.

The historical $M(t)$ series utilized in the book can be found in appendix A (Table A.16). Note that $M(t)$ assumed negative values over protracted periods: in particular, the mid-1870s and the mid–late 1890s were years of sufficiently serious depression so that gross out-migration from America took place. The simulation (chapter 4) generates a $\tilde{w}_E(t)$ series which we have seen closely corresponds to Lebergott's estimates of real manufacturing wages. The econometrics in pp. 78–83 will help us establish a plausible estimate of δ_1. Given historical observations on $M(t)$ and $\tilde{w}_E(t)$, and given an estimate of δ_1, in the language of the literature push effects could be identified. Let $D(t)$ (for Devil in 'Malthusian Devil') denote these European push effects:

$$\hat{D}(t) = M(t) - \delta_1 \tilde{w}_E(t).$$

To summarize, in conjunction with an estimate of δ_1, historical observations on $M(t)$ and $\tilde{w}_E(t)$ yield a numerical series which captures the secular movements in the excess foreign labor supply. The $\hat{D}(t)$ series by itself should prove to be of interest since it will enable us to decompose observed international migration into 'push' and 'pull' effects over time. This decomposition is central to understanding the economic–demographic interactions in American growth. Pages 237–46 are devoted entirely to this decomposition.

With $\hat{D}(t)$ and δ_1 estimated, the exogenous immigration series used in chapter 3 can be replaced by the equation

$$M(t) = \hat{D}(t) + \delta_1 \tilde{w}_E(t),$$

where $M(t)$ is fully endogenous. We can then proceed with the revised model to ask once more the counterfactuals posed in chapters 5 to 10. When foreign immigration is made endogenous, how is our analytical interpretation of American economic history revised? In particular, how important was the frontier as an international safety-value? Or, how important were demographic forces in America? In addition, the impact of European economic–demographic conditions on American growth can be isolated. How are the long-run development trends over these four decades influenced by external migration conditions? These questions are the focus of section 11.4.

All we require, then, is an estimate of δ_1. Unfortunately, the existing literature fails to supply the estimate.

11.2 Foreign immigration and trans-Atlantic economic growth

Migrant behavior and the historical literature

Given the bewildering variety of the empirical work contained in the eight articles listed in Table 11.1, it might prove helpful to review the state of migration theory and evaluate these eight contributions in that light. The most appropriate place to begin is with the human capital model itself. Define the present discounted value of the net income stream associated with a move as

$$V_{it} = \sum_{t}^{n} \frac{E_{it} - C_{it}}{(1 - r_i)^t},$$

where E refers to the earnings differential between the two employments, C refers to costs associated with the move, and r the appropriate discount rate over the remainder of the potential migrant's lifetime, t–n. Of course, the economic historian does not have the requisite data to derive V for a specific age–education class of potential migrants, and thus he must be content with a gross approximation of the human capital model, i.e., one restricted to *current* earnings differentials. Furthermore, he rarely has current earnings differentials by age, education or occupation classes and thus must deal with average variables in each economy. The exception appears to be Quigley's recent attempt to disaggregate Swedish migration into agricultural and non-agricultural streams with the relevant wages by sector.[10] Data constraints are often so severe that income per capita measures must be used as proxies for earnings. In Easterlin's words: '. . . per capita income figures include property as well as labor income and are averages over the whole population . . . This, of course, is still some way from the ideal one might desire, the discounted value of the future income stream available to

Table 11.1. *Survey of international migration literature (1961–72)*

Researcher	Country	Basic model(s)	Basic conclusion(s)
Easterlin (1961)	Many, 1850–1914	$M = M(dNs)$	Pull
Kelley (1965)	Australia, 1865–1935	$M = M(U_s, U_r, M(-1))$	Pull
Wilkinson (1967)	Sweden, 1860–1914	$M = M(Q_s, Q_r, [M(-1)])$	Push and pull
Wilkinson (1970)	Many, 1870–1914	$M = M(Q_s, Q_r, YD)$	Push
		$\frac{M}{N_s} = M(Q_s, Q_r, YD, \frac{M}{N_s}(-1))$	
Gallaway and Vedder (1971)	UK, 1860–1913	$M = M(w_s, w_r, U_s, U_r)$	Push and pull
Tomaske (1971)	Many, 1881–1900	$\frac{M}{N_s} = M(YD, \int M(-1), dN_s)$	Pull
Quigley (1972)	Sweden, 1867–1908	$\frac{M}{N_s} = M(w_s, w_r, dN_s, M(-1))$	Push and pull
Richardson (1972)	Britain, 1870–1914	$M = M(w_s, w_r)$	None

Definition of symbols:

M, migration level (usually gross)

$\frac{M}{N_s}$, migration rate

dN_s, measure of demographic effect in sending region

U_s, unemployment rate in sending region

U_r, unemployment rate in receiving region

Q_s, output level in sending region

Q_r, output level in receiving region

w_s, real wage or income per capita in sending region

w_r, real wage or income per capita in receiving region

YD, income per capita or real wage differential

$M(-1)$, lagged migration level

$\frac{M}{N_s}(-1)$, lagged migration rate

$\int M(-1)$, integral of past migration levels

229

persons of migratory age.'[11] The earnings variable can, of course, be decomposed into wages of employed workers with the ith characteristics and the unemployment rate. Since historical wage series are normally quoted for *employed* workers, both the wage and the unemployment differential should be included in the migration equation whenever the data permit as in the recent study by Gallaway and Vedder.[12] Where appropriate wage data are unavailable and an *expected* earnings differential cannot be calculated, unemployment rates by themselves appear to serve well as proxies for the variance in earnings differentials as in Kelley's study of Australian immigration.[13] Finally, in spite of the fact that V_i is not directly observable, that does not imply that an indirect improvement on the *current* earnings differential cannot be achieved by synthetic means. Much of the single equation models of international migration attempt to approximate a permanent earnings differential by the utilization of distributed lag functions.

How can the economic historian approximate migrant costs,[14] C_{it}, and the discount rate, r_i, in his formulation of a migration function? The conventional procedure has been to use the integral of all past migrations as a proxy for current migration costs. Not only are psychic costs reduced when a migrant can locate among past migrants, but his move can be financed by past migrants as well. Thus, Kelley, Wilkinson, Tomaske and Quigley all introduce lagged migration or the integral of all past migrations in their studies.[15] Unfortunately, it is difficult in practice to interpret these results since, as we shall see below in *The estimation model*, lagged migration rates also appear as a derivative from the distributed lag formulation.

This survey is sufficient to identify the problems that must be confronted in developing a *micro* analysis which can be utilized to explain nineteenth-century international migrations. Yet the more important shortcomings of the existing literature do not appear at this step in the analysis. The most serious problems have arisen when the economic historian moves from human capital theorizing to the econometric estimation of *aggregate* migrations. To our knowledge, the literature does not contain an attempt to construct a relevant *macro economic* structure within which influences on migration listed in section 11.1 can be adequately evaluated. We hope to substantiate this assertion below where we lay bare the elements of a classic identification problem embedded in recent econometric attempts to explain emigration to the New World.[16]

Aggregate forces and the identification problem

Consider a two-country world in which the two national labor markets are integrated by foreign migration. The sending and receiving regions will be denoted by the subscripts S and R, respectively. In the short run, capacity in both economies is taken as exogenously fixed. The problem for us, and for other researchers listed in Table 11.1, is to determine the equilibrium wages and employment levels in these two economies. Given information, search and psychic costs, the equilibrium wage differential need not be zero.[17] Furthermore, we shall assume that the 'native' labor forces are fixed in the short run in these two economies: i.e., the 'domestic' labor participation rate is insensitive to wage variation. This assumption is adopted for convenience but the contemporary American evidence is not inconsistent with it. Based on the period 1930–65, for example, Lucas and Rapping find that the 'assumption of a zero labor-supply elasticity is approximately correct,' at least in the long run.[18]

The labor supplies in the two regions are defined to be

$$L_S = N_S - M, \tag{1}$$

$$L_R = N_R + M, \tag{2}$$

where M is the net migration flow from S to R and N_i is the 'native' labor force. The labor demand functions in the two regions are derived from neoclassical calculus.[19] Since the underlying production functions are not known with certainty, at this stage we cannot *a priori* discriminate between alternative functional forms.[20] In any case, the proper arguments in these labor demand functions are real wages and output levels. Because of its simplicity, we shall postulate linear labor demand functions in both economies:

$$L_S = \alpha_0 + \alpha_1 w_S + \alpha_2 Q_S \tag{3}$$

and

$$L_R = \beta_0 + \beta_1 w_R + \beta_2 Q_R. \tag{4}$$

Since output levels, Q_i, are taken to be given exogenously, these labor demand functions can be utilized to explore the response of employment to real wages. If migration were ignored, then a unique national wage would be consistent with the full employment in each national labor market. Given the possibility of international migration, the equilibrium pair of wages (and thus, the wage differential) which clears both labor markets will be consistent with some unique annual emigration flow. Thus, a migration response function must now be specified to close the system.

The conventional treatment of migration is to relate it to current wage differentials. The model can, of course, be made more complex by recognizing lags, permanent income variables, and by explicit human capital theorizing. For the sake of expository simplicity, the current wage differential is taken as the potential migrant's decision variable. Net emigration presumably should be allowed to take on negative values even when $w_S = w_R$ to recognize migration costs explicitly, unless, of course, non-pecuniary gains to migration dominate the decision to move: in the latter case, δ_0 will be positive. A linear specification of the migration function is typical of other migration studies and use will be made of it here as well:

$$M = \delta_1 [w_R - w_S] - \delta_0. \qquad (5)$$

Note that the human capital model outlined above argues that only the expected wage differential (or some proxy therefore) should appear in the migration function. The two wages do not appear separately in (5). There seems to be little theoretical justification for their joint appearance in empirical analysis of migration, as they do in the papers by Kelley, Gallaway and Vedder, Quigley and Richardson.[21] Perhaps the joint appearance of both wage variables in the literature is motivated by the mistaken impression that only by doing so can the relative strengths of push and pull be evaluated.

The authors listed in Table 11.1 attempt to estimate some variant of (5). By so doing, they are implicitly assuming that the migrations themselves have no effect on employment and wage conditions in either country. This is a strong assumption indeed when we pause to consider that from 1850 to 1914 Europe lost one-quarter of its labor force to the New World from migration.[22] To see more clearly elements of a classic identification problem, consider now the reduced form expression of the system of five equations (1)–(5). Equating labor supply and demand in each market and solving for national real wages, the resulting expressions can be substituted into the migration equation (5). Algebraic manipulation yields the reduced form equation

$$M = \gamma'' + \frac{\delta_1}{\beta_1 \left[1 - \dfrac{\delta_1}{\beta_1} - \dfrac{\delta_1}{\alpha_1} \right]} N_R - \frac{\delta_1 \beta_2}{\beta_1 \left[1 - \dfrac{\delta_1}{\beta_1} - \dfrac{\delta_1}{\alpha_1} \right]} Q_R -$$

$$\qquad\qquad\qquad\qquad\qquad\qquad\qquad\qquad\qquad\qquad (6a)$$

$$- \frac{\delta_1}{\alpha_1 \left[1 - \dfrac{\delta_1}{\beta_1} - \dfrac{\delta_1}{\alpha_1} \right]} N_S + \frac{\delta_1 \alpha_2}{\alpha_1 \left[1 - \dfrac{\delta_1}{\beta_1} - \dfrac{\delta_1}{\alpha_1} \right]} Q_S$$

or

$$M = \hat{A}_0 + \hat{A}_1 N_R + \hat{A}_2 Q_R + \hat{A}_3 N_S + \hat{A}_4 Q_S. \qquad (6b)$$

Note that there are no wage variables appearing in equation (6). To the extent that our characterization of labor market behavior is reasonably accurate, single equation estimation of migration should *not* include a wage (income per capita or unemployment rate) variable. Presumably those that do are mis-specified. With the exception of the Easterlin and Wilkinson (1967) papers, all of those studies listed in Table 11.1 fail on this criterion. A specific example may illustrate the point more clearly. Economic historians have long been interested in America's role as a safety-valve for Europe after the 1830s as 'the Malthusian Devil crossed the European continent from Ireland to Germany, then to Southern and Eastern Europe where his sway was to be greatest of all.'[23] This concern has motivated historical studies which explore the impact of the birth rate twenty years earlier on current migrations. If current real wages and lagged demographic variables are introduced simultaneously into the estimating equation (as they are in the papers by Tomaske and Quigley), a low coefficient may be meaningless since a demographically-induced decline in w_S would initiate out-migration. The wage variable appears to take the credit for the 'Malthusian Devil.'

The simple theory of labor market behavior outlined above is sufficiently precise to imply the following restriction on parameters: $\alpha_1 \leqq 0, \alpha_2 \geqq 0, \beta_1 \leqq 0, \beta_2 \geqq 0$, and $\delta_1 \geqq 0$. This information implies unambiguously that

$$\hat{A}_1 = \frac{\delta_1}{\beta_1 \left[1 - \dfrac{\delta_1}{\beta_1} - \dfrac{\delta_1}{\alpha_1}\right]} \leqq 0,$$

$$\hat{A}_2 = \frac{-\delta_1 \beta_2}{\beta_1 \left[1 - \dfrac{\delta_1}{\beta_1} - \dfrac{\delta_1}{\alpha_1}\right]} \geqq 0,$$

$$\hat{A}_3 = \frac{-\delta_1}{\alpha_1 \left[1 - \dfrac{\delta_1}{\beta_1} - \dfrac{\delta_1}{\alpha_1}\right]} \geqq 0,$$

$$\text{and } \hat{A}_4 = \frac{\delta_1 \alpha_2}{\alpha_1 \left[1 - \dfrac{\delta_1}{\beta_1} - \dfrac{\delta_1}{\alpha_1}\right]} \leqq 0.$$

It may be instructive to emphasize that the empirical result that $\hat{A}_2$ is 'very small' sheds no light whatsoever on the controversy that migration is or is not to be explained by economic incentive as measured by wage differentials in general and the American wage in particular. For example, suppose the (negative) elasticity of employment to real wages is very low in America (e.g., β_1 may be a very small negative number). Under those conditions, even if the migration coefficient, δ_1, is very low, the effect would be masked by low values of $\beta_1 \left[1 - \dfrac{\delta_1}{\beta_1} - \dfrac{\delta_1}{\alpha_1}\right]$. The researcher would find high values of $\hat{A}_2$ and erroneously conclude that migrants were very responsive to employment conditions in America. By a symmetrical argument, a high negative value of $\hat{A}_4$ may be explained by a low wage elasticity in Europe (α_1), a high output elasticity in Europe (α_2), and/or a high responsiveness of European migrants to wage differentials (δ_1). It should be pointed out that the result $|\hat{A}_2| > |\hat{A}_4|$ *can* be interpreted as relatively strong pull effects, but presumably our interest is in decomposing the *sources* of such effects – if they are in fact forthcoming – into (i) low wage elasticities in the receiving region as opposed to the sending region (e.g., $\beta_1 < \alpha_1$) and/or (ii) high output elasticities in the receiving as opposed to the sending region (e.g., $\beta_2 > \alpha_2$) and/or (iii) high rates of capacity growth (and/or low rates of labor-saving technical change) in the receiving region as opposed to the sending region (e.g., $dQ_R/dt > dQ_S/dt$). Finally, note that similar precautions must be taken in interpreting coefficients on the 'demographic' variables. $\hat{A}_3$ may assume high values only because α_1 is low. That is, labor supply conditions in the sending region may appear to play a prominent role only because the wage elasticity in the labor demand function is also low in the sending region.

Examination of equation (6a) indicates that we can directly identify only α_2 and β_2, the output elasticities, from the estimation of $\hat{A}_i$. Fortunately, detailed twentieth-century studies exist which can be utilized to supply an extraneous estimate for α_1, the wage elasticity in American industry.[24] This added information makes it possible to identify the remaining parameters of interest, i.e., δ_1 and β_1.[25]

11.3 Push and pull forces in the late nineteenth century

The estimation model

The model developed in the preceding section is in equilibrium terms. It must be modified for estimation. In addition, we must account for the fact that a given sending region 'sends' migrants to countries other than the United States, and that America receives migrants from countries other than a given sending nation. In the empirical analysis, only four European countries have historical data of sufficient quality to warrant analysis: Sweden, Denmark, Germany and the United Kingdom. Let j denote one of these four countries, let $R =$ U.S., and let

$M_j =$ U.S. immigration from j,
$M^*_j =$ exogenous emigration from j to non-U.S. countries,
$M^{**}_j =$ exogenous immigration to U.S. from all other countries excluding j.

Equation (6b) is revised slightly to read

$$M_j = \hat{A}_{j0} + \hat{A}_{j1}\{N_{US} + M^{**}{}_j\} + \hat{A}_{j2}Q_{US} + \hat{A}_{j3}\{N_j - M^*{}_j\} + \hat{A}_{j4}Q_j. \quad (7)$$

A commonly used adjustment model would suggest

$$dM_j = a\{\tilde{M}_j - M_j(-1)\}$$

where $\tilde{M}_j$ is the 'optimal' current migration and $M_j(-1)$ is last year's actual migration level. Applying this adjustment model to (7), yields the estimation equation (8):

$$dM_j = \hat{B}_{j0} + \hat{B}_{j1}\{N_{US} + M^{**}{}_j\} + \hat{B}_{j2}Q_{US} + \hat{B}_{j3}\{N_j - M^*{}_j\} \quad (8)$$
$$+ \hat{B}_{j4}Q_j - \hat{B}_{j5}M_j(-1),$$

where $\hat{B}_{j1} = \hat{a}\hat{A}_{j1}$, $\hat{B}_{j2} = \hat{a}\hat{A}_{j2}$, $\hat{B}_{j3} = \hat{a}\hat{A}_{j3}$, $\hat{B}_{j4} = \hat{a}\hat{A}_{j4}$ and $\hat{B}_{j5} = \hat{a}$. This equation is estimated in the next section for five nations, 1871–1913: four European countries who sent migrants to the United States – Sweden, United Kingdom, Denmark and Germany – and the United States itself.

European migration to the United States, 1871–1913

The regression results are presented in Table 11.2. In general, they appear to be reasonably good. Only one of the Durbin–Watson statistics lies in the inconclusive range, that for Denmark. Furthermore, the signs on the $\hat{B}_j$ are correct in seventeen out of twenty cases.

Table 11.2. *Migration regression results: 1871–1913*

	Denmark	Germany	United Kingdom	Sweden
DW	1·137	1·353	1·816	1·677
R^2	0·485	0·453	0·473	0·515
$\hat{B}_{j0}$	−0·00063	+0·18497	+0·06735	+0·01154
	(0·07670)	(1·19460)	(1·41674)	(1·44892)
$\hat{B}_{j1}$	−0·00031	−0·00102	−0·00581	−0·00095
	(0·71400)	(0·10850)	(1·40812)	(0·48306)
$\hat{B}_{j2}$	+0·00008	+0·00125	+0·00077	+0·00042
	(2·72140)	(2·00640)	(2·25898)	(2·06306)
$\hat{B}_{j3}$	+0·01034	−0·03263	−0·01835	+0·11088
	(0·44140)	(0·76930)	(1·54474)	(1·08259)
$\hat{B}_{j4}$	−0·00009	−0·00008	+0·00089	−0·00063
	(1·21890)	(0·06340)	(0·96039)	(2·00314)
$\hat{B}_{j5}$	+0·13841	+0·26753	+0·18812	+0·30432
	(1·40300)	(2·46540)	(1·66156)	(2·68177)

Note: Figures in parentheses are *t*-values. The estimation equation is (8) in text.

The offenders are Germany and the United Kingdom. The foreign labor force variable has a coefficient of wrong sign in both cases, while the U.K. output variable also has the wrong sign. Yet the American labor force and output variables always have the right sign, and the same is true of the Danish and Swedish labor force and output variables.

The implied long-run output, wage and migration coefficients are given in Table 11.3. There we see that the β_2 and δ_1 coefficients are of correct theoretical sign, while α_1 is incorrect in the case of Germany and the United Kingdom, and α_2 is incorrect only in the case of Germany. Table 11.3 also displays migration elasticities, η_{Mj}, which are evaluated at mean migration and wage levels. Although we are unaware of any empirical studies with which to compare these migration elasticities, the range $(0.0836 < \eta_{Mj} < 0.3736)$ seems plausible. A weighted average of these yields $\eta_M \cong 0.25$ and this is the migration elasticity utilized in the counterfactual analysis contained in section 11.4.

It might be instructive to pause for a moment and examine these results in some detail. First, if these estimates are accepted without qualification, they imply that the English worker was the most responsive to wage differentials while the Swedes were by far the most immobile. Apparently, in the late nineteenth century it took a far larger percentage increase in wage differentials to induce the same percentage increase in Swedish emigration compared with the English. The Danes and the Germans were in the intermediate range. It should also be pointed out that the migration elasticities have a perfect positive correlation with levels of national development and industrialization. This is a common finding in contem-

Table 11.3. *Derived parameters and elasticities*

	Denmark	Germany	United Kingdom	Sweden
$\hat{A}_{ji}$	−0.00224	−0.00383	−0.03088	−0.00312
$\hat{A}_{j2}$	+0.00056	+0.00466	+0.00409	+0.00138
$\hat{A}_{j3}$	+0.07470	−0.12200	−0.09754	+0.36435
$\hat{A}_{j4}$	−0.00064	−0.00030	+0.00473	−0.00207
$\hat{\beta}_1$	−0.12790**	−0.12790**	−0.12790**	−0.12790**
$\hat{\beta}_2$	+0.25000	+1.21670	+0.10770	+0.45160
$\hat{\alpha}_1$	−0.00380	+0.00402*	+0.04994*	−0.00110
$\hat{\alpha}_2$	+0.00857	−0.00244*	+0.04860	+0.00580
$\hat{\delta}_1$	+0.00031	+0.00438	+0.00460	+0.00063
η_{Mj}	+0.1858	+0.2124	+0.3763	+0.0836

*Coefficient has the wrong sign.
**Assumed value. See text.

porary analysis of regional migration: out-migration is far less sensitive to economic inducement at low levels of skill or regional development. Second, there is absolutely no positive correlation between the migration elasticities and observed migration rates. Whether the national out-migration rate is measured as an annual percent of population or industrial employment, Sweden recorded the highest out-migration rates from 1871 to 1913 while the United Kingdom recorded the lowest. Thus, the correlation is inverse: high migration elasticities coincide with low measured out-migration rates. It obviously follows that the high measured out-migration rates from Sweden, and the low rates from the United Kingdom, are not explained by differential migration 'responsiveness' but rather by differential push effects in these sending countries. To be more precise, Table 11.3 displays a very high negative coefficient on Q_j for Sweden compared with the other countries, and, in particular, the United Kingdom. We now know why this was so. In Sweden, the (negative) wage elasticity for non-agricultural employment was far higher than in England where it was zero; output elasticities were also far higher in Sweden. Thus, any change in Swedish industrial output had a far more potent effect on migration to the United States than was true of England. The same can be said for labor force effects; $\hat{A}_{j3}$ is a larger positive number by far for Sweden than any other country, especially England. In short, impressive emigration rates from Sweden – and presumably from southern and eastern Europe as well – are as much related to the 'Malthusian Devil' and population pressure, as they are to the structure of the Swedish economy itself – that is, characterized by high wage and output elasticities.

Identifying push effects abroad

Given our estimate of η_M, we can now proceed with an accounting of the sources of American immigration in the late nineteenth century. The analysis is eased if equation (5) is restated in constant elasticity form:

$$M(t) = Z\{\tilde{w}_E(t)\}^{\eta_M} + \hat{D}(t), \qquad (9)$$

where $\tilde{w}_E(t)$ is the real wage of industrial workers in the East, $\eta_M = 0.25$, and $\hat{D}(t)$ is an index of European push conditions generated for each year up to 1910. The first term on the right-hand side of expression (9) captures the influence of American demand (i.e., P stands for pull), and it is convenient to rewrite (9) as

$$M(t) = \hat{P}(t) + \hat{D}(t).$$

Secular *changes* in annual immigration levels, our main focus, can be decomposed into

$$dM(t) = d\hat{P}(t) + d\hat{D}(t). \qquad (9a)$$

(In the discussion which follows we shall use the term 'push' to refer to that portion of the *change* in migration levels associated with *changing* conditions abroad, $d\hat{D}(t)$. 'Pull' is treated symmetrically.) Alternatively, it may prove more helpful to consider the sum of these annual immigration flows (above the 1870 level) over longer periods of time in which case

$$\sum_t dM(t) = \sum_t d\hat{P}(t) + \sum_t d\dot{\hat{D}}(t). \qquad (9b)$$

Before turning to a counterfactual analysis of total American immigration, consider a simple *ex post* accounting of push and pull limited to the cases of Great Britain, Scandinavia and Germany. Table 11.4 presents an *ex post* decomposition using the gross immigration data from *Historical Statistics*. The period covered is the thirty-five years between 1870 and 1904–7. Unemployment rates in the non-farm sector were very low at both these points in time (appendix C, Tables C.4 and C.5), so in effect we are examining the secular change in annual gross immigration levels between two full employment periods separated by three and a half decades. Treating

Table 11.4. *An ex post decomposition of the 'sources' of American gross immigration from three European regions: 1870–1907*

Variable	Immigration (000) to America from			
	Great Britain ($\eta_M = 0.3763$) (1)	Scandinavia ($\eta_M = 0.1038$) (2)	Germany ($\eta_M = 0.2124$) (3)	Three regions: Cols. (2) + (3) + (4) ($\eta_M = 0.2500$) (4)
$M_j(t)$				
1870	103.7	30.7	118.2	252.6
1904–7	70.5	55.9	40.6	167.0
$dM_j(t)$	−33.2	+25.2	−77.6	−85.6
$d\hat{P}_j(t)$	+51.9	+4.3	+33.1	+83.4
$d\hat{D}_j(t)$	−85.1	+20.9	−110.7	−169.0

Sources: The immigration data are in thousands and are taken from *Historical Statistics of the United States*, Series C, pp. 56–7. The figure for 1904–7 is an average for those four years. The η_M in cols. (1) and (3) are taken directly from Table 11.3. The elasticity utilized in col. (2) is a weighted average of Denmark and Sweden; col. (4) uses a weighted average of Great Britain, Germany, Denmark and Sweden. See text for an explanation of the derivation of $d\hat{D}_j(t)$ and $d\hat{P}_j(t)$.

the observed $M_j(t)$ as 'equilibrium' immigration flows at existing American real wages, and given our estimates of η_{Mj} while arbitrarily setting $\hat{D}_j(1870) = 0$, the impact of *changing* push conditions, $d\hat{D}_j(t)$, on changing immigration flows, $d\hat{M}_j(t)$, can be estimated. Immigration from Great Britain, Germany and Scandinavia combined *declined* from 252,600 in 1870 to an average level of 167,000 in 1904–7. Apparently, immigration to America from these three regions would have increased by 83,400 to a level of 336,000 in 1904–7 had conditions in these sending regions remained unchanged over these thirty-five years. In fact, American pull conditions were swamped by *negative* push conditions in these sending countries of north-west Europe, and these forces were tending to diminish immigration to America. Within the 'three region' group of 'old' migrants, only one exhibited a positive push: even in this case, the increase in Scandinavian immigration would have been miniscule, a little more than 4,000, had not positive push factors been present.

It would take a very large error in our estimates of η_{Mj} to reverse these results. Indeed, if $\eta_M = 0.25$ is an underestimate, then the negative European push effect is underestimated as well. The long term secular decline in late nineteenth-century trans-Atlantic migration rates from north-west Europe obviously has its source abroad, rather than in America. This result may come as a shock to many readers who have assumed all along that immigration to America is at least in part explained by *positive* European push factors. Table 11.4 shows this interpretation to be incorrect since the push factors – at least in north-west Europe – were *negative*. Had net labor market conditions remained unchanged in those regions after 1870, the inflow of immigrants to America would have been far greater. Would we get the same answer if (i) *net* immigration rates were considered, (ii) *all* countries sending migrants were included, and (iii) the calculation was performed not between full employment periods as in expression (9a), but as an aggregation of the total increase in the stock of new immigrants to America between 1870 and 1910, as in (9b)? After all, the composition of immigration by sending country changes dramatically over the late nineteenth century, shifting from the 'old' north-west – where indigenous economic development tended increasingly to retain more of the potential migrants – to the 'new' south and central European countries – where positive push presumably held sway.

The immigration series utilized in subsequent analysis is the Kuznets–Rubin estimates on the net additions to American foreign born. This is a more relevant series for our purposes for two reasons. First, the Kuznets–Rubin series is, after all, the migration data utilized in the chapters preceding this one. (The $M(t)$ series can be found in Table A.15, appendix A.) Thus, the $M(t)$ counterfactual analysis which follows deals with 'net additions to foreign born' rather than immigration as reported in *Historical Statistics*. Second, the immigration data fail to capture *return* migration to Europe and thus is a gross migration measure. Kuznets and Rubin attempt to estimate a more relevant $M(t)$ series, *net* migration. Finally, we might as well replace Lebergott's real wage series in expression (9) by the predicted $\tilde{w}_E(t)$ produced by the model, since chapter 4 documents a very close correspondence between the predicted and actual real wage series.

The results are presented in Table 11.5. The absolute figures have already been 'normalized' in chapter 4 to ease computation, but the percentages given in parentheses are invariant to the scaling. For the four decades as a whole, push effects are – once again – *negative*. Even when the analysis is expanded to include central and south-eastern Europe, push effects still are estimated to have been negative. Labor market conditions in Europe as a whole were improving sufficiently in the late nineteenth century to enhance significantly the ability of sending nations to retain potential foreign migrants at home. They still came to America in massive numbers, of course, but the point remains that had not conditions been improving in Europe, immigration to America would have been even greater. Had European employment and living standards remained at their 1870 levels, America would have had a stock of immigrants in 1910 some 20 percent larger than was in fact the case. Since this empirical result may be somewhat controversial, it would be wise to dwell on it. First, it is true that the negative push effects documented in Table 11.4 are far greater than in Table 11.5. This is as it should be. Economic growth and real wage improvement in Germany, Scandinavia and Great Britain was considerably more

Table 11.5. *Decomposition of the 'sources' of American net immigration, using the model's predicted $\tilde{w}_E(t)$: 1870–1910*

	Additions to American foreign born population:		
	Total:	Attributable to pull:	Attributable to push: $\sum_t d\hat{D}(t) = \sum_t dM(t) -$
	$\sum_t dM(t)$	$\sum_t d\hat{P}(t)$	$\sum_t d\hat{P}(t)$
Period	(1)	(2)	(3)
1870–1890	14·740(100·0)	16·827(114·2)	−2·087(−14·2)
1890–1910	14·806(100·0)	18·426(124·4)	−3·620(−24·4)
1870–1910	29·546(100·0)	35·253(119·3)	−5·707(−19·3)

impressive than in central and south-east Europe during most of these four decades. Indeed, this obviously explains why the composition of immigrants by source shifts so dramatically during the late nineteenth century: 'Why the geographic origins of migration moved across the face of Europe from North and West to South and East is not a mystery, since that is how industry, elimination of feudal land tenure, higher living standards, and declining death rates occurred in Europe.'[26]

Second, how are the results presented in Tables 11.4 and 11.5 to be reconciled with a conventional wisdom which stresses the positive push of Europeans to America? The standard historical account of nineteenth-century European emigration seems to emphasize two forces. The first of these relates to harvest conditions in general and the Irish Potato Famine in particular. No doubt poor European harvest conditions continued to push migrants to America in isolated years even after 1870, but apparently its *total* impact on immigration experience was not sufficiently important to produce net push effects over longer periods of time. The second, the 'Malthusian Devil,' has also attracted considerable attention. In Brinley Thomas's colorful language:

> The evolution of the Atlantic community could be described in terms of two frontiers – the ever-widening frontier of surplus population in the Old World and the moving frontier of economic opportunity in the New. The 'Malthusian Devil' crossed the European continent from Ireland to Germany, then to Scandinavia and finally to Southern and Eastern countries where his sway was to be greatest of all. Each crisis of overpopulation was a milestone in the process of building up the industrial strength of America.[27]

If Professor Thomas is asserting that increasing 'population pressure' was sufficiently strong in Europe to result in an increasing net push of migrants to America, we must disagree. If instead he, like Easterlin, has a counterfactual statement lurking behind his assertion, then our positions may not conflict. To be more precise, Easterlin has stressed natural population increase in Europe as a source of push, but he clearly has a demographic counterfactual in mind: 'The reasoning is that differences in natural increase rates result with a lag in differences in the rate of additions to the labor market. Relatively high additions to the labor market would be expected, *other things remaining equal*, to result in labor market slack ... and to lead to relatively high emigration.'[28] Other things were not equal, of course. Indeed, the impact of the 'Malthusian Devil' was sufficiently offset by capital accumulation and technical change to produce the negative push effect documented in Tables

11.4 and 11.5. It is quite another matter to ask what American immigration would have been had the 'Malthusian Devil' *not* been present in Europe. This chapter cannot supply an answer to this interesting question although it does supply a methodology to do so.

11.4 Immigration and economic growth: counterfactual analysis

Immigration and real wages in America: a counterfactual world with no European push

The remainder of this chapter relies on counterfactual analysis. Each counterfactual experiment utilizes the model developed in chapter 3 with only one change. Exogenous immigration is now replaced by the endogenous immigration equation laboriously estimated in the previous pages in this chapter. To summarize, we now have

$$M(t) = Z\{\tilde{w}_E(t)\}^{\eta_M} + \hat{D}(t),$$

where $\eta_M = 0.25$ and $Z = 0.745$ (i.e., Z is so selected that $\hat{D} = 0$ in 1870). Recall that $D(t)$ is derived as a residual. Given the annual values of $\tilde{w}_E(t)$ displayed in Table B.6, col. (5), and given the annual values of $M(t)$ reported in Table A.16, $\hat{D}(t)$ is uniquely determined. The series is documented in Table C.6. We are now equipped with at least one model to explore the following: (i) the impact of European push can be evaluated by setting $\hat{D}(t) = 0$, a world in which push factors were absent; (ii) the impact of European immigration on America by setting $M(t) = 0$, a world in which *no* immigrants arrived in America after 1870; (iii) the impact of conditions in America on immigration, by examining the impact of the frontier and other forces on $\tilde{w}_E(t)$ and thus $M(t)$.

Since Thomas feels that 'each crisis of overpopulation was a milestone in the process of building up the industrial strength of America,' it should be of some interest to explore the likely impact of European push on American real wages and immigration rates (*ex ante*). Suppose conditions in Europe remained unchanged between 1870 and 1910 in the sense that net push effects were zero for each of the forty years: i.e., let $\hat{D}(t) = 0$ for every year. By comparing this counterfactual world with 'actual' history, we shall have isolated the impact of European push on American performance – in particular, on the behavior of real wages and living standards. We are *not* estimating the impact on the American economy had no immigration taken place up to 1910; rather, we are restricting immigration response only to American pull conditions.

The result of this experiment is reported in Table 11.6. The implications are straightforward. Total additions to foreign born in America between 1870 and 1910 would have been some 19 percent *larger* had push conditions been absent in Europe. Although this figure may seem significant, the impact of the larger counterfactual immigration on real wages in America would have been negligible: the real wage in Eastern industry would have been lowered by only 1 percent either in 1890 or 1910. Furthermore, industrialization, GNP growth and capital formation rates are only slightly influenced as well. Even granting a large range of error in this counterfactual calculation, it is hard to see how 'each crisis of overpopulation was a milestone in the process of building up the industrial strength of America,' at least in the *long run*. Business cycles and long swings are another matter entirely.

Turner and Malthus: the impact of the American frontier and demographic forces on immigration

The Turner thesis has played an important role in historians' views of American sectional development. Extending the 'safety-valve' mechanism to international migration is an obvious step and it has been made by many historians:

... endless amounts of free or nearly free land were available throughout the nineteenth century, offering brighter opportunities at nearly any time than the European migrant could have had at home ...[29]

Up to 1860 and probably until the end of the nineteenth century, land was the most influential factor in American economic development ... The golden opportunity offered

Table 11.6. *The impact of European push on American real wages and immigration: 1870–1910*

	'Actual'		Counterfactual: $\hat{D}(t) = 0$	
Year	Total additions to foreign born population, 1870 to t: $\sum_{1870}^{t} dM(t)$	Real wage in Eastern industry at t: $w_E(t)$	Total additions to foreign born population, 1870 to t: $\sum_{1870}^{t} dM(t)$	Real wage in Eastern industry at t: $w_E(t)$
1870	0	0·975	0	0·975
1890	14·740	1·960	16·794	1·946
1910	29·546	2·646	35·140	2·634

by almost unlimited land attracted immigrants from across the ocean ... Thus the expanse of land encouraged the growth of the labor supply.[30]

Even if the American immigrant failed to farm, or had no intention of farming, 'free' land might still have lured the immigrant away from Europe. The movement of a native American to new land at the frontier obviously created a job vacancy elsewhere which the immigrant could fill. By exhuming Turner's thesis, we are in fact searching for the underlying sources of pull to America. In the short run, tight labor markets and job vacancies attracted immigrants in increasing numbers. In the long run, this pull is translated into secular increases in real earnings. Whichever the period of analysis, what role did an expanding frontier play in creating a pull?

Table 11.7 contains a tentative answer for the late nineteenth century. Two extreme counterfactuals are reported there which also appeared in chapter 8. The first column displays the net additions to the American foreign born population which actually took place up to 1910. The second indicates what it would have been had the Midwest land stock remained constant at 1870 levels. The third shows the impact had the land stock continued to grow at the very high levels obtained in the early 1870s (4 percent per annum). A quick glance at the 1910 figures confirms that conditions at the frontier had a trivial impact on real wages, job vacancy and thus immigration from Europe. Indeed, had the land stock remained constant at 1870 levels, net additions to the American foreign born population would have been only 0·3 percent below the 1910 levels actually attained! Land 'availability' appears to have had very little to do with immigration in the late nineteenth century.

A second potential influence is suggested by debate over the

Table 11.7. *The impact of the American frontier and demographic forces on immigration: two counterfactuals, 1870–1910*

	Additions to American foreign born population: $\sum_{t} dM(t)$			
		Counterfactuals		
Period	'Actual' (1)	Land stock constant at 1870 levels (2)	Land stock growth at 4 percent per annum (3)	Native labor force growth at 1870 rates (4)
1870–1890	14·740	14·727	14·740	14·631
1890–1910	14·806	14·719	14·834	14·448
1870–1910	29·546	29·446	29·574	29·079

Walker thesis and concern with 'population pressure' in Europe. A restatement of the Malthusian push thesis is in order. Thomas, for example, correlates Swedish birth rates with emigration twenty years hence and find a high positive correlation: 'The majority of the migrants were between 15 and 30 years of age, and the heaviest outflow usually came from the 20–25 age group. Emigration in these groups ... was evidently related to the level of the birth rate at the time those emigrants were born.'[31] In a similar vein, the composition of nineteenth-century immigration has been related to the 'Malthusian Devil' as it first hit Ireland, swept through north-west Europe, and touched central and southern Europe only late in the century: 'The decrease in emigration from the north-western and central European countries toward the end of the nineteenth century and their replacement by the south-eastern European countries as main sources of overseas ... migration have been explained as due ... to changes in the rate of natural increase.'[32] The magnitude of these demographic forces are documented in Table 11.8. Between the periods 1841–60 and 1871–90, the average annual rate of natural increase rises from 8·1 per thousand to 14·2 per thousand in Russia. That is, the rate rises by 6·1 per thousand. This is the *maximum* demographic change reported by Easterlin. The Italian and German rates rise, for example, by 2·5 and 2·6 per

Table 11.8. *Natural rates of population increase in Europe, 1841–60 to 1871–90*

Country	Annual average rate of natural increase per 1,000:		
	1841–60	1871–90	Change between 1841–60 and 1871–90
Norway	14·2	13·8	−0·4
Great Britain	12·0	13·6	1·6
Sweden	10·8	12·2	1·4
Denmark	11·0	12·7	1·7
Finland	9·6	14·4	4·8
Germany	9·2	11·8	2·6
Netherlands	7·3	12·6	5·3
Belgium	7·0	9·7	2·7
France	3·2	1·8	−1·4
Italy	6·2	8·7	2·5
Portugal	6·2	9·9	3·7
Switzerland	6·4	7·2	0·8
Austria	5·1	7·5	2·4
Russia	8·1	14·2	6·1

Source: Easterlin, 'Influences in European Overseas Emigration Before World War I,' table 3, p. 339.

thousand over the same period. Presumably, these rates of natural increase in *population* between 1841–60 and 1871–90 roughly translate into potential rates of *labor force* increase (net of emigration) between 1861–80 and 1891–1910, our period of analysis. Since it is on the basis of such evidence that the Malthusian explanation of the European safety-valve has gained its well established credence, consider a similar demographic variable in American history. The Eldridge and Thomas figures reported in Table A.14 show the following: between 1870–80 and 1900–10, the rate of natural increase declines from 13·2 to 8·7 in the Northeast, and from 20·4 to 10·7 in the North Central. That is, the rate declines in the Northeast by 4·5 per thousand and by 9·7 per thousand in the North Central. Obviously, the changing rate of natural increase in America is even *more* dramatic than in Europe (with the possible exception of Russia and the Netherlands). Given the attention which the 'Malthusian Devil' has attracted as a source of European push, it certainly seems plausible to hypothesize that the *declining* 'population pressure' in late nineteenth-century American must have had a powerful impact on pulling immigrants across the Atlantic.

The Malthusian hypothesis is tested in Table 11.7, under the plausible assumption that native labor force and native population growth declined at roughly the same rate after 1870. Col. (4) reports the following counterfactual: If the Northern states had maintained the high natural rates of population increase obtained in the early 1870s, what would have been the impact on immigration? The 'actual' history documented in col. (1) includes the declining natural rates as part of the pull of immigrants via a tighter labor market, while col. (4) does not. The direction of effects is certainly consistent with the thesis since the counterfactual additions to American foreign born would have been 29·079 in 1910 rather than 29·546. Thus, declining native labor force growth in the late nineteenth century did tend to foster greater real wage improvement in America, thus attracting European migrants in larger numbers. It is also true that these demographic forces had a far more potent effect on immigration than 'frontier availability.' Nevertheless, the demographic forces this side of the Atlantic could hardly be classified as fundamental: the total stock of foreign born would have been altered by only 1 percent.

It appears unlikely that indigenous American demographic forces had much at all to do with immigration from Europe. This result casts some doubt on the importance of the 'Malthusian Devil' in contributing to push conditions on the other side of the Atlantic as well. Why should a similar analysis of European countries yield different results? Perhaps this section may goad European economic historians to submit this piece of conventional wisdom on the 'Malthusian Devil' to further quantitative scrutiny.

A final remark: America without immigrants

The counterfactual analysis reported above implies that immigration to America in the late nineteenth century was not significantly influenced by either the frontier or indigenous demographic forces. Neither of these two 'exogenous' influences was important enough to have a sufficiently powerful impact on real wages, job vacancies and labor market conditions as to contribute much to long-term American pull forces. It seems apparent, therefore, that the counterfactual analysis reported in chapters 5 through 10 would not be significantly altered by an endogenous treatment of immigration. Furthermore, conditions in Europe, presumed to be exogenous to America, were far more significant than either the frontier or native demographic conditions in America. We also have tentatively suggested that 'exogenous' demographic conditions in Europe were not nearly as important a part of the migration mechanism as is conventionally thought, although no hard analysis is presented here to back up that inference. It follows, of course, that the key to European immigration experience is the relative rates of industrialization and economic growth in the trans-Atlantic economy. Relative rates of industrialization, in turn, are to be understood only by careful attention to the basic underlying rates of capital formation and technical change. An accounting of transatlantic immigration which excludes the Frontier, the 'Malthusian Devil' and the safety-valve is certainly less colorful history, but it is far more accurate history.

Note that we have nowhere asserted that immigration was inconsequential to American late nineteenth-century growth. How important *was* the exodus from Europe? An answer to this query can be found by posing a counterfactual world in which immigration was non-existent. Before doing so, it might be fruitful to recall the contribution of European immigration to increases in the American labor force. Table 11.9 displays the relevant data for both America as a whole (Easterlin) and those for the North implied by the model. These two data sets are not entirely consistent, of course. Easterlin considered the 'active' labor force participants among the immigrants and his labor force data are for America as a whole. The figures implied by the model, on the other hand, treat all immigrants as potential additions to the labor force and the labor force itself excludes those regions outside of the Northeast and North Central. Nevertheless, the secular trends and decadal fluctuations are essentially the same. While Easterlin attributes 32 percent of the labor force expansion between 1870 and 1910 to immigration, the model implies a component contribution of 26 percent.

Now consider a world in which the migration legislation imposed in the 1920s was passed in 1870. That is, consider nineteenth-century

Table 11.9.   *Average labor force growth by component, 1870–1910*

| Period | Average rate of labor force growth per decade | | Share of immigration in total labor force increase (3) |
	Total (percent) (1)	Net immigration contribution (percent) (2)	
A. *Actual data: Easterlin*			
1870–80	29·3	6·2	21·2
1880–90	29·2	9·9	33·9
1890–1900	21·9	5·8	26·5
1900–10	22·8	9·5	41·7
1870–1910	25·8	8·3	32·1
B. *Data implied by the model*			
1870–80	27·2	4·7	17·3
1880–90	24·5	7·5	30·6
1890–1900	15·3	2·3	15·0
1900–10	17·4	5·6	32·2
1870–1910	21·4	5·5	25·8

Source: Panel A is taken from Easterlin, *Population, Labor Force, and Long Swings in Economic Growth*, table A-3, p. 190.

American development under a counterfactual prohibition of European immigration. This is hardly an idle speculation since labor opposition to immigration was always strong in America and many contemporary observers felt that the arguments for tariff protection should be extended to protection against foreign labor: 'There is no protection for the carpenter or the bricklayer . . . Yet if we cared for men more than money, and were consistent with our principles of protection . . . we should exclude all foreign workmen as well as their work, and so raise the wages of native hands.'[33] The first federal immigration law was passed in 1882. It introduced the head tax and exclusion of some 'undesirables.' A reading test was finally passed by Congress in 1917 and some argue that the literacy test itself would have been sufficient to stem the post-war European tide. What happened subsequent to the Armistice is well known. American public opinion was swept up with fear of 'the formidable host fleeing the continent in the throes of political upheaval.'[34] Suppose this legislation had been passed following the Civil War? By how much would real wages have expanded in the absence of competition from new immigrant labor? Would American industrialization and urbanization have been aided or hindered? Would GNP per capita have been augmented or diminished? What *was* the impact of European immigration on American growth in the late nineteenth century?

The answers appear in Table 11.10. Apparently, immigration did foster industrialization, did suppress real wage improvement, but did not have a very significant effect on aggregate growth as measured by real GNP per capita indices. Certainly the direction of these effects would have been predicted based upon a reading of the qualitative historical literature. The magnitudes perhaps may not have been anticipated. In the absence of European immigration, real annual earnings in Eastern industries would have been higher by some 11 percent in 1910. This may seem in retrospect a small price to pay for a free immigration policy since real wages actually rose by more than 170 percent over the four decades while America absorbed the disgruntled European. But to contemporaries lobbying Congress in 1910, such a figure would hardly have diminished their energetic objection to competition from 'cheap' European immigrants. Furthermore, the resulting slower growth in the labor force would have produced a noticeable improvement in labor's share at the expense of rents, dividends and profits. This inference follows from Table 11.10 which shows that GNP per capita would have been increased by only 1 percent by 1910 while, as we have seen, real labor earnings in industry would have risen by 11 percent.

An America without immigrants indeed would have grown very differently from how in fact she did in the late nineteenth century.

Table 11.10. *The impact of immigration on American growth*

Year	Real wage in Eastern industry: $w_E(t)$		Real GNP per capita (1870 prices)		Industrialization level: $L_I(t)/L(t)$	
	'Actual' (1)	Counter-factual $M(t) = 0$ (2)	'Actual' (3)	Counter-factual $M(t) = 0$ (4)	'Actual' (5)	Counter-factual $M(t) = 0$ (6)
1870	0·975	0·975	92·5	92·5	0·507	0·507
1890	1·960	2·138	146·7	150·1	0·538	0·492
1910	2·646	2·937	208·3	214·5	0·685	0·639

Part IV The Facts of History

Appendix A: Parameter Estimation

> To this day many of our comrades still do not understand that they must attend to the quantitative aspect of things . . . They have no 'figures" in their heads and as a result cannot help making mistakes.
>
> Mao Tse-tung (1949)

A.1 Production parameters

An impressive amount of evidence has accumulated suggesting that the elasticity of substitution may be fairly close to unity in both manufacturing and agriculture. These econometric results argue for a Cobb–Douglas specification in all three production activities in our economy. The specification certainly makes estimation much easier since it is well known that output elasticities conform to observed factor income shares under competitive assumptions of marginal product pricing. Under these specifications only data on factor shares in agriculture and manufacturing during or immediately following the Civil War decade are required.

Table A.1 presents two estimates of manufacturing factor shares in the sixth and seventh decades of the nineteenth century. Placing heaviest weight on the 1869–70 estimates for manufacturing, the simulations assume $\alpha_K = 0.45$ and $\alpha_L = 0.55$ for industry in both regions.

Passell and Schmundt utilize the 1869 census to compute labor's share in agriculture, but these estimates are for the United States as a whole. They find $\beta_L = 0.68$. A very careful study of Midwestern agriculture is available to check the accuracy of the Passell and Schmundt economy-wide estimates. Agriculture is restricted to the

Table A.1. *Mid-nineteenth-century factor shares in industry*

Sector	Year	α_K	α_L
Industry:	1869–70	0·497	0·503
Manufacturing:	1869	0·440	0·560

Sources: Industry, 1869–70: Adjusted industry wages share data from E. C. Budd, 'Factor Shares, 1850–1910,' table 2, p. 371. Manufacturing: 1869 census labor shares from P. Passell and M. Schmundt, 'Pre-Civil War Land Policy and the Growth of Manufacturing,' p. 20.

Midwest in our model, and John Bowman has computed farm factor shares for those states.[1] Aggregating over the states of Illinois, Indiana, Iowa, Kansas, Michigan, Minnesota, Missouri, Nebraska, Ohio and Wisconsin yields $\beta_L = 0.705$ for 1870, certainly very close to the Passell and Schmundt estimate. Following Denison,[2] β_R is set equal to 0.10 and thus $\beta_K = 0.20$.

A.2 Technical progress parameters

Since the classic Abramovitz study of productivity growth in the American economy and Solow's pathbreaking attempts to measure sources of output expansion,[3] economic historians have made the measurement of total factor productivity growth the focus of much of their empirical work. Solow's conclusion was that as much as 90 percent of average labor productivity growth over the period 1909–49 was attributable to 'technical progress' – or more accurately, unexplained by conventional input growth. Does the American economy in the late nineteenth century produce a similar record? It was noted in chapters 3 and 5 that Murray Brown has developed evidence suggesting a much lower contribution of technical progress, at least between 1890 and World War I. How was American productivity improvement 1869–1919 shared between sectors; i.e., did agriculture attain rates of total factor productivity growth in excess of manufacturing? Surprisingly little has been done to answer these questions beyond the early efforts of Kendrick.[4]

This gap in empirical research is surprising given the emphasis which differential rates of sectoral technical change have received by many economists in explaining historical experience with industrialization and relative commodity price behavior. Economic historians have often argued, for example, that the farmers' discontent and the rapid rate of American industrialization during the late nineteenth century can in part be attributed to agriculture's success in improving productivity.[5] Shannon, when referring to the effects of agricultural productivity advance up to the 1890s, states that:

> . . . it reduced the number of people needed to feed and clothe the population of the United States and to supply its agricultural exports. Between 1860 and 1900, the cities and other nonfarm areas gained about 18,000,000 in population over the national average of growth, while the farms lost an equal number. . . . In other words, some 18,000,000 less people got their living directly from the soil than would have under the agricultural standard of 1860. . .[6]

A similar view can be found in a more recent study by Whitney:

... the measure of annual technological change in agriculture is on the order to 2·0% for the 1880's and 0·7% for the 1890's. The precipitous decline of agricultural output relative to that of manufacturing in the latter decades of the nineteenth century was accompanied by an even more pronounced shift in the factors of production since technological change in agriculture made it possible to economize on the inputs required to meet the faltering demand for farm products.[7]

What in fact was the American total factor productivity growth performance from 1869 to 1919?

Kendrick's figures are very approximate, of course, but they do offer insight into the relative magnitudes of productivity growth over the pre-World War I period. The key estimates for our purposes are presented in Table A.2 and Figure A.1. First, the private domestic non-farm sector attained total factor productivity growth (TFPG) rates averaging 1.5 percent per annum over these five decades, while the manufacturing sector was somewhat lower (1·2 percent per annum). Second, the overall performance of the farm sector was considerably less impressive over the same period, i.e. 0·75 percent per annum.[8] An identical estimate over these four

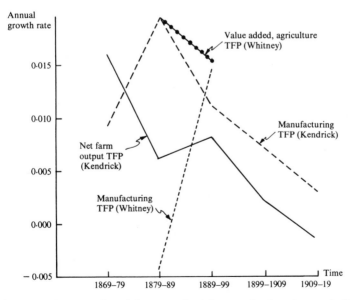

Figure A.1 Measures of total factor productivity growth: American agriculture and manufacturing, 1869–1919
(*Source:* See text.)

decades can be found in Lave's work. Furthermore, Lave shows that the relatively rapid rates of agricultural total factor productivity growth, compared to non-agriculture, is purely a twentieth-century phenomenon. Apparently, the service sector was enjoying far more rapid rates of technical progress than either manufacturing or agriculture. Yet, there is considerable nineteenth-century evidence suggesting that performance in food grains was some- what more impressive for the farm sector as a whole than for the Corn Belt and Lake States. For the decade following 1919, Kendrick shows that the farm production per man hour grew at 1·9 percent per annum in the West North Central and 1·2 percent in the East North Central compared to 1·2 percent for the United States as a whole. Lave asserts that these regional differentials persist in the earlier period, 1870–1910.[9] Both manufacturing and agri- culture exhibit declining rates of TFPG over time. The evidence reviewed above suggests support for an assumption that rates of TFPG were around 0·75 percent per annum in agriculture and 1·2 percent per annum in manufacturing, for the four decades as a whole. These estimates would be consistent with Murray Brown's view that

> ... only from 1921 to 1960 did technological progress con- tribute more to the growth in output than the increase in inputs. From 1890 to 1921, the increase in inputs was over three times as important as technological change. The relative importance of technological progress that has received much attention from economists appears to be a phenomenon of the more recent rather than the more distant past.[10]

In fact, we shall use interpolated Kendrick TFPG estimates derived from columns (2) and (3) in Table A.2. These estimates are presented

Table A.2. *Kendrick's total factor productivity growth estimates, 1869–1919*

Per annum rates of change for	(1) Private domestic non-farm	(2) Farm value added	(3) Manufacturing value added
1869–79		1·6	0·9
1879–89	3·7	0·6	1·9
1889–99	0·1	0·8	1·1
1899–1909	1·4	0·2	0·7
1909–19	0·9	neg.	0·3
1869–1909	1·53	0·75	1·18

Source: Col. (1) from J. W. Kendrick, *Productivity Trends in the United States*, table A-XXIII, pp. 338–41. Col. (2) from *ibid.*, table B–1, pp. 362–4. Col. (3) from *ibid.* table D–1, p. 464.

Table A.3. *Total factor productivity levels assumed in the simulation*

Year	$B(t)$	$A(t)$	$A'(t)$	Year	$B(t)$	$A(t)$	$A'(t)$
1870	1·466	1·025	·983	1891	1·726	1·377	1·320
1871	1·486	1·035	·992	1892	1·733	1·392	1·335
.1872	1·507	1·044	1·001	1893	1·739	1·407	1·350
1873	1·528	1·053	1·010	1894	1·746	1·423	1·364
1874	1·550	1·063	1·019	1895	1·753	1·438	1·379
1875	1·571	1·072	1·028	1896	1·760	1·454	1·395
1876	1·593	1·082	1·038	1897	1·767	1·470	1·410
1877	1·616	1·092	1·047	1898	1·775	1·480	1·420
1878	1·624	1·112	1·067	1899	1·782	1·491	1·430
1879	1·632	1·134	1·087	1900	1·789	1·501	1·440
1880	1·640	1·155	1·108	1901	1·796	1·512	1·450
1881	1·648	1·177	1·129	1902	1·803	1·522	1·460
1882	1·656	1·199	1·150	1903	1·810	1·533	1·470
1883	1·665	1·222	1·172	1904	1·818	1·544	1·480
1884	1·673	1·245	1·194	1905	1·825	1·554	1·490
1885	1·681	1·269	1·217	1906	1·832	1·565	1·501
1886	1·690	1·293	1·240	1907	1·839	1·576	1·512
1887	1·698	1·318	1·264	1908	1·847	1·587	1·522
1888	1·705	1·332	1·278	1909	1·854	1·598	1·533
1889	1·712	1·347	1·292	1910	1·862	1·610	1·544
1890	1·719	1·362	1·306				

in Table A.3 and identical rates of TFPG in Eastern and Western industry are assumed.

A.3 Depreciation parameter

Kuznets estimates the share of capital consumption in gross investment, $d^*(t)$, to be 0·42 for the period 1869–88 and 0·46 for the period 1889–1908. Since

$$d^*(t) = \frac{\delta K(t)}{I(t)},$$

then the depreciation parameter can be derived given the gross investment share in GNP and the capital–output ratio (all variables in value terms):

$$\delta = d^*(t) \left[\frac{I(t)}{G(t)} \right] \left[\frac{K(t)}{G(t)} \right]^{-1}.$$

The data presented in Table A.4 suggest a fairly stable depreciation parameter of 0·03 over these four decades. This is the rate assumed in the simulation.

Table A.4. *Estimates of δ, 1869–1908*

Years	(1) $d^*(t)$	(2) $I(t)/G(t)$	(3) $K(t)/G(t)$	(4) δ
1869–88	0·42	0·20	2·83	0·0297
1889–1908	0·46	0·22	3·00	0·0337
Average 1869–1908	—	—	—	0·0317

Sources: Col. (1) from S. Kuznets, *Capital in the American Economy: Its Formation and Financing*, table 2, p. 56. Col. (2) from L. Davis and R. Gallman, 'The Share of Savings and Investment in Gross National Product During the 19th Century,' tables 1 and 2. Col. (3) derived from Kuznets, table 6, pp. 80–1.

A.4 Interregional transport costs

Given the importance which economic historians have attached to $Z_I(t)$ and $Z_A(t)$ on American growth, special care must be taken in reconstructing these series which can then be introduced exogenously into the model. Unfortunately, $Z_I(t)$ and $Z_A(t)$ are among the most difficult historical series on which to get accurate observations. Oddly enough, in spite of the attention which economic historians have devoted to American transport development there have been few attempts to construct continuous real transport cost series for the American economy.[11] It is critically important that this gap is filled.

Recall from chapter 3 how these Z_j's link up regional commodity markets:

$$P_{IW}(t) = \left[1 + Z_I(t)\right] P_{IE}(t),$$

and

$$P_{AE}(t) = \left[1 + Z_A(t)\right] P_{AW}(t).$$

That is, the price of agricultural products in East coast cities exceeds that in the interior by some percentage Z_A which varies over time. Similarly, industrial goods' prices in the Midwest are some percent higher, $Z_I(t)$, than those in the East. The Z_j's can be estimated in one of two ways. An attempt can be made to secure direct information on transport charges applied to commodity trade between the two regions. We shall see below that this procedure raises sufficient problems to warrant searching for an alternative measure wherever possible. The alternative is to measure commodity price differentials directly. Having done so, an appeal to indirect evidence can be made to establish that the historical behavior of the Z_j's over time are primarily attributable to changes in transport charges.

Assume that grain products are shipped from some point in the

Midwest (say, Council Bluffs, Iowa) to Chicago where they are subsequently trans-shipped to New York for consumption in the Northeast or for export to Europe. This was hardly the only route utilized in historical fact but it is taken as representative. Eastern industrial goods, a far more heterogenous commodity basket, are assumed to originate in New York and go via Chicago to some consumption point in the Midwest (say, Council Bluffs, Iowa). This implies that the charges for goods moving from a variety of Eastern cities to a variety of Western towns can be captured by *one* 'average charge' for each commodity. Also, the charge on industrial goods can be broken down, without loss of generality, into its components: New York–Chicago and Chicago–Iowa. The empirical relevance of these and other assumptions must now be established.

New York and Chicago were the most important trade centers in the East and Midwest, respectively, and long haul freight rates from other Eastern cities into Chicago were patterned after New York–Chicago rates and approximately equal to them. Furthermore, long haul freight rates (for a given class) were roughly the same in both directions. From Chicago to the Mississippi (all points), a 25 percent surcharge on the New York–Chicago rate was in effect, or at least quoted. All shipments between the Mississippi and the Missouri Rivers were subjected to a flat rate of 60 cents per 100 pounds (first class, 1880–1900). Goods from all points south of Chicago, at the same distance from New York, were shipped at approximately the same long haul rate. For industrial goods shipped west of Chicago, it did not make much difference how far south or north of Council Bluffs the actual destination lay. A difference of 100 miles does not greatly disturb the accuracy of our computed 'representative' fares.[12] Finally, industrial goods were generally shipped first or fifth class. Competition for the grain traffic caused the rate to fluctuate considerably in these commodity classes, but grains generally commanded the lowest absolute tariff.[13]

Effective rates on Western grains shipped to New York: $Z_A(t)$

Grain price quotations are available for Iowa and Wisconsin (1870–1910),[14] as are yearly averages for Chicago (1880–1910) and New York (1870–1910).[15] Using spot price differentials between New York and Chicago grain markets, the following identity holds for 1880–1910:

$$P_{NY}(t) = P_{Chi}(t) + \left[P_{NY}(t) - P_{Chi}(t) \right].$$

MacAvoy has shown that these spot price differentials correlate very well with transport costs, at least for the last two decades of the nineteenth century. Unfortunately, when this relationship is extended to Council Bluffs–Chicago transport costs, the association is far less strict. This is hardly surprising since the quoted rates are less reliable in this case and they were certainly less competitive. It is well known that farmers had to pay a multitude of charges for shipment to the nearest rail connection with trunk lines to Chicago, thus driving a wedge between quoted and effective rates. As a rule, these short lines charged flat rates which were large relative to the services rendered if the tariffs on trunk lines are to be our guide. The trunk line charged whatever tariff was necessary to give it a reasonable share of the grain transported and rate wars were not uncommon.

This discussion clearly suggests the wisdom of avoiding the use of *published* tariffs as a measure of the costs involved in shipping grains East. Instead, the price differential between Iowa and New York will be used as an index of all charges incurred between the f.o.b. farm site and New York.

Table A.5 presents data on absolute price differentials between New York and both Iowa and Wisconsin. Table A.6 reports our computed $Z_A(t)$, as a percentage of the farm price. Generally, the following observations should be noted: (i) erratic short-run behavior but a sharp secular decline in *absolute* rates; (ii) erratic short-run behavior but a secular decline in percentage rates (e.g., Z_A), with sharp peaks and lows in 1871, 1881, 1887, 1891 and 1893 (Tables A.5, A.6, and Figure A.2).[16] On average, New York grain prices were almost 80 percent higher than those received in the West from 1870 to 1875. By 1910 the differential was only about 20 percent. The accuracy of the $Z_A(t)$ series may be questionable, but additional research is unlikely to improve the estimates a great deal.[17] In any case, our only concern is that the trends in $Z_A(t)$ are reasonably accurate.

Effective rates on industrial goods shipped West: $Z_I(t)$

Unfortunately, our task in constructing the $Z_I(t)$ series is far more difficult than with the $Z_A(t)$ series. The main problem lies with the heterogeneity of industrial goods. It is impossible to construct a comparable commodity price differential for a 'standard' basket of goods shipped to Western consumption points. We must rely, as a result, more heavily on published rates.

Table A.7 reports the quoted rates on first class traffic between New York and Chicago, and from there to Council Bluffs. Since this is taken as a representative series, and since first class rates were roughly related in fixed proportions to other classes of traffic, an index of transport costs is obtained on Western long haul shipments of industrial goods to Chicago. In the construction of the series presented in Table A.7 (col. 2), missing annual observations were supplied by interpolation; over the period 1896–1910, there was little

Table A.5. *Wheat spot prices in New York, Iowa, and Wisconsin, 1870–1910*

Year	Price NY	Farm price Iowa	Farm price Wisconsin	Δ Price NY–Iowa	Δ Price NY–Wisc	Δ Price Wisc–Iowa
1870	137	68	85	69	52	17
1871	158	97	108	61	50	11
1872	178	105	116	73	62	11
1873	178	94	108	84	70	14
1874	152	89	101	63	51	12
1875	140	78	95	62	45	27
1876	132	77	98	65	34	29
1877	168	102	122	66	46	20
1878	125	74	88	51	37	14
1879	122	70	85	52	37	15
1880	125	84	94	41	31	10
1881	126	90	111	36	15	11
1882	135	94	107	41	28	13
1883	128	75	88	53	40	13
1884	104	65	75	39	29	10
1885	99	59	72	40	27	13
1886	93	55	69	38	24	14
1887	90	55	67	35	23	12
1888	100	69	78	36	22	12
1889	101	68	75	33	26	7
1890	100	71	75	29	25	4
1891	107	78	85	29	22	7
1892	93	64	72	29	21	8
1893	80	49	57	31	23	8
1894	67	47	51	20	16	4
1895	68	49	55	19	13	6
1896	73	47	58	23	15	8
1897	88	62	74	26	14	12
1898	96	67	77	29	19	10
1899	79	53	63	26	16	10
1900	80	55	63	25	17	8
1901	84	56	64	28	20	8
1902	76	57	68	19	8	11
1903	92	59	71	33	21	12
1904	116	76	87	40	29	11
1905	114	79	88	35	26	9
1906	91	66	73	25	18	7
1907	104	74	81	30	23	7
1908	112	85	94	27	18	9
1909	134	99	102	35	32	3
1910	111	92	101	19	10	9

Source: All prices are *yearly* averages in cents per bushel. Col. (1): New York prices: 1870–80 from *Historical Statistics*, E101; 1881–1910 are from *Historical Statistics*, E101 plus MacAvoy's or Ripley's transport costs from Chicago to New York. MacAvoy, *The Economic Effects of Regulation*, table 6–1 gives spot differentials (average of summer and winter) for 1881–1900. The rail rate for 1900–10 is derived from Ripley, *Railroads: Rates and Regulations*, p. 431, taking 1900 = 10 cents. Col. (2): Iowa prices are from Strand, 'Prices of Farm Products in Iowa, 1851–1940.' Col. (3): Wisconsin prices are from Mortenson, 'Wisconsin Farm Prices 1841–1933,' table 3, pp. 13–14.

Table A.6. *Derivation of $Z_A(t)$ estimates, 1870–1910*

Year	Price differential as a percent of farm price: $Z_A(t)$		$Z_A(t)$ Ave. 1870–5 = 100	
	Iowa (1)	Wisconsin (2)	Iowa (3)	Wisconsin (4)
1870	101 ⎫	61 ⎫	120	113
1871	62 ⎪	46 ⎪	78	86
1872	69 ⎬ Ave: 79	53 ⎬ Ave: 54	86	99
1873	89 ⎪	64 ⎪	112	119
1874	75 ⎪	50 ⎪	94	93
1875	79 ⎭	47 ⎭	100	87
1876	84	34	106	63
1877	64	37	81	69
1878	68	42	86	78
1879	74	43	93	80
1880	48	32	60	60
1881	40	13	50	24
1882	43	26	54	48
1883	70	45	88	84
1884	60	38	79	71
1885	67	37	84	69
1886	69	34	87	63
1887	63	34	79	63
1888	56	28	71	52
1889	48	34	60	63
1890	40	33	50	61
1891	37	25	47	47
1892	45	29	57	54
1893	63	40	79	74
1894	42	31	53	58
1895	38	23	48	43
1896	48	25	60	47
1897	41	18	52	33
1898	43	24	54	45
1899	49	25	62	47
1900	45	26	57	48
1901	50	31	63	57
1902	33	12	42	22
1903	56	30	71	56
1904	53	33	67	61
1905	44	30	55	56
1906	38	27	48	50
1907	41	28	52	52
1908	32	19	40	35
1909	35	31	44	57
1910	21	10	26	19

Source: Iowa: (NY–Iowa)/Iowa, from Table A.5. Wisconsin: (NY–Wisc)/Wisc, from Table A.5. Index: 1870–5 = 100.

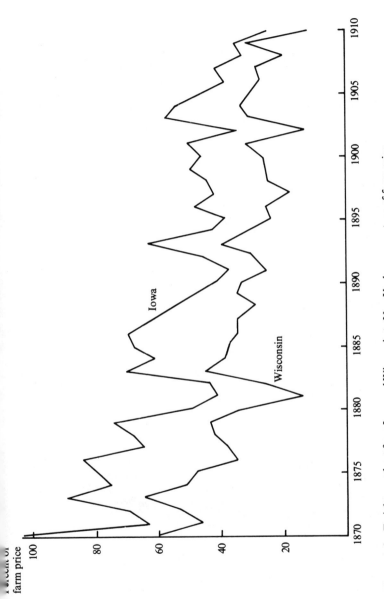

Figure A.2   Freight on wheat from Iowa and Wisconsin to New York as percentage of farm price, 1870–1910
(*Source*: Tables A.5 and A.6)

The facts of history

Table A.7.   *Movements of first class rail rates between New York and Chicago,
and Chicago and Council Bluffs, Iowa (cents per 100 pounds)*

Year	(1) New York–Chicago	(2) Chicago–Council Bluffs	(3) Total
1870	115	(120)	235
1871	77	(117)	194
1872	100	(114)	214
1873	63	(111)	174
1874	87	(108)	195
1875	65	(105)	170
1876	47	(102)	149
1877	100	(100)	200
1878	75	(98)	173
1879	(70)	(96)	166
1880	(60)	(94)	159
1881	50	(92)	142
1882	60	(90)	150
1883	75	90	165
1884	(67)	(90)	157
1885	62	(90)	152
1886	75	(90)	165
1887	75	90	165
1888	67	(90)	157
1889	(70)	(90)	160
1890	(75)	90	165
1891	75	80	155
1892	75	80	155
1893	75	80	155
1894	75	80	155
1895	75	80	155
1896–1910	75	80	155

Source: Noyes, *American Railroad Rates.*
Notes: Figures in parentheses are interpolated using the generally accepted notion that short haul rates declined slowly between 1870 and 1910. See text for a discussion of long haul rates. After 1900, changes in rates tend to be marked by changes in specifications for special discounts, such as carload ratings. It is significant that MacAvoy ceases his assessment of rate movements with 1900. As to the remarkable stability of rates, MacAvoy (*The Economic Effects of Regulation*, table 5.9 and 6.1) shows that the official rate must be viewed as a trend setter rather than as a precise index of cost changes. McCain, *The Diminished Purchasing Power of Railway Earnings*, pp. 50–8, argues that absolute rates did not vary greatly from 1897 to 1907.

or no change in the official rates for many goods.[18] Column 2 in Table A.8 converts this to a *real* index by deflating by wholesale prices; Figure A.3 graphs the index of real transport costs on industrial goods shipped West. While absolute rates in cents per pound declined considerably over time, Figure A.3 yields the surprising result that *real transport costs did not differ much in 1910 from what they were in 1870.*

Table A.8. *Real cost index for industrial goods shipped West: 1870–1910*

Year	(1) Wholesale price index (1870 = 100)	(2) Transportation index for industrial goods (1870 = 100)
1870	100	100
1871	96	86
1872	100	91
1873	99	75
1874	93	89
1875	87	83
1876	81	78
1877	79	107
1878	67	110
1879	67	105
1880	74	91
1881	76	79
1882	80	80
1883	75	93
1884	69	97
1885	63	103
1886	61	115
1887	63	111
1888	64	104
1889	60	113
1890	61	114
1891	56	114
1892	57	122
1893	58	120
1894	52	134
1895	53	132
1896	51	137
1897	51	137
1898	53	132
1899	57	122
1900	61	114
1901	60	116
1902	64	109
1903	65	107
1904	65	107
1905	65	107
1906	67	104
1907	71	98
1908	69	101
1909	74	94
1910	77	90

Sources: The wholesale index is from *Historical Statistics*, E1 and E13. Converted to base 1870 = 100. The transportation index is an index of shipping cost from New York to Council Bluffs, Iowa (1870 = 100), Table A.7, col. 3, deflated by the wholesale index.

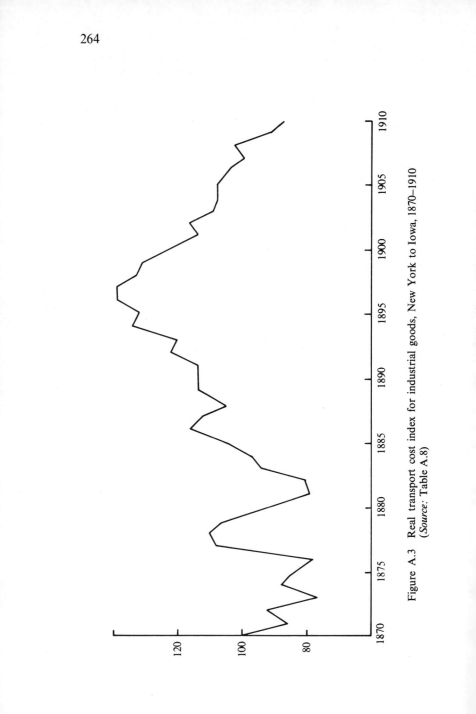

Figure A.3 Real transport cost index for industrial goods, New York to Iowa, 1870–1910 (*Source:* Table A.8)

It might be charged that this result is dominated by the questionable evidence on short haul rates (col. 3, Table A.6). Yet even if it were assumed that short haul rates declined just as rapidly as long haul rates, this result would not be significantly altered. (Table A.7, col. 2, shows that the *real* cost index was 37 percent higher in 1896 than in 1870 when short haul rates are included. Applying long haul rates alone produces a real cost index 28 percent higher in 1896.)

While the estimated long-run stability in $Z_I(t)$ over four decades may seem questionable, and certainly inconsistent with the sharp secular decline in $Z_A(t)$, Ripley also comments on the difficulties in assessing any trend over these years.[19] The next problem to confront is the *level* of $Z_I(t)$ at any point in time. Certainly as a relatively high bulk low value commodity, grains should have a higher transport cost component in delivered price. How much higher? Table A.9 presents data for 1897 giving the percent of transport costs to retail

Table A.9.   *Cost of transport for several finished goods: New York to Council Bluffs, Iowa, 1897 (cents per 100 pounds)*

Class	Commodity	Price	NY–Chicago	Chi–Iowa	Total	Z_I
4	Barbed wire	180	40	32	72	40
5	Copper and products	1500	35	27	62	4
4	Lead pipe	432	35	32	67	15
4	Zinc sheets	494	25	32	57	12
4	Pig iron (average)	50	25	32	57	100
4	Steel sheets	200	25	32	57	18
4	Iron	150	25	32	57	30
1	Rope	600	25	90	115	19
2	Candles	700	30	65	95	14
3	Paper	300	25	45	70	23
1–2	Earthenware (1 lb a piece)	325	30	65	95	30
4	Shovels (5 lb a piece)	1288	30	32	62	5
2	Cutlery (8 gross of spoons, knives)	4000	65	65	130	3
4–5	Nails (8 gross)	149	25	27	52	33
1–2	Refined sugar	300	25	65	90	30
1	Worsted yarns	8200	75	80	155	2
1	Blankets	7500	75	80	155	2
1	Flannels	3100	75	80	155	5
1	Horse blankets	5700	75	80	155	3
1–2	Cotton goods	1500	50	65	115	8

Source: New York to Chicago rates from McCain, *The Diminished Purchasing Power of Railway Earnings*, appendices B and C. Chicago to Iowa rates from Noyes, *American Railroad Rates*, p. 158. Z_I is computed by taking the ratio of 'total transport cost' to price. The prices are retail price quotations.

price. The variance is enormous among these heterogenous goods. Without detailed evidence on the composition of commodity traffic flowing West, a representative Z_I for 1897 is difficult to determine except that it must have been in excess of 5 percent. With the exception of pig iron, the rates range between 2 and 40 percent of the commodity's initial value. It seems plausible to select a value of Z_I lying somewhere between those on textiles and those on metal products. Somewhat arbitrarily we have selected approximately 20 percent as the average percent price differential for industrial products between Eastern and Western markets in 1897. This 20 percent figure for industrial goods seems reasonably consistent with the Z_A estimate for 1897 of 42 percent. In any case, the implied $Z_I(t)$ index appears to conform with the indirect evidence presented in Tables A.10 and A.11 where the real freight rate on nails and Barger's spread between producer and retail price are documented.

The $Z_A(t)$ and $Z_I(t)$ series are presented in detail in Table A.12.

A.5 Demand conditions

The structural transformation of the American economy after the Civil War has attracted much attention but apparently it is not well understood. Over the period 1879–99 alone, agriculture's share in commodity output declines by 16 percentage points (from 0·49 to 0·33) matching the 1839–59 performance, a period to which Rostow and others have attached special significance. Furthermore, the relative decline in agriculture is entirely accounted for by the expansion in manufacturing since mining and construction maintain constant shares.[20] Yet, chapters 4, 7 and 8 present quite a different characterization for the Midwest and Northeast by themselves. Whatever the evidence, domestic consumption demand

Table A.10. *Cost of shipping nails, New York to Iowa, 1883–1900*
(cents per 100 pounds)

| Year | Transport costs | | | Price | $Z_I(t)$ |
	NY–Chicago	Chicago–Iowa	Total		
1883	35	28	63	306	20
1887	30	30	60	230	26
1890	30	21	51	200	25
1895	25	27	52	211	25
1900	25	27	52	264	20

Source: Noyes, *American Railroad Rates*, pp. 166 and 168 for Class 5 to Council Bluffs. $Z_I(t)$ is computed by taking the ratio of 'total transport costs' to price.

Table A.11. *Spread between producer and retail price, 1869–1905 (in percent)*

Commodity	1869	1879	1884	1895	1905
			Year		
Groceries	27	28	28	29	29
Dry Goods	32	39	34	37	42
Furniture	37	38	38	35	39
Appliances	47	46	47	46	46
Hardware	41	41	39	38	40
Farm implements	32	33	31	30	30
Books, stationery	32	36	36	38	39

Source: H. Barger, *Distribution's Place in the American Economy Since 1869,* table B.2.

requirements in our model do not play an important role in pre-cipitating the structural transformation after 1870: they only serve to influence the volume of interregional and international trade. In any case, Engel effects must be allowed to operate in our model; the demand parameters selected must be consistent with low income (and low *price*) elasticity of demand for agricultural products.

Table A.13 displays six estimates of the income elasticity of demand for food based on late nineteenth-century evidence. The estimated income elasticity for food ranges between 0.67 and 1.04. A 'median' estimate is selected for the numerical analysis:

$$d_2 = 0.80$$
$$d_3 = -0.80$$

Table A.12. *Interregional transport cost indices assumed in the simulation*

Year	$Z_A(t)$	$Z_I(t)$	Year	$Z_A(t)$	$Z_I(t)$	Year	$Z_A(t)$	$Z_I(t)$
1870	1.00	0.25	1884	0.60	0.24	1897	0.41	0.34
1871	0.62	0.22	1885	0.67	0.26	1898	0.43	0.33
1872	0.69	0.18	1886	0.69	0.29	1899	0.49	0.31
1873	0.89	0.19	1887	0.63	0.28	1900	0.45	0.29
1874	0.75	0.22	1888	0.56	0.26	1901	0.50	0.29
1875	0.79	0.21	1889	0.48	0.28	1902	0.33	0.27
1876	0.84	0.20	1890	0.40	0.29	1903	0.56	0.27
1877	0.64	0.27	1891	0.37	0.29	1904	0.53	0.27
1878	0.68	0.28	1892	0.45	0.31	1905	0.44	0.27
1879	0.74	0.21	1893	0.63	0.30	1906	0.38	0.26
1880	0.48	0.23	1894	0.42	0.34	1907	0.41	0.25
1881	0.40	0.22	1895	0.38	0.33	1908	0.32	0.25
1882	0.43	0.20	1896	0.48	0.34	1909	0.35	0.24
1883	0.70	0.23				1910	0.21	0.23

Table A.13. *Estimates of income elasticities for food: 1875–1901*

Year	Income elasticity	Data source
1879–89	0·82	Time series based on per capita income[a]
1889–99	1·04	Time series based on per capita income[a]
1875	0·67	Survey of Massachusetts urban workers, based on expenditure per capita[b]
1901	0·71	Survey of industrial employees, family income controlled for size[c]
1888–91	0·68	Survey of industrial employees, family income controlled for size: 'normal' families[d]
1888–91	0·86	Survey of industrial employees, family income controlled for size: renters[d]

Sources: (a) Whitney, *The Structure of The American Economy*, table VI-3, p. 152.
(b) J. G. Williamson, 'Consumer Behavior in the Nineteenth Century: Carroll D. Wright's Massachusetts Workers in 1875,' table 6, p. 119.
(c) H. S. Houthakker, 'An International Comparison of Household Expenditure Patterns, Commemorating the Centenary of Engel's Law,' table II, pp. 541–2.
(d) A. Fishlow, 'Comparative Consumption Patterns, the Extent of the Market, and Alternative Development Strategies,' table 3.5, p. 65.

These parameter values are, of course, consistent with both Engel effects and low price elasticities, as well as the evidence of similar tastes between American regions.

A.6 Labor force growth

It is a common practice of both economic historians and growth theorists to specify labor force growth exogenously, at least in long-run analysis.[21] For the most part, the model developed in chapter 3 conforms to that tradition. Yet overall labor force growth in our spatial model *is* endogenously determined, since different natural rates of exogenous population growth are allowed in the two regions so that unbalanced regional growth implies variance in the aggregate labor force growth. This section attempts to establish parameter estimates for these regional rates and for the foreign immigration series, 1870–1910.[22]

Table A.14 and Figure A.4 document the behavior of rates of natural population increase per 1,000 in the Northeast and North Central from 1870 to 1910. These decadal estimates are utilized to derive $n_E(t)$ and $n_W(t)$. Both rates decline sharply over time so that the aggregate national growth rate should decline as well but at a lesser rate since the population shift was to the West where the rates were higher.

Table A.14. *Rates of natural population increase*
by regions, 1870–1910 (per 1,000)

Decade	North Central	Northeast
1870–80	224	144
1880–90	168	94
1890–1900	140	96
1900–10	112	90

Source: H. Eldridge and D. S. Thomas, *Population Redistribution*, III, table 1.14, p. 48. *North Central*: Ohio, Michigan, Indiana, Illinois, Wisconsin, Missouri, Iowa, Minnesota, N. Dakota, S. Dakota, Nebraska, Kansas. *Northeast*: New York, Pennsylvania, New Jersey, Maryland, Delaware, District of Columbia.

American (excluding Far West and South) labor force growth can be written as

$$\frac{\dot{L}(t)}{L(t)} = l(t) = \frac{\dot{L}_E(t) + \dot{L}_W(t) + M(t)}{L(t)}$$

$$= \frac{\dot{L}_E(t)}{L_E(t)}\left[1 - \eta(t)\right] + \frac{\dot{L}_W(t)}{L_W(t)}\eta(t) + \frac{M(t)}{L_E(t)}\left[1 - \eta(t)\right]$$

$$= \left[1 - \eta(t)\right]\{n_E(t) + m(t)\} + \eta(t)n_W(t),$$

where $\eta(t)$ is the share of the labor force in the Midwest, and $m(t)$ is the rate of immigration from abroad. That is, $m(t) = M(t)/L_E(t)$, i.e. the *rate* of foreign immigration to the East. Direct estimates on $M(t)$ are notably inaccurate for the nineteenth century since official series record *gross* immigration and do not effectively discriminate between migrants and visitors. Instead, the Kuznets–Rubin series (Table A.15 and Figure A.5) on net additions to foreign born are utilized. The $M(t)$ series reported in Table A.15 is introduced directly in the simulation with the exception that the series is normalized to the labor force stocks assumed initially in 1870. The native labor force growth parameters assumed in the simulation are summarized in Table A.16.

Two issues remain. First, to what extent can $M(t)$ be treated as immigration into the Northeast and North Central states? How significant was foreign immigration into the South and Far West? Second, how important was foreign migration in augmenting (at least initially) the Eastern labor force? Empirical evidence relating to the first question is surprisingly thin. While 'the most authoritative and comprehensive work on United States internal migration in the 19th century is the monumental three volume work edited by Kuznets and Thomas ...,'[23] their data supply no information

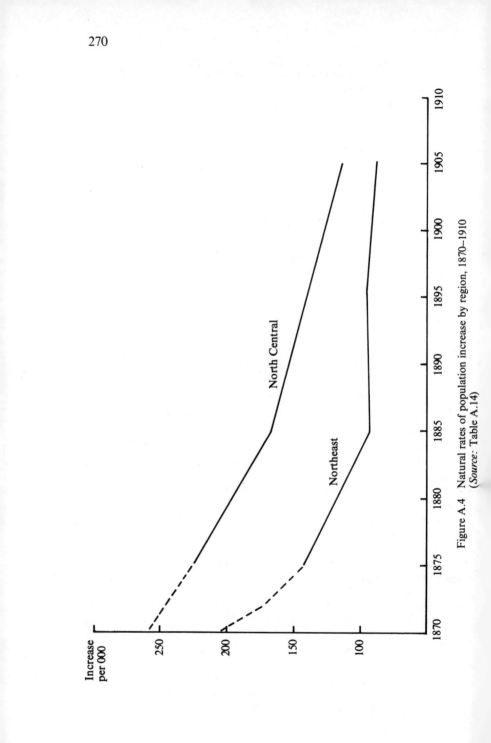

Figure A.4 Natural rates of population increase by region, 1870–1910
(*Source*: Table A.14)

Table A.15.   *External additions to United States population, 1879–1910 (000)*

Year	$M(t)$	Year	$M(t)$
1870	200	1890	120
1871	220	1891	300
1872	270	1892	350
1873	280	1893	290
1874	130	1894	20
1875	20	1895	−40
1876	−20	1896	40
1877	−60	1897	−40
1878	−40	1898	−40
1879	20	1899	50
1880	270	1900	190
1881	490	1901	70
1882	560	1902	180
1883	410	1903	300
1884	290	1904	330
1885	100	1905	440
1886	70	1906	590
1887	200	1907	510
1888	210	1908	50
1889	100	1909	310
		1910	560

Source: S. Kuznets and E. Rubin, *Immigration and the Foreign Born*, table B.6, p. 102. $M(t)$ is defined as net additions to foreign born.

on origin and destination of migrants, including foreign migrants. Recent estimates for the decade 1850–60 give us some insight to this question. Of the 1,210,467 immigrants arriving during that decade, only 10·7 percent settled in the South or Far West.[24] The vast majority of foreign immigrants, represented by our $M(t)$ series, are indeed entering labor markets in the North Central and Northeast economies.

Finally, how important were these foreign immigrations if they are treated as first augmenting the East's labor force before an interregional migration decision is made? Consider three periods of heavy foreign immigrants augmented the Eastern labor force by more than value of $m(t)$ was respectively 0·017, and 0·024 and 0·009. That is, foreign immigrants augmented the Eastern labor force by more than 2 percent each year in the early 1880s. These immigration rates were at the very least as important as native Eastern labor force growth itself in augmenting the Eastern labor force. As a result, $[n_E(t) + m(t)] > n_W(t)$ during each of these periods. This fact may not be fully appreciated in descriptions of American historical experience 1870–1910. In any case, it placed considerable stress on the opera-

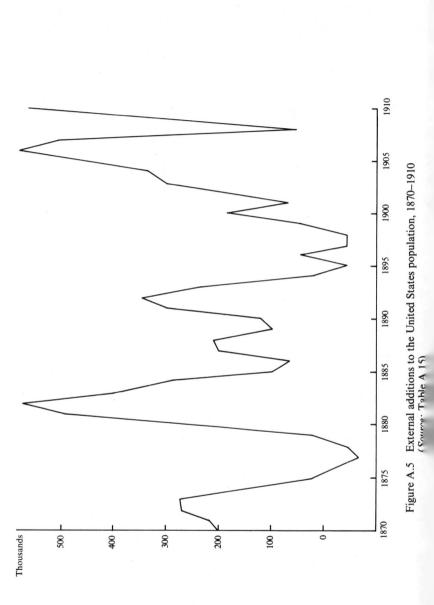

Figure A.5   External additions to the United States population, 1870–1910
(Source: Table A.15)

Table A.16.   *Labor force growth parameters assumed in the simulation*

Year	$M(t)$	$n_E(t)$	$n_W(t)$	Year	$M(t)$	$n_E(t)$	$n_W(t)$
1870	0·740	1·022	1·025				
1871	0·846	1·022	1·025	1891	1·154	1·009	1·015
1872	1·038	1·020	1·024	1892	1·346	1·010	1·014
1873	1·077	1·018	1·024	1893	0·923	1·010	1·014
1874	0·500	1·017	1·023	1894	0·077	1·010	1·014
1875	0·077	1·015	1·023	1895	−0·154	1·010	1·013
1876	−0·077	1·014	1·022	1896	0·154	1·010	1·013
1877	−0·231	1·014	1·021	1897	−0·154	1·009	1·013
1878	−0·154	1·014	1·021	1898	−0·154	1·009	1·013
1879	0·077	1·013	1·020	1899	0·192	1·009	1·013
1880	1·038	1·012	1·020	1900	0·731	1·009	1·012
1881	1·885	1·012	1·019	1901	0·269	1·009	1·012
1882	2·154	1·011	1·019	1902	0·692	1·009	1·012
1883	1·577	1·011	1·018	1903	1·154	1·009	1·012
1884	1·115	1·010	1·018	1904	1·269	1·009	1·012
1885	0·385	1·010	1·017	1905	1·692	1·009	1·011
1886	0·269	1·010	1·017	1906	2·269	1·009	1·011
1887	0·769	1·009	1·016	1907	1·962	1·009	1·011
1888	0·808	1·009	1·016	1908	0·192	1·009	1·011
1889	0·385	1·009	1·015	1909	1·192	1·009	1·011
1890	0·462	1·009	1·015	1910	1·806	1·009	1·011

tion of the interregional migration mechanism given the relatively rapid expansion of the derived demand for labor in the Midwest.

A.7 Land expansion

Our proxy for cultivated land is Tostlebe's value of physical farm assets (1910–14 prices) in land. These data are reported at census dates in Table A.17. The rate of expansion in the 'land stock'

Table A.17.   *Tostlebe's value of physical farm assets in land (1910–14 prices, in millions of dollars)*

	Year				
	1870	1880	1890	1900	1910
United States	13,627	19,115	22,937	28,020	30,215
Lake	974	1,617	1,951	2,546	2,713
Corn Belt	6,691	8,768	9,619	10,596	10,605
Great Plains	266	1,233	2,704	3,860	4,976
West	7,931	11,618	14,274	17,002	18,294

Source: A. S. Tostlebe, *Capital in Agriculture: Its Formation and Financing Since 1870*, table 9, pp. 66–9.

Table A.18. *Number of improved acres by state and region, 1870–1910*
(in th. acres)

	1870	1880	1890	1900	1910
New England	11,998	13,140	10,739	8,134	7,255
Mid-Atlantic	29,818	33,984	32,362	31,540	30,034
Southeast	29,497	35,411	40,905	45,340	47,761
North Central	43,904	58,130	59,115	63,630	64,207
South Central	28,124	37,156	44,979	52,188	57,299
Lake	20,340	24,706	30,788	41,488	44,393
Prairie	12,014	36,112	74,591	94,303	120,060
Southwest	12,095	29,395	40,539	51,970	69,493
Mountain	578	2,761	6,157	8,403	15,914
Pacific	7,528	13,343	17,560	19,974	22,039
United States	195,896	284,146	357,741	415,800	478,459

Source: M. L. Primack, 'Farm Formed Capital in American Agriculture, 1850 to 1910,' appendix, table 1, pp. 152–3.

declines over time, reflecting the gradual closing at the frontier, both in the Midwest and in the United States as a whole. Table A.18 reports Primack's improved acreage series for comparative purposes. The latter series clearly makes no effort to control for the quality of land and the extent of its improvement. The difference between the two series can best be summarized by the per annum Midwestern growth rates as follows:

	Tostlebe	*Primack*
1870–80	3·93	4·48
1880–90	2·09	3·27
1890–1900	1·75	1·92
1900–10	1·41	1·41

The complete $R(t)$ series assumed in the simulation is displayed in Table A.19.

A.8 Factor migration

The evidence on both labor migration and financial flows is very thinly documented for the late nineteenth century. In fact, even contemporary estimates are of questionable quality. Yet an attempt must be made to select migration parameters with which we can be reasonably confident. A considerable range of error is tolerable, since experiments indicate that the system may be quite insensitive to wide variance in these parameters.[25]

Table A.19. *Land stock series assumed in the simulation*

Year	$R(t)$	Rate of increase	Year	$R(t)$	Rate of increase
1870	972·157	0·000	1891	1780·393	0·019
1871	1017·848	0·047	1892	1813·330	0·018
1872	1063·651	0·045	1893	1845·970	0·018
1873	1109·388	0·043	1894	1878·274	0·017
1874	1154·873	0·041	1895	1911·144	0·017
1875	1200·259	0·039	1896	1944·589	0·017
1876	1244·669	0·037	1897	1977·647	0·017
1877	1288·232	0·035	1898	2010·278	0·016
1878	1330·744	0·033	1899	2042·443	0·016
1879	1373·328	0·032	1900	2074·100	0·015
1880	1414·528	0·030	1901	2102·101	0·013
1881	1452·720	0·027	1902	2126·275	0·011
1882	1487·585	0·024	1903	2146·474	0·009
1883	1518·824	0·021	1904	2162·573	0·007
1884	1556·795	0·025	1905	2174·467	0·005
1885	1587·931	0·020	1906	2184·252	0·004
1886	1618·895	0·019	1907	2192·989	0·004
1887	1650·464	0·019	1908	2201·761	0·004
1888	1682·648	0·019	1909	2210·568	0·004
1889	1714·618	0·019	1910	2219·410	0·004
1890	1747·196	0·019			

First, consider interregional labor migration during the 1870s. The Eldridge–Thomas volume reports *net* migration data of native and foreign born for the Northeast.[26] Their data imply a migration rate of 2·4 percent.[27] Since very few native Americans left the country, the net figure measures fairly accurately their rate of migration to the Midwest. Difficulties arise in forming estimates of *gross* out-migration by recent European immigrants from the Northeast. Thus the *net* figure for foreign born whites, 687,000, who immigrated to the Northeast is composed of a gross inflow from abroad and a gross outflow to the West. Our concern is with the latter. Let us assume that foreign immigrants migrated West at the same rate as natives; e.g., at a rate of 2·4 percent. The preceding section of this appendix suggests that the foreign immigration would have augmented the Northeastern population by 20 percent during the 1870s had no migration West taken place. Applying the native American migration rate of 0·024 to these foreign migrants yields a total (native and foreign) migration rate West, $m_{WE}(t)$, equal to approximately 0·03 during the 1870s. This, of course, is a *decade* rate of Westward migration. Although the annual rate must have varied much like the international in-migration flows, an annual Westward migration rate in the neighborhood of 0·003 cannot be far in error.

What evidence do we have on migration incentives? The average daily earnings for common laborers in 1869 were approximately the same in the Northeast and North Central: i.e., $1·57 in current prices.[28] This is in fact the annual earnings index assumed for 1870 in the simulations. Setting the Western agricultural price index at unity in this year, the real regional wage differential (West minus East) is 0·44; that is, the real wage differential is dominated totally by assumed cost of living differences.

The migration function hypothesized in chapter 3 is

$$m_{WE}(t) = 1 - e^{\varphi \tilde{w}*(t)}.$$

Table A.20 displays values for $m_{WE}(t)$, given $\tilde{w}*(t)$ and assuming $\varphi = 0·007$. (A similar migration specification is made for inter-sectoral labor mobility within the West, except labor is assumed more responsive to $\tilde{w}*$: e.g., $\varphi = 0·07$.) This estimated value of φ seems reasonably consistent with the wage and migration data: that is, it predicts for 1870 a Westward migration rate between 0·0028 and 0·0037 per annum – a range observed in the 1870s.

Potential migrants are assumed to have a three-year time horizon in formulating expectations on future earnings differentials. No evidence exists to support or deny this latter conjecture, but the econometric results presented in chapter 11 imply that foreign immigrants had a time horizon ranging from three to five years (Table 11.2, $\hat{B}_{j5}$). It is certainly difficult to imagine that potential migrants would hazard the move West on the basis of only one or two years experience given business cycle and long swing instability during these decades.

If the prerequisite data for estimating labor migration parameters are weak, they are almost non-existent for the capital market.

Table A.20. *Expected regional wage differentials and migration rates*
where $\varphi = 0·007$

$\tilde{w}*(t)$	$\varphi\tilde{w}(t)$	$e^{\varphi \tilde{w}*(t)}$	$m_{WE}(t)$
0	0	1·0000	0
−0·10	−0·0007	0·9993	0·0007
−0·20	−0·0014	0·9987	0·0013
−0·30	−0·0021	0·9979	0·0021
−0·40	−0·0028	0·9972	0·0028
−0·50	−0·0035	0·9963	0·0037
−0·60	−0·0042	0·9958	0·0042

In 1953 the Northeastern states invested 45 percent of their gross savings in other regions of the United States.[29] Surely it was far lower in the nineteenth century, but we can only guess at its value.[30] Furthermore, no estimate of τ exists for 1870. It is set arbitrarily at 0·01. Considerable documentation on regional interest rate differentials does exist, of course. Lance Davis's research[31] suggests that

$$i_W(1870) \gtreqless 1 \cdot 25 i_E(1870).$$

Given the specification developed in chapter 3,

$$\phi_{WE}(t) = 1 - e^{\mu[i^*(t)-\tau]}.$$

Table A.21 displays values for $\phi_{WE}(t)$, given $i^*(t)$, and $\mu = 4 \cdot 00$.[32] These parameter values imply that in 1870 the Northeast would have invested some 10 percent of their gross regional savings in the rest of the United States. This appears to us to be a reasonable range. Finally, as with labor migration, a three-year time horizon is assumed so that $(1 - \epsilon) = 0 \cdot 33$.

A.9 Commodity prices and terms of trade

World commodity prices are given exogenously in our model. It would be sufficient for our purposes to collect price data at the Eastern seaboard, e.g., New York City, since with the transport cost indices now estimated Western prices could be readily derived. In short, we need only estimate two price series: $P_{IE}(t)$ or $P_{IW}(t)$, and $P_{AE}(t)$ or $P_{AW}(t)$. The difficulty, of course, lies with the identification of the appropriate composite of 'industrial' and 'agricultural' goods. First, the composition of American farm exports may differ from the composition of Midwest farm output thus producing quite different *trends* in $P_{AW}(t)$ given $Z_A(t)$. Second, and perhaps more serious,

Table A.21. *Expected interest rate differentials and interregional savings flows where $\mu = 4 \cdot 00$*

$i^*(t)$	$-\mu[i^*(t) - \tau]$	$e^{-\mu[i^*(t)-\tau]}$	$\phi_{WE}(t)$
0·010	0	1·000	0
0·020	−0·040	0·961	0·039
0·025	−0·060	0·942	0·058
0·030	−0·080	0·923	0·077
0·040	−0·120	0·887	0·113
0·050	−0·160	0·852	0·148
0·060	−0·200	0·819	0·181

Table A.22.   *Farm price indices for Midwest 1870–1910 (1870 = 100)*

Year	Grains			Composite of farm products		
	(1) *Wisconsin*	(2) *Indiana*	(3) *Midwest*	(4) *Midwest*	(5) *Wisconsin*	(6) *Indiana*
1870	100	100	100	100	100	100
1871	122	98	110	87	99	87
1872	122	109	116	83	97	83
1873	120	109	115	84	95	84
1874	121	103	112	92	99	92
1875	117	99	108	92	99	92
1876	102	87	94	82	85	82
1877	123	103	113	82	94	82
1878	89	77	94	63	70	63
1879	89	82	86	64	73	64
1880			95	73	81	73
1881			119	84	89	84
1882			114	91	95	91
1883			94	83	84	83
1884			87	78	80	78
1885			82	68	71	68
1886			79	63	70	63
1887			80	75	90	75
1888			88	74	77	74
1889			74	62	67	62
1890			76	62	65	62
1891			105	71	75	71
1892			88	69	74	69
1893			73	72	77	72
1894			68	64	67	64
1895			74	59	62	59
1896			66	52	53	52
1897			79	56	56	56
1898			81	60	62	60
1899			77	59	64	59
1900			77	67	69	66
1901			77	71	73	70
1902			96	82	83	81
1903			82	77	79	76
1904			79	76	77	75
1905			83	77	78	76
1906			84	81	85	79
1907			97	86	90	84
1908			110	86	91	84
1909			104	100	103	99
1910			118	109	112	108

Source: The grain series was derived in two parts. 1870–9: Grain price indices for Indiana (P. L. Farris and R. S. Euler, *Prices of Indiana Farm Products, 1841–1955*, p. 28) and Wisconsin (Mortenson, 'Wisconsin Farm Prices, 1841–1933,' p. 76) were combined, using equal weights, and converted to 1870 = 100. Justification for the

the composition of American imports of industrial products may differ from the American industrial composition of outputs thus implying different trends in $P_{IE}(t)$. Given the relative abundance of the requisite commodity price information, this section estimates $P_{IE}(t)$ and $P_{AW}(t)$; the remaining prices are derived by utilizing $Z_I(t)$ and $Z_A(t)$. Furthermore, very similar movements in $P_{AW}(t)$ are produced whether derived from a composite index of Midwest farm products or from international trade data on crude foodstuff export prices. Our difficulties arise in deriving $P_{IE}(t)$ since a price series derived from a manufacturer's import price index and from an index based on American industrial value added weights do not coincide, especially for the period after the early 1890s and up to the latter part of the first decade of the twentieth century.

The first step is to derive $P_{AW}(t)$. Two such series are estimated as a check. One is a composite price index of Midwest products. This $P_{AW}(t)$ series is presented in Table A.22, col. (4), as a weighted average for Indiana and Wisconsin. A second $P_{AW}(t)$ series is displayed in Table A.22, col. (3), and it is based primarily on grain price indices as they enter American export trade. Figure A.6 shows how closely the two series move together at least during the years following 1876. As a result, we shall utilize the $P_{AW}(t)$ series estimated from American external grain exports.

The next step is to construct a series for $P_{IE}(t)$. The first such series is constructed from *Historical Statistics* using a weighted combination of New York quotations (Warren–Pearson) on metals and metal products, hides and leather products, and textile products. Census value added weights were used where 1870 weights were applied to 1870–75; 1880 weights were used for 1876–85; 1890 weights were used for 1886–95; etc. The weights are shares in total

---

Source to Table A.22 (*continued*)

weights comes from Perloff, *Regions, Resources and Economic Growth*, p. 203 ('wheat threshed'), which gives roughly equal production figures for the two states.

For 1880–1910, Lipsey's (*Price and Quantity Trends in the Foreign Trade of the United States*) crude food series, mainly consisting of wheat and corn (Table A.18, col. 1) was deflated by the price differential NY–Wisconsin (Table A.5, col. 2) to get the Western price. The resulting series was then linked up with the one for 1870–9.

The composite farm product series was obtained by using Mortenson, 'Wisconsin Farm Prices, 1841–1933,' table 39, and Farris and Euler, *Prices of Indiana Farm Products*, p. 28, which are given above as columns (5) and (6) (1870 = 100). From Perloff, *Regions, Resources and Economic Growth*, table B-2, p. 638, we can deduce that Indiana's farm output (value) is roughly twice as large as Wisconsin's output over the relevant years. Hence, column (4) can be computed attaching corresponding weights to columns (5) and (6).

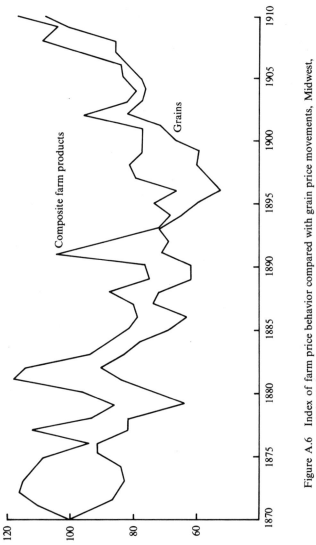

Figure A.6   Index of farm price behavior compared with grain price movements, Midwest, 1870–1910
(*Source*: Table A.23, cols. (3) and (4).)

industry value added; they are displayed in the table following:

Relative weight of value added $(\Sigma_j w_j = 1)$

Year	Textiles	Leather	Metals
1870	0·47	0·18	0·35
1880	0·45	0·15	0·40
1890	0·39	0·14	0·47
1900	0·37	0·10	0·53
1910	0·40	0·09	0·51

The resulting $P_{IE}(t)$ series is given in Table A.23. The resulting regional commodity price series is summarized in Table A.24 where the agricultural 'product' in the Midwest is taken as the numeraire $(P_{AW} = 100)$. The implied regional terms of trade are presented in Table A.25 and Figure A.7. These terms of trade indices compare quite favorably with Bowman's estimates of Midwestern farmer's terms of trade (equivalent to our $P_{AW}(t)/P_{IW}(t)$).[33]

Table A.23.   *A price index of Eastern industrial goods (1870 = 100); 1870–1910*

Year	$P_{IE}(t)$	Year	$P_{IE}(t)$
1870	100	1891	59
1871	98	1892	52
1872	108	1893	41
1873	109	1894	43
1874	100	1895	44
1875	88	1896	43
1876	78	1897	41
1877	72	1898	42
1878	65	1899	42
1879	65	1900	55
1880	79	1901	51
1881	72	1902	51
1882	73	1903	52
1883	71	1904	49
1884	65	1905	53
1885	60	1906	60
1886	59	1907	63
1887	59	1908	59
1888	59	1909	61
1889	58	1910	55
1890	59		

Source: Historical Statistics, E4, 5, 7, 17, 18 and 20, pp. 115–17, using weights described in text.

Table A.24. *Transport costs as a percent of producer price, and relative commodity prices* $(P_{AW} = 100)$ *1870–1910*

Year	(1) $Z_A(t)$	(2) $Z_I(t)$	(3) $P_{AE}(t)$	(4) $P_{IE}(t)$	(5) $P_{IW}(t)$
1870	101	25	201	100	125
1871	62	22	162	113	138
1872	69	18	169	130	153
1873	89	19	189	129	154
1874	75	22	175	108	132
1875	79	21	179	96	116
1876	84	20	184	95	114
1877	64	27	164	88	112
1878	68	28	168	103	132
1879	74	21	174	101	105
1880	48	23	148	108	96
1881	40	22	140	86	105
1882	43	20	143	80	103
1883	70	23	170	85	111
1884	60	24	160	83	121
1885	67	26	167	88	121
1886	69	29	169	94	101
1887	63	28	163	79	101
1888	56	26	156	80	120
1889	48	28	148	94	123
1890	40	29	140	95	127
1891	37	29	137	73	94
1892	45	31	145	61	80
1893	63	30	163	57	74
1894	42	34	142	67	90
1895	38	33	138	75	100
1896	48	34	148	83	111
1897	41	34	141	73	98
1898	43	33	143	70	93
1899	49	31	149	71	93
1900	45	29	145	82	106
1901	50	29	150	72	93
1902	33	27	133	62	79
1903	56	27	156	68	86
1904	53	27	153	64	81
1905	44	27	144	69	88
1906	38	26	138	74	93
1907	41	25	141	73	91
1908	32	25	132	69	86
1909	35	24	135	61	75
1910	21	23	121	50	62

Note: Decimal points are suppressed. For consistency, all figures should be divided by 100.

Sources:

Z_A: Table A.12.

Z_I: Table A.12.

P_{AE}: Derived by applying Z_A to P_{AW}, where P_{AW} is taken from Table A.22, col.(4).

P_{IE}: Table A.23, divided by P_{AW} of Table A.22, col. (3).

P_{IW}: P_{IE} adjusted by Z_I.

Table A.25. *Relative commodity prices for East and West 1870–1910*

Year	West: (1) $\dfrac{P_{IW}}{P_{AW}} \times 100$	East: (2) $\dfrac{P_{IE}}{P_{AE}} \times 100$	Year	West: (1) $\dfrac{P_{IW}}{P_{AW}} \times 100$	East: (2) $\dfrac{P_{IE}}{P_{AE}} \times 100$
1870	125	56	1890	123	68
1871	138	70	1891	94	53
1872	153	77	1892	80	42
1873	154	68	1893	74	35
1874	132	62	1894	90	47
1875	116	54	1895	100	54
1876	114	52	1896	111	56
1877	112	54	1897	98	52
1878	132	61	1898	93	49
1879	122	58	1899	93	48
1880	133	73	1900	106	57
1881	105	61	1901	93	48
1882	96	56	1902	79	47
1883	105	50	1903	86	44
1884	103	52	1904	81	42
1885	111	53	1905	88	48
1886	121	56	1906	93	54
1887	101	48	1907	91	52
1888	101	51	1908	86	52
1889	120	64	1909	75	45
			1910	62	41

Source: Table A.24, columns (3), (4) and (5).

However, the correspondence with Lipsey's index of the United States international terms of trade (equivalent to our $P_{AE}(t)/P_{IE}(t)$) is much less perfect, especially after the early 1890s (Figure A.8). This result is inevitable given the divergence between the composition of interregional and international industrial goods trade after the early 1890s.

The Lipsey terms of trade index is given in Table A.26 and Figure A.8. We have chosen to use this index in the analysis in chapter 4. The resulting price series utilized in the simulation are summarized in Table A.27.

A.10 Summary: parameter estimates

Production conditions:

$\alpha_K = 0.45$ $\beta_K = 0.20$
$\alpha_L = 0.55$ $\beta_L = 0.70$
                $\beta_R = 0.10$

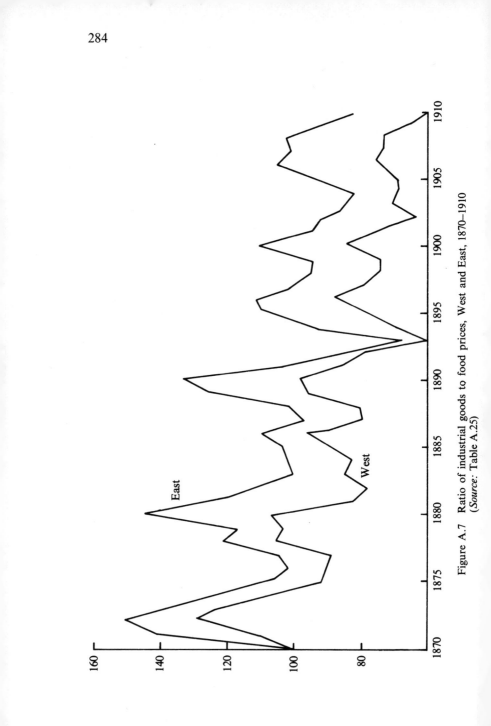

Figure A.7 Ratio of industrial goods to food prices, West and East, 1870–1910
(*Source:* Table A.25)

Table A.26. *Lipsey's price indices, 1879–1910 (1913 = 100)*

| | Prices | | Index of |
| | Crude foodstuff exports | Manufactured product imports | terms of trade |
Year	(1)	(2)	(3)
1879	93·6	102·8	116
1880	96·3	105·4	116
1881	102·9	103·2	105
1882	109·2	103·6	99
1883	104·2	101·6	102
1884	91·6	96·1	110
1885	85·6	90·7	111
1886	80·6	87·4	113
1887	81·8	87·5	112
1888	86·2	85·1	104
1889	75·5	87·6	122
1890	76·8	86·4	119
1891	100·3	86·1	90
1892	86·8	84·8	103
1893	77·9	84·6	114
1894	67·8	80·4	124
1895	69·5	80·3	122
1896	63·6	81·2	134
1897	71·5	79·4	116
1898	76·9	79·4	108
1899	73·2	82·8	119
1900	74·4	87·4	124
1901	77·4	88·6	120
1902	82·0	86·0	110
1903	81·4	87·6	112
1904	80·3	87·7	114
1905	82·4	90·1	114
1906	81·7	93·2	120
1907	95·0	97·1	107
1908	99·8	90·4	95
1909	104·2	86·3	87
1910	98·7	86·5	92

Source: R. E. Lipsey, *Price and Quantity Trends in the Foreign Trade of the United States.*

Col. (1): Table A-1, col. (2), pp. 142–3.
Col. (2): Table A-2, col. (6), pp. 144–5.
Col. (3): (2) ÷ (1), 1879 = 116.

Capital accumulation parameters:

$\delta = 0\cdot03,$

1870–1889, $\bar{s} = 0\cdot18,$
1890–1894, $\bar{s} = 0\cdot19,$
1895–1910, $\bar{s} = 0\cdot20.$

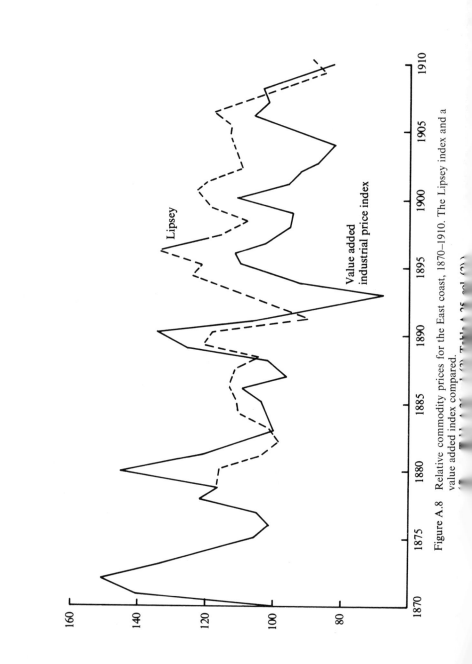

Figure A.8   Relative commodity prices for the East coast, 1870–1910. The Lipsey index and a
value added index compared.

Table A.27. *Commodity prices assumed in the simulation* $(P_{AW}(t) = 1.00)$

Year	$P_{IE}(t)$	Year	$P_{IE}(t)$	Year	$P_{IE}(t)$
1870	1·00	1884	0·92	1898	0·82
1871	1·13	1885	0·93	1899	0·90
1872	1·30	1886	0·93	1900	0·95
1873	1·29	1887	0·91	1901	0·96
1874	1·08	1888	0·81	1902	0·75
1875	0·96	1889	0·99	1903	0·89
1876	0·95	1890	0·95	1904	0·93
1877	0·88	1891	0·68	1905	0·91
1878	1·03	1892	0·80	1906	0·93
1879	1·01	1893	0·97	1907	0·84
1880	0·93	1894	0·99	1908	0·68
1881	0·73	1895	0·91	1909	0·63
1882	0·76	1896	1·03	1910	0·61
1883	0·90	1897	0·84		

Year	$P_{AE}(t)$	Year	$P_{AE}(t)$	Year	$P_{AE}(t)$
1870	2·00	1884	1·60	1897	1·41
1871	1·62	1885	1·67	1898	1·43
1872	1·69	1886	1·69	1899	1·49
1873	1·89	1887	1·63	1900	1·45
1874	1·75	1888	1·56	1901	1·50
1875	1·79	1889	1·48	1902	1·33
1876	1·84	1890	1·40	1903	1·56
1877	1·64	1891	1·37	1904	1·53
1878	1·68	1892	1·45	1905	1·44
1879	1·74	1893	1·63	1906	1·38
1880	1·48	1894	1·42	1907	1·41
1881	1·40	1895	1·38	1908	1·32
1882	1·43	1896	1·48	1909	1·35
1883	1·70			1910	1·21

Consumer demand parameters:
$$d_2 = 0.80,$$
$$d_3 = -0.80.$$

Labor migration parameters:
$$\phi_{WE} = 0.007, \qquad b = 0.33,$$
$$\phi_{IA} = 0.070.$$

Capital market parameters:
$$\mu = 4.00, \qquad (1 - \epsilon) = 0.33.$$

Transport service sector:
$$\gamma = 0.50.$$

In addition, see Tables A.3, A.12, A.16, A.19 and A.27.

Appendix B: The Simulation in Detail

Table B.1. *Real income and output*

Year	(1) GNP-T Total commodity output	(2) T Income originating in transportation	(3) Y_E Eastern income	(4) Y_W Western income	(5) Y_{AW} Western agricultural income	(6) Y_{IW} Western non-farm income
1870	308·652	53·354	132·100	176·552	104·986	71·566
1871	322·683	34·626	141·037	181·645	112·908	68·738
1872	358·278	30·498	163·104	195·174	120·045	75·129
1873	382·017	38·200	172·621	209·395	126·404	82·992
1874	376·519	49·026	159·690	216·829	132·964	83·864
1875	385·189	63·299	156·797	228·392	140·455	87·937
1876	407·098	71·376	163·682	243·415	149·199	94·216
1877	409·983	68·647	156·827	253·161	158·476	94·685
1878	449·286	60·444	178·343	270·953	166·026	104·927
1879	467·605	69·814	185·845	281·760	173·425	108·335
1880	458·353	59·751	174·710	283·642	181·058	102·585
1881	439·250	68·850	154·759	284·490	189·818	94·672
1882	469·718	72·552	169·410	300·308	199·266	101·042
1883	551·111	92·559	214·220	336·892	208·472	128·419
1884	571·748	84·182	223·995	347·753	216·957	130·796
1885	607·296	92·256	240·200	367·096	225·046	142·050
1886	635·819	96·002	251·348	384·471	232·776	151·695
1887	649·391	94·108	255·358	394·033	239·239	154·794
1888	639·357	99·889	243·502	395·855	244·727	151·128
1889	700·862	70·900	281·293	419·569	251·704	167·865
1890	705·919	67·641	278·871	427·049	255·786	171·263
1891	641·918	93·220	229·819	412·099	258·529	153·570
1892	718·932	92·207	271·409	447·523	266·416	181·107
1893	817·016	86·464	328·951	488·064	274·003	214·062
1894	834·711	61·200	334·612	500·100	278·307	221·793
1895	825·048	67·241	323·331	501·717	279·394	222·323
1896	905·432	52·420	364·995	540·437	282·545	257·892
1897	845·089	73·038	323·404	521·685	279·721	241·965
1898	858·517	75·862	326·215	532·301	281·056	251·246
1899	921·279	66·248	358·409	562·870	285·168	277·702
1900	964·031	53·018	379·938	584·093	288·648	295·445
1901	998·958	51·228	395·089	603·870	290·754	313·115
1902	889·088	68·703	332·073	557·015	287·757	269·258
1903	1018·363	65·993	398·061	620·302	295·233	325·069
1904	1068·774	53·690	422·269	646·505	300·071	346·434
1905	1080·681	49·082	425·605	655·075	302·330	352·745
1906	1119·833	39·488	445·938	673·895	304·822	369·073
1907	1090·892	55·494	429·968	660·924	303·835	357·089
1908	993·551	71·504	375·418	618·133	302·595	315·538
1909	981·328	83·959	366·142	615·185	307·692	307·494
1910	975·667	68·075	359·246	616·422	317·476	298·845

Table B.2. *Per capita income and commodity output*

Year	(1) Y_E/L_E Eastern per capita income	(2) Y_W/L_W Western per capita income	(3) GNP/L U.S. per capita income	(4) Q_{IE} Eastern industrial output	(5) Q_{IW} Western industrial output	(6) Q_{AW} Western agricultural output
1870	3·764	3·087	2·720	100·195	35·625	110·573
1871	3·856	3·125	2·724	104·603	37·439	118·242
1872	4·277	3·361	2·851	109·202	39·707	124·908
1873	4·330	3·472	2·984	114·353	42·654	130·823
1874	3·840	3·317	3·015	119·980	46·123	137·143
1875	3·673	3·310	3·100	124·914	49·547	144·419
1876	3·783	3·427	3·223	129·353	52·594	152·880
1877	3·593	3·389	3·274	133·577	55·386	161·893
1878	4·067	3·653	3·424	138·702	58·549	168·799
1879	4·209	3·738	3·481	144·563	62·118	175·867
1880	3·914	3·599	3·428	150·775	65·758	183·160
1881	3·361	3·363	3·365	159·446	69·631	191·991
1882	3·509	3·489	3·477	170·153	73·150	201·137
1883	4·222	3·966	3·818	182·203	76·674	209·692
1884	4·256	4·007	3·861	193·750	80·352	217·651
1885	4·445	4·161	3·994	205·237	84·576	225·063
1886	4·594	4·283	4·192	215·814	89·285	231·994
1887	4·619	4·305	4·123	226·732	95·528	237·687
1888	4·324	4·161	4·067	237·329	102·298	242·826
1889	4·903	4·478	4·232	247·682	108·066	247·816
1890	4·803	4·442	4·235	257·937	116·104	250·953
1891	3·905	3·977	4·019	269·594	126·196	254·674
1892	4·500	4·367	4·290	282·755	133·602	260·506
1893	5·303	4·862	4·694	296·663	140·650	265·429
1894	5·280	4·880	4·644	309·871	149·856	267·940
1895	5·058	4·761	4·588	321·759	162·354	268·509
1896	5·680	5·168	4·872	333·051	175·154	268·222
1897	4·980	4·763	4·638	346·082	190·787	266·592
1898	5·000	4·788	4·666	356·566	204·832	266·880
1899	5·469	5·083	4·865	366·908	217·554	268·318
1900	5·740	5·253	4·978	377·899	230·405	269·647
1901	5·860	5·363	5·082	391·087	244·001	270·115
1902	4·869	4·715	4·628	403·176	259·528	270·802
1903	5·737	5·323	5·088	416·741	272·152	273·857
1904	5·944	5·494	5·235	432·018	285·081	276·599
1905	5·844	5·460	5·236	447·796	299·294	278·210
1906	5·941	5·553	5·323	465·679	314·211	279·071
1907	5·518	5·296	5·160	486·555	330·599	279·563
1908	4·666	4·730	4·769	507·354	347·016	282·082
1909	4·510	4·620	4·688	522·340	361·230	288·377
1910	4·336	4·522	4·637	540·935	372·143	298·403

Table B.3. *Net physical capital stock*

Year	(1) K U.S. net capital stock	(2) K_{IE} Net Eastern industrial capital stock	(3) K_{IW} Net Western industrial capital stock	(4) K_{AW} Net Western agricultural capital stock
1870	536·149	341·572	101·463	93·114
1871	565·516	350·013	107·475	108·029
1872	593·507	358·967	114·923	119·618
1873	623·859	369·594	123·688	130·577
1874	660·847	382·486	133·411	144·951
1875	705·269	397·623	144·582	163·064
1876	753·044	413·989	156·786	182·269
1877	802·697	431·090	168·952	202·655
1878	846·331	447·575	180·788	217·968
1879	895·259	465·888	194·136	235·235
1880	946·576	484·603	207·199	254·774
1881	1013·481	506·606	221·809	285·065
1882	1082·169	530·101	236·578	315·490
1883	1147·221	556·808	252·288	338·126
1884	1211·740	585·482	267·362	358·895
1885	1278·871	617·640	283·231	378·000
1886	1347·813	652·395	299·656	395·762
1887	1419·918	688·865	317·045	414·007
1888	1502·390	728·234	337·147	437·009
1889	1569·287	763·516	353·694	452·077
1890	1645·673	803·393	373·287	468·993
1891	1751·275	850·632	400·777	499·866
1892	1845·777	896·136	426·479	523·163
1893	1929·867	940·634	450·376	538·858
1894	2009·578	984·434	473·389	551·855
1895	2105·403	1034·741	502·098	568·564
1896	2193·442	1083·057	530·294	580·091
1897	2299·393	1136·261	565·618	597·513
1898	2409·319	1189·329	604·067	615·923
1899	2513·554	1239·827	642·414	631·313
1900	2614·620	1288·529	681·052	645·040
1901	2717·118	1337·836	721·308	657·973
1902	2841·918	1390·857	770·021	681·040
1903	2956·566	1442·675	816·422	697·468
1904	3068·883	1494·458	862·327	712·098
1905	3184·492	1547·629	909·654	727·210
1906	3300·672	1601·826	957·396	741·450
1907	3430·717	1661·079	1010·055	759·583
1908	3584·343	1726·038	1070·245	788·059
1909	3752·215	1793·601	1134·917	823·698
1910	3922·003	1859·953	1197·987	864·064

Table B.4. *Gross investment and investment flows*

Year	(1) I_{WW} Western investment financed by West	(2) I_W Western investment	(3) I_{EW} Eastern investment financed by West	(4) I_E Eastern investment	(5) I_{AW} Western agricultural investment	(6) I_{AWWF} Western agricultural investment self-financed
1870	25·398	30·015	0·000	18·007	16·146	15·118
1871	23·721	26·764	0·000	18·687	17·709	14·760
1872	22·906	25·502	0·000	19·455	14·830	14·105
1873	24·557	26·760	0·000	21·397	14·548	14·547
1874	29·625	31·725	0·000	23·979	18·291	17·602
1875	35·395	37·635	0·000	26·612	22·462	21·196
1876	38·438	40·638	0·000	28·295	24·097	22·957
1877	40·777	42·724	0·000	29·521	25·854	24·859
1878	36·997	38·297	0·000	29·418	21·392	21·392
1879	41·504	42·578	0·000	31·740	23·807	23·807
1880	44·637	45·483	0·000	32·692	26·596	26·490
1881	57·502	58·761	0·000	36·542	37·934	36·904
1882	59·274	60·400	0·000	38·692	38·977	38·236
1883	54·782	54·908	0·000	42·610	32·100	32·100
1884	53·555	53·556	1·635	45·379	30·913	30·913
1885	53·760	53·761	3·317	49·722	29·872	29·872
1886	54·023	54·024	4·729	53·284	29·102	29·102
1887	56·496	56·497	5·631	56·042	30·118	30·118
1888	65·035	65·036	6·029	60·034	35·423	35·423
1889	54·838	54·839	6·099	57·129	28·178	28·178
1890	60·681	60·682	7·138	62·782	30·478	30·478
1891	83·631	83·632	7·268	71·341	44·944	44·944
1892	76·017	76·018	6·713	71·023	38·292	38·292
1893	68·081	68·082	7·105	71·382	31·390	31·390
1894	65·686	65·687	7·970	72·020	29·163	29·163
1895	76·175	76·176	8·967	79·840	33·265	33·265
1896	71·842	71·843	8·685	79·359	28·584	28·584
1897	86·057	86·058	8·907	85·696	34·824	34·824
1898	91·752	91·753	7·812	87·156	36·336	36·336
1899	90·335	90·336	6·758	86·178	33·867	33·867
1900	90·576	90·577	6·139	85·896	32·666	32·666
1901	92·972	92·973	5·887	87·964	32·285	32·285
1902	113·157	113·158	4·841	93·156	42·806	42·806
1903	106·361	106·362	4·329	93·544	36·850	36·860
1904	105·951	105·952	4·490	95·062	35·554	35·554
1905	109·670	109·671	4·706	98·005	36·474	36·474
1906	111·087	111·088	4·968	100·626	36·057	36·057
1907	121·757	121·758	5·180	107·308	40·377	40·377
1908	141·754	141·755	4·623	114·792	51·264	51·264
1909	156·059	156·060	3·356	119·344	59·281	59·281
1910	162·192	162·193	2·620	120·160	65·076	65·076

Table B.5. *Gross returns to capital and interest rates*

Year	(1) r_E Gross returns to Eastern capital	(2) r_{IW} Gross returns to Western industrial capital	(3) r_{AW} Gross returns to Western agricultural capital	(4) i_E Eastern interest rate	(5) i_{AW} Farm mortgage rate	(6) i_{IW} Western 'city' rate
1870	0·132	0·197	0·237	0·102	0·160	0·128
1871	0·152	0·216	0·219	0·104	0·129	0·127
1872	0·178	0·239	0·209	0·107	0·106	0·125
1873	0·180	0·238	0·200	0·109	0·101	0·125
1874	0·152	0·205	0·189	0·111	0·114	0·126
1875	0·136	0·179	0·177	0·111	0·122	0·124
1876	0·134	0·172	0·168	0·111	0·117	0·121
1877	0·123	0·165	0·160	0·109	0·113	0·118
1878	0·144	0·192	0·155	0·109	0·087	0·116
1879	0·141	0·176	0·150	0·110	0·092	0·114
1880	0·130	0·163	0·144	0·110	0·096	0·113
1881	0·103	0·126	0·135	0·112	0·121	0·111
1882	0·110	0·127	0·128	0·114	0·110	0·109
1883	0·133	0·151	0·124	0·117	0·082	0·107
1884	0·137	0·154	0·121	0·119	0·076	0·105
1885	0·139	0·157	0·119	0·120	0·072	0·104
1886	0·138	0·161	0·117	0·119	0·068	0·104
1887	0·135	0·158	0·115	0·118	0·069	0·106
1888	0·119	0·139	0·111	0·117	0·079	0·107
1889	0·145	0·174	0·110	0·116	0·057	0·107
1890	0·137	0·172	0·107	0·114	0·057	0·110
1891	0·097	0·124	0·102	0·113	0·086	0·112
1892	0·114	0·148	0·100	0·112	0·065	0·111
1893	0·138	0·177	0·099	0·112	0·048	0·111
1894	0·140	0·189	0·097	0·112	0·043	0·112
1895	0·127	0·176	0·094	0·110	0·048	0·116
1896	0·143	0·205	0·092	0·108	0·037	0·119
1897	0·115	0·171	0·089	0·107	0·049	0·122
1898	0·111	0·166	0·087	0·105	0·049	0·123
1899	0·120	0·180	0·085	0·103	0·042	0·122
1900	0·125	0·187	0·084	0·102	0·038	0·122
1901	0·126	0·189	0·082	0·102	0·036	0·122
1902	0·098	0·144	0·080	0·100	0·053	0·122
1903	0·116	0·170	0·079	0·100	0·039	0·120
1904	0·121	0·176	0·078	0·100	0·036	0·119
1905	0·118	0·171	0·077	0·100	0·036	0·118
1906	0·122	0·173	0·075	0·101	0·034	0·118
1907	0·111	0·155	0·074	0·102	0·040	0·117
1908	0·090	0·124	0·072	0·102	0·054	0·116
1909	0·083	0·111	0·070	0·101	0·060	0·113
1910	0·080	0·105	0·069	0·101	0·062	0·110

Table B.6. *Wage rates by sector*

Year	(1) w_E Eastern industrial wage	(2) w_{IW} Western industrial wage	(3) w_{AW} Western agricultural wage	(4) $\overline{w}_W$ Average Western wage	(5) $\tilde{w}_E$ 'Real' Eastern wage	(6) $\tilde{w}_W$ 'Real' Western wage
1870	1·570	1·570	1·570	1·570	0·975	1·411
1871	1·777	1·771	1·634	1·667	1·244	1·424
1872	2·047	2·017	1·687	1·767	1·325	1·447
1873	2·035	2·054	1·740	1·818	1·194	1·519
1874	1·714	1·783	1·803	1·799	1·105	1·609
1875	1·545	1·613	1·870	1·802	1·048	1·681
1876	1·562	1·640	1·932	1·854	1·066	1·733
1877	1·481	1·664	1·993	1·906	1·124	1·993
1878	1·792	2·052	2·022	2·030	1·300	1·743
1879	1·819	1·987	2·054	2·037	1·264	1·849
1880	1·728	1·939	2·088	2·050	1·383	1·915
1881	1·390	1·576	2·136	1·993	1·280	2·112
1882	1·473	1·690	2·178	2·055	1·386	2·170
1883	1·778	2·153	2·206	2·193	1·399	2·061
1884	1·863	2·316	2·231	2·252	1·455	2·094
1885	1·943	2·476	2·254	2·307	1·472	2·116
1886	2·018	2·627	2·277	2·361	1·512	2·140
1887	2·053	2·617	2·305	2·381	1·590	2·197
1888	1·878	2·326	2·340	2·336	1·570	2·311
1889	2·351	2·930	2·362	2·509	1·924	2·178
1890	2·321	2·847	2·394	2·518	1·957	2·265
1891	1·713	2·057	2·444	2·332	1·665	2·487
1892	2·063	2·519	2·473	2·486	1·935	2·415
1893	2·552	3·102	2·492	2·673	2·010	2·330
1894	2·662	3·288	2·520	2·757	2·194	2·369
1895	2·519	3·007	2·560	2·707	2·192	2·457
1896	2·936	3·442	2·597	2·891	2·357	2·415
1897	2·462	2·813	2·647	2·709	2·165	2·558
1898	2·465	2·749	2·692	2·715	2·247	2·587
1899	2·771	3·013	2·727	2·843	2·382	2·585
1900	2·983	3·175	2·759	2·932	2·513	2·518
1901	3·063	3·249	2·794	2·990	2·506	2·659
1902	2·438	2·538	2·839	2·705	2·358	2·773
1903	2·940	3·077	2·864	2·960	2·523	2·745
1904	3·110	3·277	2·890	3·067	2·568	2·788
1905	3·077	3·259	2·918	3·077	2·645	2·839
1906	3·173	3·356	2·949	3·143	2·785	2·873
1907	2·885	3·054	2·985	3·018	2·609	2·939
1908	2·358	2·521	3·025	2·775	2·452	3·039
1909	2·229	2·365	3·053	2·711	2·464	3·166
1910	2·191	2·366	3·070	2·727	2·643	3·267

Table B.7. *Sectoral employment and migration*

year	(1) L Total employ- ment	(2) L_{IE} Eastern industrial employ- ment	(3) L_{IW} Western industrial employ- ment	(4) L_{AW} Western agricultural employ- ment	(5) m_{WE} Migration rate East to West	(6) $\hat{m}_{IA}$ Western rural-urban migration rate
1870	100·000	35·100	15·600	49·300	0·003	0·000
1871	103·270	36·577	16·031	50·662	0·002	0·003
1872	106·588	38·139	16·613	51·836	0·002	0·010
1873	110·031	39·868	17·531	52·633	0·002	0·014
1874	113·510	41·582	18·692	53·236	0·002	0·009
1875	116·371	42·685	19·619	54·067	0·003	0·000
1876	118·783	43·270	20·108	55·406	0·004	0·000
1877	120·973	43·643	20·457	56·873	0·004	0·000
1878	122·977	43·851	20·687	58·440	0·004	0·000
1879	125·099	44·151	21·011	59·937	0·004	0·000
1880	127·369	44·635	21·338	61·395	0·004	0·000
1881	130·597	46·042	21·642	62·913	0·004	0·000
1882	134·641	48·277	21·716	64·648	0·005	0·000
1883	138·967	50·734	21·683	66·550	0·005	0·000
1884	142·690	52·633	21·768	68·290	0·005	0·000
1885	145·953	54·033	22·015	69·905	0·005	0·000
1886	148·441	54·713	22·423	71·305	0·004	0·007
1887	150·850	55·285	23·381	72·183	0·004	0·012
1888	153·645	56·311	24·683	72·652	0·005	0·008
1889	156·518	57·366	25·709	73·443	0·004	0·018
1890	158·906	58·057	27·483	73·367	0·003	0·022
1891	161·404	58·858	29·595	72·951	0·004	0·006
1892	164·625	60·307	30·566	73·753	0·004	0·005
1893	168·035	62·030	31·451	74·554	0·003	0·017
1894	171·062	63·372	33·253	74·437	0·003	0·029
1895	173·281	63·919	35·936	73·425	0·002	0·030
1896	175·188	64·256	38·631	72·301	0·002	0·039
1897	177·426	64·944	41·984	70·499	0·002	0·030
1898	179·319	65·243	44·691	69·385	0·002	0·021
1899	181·235	65·537	46·816	68·883	0·002	0·021
1900	183·521	66·195	48·916	68·410	0·002	0·023
1901	186·256	67·422	51·151	67·683	0·001	0·026
1902	188·558	68·206	53·570	66·782	0·002	0·011
1903	191·308	69·386	54·985	66·937	0·002	0·012
1904	194·549	71·043	56·507	67·000	0·002	0·017
1905	197·940	72·833	58·373	66·734	0·002	0·019
1906	201·663	75·067	60·344	66·253	0·001	0·022
1907	206·001	77·918	62·516	65·567	0·002	0·016
1908	210·073	80·458	64·341	65·274	0·002	0·000
1909	212·415	81·181	65·110	66·123	0·003	0·000
1910	215·781	82·844	64·907	68·030	0·004	0·000

Table B.8. *Employment distribution and capital–labor ratios*

Year	(1) L_W/L Share of labor in West	(2) $L_{IW} + L_{IE}/L$ U.S. industrial employment share	(3) L_{IW}/L_W Western industrial employment share	(4) K_{IE}/L_{IE} Capital–labor ratio in Eastern industry	(5) K_{IW}/L_{IW} Capital–labor ratio in Western industry	(6) K_{AW}/L_{AW} Capital–labor ratio in Western agriculture
1870	0·649	0·507	0·240	100·000	100·000	100·000
1871	0·646	0·509	0·240	112·900	103·078	98·333
1872	0·642	0·514	0·243	122·180	106·360	96·718
1873	0·638	0·522	0·250	131·354	108·477	95·264
1874	0·634	0·531	0·260	144·161	109·739	94·522
1875	0·633	0·535	0·266	159·684	113·306	95·723
1876	0·636	0·534	0·266	174·177	119·885	98·316
1877	0·639	0·530	0·265	188·661	126·981	101·503
1878	0·643	0·525	0·261	197·477	134·368	104·885
1879	0·647	0·521	0·260	207·796	142·064	108·434
1880	0·650	0·518	0·258	219·712	149·295	111·566
1881	0·647	0·518	0·256	239·905	157·577	113·068
1882	0·641	0·520	0·251	258·384	167·499	112·834
1883	0·635	0·521	0·246	269·008	178·894	112·779
1884	0·631	0·521	0·242	278·256	188·844	114·310
1885	0·630	0·521	0·240	286·297	197·807	117·463
1886	0·631	0·520	0·239	293·866	205·474	122·530
1887	0·634	0·521	0·245	303·671	208·483	128·041
1888	0·634	0·527	0·254	318·475	210·009	132·894
1889	0·633	0·531	0·259	325·906	211·526	136·770
1890	0·635	0·538	0·273	338·454	208·832	142·200
1891	0·635	0·548	0·289	362·789	208·213	148·512
1892	0·634	0·552	0·293	375·570	214·528	152·696
1893	0·631	0·556	0·297	382·677	220·171	155·828
1894	0·630	0·565	0·309	392·525	218·876	159·630
1895	0·631	0·576	0·329	409·984	214·820	166·350
1896	0·633	0·587	0·348	424·801	211·057	173·206
1897	0·634	0·603	0·373	448·744	207·138	179·790
1898	0·636	0·613	0·392	469·983	207·817	187·324
1899	0·638	0·620	0·405	485·250	210·980	194·402
1900	0·639	0·627	0·417	499·225	214·066	200·030
1901	0·638	0·637	0·430	514·708	216·813	203·904
1902	0·638	0·646	0·445	539·942	221·004	209·548
1903	0·637	0·650	0·451	551·680	228·293	213·660
1904	0·635	0·656	0·458	562·729	234·634	216·166
1905	0·632	0·663	0·467	576·960	239·596	218·356
1906	0·628	0·671	0·477	592·531	243·935	219·277
1907	0·622	0·682	0·488	613·370	248·412	219·068
1908	0·617	0·689	0·486	639·217	255·749	220·449
1909	0·618	0·689	0·496	659·548	267·998	227·036
1910	0·616	0·685	0·488	672·476	283·778	230·710

The facts of history

Table B.9. *Land values and budget shares*

Year	(1) V Land values	(2) Share of Western wage income on food	(3) Share of Eastern wage income on food
1870	0·071	0·450	0·500
1871	0·080	0·481	0·516
1872	0·111	0·518	0·566
1873	0·117	0·515	0·575
1874	0·105	0·457	0·509
1875	0·098	0·413	0·475
1876	0·105	0·404	0·472
1877	0·111	0·386	0·439
1878	0·145	0·446	0·482
1879	0·139	0·420	0·476
1880	0·135	0·397	0·436
1881	0·109	0·327	0·371
1882	0·123	0·331	0·380
1883	0·168	0·382	0·434
1884	0·183	0·389	0·432
1885	0·198	0·396	0·436
1886	0·212	0·401	0·434
1887	0·210	0·391	0·422
1888	0·183	0·353	0·388
1889	0·256	0·414	0·431
1890	0·251	0·399	0·409
1891	0·166	0·310	0·331
1892	0·221	0·353	0·368
1893	0·299	0·403	0·421
1894	0·330	0·418	0·413
1895	0·292	0·386	0·384
1896	0·373	0·423	0·417
1897	0·274	0·364	0·363
1898	0·268	0·355	0·357
1899	0·312	0·374	0·379
1900	0·340	0·383	0·388
1901	0·354	0·385	0·392
1902	0·238	0·318	0·329
1903	0·323	0·359	0·375
1904	0·358	0·369	0·382
1905	0·353	0·362	0·372
1906	0·373	0·365	0·373
1907	0·318	0·337	0·352
1908	0·236	0·289	0·305
1909	0·216	0·270	0·292
1910	0·217	0·263	0·279

Appendix C: Data Underlying the Analysis of American Immigration

C.1 Appendix tables

Table C.1. *Production indices for five countries, 1870–1913 (1899 = 100)*

Year	United States (1)	Sweden (2)	United Kingdom (3)	Germany (4)	Denmark (5)
1870	25·0	35·3	57·7	28·1	31·1
1871	26·0	29·1	59·2	32·8	32·8
1872	31·0	35·1	60·8	35·9	33·9
1873	30·0	37·3	62·3	35·9	33·2
1874	29·0	38·0	63·8	34·4	35·9
1875	28·0	36·9	65·2	34·4	36·4
1876	28·0	36·8	66·5	37·5	38·7
1877	30·0	37·2	67·7	34·4	38·4
1878	32·0	33·1	68·7	39·1	40·0
1879	36·0	34·1	69·8	40·6	41·3
1880	42·0	37·2	71·0	39·1	45·0
1881	46·0	41·0	72·0	42·2	47·5
1882	49·0	44·4	73·1	43·8	50·3
1883	50·0	43·7	74·0	46·9	53·5
1884	47·0	46·0	74·8	48·4	55·0
1885	47·0	48·6	75·8	50·0	56·2
1886	57·0	46·2	76·7	51·6	55·6
1887	60·0	49·3	77·9	54·9	57·2
1888	62·0	50·3	79·4	56·3	59·3
1889	66·0	56·1	80·8	60·9	62·3
1890	71·0	58·6	82·3	62·5	65·5
1891	73·0	60·1	83·8	64·1	68·7
1892	79·0	63·6	85·5	62·5	71·6
1893	70·0	66·3	87·4	65·6	72·2
1894	68·0	73·2	89·4	70·3	75·5
1895	81·0	74·3	91·6	75·0	82·1
1896	74·0	85·5	93·8	82·8	85·7
1897	80·0	91·9	95·9	87·5	90·9
1898	91·0	96·5	98·1	93·8	97·4
1899	100·0	100·0	100·0	100·0	100·0
1900	100·0	107·9	101·7	101·4	97·8
1901	111·0	107·7	103·2	98·8	102·8
1902	127·0	110·4	104·7	98·8	105·2
1903	126·0	111·5	105·9	100·1	112·4
1904	121·0	120·4	106·7	101·5	117·4
1905	140·0	120·8	108·2	101·5	122·3
1906	152·0	135·2	109·2	100·5	124·8
1907	156·0	138·5	110·0	105·3	124·3
1908	127·0	130·8	110·5	104·1	124·0
1909	166·0	127·4	111·0	103·0	132·9
1910	172·0	148·2	111·4	102·9	136·7
1911	162·0	153·9	111·8	101·9	145·7
1912	194·0	155·9	111·4	99·9	157·4
1913	203·0	156·0	110·9	104·1	159·7

Table C.2. *Industrial labor force for five countries, 1870–1913 (in millions)*

Year	United States (1)	Sweden (2)	United Kingdom (3)	Germany (4)	Denmark (5)
1870	6·14	0·081	5·05	5·38	0·45
1871	6·34	0·088	5·22	5·41	0·46
1872	6·55	0·098	5·29	5·44	0·47
1873	6·76	0·109	5·32	5·49	0·47
1874	6·98	0·118	5·33	5·55	0·48
1875	7·21	0·121	5·33	5·62	0·48
1876	7·45	0·120	5·30	5·69	0·48
1877	7·69	0·117	5·28	5·76	0·49
1878	7·94	0·108	5·20	5·83	0·49
1879	8·20	0·103	4·98	5·90	0·50
1880	8·47	0·113	5·35	5·96	0·50
1881	8·87	0·123	5·50	6·01	0·51
1882	9·28	0·128	5·65	6·05	0·52
1883	9·71	0·132	5·70	6·17	0·52
1884	10·16	0·135	5·12	6·28	0·53
1885	10·64	0·136	5·45	6·41	0·53
1886	11·13	0·138	5·46	6·53	0·54
1887	11·65	0·139	5·69	6·65	0·55
1888	12·19	0·152	5·78	6·78	0·55
1889	12·76	0·170	6·20	6·91	0·56
1890	13·36	0·178	6·28	7·04	0·57
1891	13·59	0·193	6·27	7·18	0·58
1892	13·83	0·191	6·19	7·32	0·59
1893	14·07	0·193	6·22	7·46	0·60
1894	14·32	0·203	6·37	7·60	0·61
1895	14·57	0·218	6·56	7·74	0·62
1896	14·83	0·238	6·85	7·91	0·63
1897	15·09	0·258	6·96	8·09	0·64
1898	15·35	0·277	7·12	8·27	0·66
1899	15·62	0·289	7·29	8·46	0·67
1900	15·90	0·298	7·38	8·65	0·69
1901	17·03	0·295	7·45	8·84	0·70
1902	18·05	0·296	7·48	9·04	0·72
1903	18·63	0·304	7·50	9·24	0·72
1904	18·67	0·311	7·48	9·45	0·74
1905	19·73	0·314	7·65	9·67	0·75
1906	21·16	0·317	7·85	9·87	0·76
1907	21·75	0·319	7·93	10·11	0·78
1908	20·90	0·322	7·67	10·34	0·79
1909	22·73	0·326	7·77	10·57	0·80
1910	23·30	0·329	8·11	10·81	0·81
1911	23·85	0·332	8·34	11·05	0·82
1912	25·04	0·336	8·42	11·30	0·84
1913	26·03	0·339	8·61	11·54	0·85

Table C.3. *Migration from four European countries to America, 1870–1913*
(*in millions*)

Year	Sweden (1)	United Kingdom (2)	Germany (3)	Denmark (4)
1870	0·0134	0·0888	0·1182	0·0041
1871	0·0107	0·0790	0·0826	0·0020
1872	0·0135	0·0849	0·1411	0·0037
1873	0·0143	0·0895	0·1497	0·0049
1874	0·0057	0·0620	0·0873	0·0031
1875	0·0056	0·0479	0·0478	0·0027
1876	0·0056	0·0293	0·0319	0·0016
1877	0·0050	0·0236	0·0293	0·0017
1878	0·0054	0·0222	0·0293	0·0021
1879	0·0110	0·0300	0·0346	0·0035
1880	0·0392	0·0733	0·0846	0·0066
1881	0·0498	0·0814	0·2105	0·0091
1882	0·0646	0·1030	0·2506	0·0116
1883	0·0383	0·0766	0·1948	0·0103
1884	0·0266	0·0660	0·1797	0·0092
1885	0·0223	0·0577	0·1244	0·0061
1886	0·0278	0·0629	0·0844	0·0062
1887	0·0428	0·0934	0·1069	0·0085
1888	0·0547	0·1087	0·1097	0·0090
1889	0·0354	0·0880	0·0995	0·0087
1890	0·0296	0·0697	0·0924	0·0094
1891	0·0367	0·0666	0·1136	0·0107
1892	0·0419	0·0422	0·1192	0·0101
1893	0·0357	0·0352	0·0788	0·0077
1894	0·0183	0·0225	0·0540	0·0050
1895	0·0154	0·0289	0·0322	0·0039
1896	0·0212	0·0246	0·0319	0·0032
1897	0·0132	0·0128	0·0225	0·0021
1898	0·0124	0·0129	0·0171	0·0020
1899	0·0128	0·0127	0·0175	0·0027
1900	0·0187	0·0125	0·0185	0·0029
1901	0·0233	0·0150	0·0217	0·0037
1902	0·0309	0·0169	0·0283	0·0057
1903	0·0460	0·0336	0·0401	0·0072
1904	0·0278	0·0515	0·0464	0·0085
1905	0·0266	0·0842	0·0406	0·0090
1906	0·0233	0·0672	0·0376	0·0077
1907	0·0206	0·0790	0·0378	0·0072
1908	0·0128	0·0628	0·0323	0·0050
1909	0·0145	0·0468	0·0255	0·0044
1910	0·0238	0·0689	0·0313	0·0070
1911	0·0208	0·0734	0·0321	0·0076
1912	0·0127	0·0572	0·0278	0·0062
1913	0·0172	0·0603	0·0343	0·0065

United States

Industrial labor force.   S. Lebergott, *Manpower in Economic Growth*, pp. 510–12. For 1870–90, industrial labor force was found by subtracting the agricultural labor force from the total labor force which was given for 1870, 1880 and 1890 (table A.1, p. 510). For the interim years, growth tables were applied to the ten-year values. For 1890–9, the figure for 1890 was found as above on p. 510, and the figure for 1900 was the 'non-farm employment' number for 1900 on p. 512. The interim year figures were arrived at through the use of growth tables. For 1900–13, the figures were the non-farm employment numbers on p. 512, table A.4.

Index of production.   E. Frickey, *Production in the United States, 1860–1914*, table 6, p. 54.

Sweden

Migration: I. Ferenczi and W. Wilcox, *International Migrations*, vol. I, tables 2 and 3, pp. 384–91.

Industrial labor force: G. Bagge, E. Lundberg and I. Svennilson, *Wages in Sweden 1860–1930*, vol. II, part II, table 190, pp. 240–1. Number of workers in manufacturing and mining.

Index of production: O. Johansson, *The Gross Domestic Product of Sweden and its Composition*, table 6, pp. 48–9. The gross output of manufacturing industry and handicrafts was deflated by the cost of living index in E. Lindahl, E. Dahlgren and K. Kock, *National Income of Sweden 1861–1930*, table 5, p. 247.

United Kingdom

Migration: Ferenczi and Wilcox, *International Migrations*, vol. I, tables 2 and 3, pp. 384–91. For 1870 and 1871, the number of migrants from the whole United Kingdom was decreased by an estimated figure for Irish emigrants. The number of Irish emigrants for 1870 and 1871 was estimated by finding the percentage of Irish migrants of total U.K. migrants into the U.S. for 1872 and applying it to the number of total migrants to the U.S. for 1870 and 1871. For 1872–1913, the migration figure is that for England, Scotland and Wales.

Industrial labor force: P. Deane and W. A. Cole, *British Economic Growth 1688–1959*, table 31, p. 143, and B. R. Mitchell and P. Deane, *Abstract of British Historical Statistics*, p. 64. First the ten-year data for persons working in mining and quarrying, manufactures, and building were used for 1871, 1881, 1891, 1901 and 1911. Growth tables were applied to these figures to get interim year figures as well as figures for 1870, 1912 and 1913. Using the figures of column A for 1870–90 inclusive, and column B for 1891–1913 inclusive for the percentage unemployed of all unions making returns (Mitchell and Deane), the employed labor force for industry found above was decreased to take unemployment into account.

Index of production: Mitchell and Deane, *Abstract of British Historical Statistics*, pp. 271–2. The data used were from the Hoffman index including building for 1870–1913.

Germany

Migration: Ferenczi and Wilcox, *International Migrations*, vol. I, tables 2 and 3, pp. 384–91.

Industrial labor force: G. Bry, *Wages in Germany 1871–1945*, p. 26. This provided data for the following years: 1882, 1895 and 1907. For 1870–81 inclusive, the industrial labor force was interpolated by applying the same year-by-year changes in population. The percentage change in population was computed on the basis of the population figures in W. G. Hoffman and J. H. Miller, *Das Deutsche Volkseinkommen*, table 14, pp. 39–40. The industrial labor force for 1883–94 and 1896–1904 was interpolated through the use of growth tables on the given data for 1882, 1895 and 1907. For 1908–13, the compound growth rate used for the industrial labor force for 1894–1907 was applied to 1907 and successive years.

Index of production: Bry, *Wages in Germany 1871–1945*, pp. 325–6.

Denmark

Migration: Ferenczi and Wilcox, *International Migrations*, vol. I, tables 2 and 3, pp. 384–91.

Industrial labor force: K. Bjerke and N. Ussing, *Studies Over Denmarks Nationalprodukt 1870–1915*, table 1, p. 143.

Index of production: Ibid., table 2, p. 144. The net domestic product of 'other' industries at current prices was deflated by a price index (*ibid.*, table 73, pp. 126–7).

C.3 Reconstructing an unemployment rate for the non-farm sector, 1870–99

An annual unemployment statistic for the non-farm sector does not exist prior to 1900. Lebergott does supply estimates for selected years and for decade averages in the nineteenth century, but annual estimates do not appear until after 1899. (See Table C.4.) This section derives such a series by utilizing the more detailed historical data in the decade and a half preceding World War I.

The following notation will prove helpful:

$F(t)$ = annual index (Frickey) of industrial production,
$w(t)$ = annual real earnings of industrial workers employed,

Table C.4. *Wages, unemployment and capacity utilization: 1900–13*

Year	Frickey index (1900=100): $F(t)$ (1)	Capacity utilization index (percent) $c(t)$ (2)	Real annual earnings employed workers (1914 prices): $w(t)$ (3)	Real annual earnings all workers (1914 prices): $w^*(t)$ (4)	Industrial unemployment rate: $u(t)$ (5)
1900	100	−8·09	$573	$523	0·087
1901	111	−1·33	582	546	0·062
1902	127	+7·66	612	583	0·047
1903	126	+2·82	607	575	0·053
1904	121	−5·81	606	555	0·084
1905	140	+4·28	621	582	0·063
1906	152	+7·64	627	618	0·014
1907	156	+5·67	631	613	0·029
1908	127	−21·50	631	545	0·136
1909	166	+2·49	657	604	0·081
1910	172	+1·27	669	608	0·091
1911	162	−9·98	676	612	0·095
1912	194	+3·65	676	619	0·084
1913	203	+3·42	695	649	0·066

Sources: Col. (1); from Frickey, *Production in the United States 1860–1914*, table 6, p. 54.

Col. (2); $c(t) = \dfrac{F(t) - \hat{F}(t)}{F(t)}$, where $\hat{F}(t)$ derived as in text.

Col. (3); from Lebergott, *Manpower in Economic Growth*, table A-17, p. 524.

Col. (4); *Ibid.*

Col. (5); $u(t) = \dfrac{w(t) - w^*(t)}{w(t)}$.

$w^*(t)$ = annual real earnings of industrial labor force, including unemployed.

$F(t)$ and $w(t)$ are available for all years 1870–1913, but $w^*(t)$ is available only for the years 1900–13. We wish to reconstruct $w^*(t)$ for 1870–99. Having done so, we shall have an estimate of the non-farm unemployment rate since

$$u(t) = \frac{w(t) - w^*(t)}{w(t)}.$$

Given the reasonable premise that the unemployment rate should be closely related to an index of industrial capacity, the procedure entails the construction of an industrial capacity index, $c(t)$, which can then be related to labor market conditions.

First, the trend is removed from the Frickey index for 1900–13, using

$$F(t) = \alpha_0 + \alpha_1 t + \alpha_2 t^2.$$

An index of industrial capacity utilization is then estimated by expressing the percentage deviations of actual $F(t)$ from its predicted value, $\hat{F}(t)$:

$$\hat{c}(t) = \frac{\hat{C}(t)}{F(t)} = \frac{F(t) - \hat{F}(t)}{F(t)},$$

where $\hat{c}(t)$ is in percent. The unemployment rate is then regressed on the capacity utilization index yielding (1900–13)

$$u(t) = 0.069 - 0.003\,\hat{c}(t), \quad R^2 = 0.70, \quad DW = 1.447. \quad \text{(C.1)}$$
$$(14.835) \quad (5.264)$$

From a statistical point of view, these results are excellent since t-values, the R^2, and the Durbin–Watson statistic are all acceptable. The economics also makes sense since the estimated equation implies that a 3.33 percent increase in $\hat{c}(t)$ was associated on average with a decline in the unemployment rate by 1 percentage point. This statistical relationship has been reproduced frequently enough in the post-World War II years to warrant the term Okun's Law. Assuming that relation (C.1) holds approximately for the period 1870–99, it becomes a simple matter to reconstruct an estimated $\hat{u}(t)$ series for the three decades prior to 1900.

Once again we construct a $\hat{c}(t)$ index, this time for the period 1870–99, by removing the trend from the Frickey index and computing residuals as a percent of $F(t)$. Expression (C.1) then permits us to calculate both $\hat{w}^*(t)$ and $\hat{u}(t)$ for the three decades prior to 1900:

$$\hat{w}^*(t) = w(t)\,\{0.069 - 0.003\,\hat{c}(t)\},$$

and

$$\hat{u}(t) = \frac{w(t) - \hat{w}^*(t)}{w(t)},$$

where $w(t)$ and $\hat{c}(t)$ are historical observables, and $\hat{w}^*(t)$ and $\hat{u}(t)$ are estimated.

Table C.5. *Wages, unemployment and capacity utilization: 1870–99*

Year	Frickey index (1900=100): $F(t)$ (1)	Capacity utili- zation index (percent) $c(t)$ (2)	Real annual earnings employed workers (1914 prices): $w(t)$ (3)	Real annual earnings all workers (1914 prices): $w^*(t)$ (4)	Industrial unemploy- ment rate: $u(t)$ (5)
1870	25	+7·21	$375	$357	0·047
1871	26	+5·05	386	365	0·054
1872	31	+15·35	416	406	0·023
1873	30	+7·13	407	387	0·048
1874	29	−1·88	403	373	0·075
1875	28	−11·77	403	361	0·104
1876	28	−18·25	393	344	0·124
1877	30	−16·63	388	342	0·119
1878	32	−15·42	397	351	0·115
1879	36	−8·18	391	354	0·094
1880	42	+2·33	395	371	0·062
1881	46	+6·17	415	394	0·050
1882	49	+7·42	431	411	0·047
1883	50	+4·73	459	434	0·055
1884	47	−6·32	478	436	0·088
1885	47	−11·43	492	441	0·103
1886	57	+3·80	499	470	0·058
1887	60	+4·39	509	480	0·056
1888	62	+3·29	505	475	0·059
1889	66	+5·12	510	482	0·054
1890	71	+7·96	519	496	0·045
1891	73	+6·66	525	499	0·049
1892	79	+10·13	527	506	0·039
1893	70	−5·60	505	462	0·086
1894	68	−13·90	484	432	0·108
1895	81	+1·29	520	486	0·065
1896	74	−12·26	521	466	0·106
1897	80	−7·81	529	480	0·092
1898	91	+1·65	527	493	0·064
1899	100	+7·19	563	537	0·047

Source: See notes to Table C.4 and text.

Table C.6.   *Index of immigration push effects, $\hat{D}(t)$*

Year	$\hat{D}(t)$	Year	$\hat{D}(t)$
1870	0	1891	+0·308
1871	+0·060	1892	+0·468
1872	+0·240	1893	+0·037
1873	+0·299	1894	−0·829
1874	−0·263	1895	−1·060
1875	−0·676	1896	−0·768
1876	−0·833	1897	−1·057
1877	−0·997	1898	−1·065
1878	−0·949	1899	−0·733
1879	−0·712	1900	−0·206
1880	+0·231	1901	−0·667
1881	+1·093	1902	−0·230
1882	+1·346	1903	+0·216
1883	+0·768	1904	+0·327
1884	+0·298	1905	+0·743
1885	−0·435	1906	+1·308
1886	−0·556	1907	+1·016
1887	−0·067	1908	−0·739
1888	−0·025	1909	+0·260
1889	−0·492	1910	−0·949
1890	−0·418		

Note: This series is derived residually from the equation

$$D(t) = M(t) - Z\{\tilde{w}_E(t)\}^{\eta_M},$$

where $M(t)$ is taken from Table A.16, $Z = 0.745$, $\tilde{w}_E(t)$ is taken from Table B.6, col. 5, and $\eta_M = 0.25$. See text to chapter 11.

Notes

Part I: The issues

2 Counterfactual history

1 This chapter draws heavily on A. Kelley and J. G. Williamson, *Lessons from Japanese Development: An Analytical Economic History*, chapter 5.
2 W. W. Rostow, 'The Take-off Into Self-Sustained Growth' and *The Stages of Economic Growth.*
3 See the relevant pages in W. W. Rostow, *The Economics of Take-off into Sustained Growth.* For more recent attempts at measurement see the following: R. Fogel, *Railroads and American Economic Growth*, pp. 114–21; S. Kuznets, *Modern Economic Growth*, pp. 86–153; W. G. Whitney, *The Structure of the American Economy in the Late Nineteenth Century*; D. C. North, 'Industrialization in the United States'; P. A. David, 'The Growth of Real Product in the United States Before 1870: New Evidence, Controlled Conjectures,' pp. 151–97.
4 J. G. Williamson, 'Antebellum Urbanization in the American Northeast' and G. R. Taylor, 'American Urban Growth Preceding the Railway Age.'
5 R. W. Fogel, *Railroads and American Economic Growth.*
6 Fogel, 'The Specification Problem in Economic History,' p. 284.
7 In addition to Fogel's research see the following partial listing: A. H. Conrad and J. R. Meyer, *The Economics of Slavery*; A. Fishlow, *American Railroads and the Transformation of the Ante-Bellum Economy*; P. David, 'The Mechanization of Reaping in the Ante-Bellum Midwest'; P. Temin, *Iron and Steel in Nineteenth-Century America.*
8 Fogel, 'The Specification Problem in Economic History,' p. 285.
9 F. Redlich, 'New and Traditional Approaches to Economic History and Their Interdependence,' p. 487.
10 Fogel, 'The Specification Problem in Economic History,' pp. 283–4 and 297.
11 J. G. Williamson, 'The Railroads and Midwestern Development: A General Equilibrium History.'
12 Fogel, 'The Specification Problem in Economic History,' pp. 297–308; P. Passell and M. Schmundt, 'Pre-Civil War Land Policy and the Growth of Manufacturing'; J. G. Williamson, 'Late Nineteenth Century American Retardation: A Neoclassical Analysis.'
13 C. Pope, 'The Impact of the Ante Bellum Tariff on Income Distribution,' and J. Green, 'The Effect of the Iron Tariff in the United States, 1847–1859.'
14 Fogel, 'The Specification Problem in Economic History,' p. 297.
15 With considerable immodesty, the only exceptions appear to be A. C.

Kelley and J. G. Williamson, 'Writing History Backwards: Meiji Japan Revisited'; P. Temin, 'General-Equilibrium Models in Economic History,' and my own work cited above.

Part II: The framework

3   A model of late nineteenth-century American regional growth

1   R. Jones, 'The Structure of Simple General Equilibrium Models,' and 'General Equilibrium with Three Factors of Production'; G. Hueckel, 'The Napoleonic Wars and Factor Returns Within the English Economy.'

2   Presumably, Ames and Rosenberg would object and insist that agricultural goods be utilized as intermediate inputs to manufacturing activities as well. See E. Ames and N. Rosenberg, 'The Enfield Arsenal in Theory and History,' and D. L. Brito and J. G. Williamson, 'Skilled Labor and Nineteenth Century Anglo-American Managerial Behavior.'

3   The reader interested in the derivation of the equations which follow is advised to examine the papers by Jones and Hueckel where they are treated in detail.

4   F. J. Turner's views can be found in *The Frontier in American History*; *The Significance of Sections in American History*; *The Rise of the New West, 1811–1829*; and *The United States 1830–1850*. H. J. Habakkuk, *American and British Technology in the Nineteenth Century*.

5   In addition to the papers cited, there have been some recent applications of general equilibrium analysis to ante bellum United States. The include the following papers read at the 1970 Cliometrics Conference (Madison, Wisconsin, 30 April–2 May): C. Pope, 'The Impact of the Antebellum Tariff on Income Distribution'; P. Passell and M. Schmundt, 'Pre-Civil War Land Policy and the Growth of Manufacturing'; and J. Green, 'The Effect of the Iron Tariff in the United States, 1847–1859: The Estimation of a General Equilibrium System with Non-traded Goods.'

6   The notation used in this section is defined on pp. 45–6. An earlier version of the model developed in this chapter first appeared in published form in J. A. Swanson and J. G. Williamson, 'Explanations and Issues: A Prospectus for Quantitative Economic History.'

7   Z. Griliches, 'Production Functions in Manufacturing: Some Preliminary Results' and P. Zarembka, 'On the Empirical Relevance of the CES Production Function.'

8   C. Kennedy, 'Induced Bias in Innovation and the Theory of Distribution'; M. Morishima and M. Saito, 'An Economic Test of Sir John Hicks' Theory of Biased Induced Innovations'; M. Brown, *On the Theory and Measurement of Technological Change*; Y. Hayami and V. Ruttan, 'Factor Prices and Technical Change in Agricultural Development: The United States and Japan, 1880–1960.'

9   For example, H. J. Habakkuk, *American and British Technology in the Nineteenth Century*.

10 F. A. Shannon, *The Farmer's Last Frontier: Agriculture, 1860–1897*, chapter 6; L. Rogin, *The Introduction of Farm Machinery in Its Relation to the Productivity of Labor in Agriculture*; P. A. David, 'The Mechanization of Reaping in the Antebellum Midwest.'

11 These models do not introduce capital into agricultural activities. See P. Temin, 'Labor Scarcity and the Problem of American Industrial Efficiency in the 1850's' and R. Jones, 'The Structure of Simple General Equilibrium Models.'

12 E. C. Budd, 'Factor Shares, 1850–1910,' table 2, p. 373.

13 We do *not*, however, completely ignore long swings in American growth. Another issue which this model may effectively confront is the role of world market conditions, rates of land expansion and rates of foreign immigration on cycles in American growth rates. Considerable attention is devoted to that issue in chapters 5 and 10. If we can successfully reproduce the poor *growth* performance of the American economy centered on the mid-1870s, the mid-1880s, the early mid-1890s, and the years immediately preceding World War I, then perhaps we can shed some light on the determinants of those swings. See M. Abramovitz, 'Long Swings in American Economic Growth.'

14 For example, see R. Zevin, 'The Growth of Cotton Textile Production After 1815'; A. Fishlow, *American Railroads and the Transformation of the Antebellum Economy*, pp. 288–97; R. Fogel, *Railroads and American Economic Growth: Essays in Econometric History*.

15 Fishlow, *American Railroads and the Transformation of the Ante-Bellum Economy* and Fogel, *Railroads and American Economic Growth: Essays in Econometric History*.

16 Total revenue from transport activity, $T(t)$, is derived by summing revenues from these two sources. How do we allocate these revenues between regions? We have $T_E(t) = \gamma T(t)$ and $T_W(t) = (1-\gamma)T(t)$. In the chapters which follow we arbitrarily assume $\gamma = 0.5$. It should be clear that transport revenues are treated here in much the same way that tariff revenues are treated in trade theory. Furthermore, since demand conditions play a passive role in the model, the distribution of transport revenue is not in any way crucial.

17 This would hardly be a relevant assumption for cotton exports in the ante bellum period. An inelastic foreign demand for cotton becomes a critical element in Clayne Pope's analysis of ante bellum tariffs in his general equilibrium framework. See Pope, 'The Impact of the Antebellum Tariff on Income Distribution.'

18 G. Borts, 'Returns Equalization and Regional Growth.'

19 S. Lebergott, *Manpower in Economic Growth*, pp. 133–7. Lebergott presents regional data on the average monthly earnings (with board) for farm laborers which for our regions are consistent with the generalizations for the American labor as a whole. (*Ibid.*, table A-23, pp. 539–40.)

20 A similar treatment of interregional migration can be found elsewhere in A. C. Kelley, J. G. Williamson and R. J. Cheetham, *Dualistic Economic Development: Theory and History*, chapter 7. This specification ignores the cost-of-living component of the real wage differential, however.

21 This may or may not be an important inclusion depending on the relative change in migration costs over time, as opposed to their levels at any point in time. In reference to the 1860s 'transportation alone for a family of five would be the equivalent of half a year's wages' in migrating from the crowded East to the Gulf states. Shannon, *The Farmer's Last Frontier*, p. 54.

22 A. C. Kelley, 'International Migration and Economic Growth: Australia, 1865–1935.'

23 M. Wilkinson, 'European Migration to the United States: An Econometric Analysis of Aggregate Labor Supply and Demand.'

24 This is hardly a completely realistic characterization of the location of intermediaries, especially after the 1880s. The assumption is not critical, however, since our results do not prove to be sensitive to it. In any case, *intra*regional Western intermediation is assumed to be performed by Western cities and returns to such intermediation accrue to Western 'industrialists.' See L. Davis, 'The Investment Market, 1870–1914: The Evolution of a National Market;' A. Bogue, *Money at Interest*; H. F. Williamson and O. A. Smalley, *Northwestern Mutual Life: A Century of Trusteeship*.

25 Total GNP for the economy as a whole is simply

$$\text{GNP}(t) = Y_E(t) + Y_W(t) = \{w_E(t)L_E(t) + w_{AW}(t)L_{AW}(t) + \\ + w_{IW}(t)L_{IW}(t)\} + d(t)R(t) + T(t) + \{r_E(t)K_{IE}(t) + \\ + r_{AW}(t)K_{AW}(t) + r_{IW}(t)K_{IW}(t)\} = [\text{Wage income}] + \\ + [\text{Land rents}] + [\text{Factor payments to transport inputs}] + \\ + [\text{Gross returns to capital assets}].$$

26 It was already noted on pages 29–30 that rates of total factor productivity growth are determined exogenously – following a time-honored convention introduced with the 'residual' calculations initially performed by Abramovitz and Solow some fifteen years ago. In chapters 5 and 7 the impact of technical progress on American development is explored in detail.

27 M. L. Primack, 'Land Clearing Under Nineteenth-Century Techniques: Some Preliminary Calculations,' 'Farm Construction as a Use of Farm Labor, 1850–1910' and 'Farm Capital Formation as a Use of Farm Labor, 1850–1910.' Capital formation in land clearing, farm building, fencing, drainage and irrigation were very large components of capital formation in agriculture, although the main input was farm labor. As late as 1869–78, a little less than 10 percent of United States capital formation was in this form. L. Davis and R. Gallman, 'The Share of Savings and Investment in Gross National Product During the 19th Century,' p. 3.

28 P. Kenen, 'Nature, Capital, and Trade.'

29 The 'Walker effect' appears to us to have been discredited. See, however, L. Neal and P. Uselding, 'Immigration: A Neglected Source of American Economic Growth; 1790–1912.'

30 L. Davis and R. Gallman, 'The Share of Savings and Investment in Gross National Product,' Tables 1 and 2. Although our model is open to foreign trade, we exclude foreign capital inflows. Are we justified in ignoring external sources of finance from abroad following 1869?

Were not foreign capital inflows critical determinants of the gross domestic capital formation ratio? Surely they were during *peak* decades of capital inflow used to finance the expanding railroad network, but Gallman shows that they were negligible over longer periods. R. Gallman, 'Gross National Product in the United States 1834–1909.' See also J. G. Williamson, *American Growth and the Balance of Payments, 1820–1913.*

31 Temin, 'General-Equilibrium Models in Economic History,' pp. 72–4. We shall return to this point below.

32 Davis and Gallman, 'The Share of Savings and Investment in Gross National Product.'

33 *Ibid.*, p. 22.

34 *Ibid.*, p. 25.

35 In fact the so called 'Great Depression' during the late nineteenth century can be readily explained by such a framework. See chapter 5.

36 The depreciation rate, δ, is assumed constant. This assumption is common, but earlier thoughts on the problem make the author a bit uneasy at this point. See J. G. Williamson, 'Optimal Replacement of Capital Goods: The Early New England and British Textile Firm.'

37 This relative price decline is also evident for ante bellum textiles. Most historical accounts ignore the impact of the relative decline in capital goods' prices over time. In contrast, see D. L. Brito and J. G. Williamson, 'Skilled Labor and Nineteenth Century Anglo-American Managerial Behavior;' J. G. Williamson, 'Watersheds and Turning Points: Nineteenth Century Capital Formation, Relative Prices, and the Civil War'; and A. Kelley and J. G. Williamson, *Lessons From Japanese Development: An Analytical History*, chapter 6.

38 M. Friedman, *Essays in Positive Economics.*

39 H. S. Perloff, E. S. Dunn, E. E. Lampard and R. F. Muth, *Regions, Resources and Economic Growth*, chapter 12.

40 Calculated from S. Kuznets, *Modern Economic Growth: Rate, Structure, and Spread*, tables 3.1 and 3.5, pp. 88–93 and 131–2.

41 Easterlin's estimates are based on income originating in commodity production and distribution. His industry category includes mining, construction, manufacturing, transportation and public utilities. R. A. Easterlin, 'Interregional Differences in Per Capita Income Population, and Total Income, 1840–1950,' appendix A, pp. 97–104.

42 The nominal rates are taken from J. Bowman, 'Trends in Midwestern Farm Land Values, 1860–1900,' table II, chapter III, p. III-14. The real rates include the influence of the observed rate of price change where the preceding five years are utilized as an average. The price changes are based on the Warren–Pearson all commodity index. See chapters 5 and 7 for further discussion of these interest rate calculations.

43 R. H. Keehn, 'Nineteenth Century Wisconsin Banking,' chapter 6, tables 1–3.

44 This differential prevailed in 1880 and is based on regional mortgage rate differences. Davis, 'The Investment Market, 1870–1914: The Evolution of a National Market,' table 7, p. 375. Other evidence

presented in Davis's article implies that this differential was roughly the same in the early 1870s.

45 Lebergott, *Manpower in Economic Growth*, Table A-25, p. 541.
46 Calculated from A. S. Tostlebe, *Capital in Agriculture: Its Formation and Financing Since 1870*, tables 7 and H-3, pp. 65–7 and 214–16.
47 S. Kuznets, *Capital in the American Economy*, table 27, pp. 198–9.
48 Industry is defined broadly in Table 3.3 to include all urban oriented non-agricultural activities.
49 Budd, 'Factor Shares, 1850–1910.'
50 Davis and Gallman, 'The Share of Savings and Investment in Gross National Product During the 19th Century,' table 1, p. 2.
51 Kuznets, *Capital in the American Economy*, table 2, p. 56.
52 In the Massachusetts urban workers sample, 55·5 percent was spent on food in 1875. J. G. Williamson, 'Consumer Behavior in the Nineteenth Century: Carroll D. Wright's Massachusetts Workers in 1875,' table 4, p. 116.
53 A. Fishlow, 'Comparative Patterns, the Extent of the Market, and Alternative Development Strategies.'
54 R. Lipsey, *Price and Quantity Trends in the Foreign Trade of the United States*, table G-14, p. 436. The figure is an average over 1870–4.
55 Kuznets, *Capital in the American Economy*, tables R-21 and R-27, pp. 553 and 565. The figures are in current prices and the 'variant I' estimate excludes services.

4 *American economic history rewritten: fact or fiction?*

1 H. Theil, *Economic Forecasts and Policy*, p. 207.
2 Unless otherwise noted, for the remainder of this book we shall refer to our Midwest and Northeast as the American economy.
3 R. W. Fogel, 'The Specification Problem in Economic History,' pp. 297–8.
4 Fogel, 'The Specification Problem in Economic History,' pp. 283–97.
5 The recent applications to ante bellum United States include the following papers read at the Cliometrics Conference (Madison, Wisconsin, 30 April–2 May, 1970): C. Pope, 'The Impact of the Antebellum Tariff on Income Distribution'; P. Passell and M. Schmundt, 'Pre-Civil War Land Policy and the Growth of Manufacturing'; and J. Green, 'The Effect of the Iron Tariff in the United States, 1847–1859: The Estimation of a General Equilibrium System with Non-Traded Goods.'
6 P. Temin, 'Labor Scarcity in America,' p. 264.
7 Professor Kelley and the author have tried to meet this test in writing an analytical history of Meiji Japan: 'Writing Economic History Backwards: Meiji. Japan Revisited;' *Lessons from Japanese Development: An Analytical Economic History*, ch. 4.
8 Temin, 'Labor Scarcity in America,' p. 264.
9 A. Fishlow, *American Railroads and the Transformation of the Ante-*

Bellum Economy and R. W. Fogel, *Railroads and American Economic Growth.*

10 Fishlow, *American Railroads and the Transformation of the Ante-Bellum Economy*, p. 30.

11 We do not mean to imply that qualitative analysis will be absent from the remainder of this book. For example, in chapter 5 we shall make every effort to analyze the model developed in chapter 3 prior to reverting to simulation. In chapter 3, we have purposely retained conventional economists' notation to maximize the potential usefulness of qualitative analysis.

12 T. M. Brown, *Specification and Uses of Econometric Models*, p. 50.

13 Although there is nothing unique about the specification problem in historical analysis, Fogel does usefully emphasize the relative importance of the 'efficiency criteria' in historical model building. Fogel, 'The Specification Problem in Economic History,' pp. 297–8.

14 Theil, *Economic Forecasts and Policy*, p. 205, italics added.

15 A large share of this section is taken from Professor Theil's excellent book *Economic Forecasts and Policy*, especially chapter 2, pp. 6–30, and chapter 3, pp. 64–76. The interested reader is also urged to consult H. Theil, *Principles of Econometrics*, pp. 540–602.

16 H. Theil, *Economic Forecasts and Policy*, p. 71. In a comparable study of Meiji Japan, Professor Kelley and the author achieved accurate turning point performance about 75 percent of the time as judged by ϕ_1. See A. Kelley and J. G. Williamson, 'Writing Economic History Backwards: Meiji Japan Revisited,' and *Lessons from Japanese Development*, ch. 4.

17 H. Theil, *Economic Forecasts and Policy*, p. 73 and chapter 5.

18 *Ibid.*, pp. 69–70.

19 Theil, *Economics and Information Theory*, pp. 24–48.

20 See, for example, M. Abramovitz, 'The Nature and Significance of Kuznets Cycles'; R. A. Easterlin, 'Economic-Demographic Interactions and Long Swings in Economic Growth'; J. G. Williamson, *American Growth and the Balance of Payments, 1820–1913.*

21 M. Abramovitz, 'Long Swings in American Growth,' table 1, p. 402.

22 By the 1880s, the regions outside of the Northeast and Midwest were increasing their share of the national wealth stock. This was surely not the case in the 1860s. See E. Lee, *et al.*, *Population Redistribution and Economic Growth, United States, 1870–1950*, I, table 4.6, pp. 729–33.

23 C. Clark, *Conditions of Economic Progress*. H. B. Chenery, 'Patterns of Industrial Growth'. S. Kuznets, *Modern Economic Growth*, pp. 86–153. R. W. Fogel, *Railroads and American Economic Growth: Essays in Econometric History*, pp. 114–21.

24 See H. Theil, *Economics and Information Theory*, pp. 24–8.

25 The discussion in appendix A indicates the difficulty in securing relevant measures of out-migration from the Northeast. Nevertheless, the evidence presented in Eldridge and Thomas, when adjusted for *gross* rates of out-migration by foreign immigrants, suggests the following: a rise in the rate of out-migration from the 1870s to the

1880s, a very sharp fall in that rate during the 1890s, and a mild rise again in the 1900–10 decade. These trends are roughly reproduced in the simulation. See H. Eldridge and D. Thomas, *Population Redistribution and Economic Growth, United States, 1870–1950*, III, table 1.22, p. 68.

26 The Midatlantic includes New York, New Jersey, Pennsylvania, Delaware, Maryland and the District of Columbia. The Midwest includes all the East North Central States plus Wisconsin, Minnesota, Iowa and Missouri.

27 Unfortunately, what little empirical information we have on this point is in a form which includes *foreign* capital imports (gross) from abroad. See. E. S. Lee, *et al.*, *Population Redistribution and Economic Growth in the United States, 1870–1950*, I, pp. 729–33; II, pp. 179–81.

28 An exception can be found in the author's collaborative research with Allen Kelley on Meiji Japan cited earlier.

29 Their independence is hardly complete, however, Shifting regional demand parameters influence the volume of interregional trade and thus transport revenue. The disposition of this revenue has an impact on regional savings and thus interregional financial flows and interest rate differentials in subsequent time periods.

Part III: The lessons of history

5 The Great Depression 1870–96

1 D. N. McCloskey, 'Did Victorian Britain Fail?'

2 The comparability between British and American experience has been noted, but apparently forgotten in other writings, by many economic historians. See, for example, B. Weber and S. J. Handfield-Jones, 'Variations in the Rate of Economic Growth in the U.S.A., 1869–1939'; E. Phelps-Brown and S. J. Handfield-Jones, 'The Climacteric of the 1890's'; D. J. Coppock, 'The Climacteric of the 1870's'; R. Fels, *American Business Cycles*, ch. 5.

3 In chapter 7, even this contention will be evaluated. Our conclusions there coincide with the revisionist view summarized in R. Fogel and J. Rutner, 'The Efficiency Effects of Federal Land Policy, 1850–1900: A Report of Some Provisional Findings.'

4 S. Engerman, 'The Economic Impact of the Civil War,' p. 181.

5 See appendix A, Table A. 23.

6 While the per annum labor force growth rate during the 1870s was 2·84 percent, the rate for the 1880s was 3·02 percent, for the 1890s 2·36 percent and for the 1900s 2·57 percent (Table 4.3).

7 T. J. Sargent, 'Interest Rates and Prices in the Long Run: A Study of the Gibson Paradox,' p. 1. See also his 'Anticipated Inflation and the Nominal Rates of Interest.'

8 *Ibid.*, p. 2. As with our model developed in chapter 3, Fisher assumed in his empirical analysis that the real rate was independent of current

and past rate of inflation. I. Fisher, *The Theory of Interest*. See also P. Cagan, 'The Monetary Dynamics of Hyper-Inflation,' and M. Friedman, *A Theory of the Consumption Function*.

9   Fisher, *The Theory of Interest*, p. 415.

10 The reference here, of course, is to S. B. Saul, *The Myth of the Great Depression*, 1873–1896.

11 P. Temin, 'General-Equilibrium Models in Economic History,' pp. 70–4.

12 M. Friedman and A. J. Schwartz, *A Monetary History of the United States, 1867–1960*, p. 92.

13 See, for example, A. C. Kelley and J. G. Williamson, 'Writing History Backwards: Meiji Japan Revisited'; idem, *Lessons from Japanese Development: An Analytical Economic History*, ch. 9.

14 M. Abramovitz, 'Resource and Output Trends in the United States Since 1870'; R. M. Solow, 'Technical Change and the Aggregate Production Function'; E. F. Denison, *The Sources of Economic Growth in the United States*; D. N. McCloskey, 'Did Victorian Britain Fail?'

15 Kuznets, Weber and Handfield-Jones provide arguments in favor of this effect. S. Kuznets, *Modern Economic Growth*. Weber and Handfield-Jones, 'Variations in the Rate of Economic Growth in the U.S.A., 1869–1939.'

16 Not every economic historian who practises total factor productivity growth accounting is unaware of the crucial importance of factor growth interdependence. For example, in evaluating public land policy on national income, Fogel and Rutner have stressed: 'The answer depends on whether or not population growth was independent of land policy during the specific period under consideration.' Fogel and Rutner, 'The Efficiency Effects of Public Land Policy, 1850–1900,' p. 32.

17 Abramovitz, 'Resource and Output Trends in the United States Since 1870.' Solow, 'Technical Change and the Aggregate Production Function.'

18 M. Abramovitz and P. David, 'Towards Historically Relevant Parables of Growth,' table 1, p. 12.

19 J. W. Kendrick, *Productivity Trends in the United States*, pp. 137–40.

20 The declining rate of capital formation thesis appears in literature much too abundant to cite here. See Coppock, 'The Climacteric of the 1870's.'

21 McCloskey, 'Did Victorian Britain Fail?' p. 458. The decadal rate of capital stock growth does not appear to decline from 1860 to 1910.

22 Temin, 'General-Equilibrium Models in Economic History,' pp. 70–4.

23 R. E. Gallman, 'Commodity Output, 1839–1899' and 'Gross National Product in the United States, 1834–1909.'

24 Much of this paragraph is taken from Engerman, 'The Economic Impact of the Civil War,' pp. 178–83.

25 For a recent accounting of the enormous cost of the Civil War, see C. Goldin and F. Lewis, 'The Economic Costs of the American Civil War: Estimation and Implications.'

26 The remainder of this paragraph is taken from Engerman, 'The Economic Impact of the Civil War,' p. 184.

27 J. G. Williamson, 'Late Nineteenth Century American Retardation: A Neoclassical Analysis' and 'Watersheds and Turning Points: Nineteenth Century Capital Formation, Relative Prices and the Civil War.' Temin, 'General-Equilibrium Models in Economic History,' pp. 72–4; L. Davis and R. Gallman, 'The Share of Savings and Investment in Gross National Product During the 19th Century.'

28 Gallman's constant price shares exhibit similar discontinuity when the farm-formed capital is included. Gallman, 'Gross National Product in the United States, 1834–1909,' table 3, p. 11.

29 Gallman's data reproduced in Table 5.3 exclude, for example, farm-formed capital and assets accumulated in the form of slave values.

30 Williamson, 'Watersheds and Turning Points: Nineteenth Century Capital Formation, Relative Prices, and the Civil War.'

31 P. McGouldrick, *New England Textiles in the 19th Century*, table 46, pp. 240–1, deflated by textile price index reported in *Historical Statistics*, E-5, p. 115.

32 Calculated from Gallman, 'Gross National Product in the United States, 1834–1909,' table A-3, p. 34.

33 R. A. Gordon, 'Differential Changes in the Prices of Consumers' and Capital Goods.'

34 *Ibid.*, p. 937.

35 This, of course, is an aspect of the post-war period upon which Hacker dwells at length, and rightly so. See, for example, L. M. Hacker, *The Triumph of American Capitalism*, pp. 402ff.

36 Davis and Gallman, 'The Share of Savings and Investment in Gross National Product During the 19th Century,' tables 1 and 2.

37 For a detailed discussion of this point see Kelley and Williamson, 'Writing Economic History Backwards: Meiji Japan Revisited,' pp. 737–8.

38 Engerman, 'The Economic Impact of the Civil War,' p. 181.

39 R. Higgs, *The Transformation of the American Economy, 1865–1914*, pp. 26 and 32, italics added.

40 The experiment does not assume constant total factor productivity growth for the economy as a whole, but rather for individual sectors. It was argued above that industrialization itself would increase the relative importance of the sector enjoying more rapid rates of total factor productivity growth. From this source alone, aggregate growth rates still receive an increasing positive stimulus over time.

41 *Ibid.*, p. 26.

42 The 'monetarist' view can be found in R. P. Higonnet, 'Bank Deposits in the United Kingdom'; Friedman and Schwartz, *A Monetary History of the United States*; and P. Cagan, *Determinants and Effects of Changes in the Stock of Money, 1875–1960*.

43 Sargent, 'Interest Rates and Prices in the Long Run,' p. 57.

44 For example, see A. Hansen, *Business Cycles and National Income*, ch. 4.

45 J. R. Meyer, 'An Input–Output Approach to Evaluating British Industrial Production in the Late 19th Century' and A. H. Conrad, 'Income Growth and Structural Change.'

46 McCloskey, 'Did Victorian Britain Fail?' p. 446.

47 *Ibid.*, p. 448.

48 Conrad, 'Income Growth and Structural Change,' p. 34. There are other aggregate demand explanations, of course, and Conrad's emphasis on capital intensity is selected as only one example. Demand insufficiency, and retarding output growth, has also been linked to population growth decline and natural resource exploitation as they relate to 'autonomous' investment.

49 S. Lebergott, *Manpower in Economic Growth*, p. 187.

50 *Ibid.*, p. 189.

51 D. S. Landes, *The Unbound Prometheus: Technological Change and Industrial Development in Western Europe*, p. 231.

52 M. Brown, *On the Theory and Measurement of Technological Change*, pp. 143–91; Kendrick, *Productivity Trends in the United States*, pp. 59–137; M. Morishima and M. Saito, 'An Economic Test of Hicks' Theory of Biased Induced Inventions.'

6 Financial intermediation, capital immobilities and economic growth

1 L. E. Davis, 'The Investment Market, 1870–1914: The Evolution of a National Market,' p. 355.

2 For example, C. Pope, 'The Impact of the Ante Bellum Tariff on Income Distribution.'

3 D. W. Jorgenson and J. A. Stephenson, 'Investment Behavior in U.S. Manufacturing, 1947–1960,' pp. 173–9.

4 This can be easily shown since

$$\frac{\partial I^N}{\partial i} = \frac{-\alpha_K Z}{i^2}$$

$$\frac{\partial I^N}{\partial i} \cdot \frac{i}{I^N} = \frac{-\alpha_K Z}{i^2} \cdot \frac{i}{\dfrac{\alpha_K Z}{i}} = -1.$$

Thus, given the Cobb–Douglas specification, the investment demand elasticity is *always* minus unity.

5 L. Davis and R. Gallman, 'The Share of Savings and Investment in Gross National Product During the 19th Century,' p. 25.

6 L. E. Davis, 'Capital Immobilities and Finance Capitalism: A Study of Economic Evolution in the United States, 1820–1920,' pp. 584–5.

7 I. Fisher, *The Theory of Interest*, pp. 389–90.

8 R. Cameron *et al.*, *Banking in the Early Stages of Industrialization: A Study in Comparative Economic History*, p. 8.

9 *Ibid.*, p. 292.

10 *Ibid.*

11 R. Sylla, 'Federal Policy, Banking Market Structure, and Capital Mobilization in the United States, 1863–1913,' p. 657. The reference,

of course, is to A. Gerschenkron, *Economic Backwardness in Historical Perspective.*

12 Davis, 'Capital Immobilities and Finance Capitalism: A Study of Economic Evolution in the United States, 1820–1920,' pp. 582–3, italics ours.

13 S. Kuznets, *Capital in the American Economy: Its Formation and Financing*, p. 264.

14 L. E. Davis, 'Capital Mobility and American Growth,' p. 288.

15 L. E. Davis, 'The Capital Markets and Industrial Concentration: The U.S. and U.K., a Comparative Study,' p. 664.

16 Stigler is critical of Davis's research and his reliance on interest rate differentials as a measure of market imperfection: '. . . if prices at two points differ by less than transportation costs, the movement of goods is uneconomic.' G. Stigler, 'Imperfections in the Capital Market,' p. 288. Stigler's criticism appears to miss the historians' emphasis on *disequilibrium* completely. Stigler's criticism is all the more curious given that he (Stigler) proposes we use dispersion of industry rates of return as a measure of current disequilibrium in post-World War II American industry. G. Stigler, *Capital and Rates of Return in Manufacturing Industries.*

17 Davis, 'Capital Immobilities and Finance Capitalism,' pp. 582–3.

18 New evidence on this issue can be found in W. G. Smiley, 'The Evolution and Structure of the National Banking System, 1870–1913.'

19 Sylla, 'Federal Policy, Banking Market Structure, and Capital Mobilization,' pp. 657 and 685.

20 R. Keehn, 'Nineteenth Century Wisconsin Banking.'

21 Davis, 'The Investment Market, 1870–1914,' pp. 370–3.

22 Davis, 'The Investment Market, 1870–1914.' p. 375.

23 R. W. Fogel, *Railroads and American Economic Growth: Essays in Econometric History*, p. 121. In table 4.6, Fogel documents the percentage point increase in manufacturing's share of commodity output. The average increase per quinquennium 1839–99 is 3·0 percentage points. The rate for 1869–74 is 6·4 percentage points.

24 For a clear statement of this issue, see R. Higgs, *The Transformation of the American Economy, 1865–1914: An Essay in Interpretation*, especially pp. 15–17, 47–9 and 86–102.

25 Davis, 'The Investment Market, 1870–1914,' p. 355.

26 Davis, 'Capital Immobilities and Finance Capitalism,' p. 581.

27 Davis, 'Capital Mobility and American Growth,' p. 299.

28 Both models start from a per capita income base of 3·087 in 1870. Assuming no technical progress, the world of 'perfect' mobility would have obtained an average per capita income of 3·324 from 1871 to 1875 while under our capital market immobility specification the figure is 3·317 over the same five years.

29 D. Suits, 'The Determinants of Consumer Expenditures: A Review of Present Knowledge': T. Mayer, 'Multiplier and Velocity Analysis: An Evaluation.'

30 C. Wright, 'Some Evidence on the Interest Elasticity of Consumption.'

31 L. Davis, J. Hughes and D. McDougall, *American Economic History*, p. 199.

32   See, for example, Cameron, *Banking in the Early Stages of Industrialization*; R. Sylla, 'American Banking and Growth in the Nineteenth Century: A Partial View of the Terrain.' Davis and Gallman, 'The Share of Savings and Investment in Gross National Product During the 19th Century, United States of America.'

33   *Ibid.*, pp. 22 and 25.

34   'In his *Study of Savings*, Goldsmith has shown the impact of a number of structural shifts on the savings/income ratio during the 20th century ... For the first sixteen years of the period studied by Goldsmith (1897–1913) ... the farm sector ... yielded very small net savings. In fact, while nonfarm persons saved over 12 percent, the farm sector's savings ratio was only 2·7 percent. If these ratios had held during the period 1830–1880 the intersectoral shift out of agriculture would have increased the personal savings ratio.' *Ibid.*, p. 19.

35   *Ibid.*

36   Cameron, *Banking in the Early Stages of Industrialization*, p. 292.

7   Farmers' discontent and agricultural performance: facts, issues and an agenda

1   A. Mayhew, 'A Reappraisal of the Causes of Farm Protest in the United States, 1870–1900.'

2   J. D. Bowman, 'The Embattled Farmer Revisited: A Test for the Great Depression in Midwestern Agriculture, 1870–1900.' The literature on this topic is large. See, for example, S. J. Buck, *The Agrarian Crusade*; R. Hofstadter, *The Age of Reform*; N. Pollack, *The Populist Response to Industrial America*; F. A. Shannon, *The Farmer's Last Frontier: Agriculture, 1860–1897*. For very recent and excellent surveys see R. Higgs, *The Transformation of the American Economy, 1865–1914* and Mayhew, 'A Reappraisal of the Causes of Farm Protest.'

3   For useful summaries see J. D. Bowman, 'Trends in Midwestern Farm Land Values, 1860–1900' and D. C. North, *Growth and Welfare in the American Past*, chapter 11.

4   North, *Growth and Welfare in the American Past*, pp. 137–9.

5   The modern view can be found in North, *Growth and Welfare in the American Past*, pp. 137–9 and in J. D. Bowman and R. H. Keehn, 'Agricultural Terms of Trade in Four Midwestern States: 1870–1900.' Among the earlier historical accounts, skepticism of the deteriorating terms of trade thesis have been voiced by Shannon, *The Farmer's Last Frontier*, pp. 291–5 and even T. Veblen, 'The Price of Wheat Since 1867.'

6   Appendix A, Table A.22.

7   G. K. Holmes, 'The Course of Prices of Farm Implements and Machinery for a Series of Years,' pp. 15, 19 and 22–3. Dorothy Brady presents data consistent with this relative price characterization in 'Price Deflators for Final Product Estimates,' tables 1a–2b, pp. 106–11.

8   R. H. Keehn, 'Nineteenth Century Wisconsin Banking.' This issue is discussed at greater length in chapter 6.

9   Few farmers in the Midwest had, in fact, high debt–asset ratios during the late nineteenth century. The real interest rate facing farmers, in contrast to the quoted rate, must have been the issue. For the revisionist position see Bowman, 'Trends in Midwestern Farm Land Values, 1860–1900,' ch. 1; North, *Growth and Welfare in the American Past*, ch. 11; R. W. Fogel and J. Rutner, 'The Efficiency Effects of Federal Land Policy, 1850–1900: A Report of Some Provisional Findings,' p. 19.

10   Fogel and Rutner, 'The Efficiency Effects of Federal Land Policy,' table 3, p. 12. Fogel and Rutner use the wholesale price index as a deflator. The regional income estimates are constructed by applying Easterlin's state relatives to Gallman's value added per worker.

11   These economy-wide rates are for the period 1869/78–1899/1908. See chapter 4, Table 4.1.

12   Agriculture in the Midwest was dominated by owner-operator status rather than cash or share tenancy. Thus, the farmer's income is the sum of imputed agricultural wages *and* rents. In 1880, the share of farms under the owner-operator status was:

Illinois	68·6	Missouri	72·7
Indiana	76·3	Nebraska	82·0
Iowa	76·2	Dakotas	96·1
Kansas	83·6	Ohio	80·7
Michigan	90·0	Wisconsin	90·9
Minnesota	90·8		

This census data is conveniently reported in Bowman, 'The Embattled Farmer Revisited,' table I, p. 10.

13   *Ibid.*, p. 19.

14   This experiment is certainly informative, but it is an *improper counterfactual*. Had farm mortgage rates remained at their very high 1870 levels, the rate of farm mechanization would have been severely restricted and land rents would have risen at even lower rates in consequence (since average land productivity growth would have been inhibited).

15   Shannon, *The Farmer's Last Frontier*, pp. 306–7.

16   Higgs, *The Transformation of the American Economy*, p. 91. Not all historians accept the traditional view of land speculation. For an outstanding counterexample see A. G. Bogue, *From Prairie to Corn Belt*, p. 51.

17   C. R. Chambers, 'Farm Land Income and Farm Land Values.'

18   He would, of course, have been very disappointed with the results of 'monetary reform.' Had he lobbied successfully for price stability or even an inflation policy (by casting aside 'the cross of gold'), the nominal rate of interest would have risen to offset the change in price level growth.

19   L. Christensen, 'A New Look at Farm Income in the United States,' p. 1.

20   *Ibid.*

21   Higgs apparently would characterize *all four decades* prior to World War I as analogous to the twentieth-century farm problem: 'Much of

what is nowadays described as the "farm problem" is nothing more than an attempt to resist the transformation of agriculture, to maintain a larger amount of resources in farming than can be supported there without assistance from the government. Many modern farmers surely understood this dilemma; their political actions furnish a good example of a well-informed effort to obstruct the economy's transformation.' (Higgs, *The Transformation of the American Economy*, p. 17.) Obviously we disagree, certainly as regards the 1860s and early 1870s, a period when agrarian discontent, after all, took root. Was not the political action during the seventies a 'well-informed' reaction to a market failure which hindered agriculture's expansion?

22   Higgs, *The Transformation of the American Economy*, p. 101.
23   North, *Growth and Welfare in the American Past*, p. 141.
24   A. S. Tostlebe, *Capital in Agriculture: Its Formation and Financing Since 1870*, table 7, pp. 54–7. The figure is for the combined areas of the Lake, Corn Belt and Great Plains States.
25   Fogel and Rutner, 'The Efficiency Effects of Public Land Policy,' p. 17, estimate the rate of capital gains to have been 2·8 percent per annum.
26   See Christensen, 'A New Look at Farm Income,' table C, p. 8.
27   D. A. Nichols, 'Land and Economic Growth,' p. 332.

8   Elements of agricultural performance: land expansion and productivity growth

1   R. Higgs, *The Transformation of the American Economy, 1865–1914*.
2   The literature is too voluminous to cite fully here. See, for example, the following works: P. W. Gates, *History of Public Land Law Development*; T. Saloutas, 'Land Policy and its Relation to Agricultural Production and Distribution'; F. A. Shannon, *The Farmer's Last Frontier*; R. W. Fogel and J. Rutner, 'The Efficiency Effects of Federal Land Policy, 1850–1900.'
3   In fact, new lands were of lower quality during most of the years following 1870, at least in the Midwest as we have defined it. Parker and Klein have shown that 'the relative growth of the plains states between 1890 and 1910 exercised a downward pressure on regional yields.' The fact does not influence the arguments given above in the text. W. N. Parker and J. Klein, 'Productivity Growth in Grain Production in the United States, 1840–60 and 1900–10,' p. 541.
4   Fogel and Rutner, 'The Efficiency Effects of Federal Land Policy,' p. 13. This result is consistent with Christensen's research on the period following 1929. The interesting decades, however, are the transitional ones from the late 1880s to the 1930s.
5   *Ibid.*, p. 20. The highest rates are obtained in the West, at least in 1899, where the Western states are Montana, Wyoming, Colorado, New Mexico, Arizona, Utah, Nevada, Idaho, Washington, Oregon and California. The lowest by far were those prevailing in the North Atlantic states.
6   *Ibid.*, p. 29.
7   E. V. Nardcoff, 'The American Frontier as a Safety-Valve,' p. 138.

8   Shannon, *The Farmer's Last Frontier*, p. 35.
9   F. D. Lewis, 'Explaining Rural Emigration in the Late Nineteenth Century.'
10 Parker and Klein, 'Productivity Growth in Grain Production,' pp. 544–5.
11 *Ibid.*, table 11, p. 543.
12 See, for example, H. J. Habakkuk, *American and British Technology in the Nineteenth Century*. Compare our results with Paul David's for the ante bellum period: 'The Mechanization of Reaping in the Ante-Bellum Midwest.'
13 R. A. Easterlin, 'Regional Income Trends, 1840–1950' and 'Inter-regional Differences in Per Capita Income, 1840–1950.'
14 His views can be found in *The Frontier in American History; The Significance of Sections in American History; The Rise of the New West, 1811–1829*; and *The United States 1830–1850*.
15 Turner, *The Frontier in American History*, p. 271.
16 For example, F. A. Shannon, 'A Post Mortem on the Labor-Safety-Valve-Theory'; C. H. Danhof, 'Farm Costs and the Safety-Valve, 1850–1860' and 'Economic Validity of the Safety-Valve Doctrine'; R. S. Tucker, 'The Frontier as an Outlet for Surplus Labor.' The best sympathetic recent survey of the debate can be found in G. Murphy and A. Zellner, 'The Case for Exhuming the Labor-Safety-Valve-Doctrine,' which we have used extensively in the text.
17 Habakkuk, *American and British Technology in the Nineteenth Century*.
18 Lest we be accused of raising a counterfactual which fails adequately to capture the 'unique' resource endowment conditions of nineteenth century America, consider the following: the land stock implied by the land scarcity counterfactual would, by 1910, have been only 44 percent of the actual level! If this counterfactual fails to represent a world with significantly reduced land endowment, it is difficult to imagine a case that would do so.
19 Shannon, *The Farmer's Last Frontier*, p. 35.
20 Using the 1899 industrial employment distribution as weights, the model estimates the 'surplus' to be approximately 15 percent. Fogel and Rutner calculate the 'surplus' in 1899 to be in the neighborhood of 10 percent, reasonably close to our·estimates based on the model's predictions. Fogel and Rutner, 'The Efficiency Effects of Federal Land Policy,' p. 23. In fact there is reason to suspect that the Fogel-Rutner calculation is on the low side. With instantaneous migration response and no migration costs, potential off-farm migrants respond to *real* rather than money wage differentials. Fogel and Rutner take the money wage differential existing in the 1850s as a constant equilibrium differential reflecting, among other things, that the cost of living is lower in rural areas. Yet up to 1899, transport improvements had a bias which lowered the cost of living differential markedly: namely, bulky foodstuffs – a key wage good – were most greatly influenced. Thus, the 'equilibrium' differential in 1899 must have been lower than in the 1850s.
21 See, for example, A. C. Kelley, J. G. Williamson and R. J. Cheetham, *Dualistic Economic Development: Theory and History*; and A. C. Kelley

and J. G. Williamson, *Lessons From Japanese Development: An Analytical Economic History.*

22 For excellent summaries, see the unpublished papers by Frank Lewis at the University of Rochester: 'The Shift of Labour From Agriculture to Manufacturing: 1869–1899'; 'The Relative Movement of Labour from Agriculture to Manufacturing in the United States: 1869–1899'; 'Explaining Rural Emigration in the Late Nineteenth Century.' This section has found Lewis's thesis research very helpful in clarifying the issues.

23 S. Kuznets, *Modern Economic Growth*, p. 121. This view is shared by C. H. Danhof, 'Agriculture', p. 121 and H. V. Faulkner, *American Economic History*, p. 383.

24 R. E. Gallman, 'Commodity Output, 1839–1899,' pp. 27–8. Italics added.

25 C. W. Wright, *Economic History of the United States*, p. 588.

26 Parker and Klein, 'Productivity Growth in Grain Production,' p. 524.

9 Transportation and American development during the Gilded Age: 1870–90.

1 A. Fishlow, *American Railroads and the Transformation of the Ante-Bellum Economy.*

2 R. W. Fogel, *Railroads and American Economic Growth*; *The Union Pacific Railroad: A Case in Premature Enterprise.* See also L. J. Mercer, 'Land Grants to American Railroads: Social Cost or Social Benefit.'

3 The best critical evaluation, from this writer's point of view, can be found in Fishlow's, *American Railroads and the Transformation of the Ante-Bellum Economy*, chapter 2. See also: M. Nerlove, 'Railroads and American Economic Growth'; S. Lebergott, 'United States Transport Advance and Externalities.' Much of the remainder of this section relies heavily on Fishlow's critique.

4 Fishlow, *American Railroads and the Transformation of the Ante-Bellum Economy*, p. 27.

5 *Ibid.*, p. 30.

6 Fogel himself has suggested a linear approximation to the approach taken in this chapter. He argues that a linear programming model would be an attractive method for attacking the problem but never utilizes the approach. Fogel, *Railroads and American Economic Growth*, pp. 26–7. In any case, we have rejected linearization of our system as inappropriate for long term historical analysis.

7 R. Higgs, 'Railroad Rates and the Populist Uprising' and *The Transformation of the American Economy, 1865–1914*, pp. 87–90. In fact, neither corn nor cotton was significant enough in East–West railroad trade to affect his cost series.

8 A detailed discussion of these points can be found in appendix A and in W. Z. Ripley, *Railroads: Rates and Regulations*, chapters 2–8; F. A. Shannon, *The Farmer's Last Frontier*, pp. 173–9 and 295–303; C. C. McCain, *The Diminishing Purchasing Power of Railway Earnings.*

9 Fishlow has documented a 50 percent increase in total factor productivity in the rails from 1870 to 1890. A. Fishlow, 'Productivity and

Technological Change in the Railroad Sector, 1840–1910,' p. 626.
10 Fishlow adopts this view in *American Railroads and the Transformation of the Ante-Bellum Economy*, p. 45: 'Changed regional terms of trade over this [ante bellum] period largely reflect improved transport conditions: western farmers far from the market received relatively more for their output than eastern farmers closer in. Calculation of the effect upon income of the more favorable later terms of trade then will approximate the change due to better transportation.'
11 J. G. Williamson, *American Growth and the Balance of Payments: 1820–1913*, pp. 138–9.
12 W. W. Rostow, *The Process of Economic Growth* and *The Stages of Economic Growth*.
13 Fogel, *Railroads and American Economic Growth*, chapters 4–6.
14 That is, we continue to assume that the terms of trade in the East is determined by world market conditions. Interregional transport cost changes have an impact only on Midwestern relative prices under those assumptions.

10 Exports, world markets and American development

1 I. B. Kravis, 'The Role of Exports in Nineteenth-Century United States Growth,' p. 387.
2 R. Nurkse, *Equilibrium Growth in the World Economy*. See also I. B. Kravis, 'Trade as a Handmaiden of Growth: Similarities Between the Nineteenth and Twentieth Centuries.'
3 The remainder of this section relies heavily on R. E. Caves, 'Vent for Surplus Models of Trade and Growth.'
4 H. Myint, 'The "Classical Theory" of International Trade and the Underdeveloped Countries.'
5 D. C. North, 'Location Theory and Regional Economic Growth'; M. H. Watkins, 'A Staple Theory of Economic Growth'; G. W. Bertram, 'Economic Growth in Canadian Industry, 1870–1915: The Staple Model and the Take-off Hypothesis'; D. C. North, *The Economic Growth of the United States, 1790–1860*; C. P. Kindleberger, *Foreign Trade and the National Economy*; R. E. Baldwin, *Economic Development and Export Growth*.
6 Caves, 'Vent for Surplus Models of Trade and Growth,' p. 101.
7 *Ibid.*
8 *Ibid.*, p. 102.
9 Kravis, 'The Role of Exports in Nineteenth-Century United States Growth,' p. 393.
10 E. J. Chambers and D. R. Gordon, 'Primary Products and Economic Growth: An Empirical Measurement.'
11 R. W. Fogel and S. Engerman, 'A Model for the Explanation of Industrial Expansion During the Nineteenth Century: With Application to the American Iron Industry.'
12 C. Pope, 'The Impact of the Ante-Bellum Tariff on Income Distribution.'
13 G. Hueckle, 'The Napoleonic Wars and Factor Returns Within the English Economy.'

14 R. E. Caves, 'Export-Led Growth and the New Economic History,' pp. 407–19.

15 *Ibid.*, p. 408.

16 R. E. Gallman, 'Commodity Output, 1839–1899,' pp. 27–8. Italics added.

17 A. Bogue, *From Prarie to Corn Belt*, p. 283.

18 P. Temin, 'General-Equilibrium Models in Economic History," pp. 63–70.

19 For a detailed theoretical analysis of this point, see W. M. Corden, 'The Effects of Trade on the Rate of Growth.'

20 J. G. Williamson, *American Growth and the Balance of Payments, 1820–1913* and D. C. North, *The Economic Growth of the United States, 1790–1860.*

21 The positive impact on land values is *not* evident in the early 1890s. The explanation for this result is that farm mortgage rates would have been higher in the counterfactual world than they were in fact. We shall see that this result was inevitable given the farm sector's greater demand for credit to finance mechanization under the more favorable farm commodity price conditions.

22 H. Perloff *et al.*, *Regions, Resources and Economic Growth*, chapter 12.

23 R. W. Fogel, *Railroads and American Economic Growth*, pp. 114–29.

24 W. G. Whitney, *The Structure of the American Economy in the Late Nineteenth Century.*

25 *Ibid.*, p. 76.

26 *Ibid.*, p. 60. The 'prevailing historical opinion' has been expressed by Douglass North, "Industrialization in the United States,' pp. 694–5.

27 M. Simon and D. E. Novak, "Some Dimensions of the American Commercial Invasion of Europe, 1871–1914: An Introductory Essay,' p. 593. Our model does not distinguish between heavy and light industrial goods, but imports of manufactured products are to be viewed as imports net of exports of such products.

28 F. M. Fisher and P. Temin, 'Regional Specialization and the Supply of Wheat in the United States, 1867–1914,' pp. 142–3.

29 True, Britain was America's best customer since she absorbed about one half of America's wheat and flour exports from 1870 to 1914. But America was competing directly with Russia, Argentina, Canada and even India both in Britain and on the Continent. Indeed, after 1900 the U.S. role in British markets was relatively minor. M. Rothstein, 'America in the International Rivalry for the British Wheat Market, 1860–1914.'

30 *Ibid.*, pp. 291–2.

31 *Ibid.*, p. 294.

11 Immigration and American growth

1 H. Jerome, *Migration and Business Cycles*; W. Willcox and I. Ferenczi, *International Migration*, vols. I and II; D. S. Thomas, *Social and Economic Aspects of Swedish Population Movements.*

2 The literature is extensive. See, for example, S. Kuznets, 'Long Swings in the Growth of Population and in Related Economic Variables'; M. Abramovitz, 'The Nature and Significance of Kuznets Cycles'; R. A. Easterlin, 'Influences in European Overseas Emigration Before World War I'; and M. Wilkinson, 'Evidence of Long Swings in the Growth of Swedish Population and Related Economic Variables.'

3 B. Bolch, R. Fels, and M. McMahon, 'Housing Surplus in the 1920's?' R. A. Gordon, 'Cyclical Experience in the Interwar Period: The Investment Boom of the Twenties' and 'Population Growth and the Capital Coefficient.'

4 R. A. Easterlin, 'Economic–Demographic Interactions and Long Swings in Economic Growth' and *Population, Labor Force, and Long Swings in Economic Growth.*

5 Easterlin, 'Influences in European Overseas Emigration Before World War I,' pp. 345–6.

6 M. Wilkinson, 'European Migration to the United States: An Econometric Analysis of Aggregate Labor Supply and Demand,' p. 275.

7 H. J. Habakkuk, *American and British Technology in the Nineteenth Century.*

8 S. Lebergott, *Manpower in Economic Growth*, p. 41.

9 L. Neal and P. Uselding, 'Immigration: A Neglected Source of American Economic Growth; 1790–1912.'

10 J. M. Quigley, 'An Economic Model of Swedish Emigration.' A test of the human capital model on modern data can be found in S. Bowles, 'Migration as Investment: Empirical Tests of the Human Investment Approach to Geographical Mobility.'

11 Easterlin, 'Influences in European Overseas Emigration,' pp. 332–3.

12 L. E. Gallaway and R. K. Vedder, 'Emigration from the United Kingdom to the United States: 1860–1913.'

13 A. C. Kelley, 'International Migration and Economic Growth: Australia, 1865–1935.' The unemployment variables work well in empirical analysis of contemporary migration as well.

14 Search costs associated with frictional unemployment while seeking a job are not included in C_{it}, but appear directly in E_{it}. That is, E_{it} may be negative in the initial period of job search.

15 Kelley, 'International Migration and Economic Growth;' M. Wilkinson, 'Evidence of Long Swings' and 'European Migration to the United States: An Econometric Analysis of Aggregate Labor Supply and Demand'; J. A. Tomaske, 'The Determinants of Intercountry Differences in European Migration: 1881–1900'; Quigley, 'An Economic Model of Swedish Emigration.'

16 Assuming our arguments to be correct, this shortcoming in the migration literature is hardly unique to studies of nineteenth-century European emigration. The cliometrician can take solace in the recognition that the same weakness can be found in economic analyses of contemporary migrations as well. See, for example, B. Fleisher, 'Some Economic Aspects of Puerto Rican Migration.' For an exception, see G. S. Sahota, 'An Economic Analysis of Internal Migration in Brazil.' The same could be said, of course, for the older literature

which attempts to explain nineteenth-century Anglo-American capital flows, including, unfortunately, my own: J. G. Williamson, *American Growth and the Balance of Payments, 1820–1913*, pp. 145–58.

17 G. J. Stigler, 'Information in the Labor Market,' pp. 102–3.

18 R. E. Lucas and L. A. Rapping, 'Real Wages, Employment, and Inflation,' p. 282.

19 Wilkinson's work motivates our own approach although he does not fully explore the implications of the neoclassical model. Wilkinson, 'European Migration to the United States.'

20 For example, see F. Brechling, 'The Relationship Between Output and Employment in British Manufacturing Industries' or J. G. Williamson, 'Capital Accumulation, Labor Saving, and Labor Absorption Once More.'

21 Kelley, 'International Migration and Economic Growth;' Gallaway and Vedder, 'Emigration from the United Kingdom to the United States;' Quigley, 'An Economic Model of Swedish Emigration;' H. W. Richardson, 'British Emigration and Overseas Investment, 1870–1914.' Of course, w_R may appear separately as a measure of the ability of a potential migrant to finance the move in a world of very imperfect capital markets. The authors listed above do not explicitly consider this possibility.

22 Easterlin, 'Influences in European Overseas Emigration,' p. 331.

23 B. Thomas, *Migration and Economic Growth*, p. 224.

24 Lucas and Rapping ('Real Wages, Employment, and Inflation,' pp. 280–1) estimate that the elasticity of non-agricultural employment demand to the real wage (1930–65) is -0.46. Given mean wage and employment figures in American industry from 1870 to 1913, this implies $\hat{\alpha} = -0.1279$.

25 No attempt was made to estimate the system (1)–(5) simultaneously since the historical data on $w_i(t)$ are of doubtful value. Estimation of the reduced form equation is advantageous since wage variables do not appear in it.

26 J. R. T. Hughes, *Industrialization and Economic History: Theses and Conjectures*, pp. 148–9.

27 Thomas, *Migration and Economic Growth*, p. 224.

28 Easterlin, 'Influences in European Overseas Emigration Before World War I,' p. 332, italics ours.

29 Lebergott, *Manpower in Economic Growth*, p. 41.

30 H. Krooss, *American Economic Development*, p. 81.

31 Thomas, *Migration and Economic Growth*, p. 117.

32 United Nations, Department of Social Affairs, *The Determinants and Consequences of Population Trends*, p. 118.

33 New England political rhetoric attributed to Theodore Parker in Lebergott, *Manpower in Economic Growth*, p. 162.

34 Thomas, *Migration and Economic Growth*, p. 191. Thomas's discussion in chapter 12 is especially good on the rise of American immigration restrictions.

Part IV: The facts of history

Appendix A: Parameter estimation

1   J. Bowman, 'Gross Agricultural Output, Value Added and Factor Shares in Twelve Midwestern States: 1870–1900.'

2   E. F. Denison, *The Sources of Economic Growth in the United States*, p. 88.

3   M. Abramovitz, 'Resource and Output Trends in the United States,' and R. M. Solow, 'Technical Change and the Aggregate Production Function.'

4   J. W. Kendrick, *Productivity Trends in the United States*. The recent research of Professors Abramovitz and David is discussed at length in chapter 5.

5   H. V. Faulkner, *American Economic History*, p. 383. F. A. Shannon, *The Farmer's Last Frontier*, ch. 12. This view is challenged in chapter 8 of the present book.

6   Shannon, *The Farmer's Last Frontier*, pp. 145–6.

7   W. G. Whitney, *The Structure of the American Economy in the Late Nineteenth Century*.

8   L. B. Lave, *Measurement of Technological Change in American Agriculture*, table 2, pp. 8 and 17ff.

9   Kendrick, *Productivity Trends in the United States*, table 42, p. 158 and Lave, *Measurement of Technological Change*, table III, p. 41.

10 Brown, *On the Theory and Measurement of Technological Change*, pp. 161–2. See also Whitney, *The Structure of the American Economy*, chapter 4 and Lave, *Measurement of Technological Change*, table 2, p. 8.

11 A recent study by R. Higgs, 'Railroad Rates and the Populist Uprising' is an exception. His results are discussed below.

12 W. C. Noyes, *American Railroad Rates*, p. 168.

13 A detailed discussion of the points raised in this section can be found in W. Z. Ripley, *Railroads: Rates and Regulations*, chs. II, III, IV–VIII. See also Shannon, *The Farmer's Last Frontier*, pp. 173–9 and 295–303.

14 N. V. Strand, 'Prices of Farm Products in Iowa, 1851–1940.' W. P. Mortenson, H. H. Erdman and J. H. Drazler, 'Wisconsin Farm Prices, 1841–1933.'

15 U.S. Department of Commerce, *Historical Statistics of the United States*, E101, and P. W. MacAvoy, *The Economic Effects of Regulation*.

16 A further step would entail a detailed evaluation of geographical spread of grain crops, penetration of the railroads, and differences in quality. For our purposes, the $Z_A(t)$ index should be sufficient.

17 In 'Railroad Rates and the Populist Uprising,' Higgs finds little evidence of declining real transport costs during the Gilded Age. His results are based, however, on railroad rates rather than inter-regional price differentials. For our purposes, the observed spatial

price differentials are more appropriate than the use of questionable quoted rates.

18   C. C. McCain, *The Diminished Purchasing Power of Railway Earnings*, pp. 50–8.
19   Ripley, *Railroads: Rates and Regulations*, pp. 413 and 429.
20   Whitney, *The Structure of the American Economy*, ch. 3.
21   This is not true, of course, in analysis of business cycles and long swings. For an outstanding example see R. A. Easterlin, *Population, Labor Force, and Long Swings in Economic Growth*.
22   We should emphasize again our assumption that population and labor force growth can be used interchangeably. In fact, the labor participation rate *did* vary considerably over the period. The share of the labor force in resident population is

| 1870 | 0·324 | 1890 | 0·370 | 1910 | 0·399 |
| 1880 | 0·346 | 1900 | 0·374 | | |

L. E. Davis, J. R. T. Hughes and D. M. McDougall, *American Economic History*, table 4.1, p. 86.
23   R. Sutch, R. Roehl, J. Lyons and M. Boskin, 'Urban Migration in the Process of Industrialization,' p. 8.
24   *Ibid.*, table D.10, pp. 110–13.
25   Chapter 6 and see also A. C. Kelley, J. G. Williamson and R. J. Cheetham, *Dualistic Economic Development: Theory and History*, chapter 7.
26   Eldridge and Thomas, *Population Redistribution*, vol. III, table 1.21, p. 65.
27   *Ibid.*, table 1.22, p. 68.
28   S. Lebergott, *Manpower in Economic Growth*, table A-25, p. 54.
29   J. T. Romans, *Capital Exports and Growth Among US Regions*, table VIII, p. 68 and table XII, p. 72.
30   There are, of course, isolated estimates. '... Champaign County [Illinois] drew on eastern investors for about 40 percent of its long-term mortgage funds after 1870, but the peak eastern investment in Tippecanoe County was only half that amount, and on the average was less than one fourth.' L. Davis, 'The Investment Market, 1870–1914: The Evolution of a National Market,' p. 376.
31   Davis, 'The Investment Market,' table 4, p. 362. The differential is computed for 1869 and based on Davis's regions II and IV (i.e., the Mid-Atlantic and the East North Central states).
32   Table A.21 evaluates $\phi_{WE}(t)$ around $i_W(t) = 0·14$ and $i_E(t) = 0·10$ since these are *real* rates of interest.
33   Bowman's index can be found in J. D. Bowman and R. H. Keehn, 'Agricultural Terms of Trade in Four Midwestern States: 1870–1900', and applies to Indiana.

Bibliography

Abramovitz, M. 'Resource and Output Trends in the United States Since 1870.' *American Economic Review* 46 (May 1956): 5–23.
'The Nature and Significance of Kuznets Cycles.' *Economic Development and Cultural Change* 9 (April 1961): 225–48.
'Long Swings in American Growth.' In *New Views on American Economic Development*, edited by R. Andreano. Cambridge: Schenkman, 1965.
Abramovitz, M. and David, P. 'Towards Historically Relevant Parables of Growth.' Paper presented to Southern Economic Association Meetings, Miami, Miami Beach, Florida, 4–6 November 1971.
Ames, E. and Rosenberg, N. 'The Enfield Arsenal in Theory and History.' *Economic Journal* 77 (December 1968): 827–42.
Bagge, G., Lundberg, E. and Svennilson, I. *Wages in Sweden*, vol. II, part II, London: P. S. King and Son Ltd., 1933.
Baldwin, R. E. *Economic Development and Export Growth: A Study of Northern Rhodesia, 1920–1960.* Berkeley: University of California Press, 1966.
Barger, H. *Distribution's Place in the American Economy Since 1869.* New York: National Bureau of Economic Research, 1955.
Beard, C. A. and Beard, M. R. *The Rise of American Civilization.* New York: Macmillan, 1930.
Bertram, G. W. 'Economic Growth in Canadian Industry, 1870–1915: The Staple Model and the Take-off Hypothesis.' *Canadian Journal of Economics and Political Science* 29 (May 1963): 159–84.
Bjerke, K. and Ussing, N. *Studier Over Denmaks Nationalprodukt 1870–1950.* Kobenhavn: Universitits Okonomiske Institut, 1958.
Bogue, A. G. *Money at Interest.* Ithaca: Cornell University Press, 1955.
From Prairie to Corn Belt. Chicago: University of Chicago, 1963.
Bolch, B., Fels, R. and McMahon, M. 'Housing Surplus in the 1920's?' *Explorations in Economic History* 8 (Spring 1971): 259–83.
Borts, G. 'Returns Equalization and Regional Growth.' *American Economic Review* 50 (June 1960): 319–47.
Bowles, S. 'Migration as Investment: Empirical Tests of the Human Investment Approach to Geographical Mobility.' *Review of Economics and Statistics* 52 (November 1970): 356–62.
Bowman, J. D. 'Trends in Midwestern Farm Land Values, 1860–1900.' Ph.D. dissertation, Yale University, 1964.
'Gross Agricultural Output, Value Added and Factor Shares in Twelve Midwestern States: 1870–1900.' Mimeographed, n.d.
'The Embattled Farmer Revisited: A Test for the Great Depression in Midwestern Agriculture, 1870–1900.' Mimeographed, n.d.
Bowman, J. D. and Keehn, R. H. 'Agricultural Terms of Trade in Four Midwestern States: 1870–1900.' Mimeographed, n.d.

Brady, D. 'Price Deflators for Final Product Estimates.' In *Output, Employment and Productivity in the United States After 1800*. New York: National Bureau of Economic Research, 1966.

Brechling, F. 'The Relationship Between Output and Employment in British Manufacturing Industries.' *Review of Economic Studies* 47 (July 1965): 187–216.

Brito, D. L. and Williamson, J. G. 'Skilled Labor and Nineteenth Century Anglo-American Managerial Behavior.' *Explorations in Economic History* 10 (Spring 1973): 235–51.

Brown, M. *On the Theory and Measurement of Technological Change*. Cambridge: Cambridge University Press, 1966.

Brown, T. M. *Specification and Uses of Econometric Models*. New York: St. Martin's Press, 1970.

Bry, G. *Wages in Germany 1871–1945*. New York: National Bureau of Economic Research, 1960.

Buck, S. J. *The Agrarian Crusade*. New Haven: Yale University Press, 1920.

Budd, E. C. 'Factor Shares, 1850–1910.' In *Trends in the American Economy in the Nineteenth Century*. Princeton: Princeton University Press, 1960.

Cagan, P. 'The Monetary Dynamics of Hyper-Inflation.' In *Studies in the Quantity Theory of Money*, edited by M. Friedman. Chicago: University of Chicago Press, 1956.

Determinants and Effects of Changes in the Stock of Money, 1875–1960. New York: Columbia University Press, 1965.

Cameron, R. *et al.*, *Banking and the Early Stages of Industrialization: A Study in Comparative Economic History*. New York: Oxford University Press, 1967.

Caves, R. E. 'Vent for Surplus Models of Trade and Growth.' In *Trade, Growth, and the Balance of Payments*, edited by R. E. Caves, H. G. Johnson, and P. B. Kenen. Amsterdam: North-Holland, 1965.

'Export-Led Growth and the New Economic History.' In *Trade, Balance of Payments and Growth*, edited by J. N. Bhagwati *et al.* Amsterdam: North-Holland, 1971.

Chambers, C. R. 'Farm Land Income and Farm Land Values.' *American Economic Review* 15 (December 1924): 673–98.

Chambers, E. J. and Gordon, D. F. 'Primary Products and Economic Growth: An Empirical Measurement.' *Journal of Political Economy* 74 (August 1966): 315–22.

Chenery, H. B. 'Patterns of Industrial Growth.' *American Economic Review* 50 (September 1960): 624–54.

Christensen, L. 'A New Look at Farm Income in the United States.' EME 7112, Social Systems Research Institute. Mimeographed. Madison, Wis.: University of Wisconsin, June 1971.

Clark, C. *Conditions of Economic Progress*, 3rd ed. New York: Macmillan, 1957.

Conrad, A. H. 'Income Growth and Structural Change.' In *American Economic History*, edited by S. Harris. New York: McGraw-Hill, 1961.

Conrad, A. H. and Meyer, J. R. *The Economics of Slavery*. Chicago: Aldine, 1964.

Coppock, D. J. 'The Climacteric of the 1870's.' *The Manchester School of Economic and Social Studies* 24 (January 1956): 21–31.

Corden, W. M. 'The Effects of Trade on the Rate of Growth.' In *Trade, Balance of Payments and Growth*, edited by J. N. Bhagwati *et al.* Amsterdam: North-Holland, 1971.

Danhof, C. H. 'Economic Validity of the Safety-Valve Doctrine.' *Journal of Economic History* 1 (December 1941): 96–106.

'Farm Costs and the Safety-Valve, 1850–1860.' *Journal of Political Economy* 49 (June 1941): 317–59.

'Agriculture.' In *The Growth of the American Economy*, edited by H. F. Williamson. New York: Prentice-Hall, 1951.

David, P. A. 'The Mechanization of Reaping in the Ante-Bellum Midwest.' In *Industrialization in Two Systems*, edited by H. Rosovsky. New York: Wiley, 1966.

'The Growth of Real Product in the United States Before 1840: New Evidence, Controlled Conjectures.' *Journal of Economic History* 27 (June 1967): 151–97.

Davis, L. 'The Investment Market, 1870–1914: The Evolution of a National Market.' *Journal of Economic History* 25 (September 1965): 355–99.

'The Capital Markets and Industrial Concentration: The U.S. and U.K., a Comparative Study.' *Economic History Review*, Second Series, 19 (1966). Reprinted in *Purdue Faculty Papers in Economic History, 1956–1966*. Homewood: Richard D. Irwin, 1967.

'Capital Immobilities and Finance Capitalism: A Study of Economic Evolution in the United States, 1820–1890.' *Explorations in Entrepreneurial History*, 1 (Fall 1963): 88–105. Reprinted in *Purdue Faculty Papers in Economic History, 1956–1966*. Homewood: Richard D. Irwin, 1967.

'Capital Mobility and American Growth.' In *The Reinterpretation of American Economic History*, edited by R. Fogel and S. Engerman. New York: Harper & Row, 1971.

Davis, L. and Gallman, R. E. 'The Share of Savings and Investment in Gross National Product During the Nineteenth Century.' Stanford Research Center in Economic Growth, Memorandum No. 63 (July 1968).

Davis, L., Hughes, J. R. and McDougall, D. *American Economic History.* Homewood: Richard D. Irwin, 1969.

Deane, P. and Cole, W. A. *British Economic Growth 1688–1959: Trends and Structure.* Cambridge: Cambridge University Press, 1962.

Denison, E. F. *The Sources of Economic Growth in the United States.* New York: Committee for Economic Development, 1962.

Easterlin, R. A. 'Interregional Differences in Per Capita Income, Population, and Total Income, 1840–1950.' In *Trends in the American Economy in the Nineteenth Century*. Princeton: Princeton University Press, 1960.

'Influences in European Overseas Emigration Before World War I.' *Economic Development and Cultural Change* 9 (April 1961): 331–51.

'Regional Income Trends, 1840–1950.' In *American Economic History*, edited by S. Harris. New York: McGraw-Hill, 1961.

'Economic–Demographic Interactions and Long Swings in Economic Growth.' *American Economic Review* 56 (December 1966): 1063–104.

Population, Labor Force, and Long Swings in Economic Growth: The American Experience. New York: National Bureau of Economic Research, 1968.

Eldridge, H. and Thomas, D. S. *Population Redistribution and Economic Growth, United States, 1870–1950* III. Philadelphia: American Philosophical Society, 1964.

Engerman, S. 'The Economic Impact of the Civil War.' *Explorations in Entrepreneurial History* 3 (Spring/Summer 1966): 178–83.

Farris, P. L. and Euler, R. S. 'Prices of Indiana Farm Products, 1841–1955.' *Station Bulletin No. 644.* Lafayette, Indiana: Purdue University Agricultural Experiment Station, 1957.

Faulkner, H. F. *American Economic History.* 8th ed. New York: Harper and Brothers, 1960.

Fels, R. *American Business Cycles.* Chapel Hill: University of North Carolina Press, 1959.

Fisher, F. M. and Temin, P. 'Regional Specialization and the Supply of Wheat in the United States, 1867–1914.' *Review of Economics and Statistics* 52 (May 1970): 134–49.

Fisher, I. *The Theory of Interest.* New York: Kelley and Millman, 1954.

Fishlow, A. *American Railroads and the Transformation of the Ante-Bellum Economy.* Cambridge: Harvard University Press, 1965.

'Productivity and Technological Change in the Railroad Sector, 1840–1910.' In *Output, Employment, and Productivity in the United States After 1800.* New York: Columbia University Press, 1966.

'Comparative Consumption Patterns, The Extent of the Market, and Alternative Development Strategies.' In *Micro Aspects of Development,* edited by E. B. Ayal. New York: Praeger, 1973.

Fleisher, B. 'Some Economic Aspects of Puerto Rican Migration.' *Review of Economics and Statistics* 45 (August 1963): 245–53.

Fogel, R. W. *The Union Pacific Railroad: A Case in Premature Enterprise.* Baltimore: Johns Hopkins Press, 1960.

Railroads and American Economic Growth: Essays in Econometric History. Baltimore: Johns Hopkins University Press, 1964.

'The Specification Problem in Economic History.' *Journal of Economic History* 27 (September 1967): 283–308.

Fogel, R. W. and Engerman, S. 'A Model for the Explanation of Industrial Expansion During the Nineteenth Century: With Application to the American Iron Industry.' *Journal of Political Economy* 77 (May/June 1969): 306–28.

Fogel, R. W. and Rutner, J. 'The Efficiency Effects of Federal Land Policy, 1850–1900: A Report of Some Provisional Findings.' Report 7027, Center for Mathematical Studies in Business and Economics, University of Chicago, June 1970.

Frickey, E. *Production in the United States 1860–1914.* Cambridge: Cambridge University Press, 1947.

Friedman, M. *Essays in Positive Economics.* Chicago: University of Chicago Press, 1953.

A Theory of the Consumption Function. New York: N.B.E.R., 1956.

Friedman, M. and Schwartz, A. J. *A Monetary History of the United States 1867–1960.* Princeton: Princeton University Press, 1963.

Gallaway, L. E. and Vedder, R. K. 'Emigration from the United Kingdom to the United States: 1860–1913.' *Journal of Economic History* 31 (December 1971): 885–97.

Gallman, R. E. 'Commodity Output, 1839–1899.' In *Trends in the American Economy in the Nineteenth Century.* Princeton: Princeton University Press, 1960.

'Gross National Product in the United States 1834–1909.' In *Output, Employment, and Productivity in the United States After 1800.* New York: Columbia University Press, 1966.

Gates, P. W. *History of Public Land Law Development.* Washington, D.C. U.S. Government Printing Office, 1968.

Gerschenkron, A. *Economic Backwardness in Historical Perspective.* Cambridge: Harvard University Press, 1962.

Goldin, C. and Lewis, F. 'The Economic Costs of the American Civil War: Estimation and Implications.' EH 73–19, Graduate Program in Economic History. Mimeographed. Madison, Wis.: University of Wisconsin, March 1973.

Goldsmith, R. W. *A Study of Savings in the United States.* Princeton: Princeton University Press, 1955.

Gordon, R. A. 'Cyclical Experience in the Interwar Period: The Investment Boom of the Twenties.' In *Conference on Business Cycles.* New York: National Bureau of Economic Research, 1951.

'Population Growth and the Capital Coefficient.' *American Economic Review* 46 (June 1956): 307–22.

'Differential Prices of Consumers' and Capital Goods.' *American Economic Review* 51 (December 1961): 937–57.

Green, J. 'The Effect of the Iron Tariff in the United States.' Paper presented to the Cliometrics Conference, Madison, Wisconsin, 29 April–2 May 1970.

Griliches, Z. 'Production Functions in Manufacturing: Some Preliminary Results.' In *The Theory and Empirical Analysis of Production,* Studies in Income and Wealth, vol. 31. New York: N.B.E.R., 1967.

Habakkuk, H. J. *American and British Technology in the Nineteenth Century.* Cambridge: Cambridge University Press, 1962.

Hacker, L. M. *The Course of American Economic Growth and Development.* New York: Wiley, 1970.

The Triumph of American Capitalism. New York: Columbia University Press, 1947.

Hansen, A. *Business Cycles and National Income.* New York: Norton and Company, 1951.

Hayami, Y. and Ruttan, V. 'Factor Prices and Technological Change in Agriculture: The United States and Japan, 1880–1960.' *Journal of Political Economy* 78 (September/October 1970): 1115–41.

Higgs, R. 'Railroad Rates and the Populist Uprising.' *Agricultural History* 44 (July 1970): 291–7.

The Transformation of the American Economy, 1865–1914: An Essay in Interpretation. New York: Wiley, 1971.

Higonnet, R. P. 'Bank Deposits in the United Kingdom.' *Quarterly Journal of Economics* 71 (August 1957): 329–67.

Hoffmann, W. G. and Miller, J. H. *Das Deutsche Volkseinkommen 1851–1957.* Tübingen: 1959.

Hofstadter, R. *The Age of Reform.* New York: Knopf, 1956.

Holmes, G. K. 'The Course of Prices of Farm Implements and Machinery for a Series of Years.' *Miscellaneous Series Bulletin No. 18.* U.S. Department of Agriculture, Division of Statistics. Washington: GPO, 1901.

Homer, S. *A History of Interest Rates.* New Brunswick: Rutgers University Press, 1963.

Houthakker, H. S. 'An International Comparison of Household Expenditure Patterns, Commemorating the Centenary of Engel's Law.' *Econometrica* 25 (October 1957): 532–51.

Hueckel, G. 'The Napoleonic Wars and Factor Returns Within the English Economy.' Paper presented at the Cliometrics Conference, Madison, Wisconsin, 27–9 April 1972.

Hughes, J. R. T. *Industrialization and Economic History: Theses and Conjectures.* New York: McGraw-Hill, 1972.

Jerome, H. *Migration and Business Cycles.* New York: N.B.E.R., 1926.

Johansson, O. *The Gross Domestic Product of Sweden and Its Composition.* Stockholm: Almquist and Wiksell, 1967.

Jones, R. 'The Structure of Simple General Equilibrium Models.' *Journal of Political Economy* 73 (December 1965): 557–72.

'General Equilibrium With Three Factors of Production.' Unpublished. University of Rochester.

Jorgenson, D. W. and Stephenson, J. A. 'Investment Behavior in U.S. Manufacturing, 1947–1960.' *Econometrica* 35 (April 1967): 173–9.

Keehn, R. H. 'Nineteenth Century Wisconsin Banking.' Ph.D. dissertation, University of Wisconsin, 1971.

Kelley, A. C. 'International Migration and Economic Growth: Australia, 1865–1935.' *Journal of Economic History* 25 (September 1965): 333–54.

Kelley, A. C. and Williamson, J. G. 'Writing History Backwards: Meiji Japan Revisited.' *Journal of Economic History* 31 (December 1971): 729–76.

'Sources of Growth Methodology in Low-Income Countries: A Critique.' *Quarterly Journal of Economics* 87 (February 1973): 138–47.

Lessons From Japanese Development: An Analytical Economic History. Chicago: University of Chicago Press, 1974.

Kelley, A. C., Williamson, J. G. and Cheetham, R. J. *Dualistic Economic Development: Theory and History.* Chicago: University of Chicago Press, 1972.

Kendrick, J. *Productivity Trends in the United States.* New York: N.B.E.R., 1961.

Kenen, P. 'Nature, Capital, and Trade.' *Journal of Political Economy* 73 (October 1965): 437–60.

Kennedy, C. 'Induced Bias in Innovation and the Theory of Distribution.' *Economic Journal* 74 (September 1964): 541–7.

Kindleberger, C. P. *Foreign Trade and the National Economy.* New Haven: Yale University Press, 1967.

Kravis, I. B. 'Trade as a Handmaiden of Growth: Similarities Between the Nineteenth and Twentieth Centuries.' *Economic Journal* 70 (December 1970): 850–72.

'The Role of Exports in Nineteenth Century United States Growth.' *Economic Development and Cultural Change* 20 (April 1972): 387–405.

Krooss, H. *American Economic Development*. Englewood Cliffs: Prentice-Hall, 1955.

Kuznets, S. 'Long Swings in the Growth of Population and in Related Economic Variables.' *Proceedings of the American Philosophical Society* 102 (February 1958): 31–6.

Capital in the American Economy: Its Formation and Financing Since 1870. Princeton: Princeton University Press, 1961.

Modern Economic Growth: Rate, Structure, and Spread. New Haven: Yale University Press, 1966.

Kuznets, S. and Rubin, E. *Immigration and the Foreign Born*. New York: N.B.E.R. Occasional Paper 46, 1954.

Landes, D. S. *The Unbound Prometheus: Technological Change and Industrial Development in Western Europe From 1750 to the Present*. Cambridge: Cambridge University Press, 1969.

Lave, L. B. *Measurement of Technological Change in American Agriculture*. Ph.D. dissertation, Harvard University, 1963.

Lebergott, S. *Manpower in Economic Growth: The United States Record Since 1800*. New York: McGraw-Hill, 1964.

'United States Transport Advance and Externalities.' *Journal of Economic History* 26 (December 1966): 437–61.

Lee, E. *et al. Population Redistribution and Economic Growth, United States, 1870–1950*, I. Philadelphia: American Philosophical Society, 1960.

Lewis, F. D. 'The Relative Movement of Labour From Agriculture to Manufacturing in the United States: 1869–1899.' Ph.D., University of Rochester, 1971.

'The Shift of Labour From Agriculture to Manufacturing: 1869–1899.' University of Rochester. Mimeographed.

'Explaining Rural Emigration in the Late Nineteenth Century.' University of Rochester, October, 1971. Mimeographed.

Lindahl, E., Dahlgren, E. and Kock, K. *National Income of Sweden 1861–1930*. Part One. London: P. S. King & Son Ltd, 1933.

Lipsey, R. E. *Price and Quantity Trends in the Foreign Trade Sector of the United States*. Princeton: Princeton University Press, 1963.

Lucas, R. E. and Rapping, L. A. 'Real Wages, Employment, and Inflation.' In *Microeconomic Foundations of Employment and Inflation Theory*, edited by E. H. Phelps *et al.* New York: W. W. Norton, 1970.

MacAvoy, P. W. *The Economic Effects of Regulation*. Cambridge: M.I.T. Press, 1965.

Mayer, T. 'Multiplier and Velocity Analysis: An Evaluation.' *Journal of Political Economy* 72 (December 1964): 563–74.

Mayhew, A. 'A Reappraisal of the Causes of Farm Protest in the United States, 1870–1900.' *Journal of Economic History* 32 (June 1972): 464–76.

McCain, C. C. *The Diminishing Purchasing Power of Railway Earnings.* New York: 1909.

McCloskey, D. N. 'Did Victorian Britain Fail?' *Economic History Review* 23 (1970): 446–58.

McGouldrick, P. *New England Textiles in the Nineteenth Century.* Cambridge: Harvard University Press, 1968.

Mercer, L. J. 'Land Grants to American Railroads: Social Cost or Social Benefit.' *Business History Review* 43 (Summer 1969): 134–51.

Meyer, J. R. 'An Input–Output Approach to Evaluating British Industrial Production in the Late 19th Century.' *Explorations in Entrepreneurial History* 8 (1955): 12–34.

Miller, A. R. 'Labor Force Trends and Differentials.' In *Population Redistribution and Economic Growth, United States, 1870–1950*, II, edited by S. Kuznets *et al.* Philadelphia: American Philosophical Society, 1960.

Mitchell, B. R. and Deane, P. *Abstract of British Historical Statistics,* Cambridge: Cambridge University Press, 1962.

Morishima, M. and Saito, M. 'An Economic Test of Sir John Hicks' Theory of Biased Induced Innovations.' In *Value, Capital and Growth*, edited by J. N. Wolfe. Chicago: Aldine, 1968.

Mortenson, W. P., Erdman, H. H. and Drazler, A. H. 'Wisconsin Farm Prices, 1841–1933.' *Research Bulletin No. 119.* University of Wisconsin Agricultural Experiment Station, November 1933.

Murphy, G. and Zellner, A. 'The Case for Exhuming the Labor-Safety-Valve-Doctrine.' University of Washington, 1958. Mimeographed.

Myint, H. 'The "Classical Theory" of International Trade and the Underdeveloped Countries.' *Economic Journal* 68 (June 1958): 317–37.

Nardcoff, E. V. 'The American Frontier as a Safety-Valve.' *Agricultural History* 36 (July 1962): 123–42.

Neal, L. and Uselding, P. 'Immigration: A Neglected Source of American Economic Growth, 1790–1912.' *Oxford Economic Papers* 24 (March 1972): 68–88.

Nerlove, M. 'Railroads and American Economic Growth.' *Journal of Economic History* 26 (March 1966): 107–15.

Nichols, D. A. 'Land and Economic Growth.' *American Economic Review* 60 (June 1970): 332–40.

North, D. C. 'Location Theory and Regional Economic Growth.' *Journal of Political Economy* 62 (June 1955): 243–58.

North, D. C. *The Economic Growth of the United States, 1790–1860.* Englewood Cliffs: Prentice-Hall, 1961.

'Industrialization in the United States.' In *Cambridge Economic History of Europe*, vol. VI, edited by M. Postan and H. J. Habakkuk. Cambridge: Cambridge University Press, 1965.

Growth and Welfare in the American Past. Englewood Cliffs: Prentice-Hall, 1966.

Noyes, W. C. *American Railroad Rates.* Boston: Little, Brown and Company, 1906.

Nurkse, R. *Equilibrium and Growth in Underdeveloped Countries.* Oxford: Basil Blackwell, 1958.

Okun, A. M. 'Potential GNP: Its Measurement and Significance.' In *Readings in Money, National Income, and Stabilization Policy.* Homewood: Richard D. Irwin, 1970.

Parker, W. N. and Klein, J. 'Productivity Growth in Grain Production in the United States, 1840–1860 and 1900–1910.' In *Output, Employment and Productivity in the United States After 1800.* New York: Columbia University Press, 1966.

Passell, P. and Schmundt, M. 'Pre-Civil War Land Policy and the Growth of Manufacturing.' *Explorations in Economic History 9* (Fall 1971): 35–48.

Perloff, H. S., Dunn, E. S., Lampard, E. E. and Muth, R. F. *Regions, Resources and Economic Growth.* Baltimore: Johns Hopkins Press, 1960.

Phelps-Brown, E. H. *A Century of Pay.* London: Macmillan, 1968.

Phelps-Brown, E. H. and Handfield-Jones, J. J. 'The Climacteric of the 1890's.' *Oxford Economic Papers* 4 (October 1952): 279–89.

Pollack, N. *The Populist Response to Industrial America.* Cambridge: Harvard University Press, 1962.

Pope, C. 'The Impact of the Ante Bellum Tariff on Income Distribution'. Ph.D. dissertation, University of Rochester, 1971.

Pope, C. 'The Impact of the Ante Bellum Tariff on Income Distribution.' *Explorations in Economic History 9* (Summer 1972): 375–422.

Primack, M. L. 'Land Clearing Under Nineteenth-Century Techniques: Some Preliminary Calculations.' *Journal of Economic History 22* (December 1962): 484–97.

'Farm Formed Capital in American Agriculture, 1850–1910.' Ph.D. dissertation, University of North Carolina, 1962.

'Farm Capital Formation as a Use of Farm Labor, 1850–1910.' *Journal of Economic History 26* (September 1966): 348–62.

'Farm Construction as a Use of Farm Labor, 1850–1910.' *Journal of Economic History 25* (March 1965): 114–25.

Quigley, J. M. 'An Economic Model of Swedish Emigration.' *Quarterly Journal of Economics* 86 (February 1972): 111–26.

Redlich, F. 'New and Traditional Approaches to Economic History and Their Interdependence.' *Journal of Economic History 25* (December 1965): 480–95.

Richardson, H. W. 'British Emigration and Overseas Investment, 1870–1914.' *Economic History Review* 25 (February 1972): 99–113.

Ripley, W. Z. *Railroads: Rates and Regulations.* New York: Longmans and Green, 1912.

Rogin, L. *The Introduction of Farm Machinery in Its Relation to the Productivity of Labor in Agriculture of the United States During the Nineteenth Century.* Berkeley: University of California Press, 1931.

Romans, J. T. *Capital Exports and Growth Among U.S. Regions.* Middletown: Wesleyan University Press, 1965.

Rostow, W. W. 'The Take-off Into Self-Sustained Growth.' *Economic Journal* 66 (March 1956): 25–48.

The Process of Economic Growth. Cambridge: Cambridge University Press, 1960.

The Stages of Economic Growth. Cambridge: Cambridge University Press, 1960.

(ed.), *The Economics of Take-off into Sustained Growth.* London: Macmillan, 1964.

Rothstein, M. 'America in the International Rivalry for the British Wheat Market, 1860–1914.' *The Mississippi Valley Historical Review* 47 (December 1960): 401–18.

Sahota, G. S. 'An Economic Analysis of Internal Migration in Brazil.' *Journal of Political Economy* 76 (March/April 1968): 218–45.

Saloutas, T. 'Land Policy and Its Relation to Agricultural Production and Distribution, 1862 to 1933.' *Journal of Economic History* 22 (December 1962): 445–60.

Sargent, T. J. 'Interest Rates and Prices in the Long Run: A Study of the Gibson Paradox.' Paper presented to a Universities-National Bureau Committee for Economic Research, New York, 5–6 November 1971.

'Anticipated Inflation and the National Rates of Interest.' *Quarterly Journal of Economics* 86 (May 1972): 212–25.

Saul, S. B. *The Myth of the Great Depression, 1873–1896.* New York: St Martin's Press, 1969.

Solow, R. M. 'Technical Change and the Aggregate Production Function.' *Review of Economics and Statistics* 39 (August 1957): 312–20.

Shannon, F. A. 'A Post Mortem on the Labor-Safety-Valve-Theory.' *Agricultural History* 19 (January 1945): 31–7.

The Farmer's Last Frontier: Agriculture, 1860–1897. New York: Harper and Row, 1968.

Simon, M. and Novak, D. E. 'Some Dimensions of the American Commercial Invasion of Europe, 1871–1914: An Introductory Essay.' *Journal of Economic History* 24 (December 1964): 591–605.

Smalley, O. A. *Northwestern Mutual Life: A Century of Trusteeship.* Evanston: Northwestern University Press, 1957.

Smiley, W. G. 'The Evolution and Structure of the National Banking System, 1870–1913.' Ph.D. dissertation, University of Iowa, 1973.

Stigler, G. J. 'Information in the Labor Market.' *Journal of Political Economy* 70 (October 1962 Supplement): 94–105.

Capital and Rates of Return in Manufacturing Industries. Princeton: Princeton University Press, 1963.

'Imperfections in the Capital Market.' *Journal of Political Economy* 75 (June 1967): 287–92.

Strand, N. V. 'Prices of Farm Products in Iowa, 1851–1940.' *Research Bulletin No. 383.* Iowa Agricultural Experiment Station, n.d.

Suits, D. 'The Determinants of Consumer Expenditures: A Review of Present Knowledge.' In *Impacts of Monetary Policy.* Englewood Cliffs: Richard D. Irwin, 1963.

Sutch, R., Roehl, R., Lyons, J. and Boskin, M. 'Urban Migration in the Process of Industrialization: Britain and the United States in the Nineteenth Century.' Working Paper No. 162, Center for Research in Management Science. Berkeley, California: University of California, August, 1970.

Swanson, J. A. and Williamson, J. G. 'Explanations and Issues: A Prospectus for Quantitative Economic History.' *Journal of Economic History* 31 (March 1971): 43–57.

Sylla, R. 'Federal Policy, Banking Market Structure, and Capital Mobilization in the United States, 1863–1913.' *Journal of Economic History* 29 (December 1969): 657–86.

'American Banking and Growth in the Nineteenth Century: A Partial View of the Terrain.' *Explorations in Economic History* 9 (Winter 1972): 197–228.

Taylor, G. R. 'American Urban Growth Preceding the Railway Age.' *Journal of Economic History* 27 (September 1967): 309–39.

Temin, P. *Iron and Steel in Nineteenth Century America.* Cambridge: M.I.T. Press, 1964.

'Labor Scarcity and the Problem of American Industrial Efficiency in the 1850's.' *Journal of Economic History* 26 (September 1966): 277–98.

'General-Equilibrium Models in Economic History.' *Journal of Economic History* 31 (March 1971): 58–75.

'Labor Scarcity in America.' *Journal of Interdisciplinary History* 1 (Winter, 1971): 251–64.

Theil, H. *Economic Forecasts and Policy.* Amsterdam: North-Holland, 1965.

Economics and Information Theory. Amsterdam: North-Holland, 1967.

Principles of Econometrics. New York: John Wiley & Sons, 1971.

Thomas, B. *Migration and Economic Growth.* Cambridge: Cambridge University Press, 1954.

Thomas, D. S. *Social and Economic Aspects of Swedish Population Movements.* New York: Macmillan, 1941.

Tomaske, J. A. 'The Determinants of Intercountry Differences in European Migration: 1881–1900.' *Journal of Economic History* 31 (December 1971): 840–53.

Tostlebe, A. S. *Capital in Agriculture: Its Formation and Financing Since 1870.* New York: N.B.E.R. 1957.

Tucker, R. S. 'The Frontier as an Outlet for Surplus Labor.' *Southern Economic Journal* 7 (October 1940): 158–86.

Turner, F. J. *The Rise of the New West, 1819–1829.* New York: Harper and Brothers, 1906.

The Frontier in American History. New York: H. Holt and Company, 1920.

The Significance of Sections in American History. New York: H. Holt and Company, 1932.

The United States 1830–1850: the Nation and Its Sections. New York: H. Holt and Company, 1935.

United Nations, Department of Social Affairs. *The Determinants of Population Trends.* New York: 1952.

U.S. Bureau of the Census, *Historical Statistics of the United States, Colonial Times to 1957.* Washington, D.C.: 1960.

Veblen, T. 'The Price of Wheat Since 1867.' *Journal of Political Economy* 1 (1892): 68–103.

Watkins, M. H. 'A Staple Theory of Economic Growth.' *Canadian Journal of Economics and Political Science* 29 (May 1963): 141–58.

Weber, B. and Handfield-Jones, S. J. 'Variations in the Rate of Economic Growth in the U.S.A., 1869–1939.' *Oxford Economic Papers* 6 (June 1954): 101–32.

Whitney, W. G. 'The Structure of the American Economy in the Late Nineteenth Century.' Ph.D. dissertation, Harvard University, 1968.

Wilcox, W. and Ferenczi, I. *International Migration,* vols. I and II. New York: N.B.E.R., 1929 and 1931.

Wilkinson, M. 'Evidence of Long Swings in the Growth of Swedish Population and Related Economic Variables.' *Journal of Economic History* 27 (March 1967): 17–38.

'European Migration to the United States: An Econometric Analysis of Aggregate Labor Supply and Demand.' *Review of Economics and Statistics* 52 (August 1970): 272–9.

Williamson, J. G. *American Growth and the Balance of Payments, 1820–1913.* Chapel Hill: University of North Carolina Press, 1964.

'Antebellum Urbanization in the American Northeast.' *Journal of Economic History* 25 (December 1965): 592–608.

'Consumer Behavior in the Nineteenth Century: Carroll D. Wright's Massachusetts Workers in 1875.' *Explorations in Entrepreneurial History* 4 (Winter 1967): 98–135.

'Capital Accumulation, Labor Saving, and Labor Absorption Once More.' *Quarterly Journal of Economics* 85 (February 1971): 40–65.

'The Railroads and Midwestern Development: A General Equilibrium History.' EH 72–7, Graduate Program in Economic History. Mimeographed. Madison, Wis.: University of Wisconsin, August, 1972.

'Optimal Replacement of Capital Goods: The Early New England and British Textile Firm.' *Journal of Political Economy* 80 (September 1972): 1320–34.

'Watersheds and Turning Points: Nineteenth Century Capital Formation, Relative Prices and the Civil War.' *Journal of Economic History,* forthcoming.

'Late Nineteenth Century American Retardation: A Neoclassical Analysis.' *Journal of Economic History* 33 (September 1973): 581–607.

Wright, C. 'Some Evidence on the Interest Elasticity of Consumption.' *American Economic Review* 57 (September 1967): 850–5.

Wright, C. W. *Economic History of the United States,* 2nd ed. New York: McGraw-Hill, 1949.

Zarembka, P. 'On the Empirical Relevance of the CES Production Function.' *Review of Economics and Statistics* 52 (February 1970): 47–53.

Zevin, R. 'The Growth of Cotton Textile Production After 1815.' In *The Reinterpretation of American Economic History,* edited by R. Fogel and S. Engerman. New York: Harper and Row, 1971.

Index